Advance Praise for
THE BEST OF ACOUSTIC & DIGITAL PIANO BUYER

"An integral part of playing the piano well is to buy and care for it well. Towards that goal, this exhaustive resource, uniting the work of so many people dedicated to the art of the piano, is an invaluable tool. By simply reading it, one has already moved further down the path to becoming a better pianist."

–Frederic Chiu, concert pianist and Yamaha Artist

"Larry Fine is unique in his ability to provide information that is relevant to novice and sophisticated piano buyers alike. The articles he has published over the years, now collected in one convenient 'Best of' volume, include a staggering range of pertinent and valuable topics. From the intricacies of buying a new or used acoustic, digital, hybrid, or player piano, to deciding whether to rebuild a piano, to the tax implications of donating a piano, to institutional pianos, piano care, and piano moving, you will learn about the piano market in a way that you couldn't do anywhere else. *The Best of Acoustic & Digital Piano Buyer* is required reading for anyone buying or owning a piano."

—Mario Igrec, RPT, MMus, Chief Piano Technician,
The Juilliard School, and author, Pianos Inside Out

"A highly informative and practical resource for anyone interested in the world of pianos."

—Brian Chung, Senior Vice President,
Shigeru Kawai Piano Company

"Larry Fine's new book, *The Best of Acoustic & Digital Piano Buyer,* is a treasure trove of useful information about buying, maintaining, and eventually disposing of nearly any kind of piano. It is truly the indispensable guide to all things piano."

—Steve Brady, RPT, author, Under the Lid:
The Art and Craft of the Concert Piano Technician

"An incredibly valuable resource—whether you're a novice just figuring out how to buy a piano, or a seasoned professional requiring specific information."

—Robert Estrin, LivingPianos.com

"Absolutely filled with piano information—from buying to caring for one, rebuilding vs. purchasing new, acoustic vs. digital—plus ratings and profiles for every brand. Great, informative articles by veteran keyboard technicians."

—David Betts, RPT, Department Head,
Piano Technology, North Bennet Street School

"The piano industry is in a state of flux. Most manufacturing has moved offshore, and brand names that were once revered are now almost meaningless. We hear that once-great piano brands are no longer great, and we're confronted with brands we've never heard of. We shop for a new high-end piano and someone tells us that the only way to get a great piano is to buy one built during the 'golden age' of pianos—whenever that was.

"Enter *Piano Buyer* magazine, edited by Larry Fine—the industry's most complete and definitive resource for today's piano buyer. This book brings together some of the best articles that have appeared in the magazine to date. There is something in here for everyone. Each article has been thoroughly researched, and is based on years of experience by some of the best technicians and experts in the industry today.

"I've been in this business for more than five decades, and I still read each issue that comes out. I've learned something from all of these authors; you will too."

—Delwin D. Fandrich, RPT, Piano Design
& Manufacturing Consultant;
former Director of Research & Development,
Baldwin Piano & Organ Co.

FIRST EDITION

THE BEST OF

Acoustic & Digital

PIANO BUYER ®

THE DEFINITIVE GUIDE TO BUYING & CARING FOR A PIANO OR DIGITAL PIANO

Successor to **THE PIANO BOOK**

Larry Fine, Editor

WWW.PIANOBUYER.COM

Acoustic & Digital Piano Buyer is published by:

Brookside Press LLC   619.738.4155   619.810.0425 (fax)
P.O. Box 601041   www.pianobuyer.com
San Diego, CA 92160 USA   info@pianobuyer.com

Distributed to the book trade by Independent Publishers Group, 814 North Franklin St., Chicago, IL 60610
(800) 888-4741 or (312) 337-0747

See **www.PianoBuyer.com** for more information.

"The Piano Book" is a Registered Trademark of Lawrence Fine
"Piano Buyer" is a Registered Trademark of Brookside Press LLC

Printed in the United States of America

Publisher and Editor, Advertising Director: Larry Fine
Piano Review Editor: Dr. Owen Lovell
Contributing Editor and Piano Industry Consultant: Steve Cohen
Copyeditor: Richard Lehnert
Design and Production: Julie Gallagher
Acoustic Piano Technical Consultants: Sally Phillips, Del Fandrich
Digital Piano Technical Consultants: Alden Skinner, Stephen Fortner

ISBN 978-1-92914568-3

First Edition

26 25 24 23 22 21 20 19 18   10 9 8 7 6 5 4 3 2 1

SAUTER
designed by

AMBIENTE
100% made in Germany

CONTENTS

Editor's Preface   xiii

Introduction: 1
The Prodigious Power of Piano Playing by Brian Chung

The author, a top executive of a major piano manufacturer, discards the old adage "practice makes perfect" in favor of an updated version: "practice makes prosperous." He boldly declares that those who play the piano are far more likely to flourish, thrive, and experience success in life than those who do not.

BASICS

Acoustic or Digital: 5
What's Best For Me? by Alden Skinner and Larry Fine

Should you buy an acoustic (traditional) piano or a digital (electronic) piano? For many, there will be no easy answer to this question—many factors play into this seemingly simple decision. However, careful consideration of the advantages and disadvantages of each will probably reveal which will be best for you.

Piano Buying Basics by Larry Fine   9

The purpose of this article is modest: to provide an overview of the process of buying an acoustic (traditional) piano, with an emphasis on the decisions you'll have to make along the way, and on the factors that will affect any acoustic piano purchase. References are given to other articles in this publication, or to *The Piano Book*, for further information on selected topics.

NEW ACOUSTIC PIANOS

The New-Piano Market Today by Larry Fine   29

This article summarizes the history of U.S. piano sales, manufacturing, and imports over the last 50 years, and describes today's global piano industry, including which brands are made where and by whom, and the effect of globalization on quality and selection.

A Map of the Market for New Pianos ("Ratings") *by Larry Fine* 39

The chart and commentary that follow are intended to provide the newcomer to the piano market with a simple summary of how this market is organized. This summary is intended less as a ranking of quality than as a description of how manufacturers and dealers position their products in the marketplace. That is, if a dealer carried every brand, how would he or she position those brands, in terms of relative quality, when presenting them to prospective purchasers?

About New-Piano Pricing *by Larry Fine* 45

The subject of piano pricing is difficult, complicated, and controversial. One of the major problems is that piano dealers tend to prefer that list prices be as high as possible so they can still make a profit while appearing to give very generous discounts. Honesty about pricing is resisted. But even knowing what is "honest" is a slippery business because many factors can have a dramatic effect on piano pricing.

Sales Talk *by Larry Fine* 49

Certain technical features of pianos are frequently the subject of sales talk, either to persuade you to buy a particular piano, to upgrade to a more costly model, or not to buy a competitor's piano. Untangling the truth from the salesmanship can be difficult, even for professionals in the business. Here I discuss just three examples: laminated vs. solid soundboards, wet-sand-cast vs. vacuum-cast plates, and issues related to the wood used in grand piano rims.

USED & RESTORED PIANOS

Buying a Used or Restored Piano *by Larry Fine* 53

This basic article begins with an overview of the different historical eras represented in the used-piano market, followed by descriptions of the various methods of finding an appropriate used piano for sale. Piano restoration, and buying a restored piano, are also covered. The article concludes with a lengthy discussion of how to figure the value of a used piano. The valuation tables and charts in this section are widely used in the piano business as appraisal tools.

Advice About Used Pianos for Parents of Young 69
Beginning Piano Students *by Sally Phillips*

There are many common misconceptions about buying pianos for young students, and one of them is that a suitable piano can be had for only a few hundred dollars. The truth is that, to progress, young students need *better* pianos, not worse. Although good and bad pianos have been made in every decade, and every used piano must be evaluated on its own merits, certain decades or categories of piano frequently found in today's used-piano market should raise red flags.

How to Sell or Donate Your Piano *by Steve Cohen and Piano Buyer staff* 73

Selling a used piano can be a challenge: Since the Recession, used pianos at all price levels have plummeted in value. Used pianos for sale far outnumber shoppers to buy them, making it a buyer's market. Several conditions—some inherent to used-piano sales and some specific to current times—have tended to increase supply and/ or drive down the prices of used pianos. In his article, Cohen, with the help of other *Piano Buyer* staff, advises how to make the most of a difficult market.

Donating, Converting, or Recycling Your Piano *by Karen Lile* 79

In my 31 years of experience as a piano appraiser and broker, and as a partner in a piano-rebuilding business, I have daily encountered people who are considering donating or otherwise disposing of their pianos. In this article I outline some of the options available to those who have a piano they don't want to keep or sell, but who would like to see it go somewhere other than the dump or local landfill.

Taking a Tax Deduction When Donating a Piano *by Larry Fine* 83

There was once a time when, for tax-deduction purposes, if you needed to know the value of a piano you were donating to an institution or charity, you would just contact your piano technician or dealer, and you could be more or less assured that this "expert" opinion would not be challenged by the Internal Revenue Service. While such a process is still acceptable for some kinds of transactions, it can no longer be used to value noncash, tax-deductible contributions when the value claimed is over $5,000.

Everything Old is New Again *by Stuart Isacoff* 85

Is older better? Archeologists, antique dealers, and even aging writers will tell you so. And many pianists agree, especially when one finds a certain special instrument with which he or she can form the musical partnership of a lifetime. But even legendary wines can turn to vinegar. So when dealing with the acquisition—or restoration—of a vintage piano, it's important to get the advice of experts.

Should I Have My Piano Rebuilt? *by Sally Phillips* 91

It turns out that, from a financial point of view, except for premium-quality instruments, most pianos are not worth a private owner's investment in their rebuilding. Putting thousands of dollars into a low-quality instrument won't increase its value by much, and there's no guarantee that any of the cost of rebuilding can be recouped in resale.

Three Approaches to Piano Restoration 97
by Bill Shull, David G. Hughes, and Delwin D. Fandrich

When rebuilding a piano, the restorer is presented at every turn with questions concerning the extent to which the piano's original design, parts, and materials should be preserved or, conversely, altered or replaced. The philosophies that guide these decisions fall, roughly, into three camps, which might be called, respectively, Conservative, Modern, and Innovative. In this article, several well-respected piano restorers, each approximately representing one of the above positions, explain their approaches to restoration in general and, specifically, how they might be applied to various eras of Steinway grands.

HIGH-END & INSTITUTIONAL PIANOS

The Uncompromising World of High-End Pianos *by Sally Phillips* 105

Those who've found themselves in a showroom full of beautifully crafted, prestige and high-performance pianos know that the experience can be both impressive and unnerving—impressive for obvious reasons, unnerving because of the extraordinary prices these instruments command: from $50,000 to $150,000 or more. Sometimes, novice buyers question whether the prices are justified—or are merely the result of the clever marketing of well-known brand names. In this article, I explain what sets high-end pianos apart from less costly ones that might, at least superficially, look the same, and why the higher price can be justified.

The Best Piano: A Story *by Ori Bukai* 113

The great American pianos, having come of age during the Romantic era, tend toward the Romantic tonal tradition. The great European piano makers, however, embedded in a culture steeped in centuries of musical tradition, have long had to satisfy the conflicting tonal styles of different ages, and this has resulted in a wide variety of instruments with different musical qualities. The good news is that the best way to find the right piano for you is to play as many as you can—a simply wonderful experience! What follows is a story with a valuable perspective from a well-respected dealer of performance-quality instruments.

Buying Pianos For an Institution *by George Litterst* 119

The purchase of pianos for institutional use differs in important ways from those intended for the home. This article covers considerations in the institutional setting of size, new vs. used, acoustic vs. digital, budget, decision making, and piano loan programs.

Piano Maintenance in Institutions *by Chris Solliday* 127

The maintenance of pianos for institutional use differs in important ways from those intended for the home. This article covers considerations in the institutional setting of servicing, climate control, and choice of technician.

Piano Purgatory: The Donated Piano *by Sally Phillips* 129

Piano technicians will tell you that the worst pianos they are asked to service are usually found in houses of worship and other institutions that accept pianos as donations. How do such institutions become populated with so many inappropriate instruments? This article helps institutions develop a plan for fulfilling their piano-related needs, including valuable guidelines for the donation of used pianos, so they will not be sitting ducks for well-intended but inappropriate donations.

Selecting a Performance Piano for Concert Hall or Home 135
by Sally Phillips

The selection of a concert grand usually falls to piano faculty at a university, the music director at a church, or pianists hired to choose an instrument for an orchestra. Occasionally these pianos are selected for homes. This article, which attempts to define and shorten the selection process, assumes that you have chosen a brand and model, and are now about to select a specific instrument from among several examples.

Regulation & Voicing: What Buyers of Performance-Quality Pianos Should Know *by Sally Phillips* 141

Many pianists believe a piano's action or tone can't be changed, or that the performance quality of a piano or action is determined solely by its brand. But any piano's action can go out of regulation, become dirty and worn, suffer from neglect, or merely vary within a normal range—top-rated brands are no exceptions. Many wonderful instruments, new and used, are rejected by buyers because a lack of recent or competent service—or both—is disguising their true potential. Many a hidden gem is available to the buyer who asks the right questions, and can find the right technician to solve an instrument's problems.

PIANO CARE

Caring For Your Piano *by Larry Fine* 147

A piano may look large and imposing, but there is a great deal inside it that is delicate, and sensitive to use and changes in environmental conditions. You have made a considerable investment in the instrument; now you should protect that investment, and maximize your enjoyment of it, by properly caring for it. This article describes the major types of regular servicing that pianos require: tuning, regulating, voicing, cleaning and polishing, and humidity control.

Piano Tuning: An Introduction *by Sally Phillips* 151

To the uninitiated, tuning a piano may seem a simple, straightforward procedure, but it isn't. The process is complicated by the sheer number of strings and tuning pins, by the high tension under which the strings are stretched, by the tightness with which the tuning pins are anchored in the pinblock, and by the friction points over which the taut strings must slide as they're being tuned. All of these factors are obstacles not only to tuning, but also to creating a tuning that will be stable for a reasonable length of time, given the piano's use and environment.

Voicing and Tone: What Piano Buyer's and Owners Should Know *by Sally Phillips* 155

To most piano buyers and owners, a piano's tone is probably its most important aspect, but also the most difficult to quantify or describe. Likewise, the shaping of the tone by the technician through the procedure known as voicing involves unfamiliar terminology, and techniques that are difficult for technicians to communicate to the customer. The purpose of this article is to provide information about tone and voicing, and to define some commonly used terms so that piano owners and technicians can better communicate with each other, and piano shoppers can make more informed buying decisions.

Cleaning and Polishing a Piano's Finish *by Dave Swartz* 161

The purpose of this article is to explain the proper care of the three most common piano finishes today: satin, high gloss, and open pore. To best care for your piano's finish, you need to know what kind of finish it is, and what its special requirements are.

Benches, Lamps, Accessories, and Problem Solvers *by Larry Fine* 165

This article describes the different types of benches, lamps, and other accessories available for pianos, as well as devices for solving problems with heavy touch.

Ten Ways to Voice a Room *by Christopher Storch* 171

Have you noticed that your newly purchased piano doesn't sound quite the same as when you tried it in the showroom? Not all problems with piano tone are best solved by voicing the instrument—it may be your room that needs voicing. Some of the factors that can significantly affect the sound of your piano room are: the size of the room, including ceiling height; the sound-absorbing and -reflecting materials in the room, which give it its reverberant character; and the number and orientation of objects in the room, which affect how sound is scattered or diffused.

Moving the Family Piano *by Russ Vitt* 175

Most of us have seen or heard a humorous story of ordinary people attempting to move the heaviest thing ever made: a piano. Just thinking about it can give otherwise macho adults lower-back pain. While pianos are abnormally heavy, their thousands of moving parts make them fragile as well. Additionally, many pianos have fine finishes that are sensitive to extremes of temperature and humidity. Then, to make things even more interesting, there are obstacles to maneuver, such as steps, turns, overhangs, hills, culs-de-sac, wet grass, and long gravel driveways. So, as someone who needs a piano moved, what are your options?

DIGITAL, SOFTWARE, HYBRID, AND ELECTRONIC PLAYER PIANOS

Buying a Digital Piano *by Alden Skinner*   179

There are currently over 200 models of digital piano on the market. Narrowing the field requires exploring some basic issues. This article covers, at a basic, nontechnical level, the needs of both entry-level shoppers and those interested in more sophisticated, feature-laden models. Subjects include: style and price, taking stock of your musical needs, instrumental voices, acoustic-piano realism, connecting to a computer and to the Internet, shopping options, and tips for the serious shopper, among others.

My Other Piano is a Computer: *An Introduction to Software Pianos* *by Alden Skinner*   191

A digital piano is generally sold as a complete instrument that's ready to play right out of the box. However, if viewed as separate components of a piano kit, a personal computer can take on the role of memory and processing, piano software becomes the sound source, a keyboard (very possibly your digital piano) provides control, and powered monitor speakers and/or headphones let you hear your new invention. If you have a digital piano (or an acoustic piano with hybrid features) and a personal computer (Mac or Windows), you already have most of the ingredients of a software-based piano.

Hybrid Pianos *by Alden Skinner and Larry Fine*   193

A hybrid piano combines electronic, mechanical, and/or acoustical aspects of both acoustic and digital pianos, in order to improve or expand the capabilities of the instrument. A hybrid piano can be created from either an acoustic or a digital piano. An acoustic-based hybrid is created by adding electronic components to an acoustic piano to turn it into a MIDI controller with a sound module, and by adding a mechanical silencer to optionally mute the acoustic-piano sound. A digital-based hybrid is created by designing a digital piano's action, speaker system, cabinet, and other components to replicate as faithfully as possible the experience of playing an acoustic piano.

Buying an Electronic Player-Piano System *by Larry Fine*   197

As with so many other devices, technology has revolutionized the player piano, replacing the pneumatic pressure and rolls of punched paper with electronics, smartphones, iPads, and MP3 files. Today, nearly one out of every four new grand pianos is sold with an electronic player-piano system installed. The capabilities of these systems range from those that simply play the piano, all the way to those that allow composers to create, play, and print entire orchestral scores without ever leaving the piano bench. The features and technological capabilities are already vast and are still evolving.

BRAND & COMPANY PROFILES

This section contains brief descriptions, or profiles, of most brands of acoustic, digital, and electronic player piano distributed nationwide in the United States and Canada. Some brands that are associated with a single dealer, or otherwise have marginal distribution, have been omitted.

Acoustic Pianos   205

Digital Pianos   241

Electronic Player Pianos   246

About the Staff and Contributors   251

Other Articles on Our Website You May Enjoy   253

Advertiser Index   256

CFX

The pinnacle of Yamaha craftsmanship, the CFX boasts
a wide range of tonal colors and a powerful presence
that adds elegance to any concert hall.

YamahaPianos.com

EDITOR'S PREFACE

Larry Fine

WELCOME TO *The Best of Acoustic & Digital Piano Buyer*, a collection of the best and most useful articles we've published in the past nine years on buying a new, used, or restored piano or digital piano.

Some history might be helpful here: In 1987, I published *The Piano Book: Buying & Owning a New or Used Piano*, at a time when many, if not most, new pianos were poorly made by today's standards, and the methods of selling them often bordered on the unethical. The book was groundbreaking in its exposure of all that, as well as unusually comprehensive and technically accessible to the layperson, and over the next 20 years, it was published in three updated editions, supplemented by annual model-and-price guides.

By about 2005, globalization and computerization had so transformed the manufacturing landscape that defective and substandard pianos were largely things of the past, at least for pianos sold in the West; sales practices, too, had also considerably improved. Technology was also beginning to blur the distinctions between digital pianos and traditional acoustic pianos. All of this had the effect of rendering outdated much of the editorial basis for *The Piano Book*, at least as far as its treatment of new pianos was concerned. At the same time, the Internet had transformed people's reading habits; increasingly they preferred digital media to printed books, and demanded that information be provided *now* and *free*. I responded to these challenges by rewriting all of my material for the 21st century, putting it online for free, and turning the work into a collaborative effort among many authors with diverse areas of expertise. Thus was born, in 2009, *Acoustic & Digital Piano Buyer*, an advertising-supported, free online magazine

(**www.pianobuyer.com**) with a semiannual print component.

As the public continues to migrate online, publishing a four-color magazine twice a year has become increasingly costly and unnecessary. At the same time, over the past nine years of publishing, we've accumulated in our Archive a considerable body of excellent articles that we feel would greatly benefit a wider audience. We also believe that, despite the trend toward digital, having a printed version of the articles continues to be worthwhile, as there are many people who do not enjoy reading onscreen for extended periods of time, or who prefer to find their reading materials in bookstores and libraries. Our response has been to separate our printed materials into two publications: this book, with its collection of articles that age well and thus will last for a number of years; and a separate, smaller, and simpler *Piano Buyer Model & Price Supplement*, published twice a year and containing exactly what its title implies: comprehensive and up-to-date listings of acoustic-piano models and prices and digital-piano specifications and prices.

Of course, *all* of our materials—articles, instrument reviews, models, prices, specifications, databases, stories, etc.—will continue to be available online for free.

Now, I can imagine one asking: Why is it necessary to publish dozens of articles about buying a piano? Is the subject really that complicated?

Well, yes, it is—for several reasons. First, the subject can be segmented into a large number of specialized interests: new pianos, used pianos, restored pianos, digital (and hybrid, software, and electronic player) pianos; pianos for institutions, for performance use, for beginning students; caring for a piano (tuning, regulating, voicing, cleaning, humidity control), piano accessories, piano moving; establishing a value for a piano, and selling, donating, or disposing of a piano; room acoustics; and so forth.

Second, each of these interests can be further subdivided almost without limit. For example, treatment of the subject of new pianos requires some description of each of the dozens of brands in the marketplace. The treatment of used pianos requires a description of each era of the past 150 or so years that is still represented in the used-piano market.

Third, most of the above subjects can be discussed at a number of different technical levels, from basic, nontechnical information for the casual buyer, to more in-depth information for piano professionals and aficionados.

Of course, no single volume could possibly cover all of these topics comprehensively, but this book makes a good start. It covers almost every significant area of interest, and some more minor ones, at at least a basic level, and several at more advanced levels. It also touches on a number of topics of great importance that, to my knowledge, have never before been written about—such as how an institution can avoid getting stuck with donations of inappropriate instruments, how to select a concert grand from several of the same brand, taking a tax deduction when donating a piano, and why, from a financial point of view, most pianos are not worth an owner's investing in their rebuilding.

This broad treatment of the subject at a variety of technical levels, combined with coverage of significant niche topics, makes this volume suitable for a very wide audience: from first-time buyers to professional pianists, dealers, and technicians, and from administrators and faculty at colleges and conservatories to piano students at those same institutions. Each will find ample material here to answer their questions, guide their purchases, help them do their jobs, and/or enable them to advise others.

And, while you're reading, please visit us online at **www.pianobuyer.com**, where you'll find additional articles, instrument reviews, searchable databases, classified ads, and other shopping tools.

—Larry Fine, *Editor*

INTRODUCTION
The Prodigious Power of Piano Playing

Brian Chung

PRACTICE MAKES PERFECT. You've probably heard that saying a hundred times, especially if you've ever studied the piano. Mom said it, so it must be true, right?

Well, hold on a minute—nothing against Mom, but let's get real: "Practice makes perfect" is a terrible motto for piano players. First of all, it's incorrect—how can anything become "perfect" if, every time, you practice it *wrong*? And second, it can't even come close to capturing the prodigious power of playing the piano. So, with all due respect to that venerable axiom, trash it—and make way for a motto that proclaims the *real* benefits of piano playing: *Practice makes prosperous*.

People usually associate the word *prosperous* with wealth. While that's certainly part of its meaning, many dictionaries suggest a broader definition: to be *prosperous* is to *flourish*, to *thrive* . . . to *be successful*. Therefore, the phrase *practice makes prosperous* declares boldly that *those who play the piano are far more likely to flourish, thrive, and experience success in life than those who do not*. Quite a stretch, you say? Read on.

Thriving Children

Consider what happens when eight-year-old Bobby decides to embrace serious piano practice. Not only does he embark upon a wondrous musical adventure (possibly the greatest benefit of all) but, perhaps unconsciously, he acquires a diversity of skills far beyond the musical notes:

- **He learns to *work hard*.** Anyone who excels at the piano has made a commitment to practice with vigor and determination.

- **He learns to *focus*.** In a world where iPads, Facebook, Twitter, Instagram and mobile texting have made multi-tasking the de facto way of life, young people are at risk of losing the art of concentration. Piano practice reminds Bobby how to focus on *one thing*—and do it well.

- **He learns to be *responsible*.** Serious pianists learn that faithful, consistent practice—even when they don't *feel* like doing it—will bring great satisfaction over time.

- **He learns to *pay attention to details*.** As his skills mature, Bobby learns to observe the fine points and use the most subtle nuances to create art.

- **He learns to be *self-reliant*.** While practicing, Bobby can't always rely on Mom and Dad for help. To succeed, he must learn to work well on his own.

- **He learns to be *creative*.** Creativity is a musician's lifeblood. Pianists use it not only to express musical ideas, but also to conquer the physical and mental obstacles that arise when learning new music.

- **He learns to *persevere*.** There is little satisfaction in learning only *half* of a piece of music. The determined pianist finds joy in following through to the very end.

These are only some of the skills Bobby will acquire as he devotes himself to diligent piano practice. So, how will such practice make him prosperous?

Ask employers what they look for when interviewing young job candidates for their top positions. Most are looking for a well-defined set of character traits. Specifically, they want people who know how to work hard, can focus well and avoid distractions, are responsible, will pay attention to details, are self-reliant and creative, and will persevere on a project from start to finish. Sound familiar?

You see my point. The skills Bobby learns by practicing the piano will be of immeasurable value to him not only in job interviews, but in every area of his life.

Wm. Knabe & Co.

ESTABLISHED 1837

Exceptional. Elegant. Extraordinary.

"They reflect monumental credit on American achievement; they are perfection."

- Richard Strauss,
Renowned German composer

People who have these skills are more likely to flourish in college, thrive in the work world, advance in their careers—and generally enjoy success in any field of endeavor.

Test scores support this contention. Studies show that students of music typically score higher on SATs than do non-music students—on average, 57 points higher on the verbal section and 41 points higher in math.[1] Further, a 1994 study showed that college undergraduate students who majored in music had the highest rate of acceptance to medical school (66%).[2] *Practice makes prosperous.* Prepare your children for success in life: Introduce them to the piano.

Thriving Adults

But how about *you*? Are you among the 82% of adults who have always wanted to learn how to play an instrument?[3] Did you know that adults can gain as much as younger people from playing the piano?

Even if you've already achieved career success and significant wealth, there can be so much more to a prosperous life. Consider what happens when Nancy, a baby boomer and successful business owner, decides to join a recreational group piano class for adults:

- **She immediately feels *relief from stress*.** After hours of intense daily pressure at work, Nancy finds it easy to unwind at the piano. The class moves at a comfortable pace and no one is ever required to play solo—which means zero stress. In her personal practice and in class, Nancy can just relax and have fun.

- **She's *making new friends*.** Because recreational piano classes are taught in groups, Nancy enjoys getting to know others who share a common interest. Many of her classmates are professional people like her who, after raising a family, are finally getting to try the things they've always wanted to do. The warm camaraderie among class members is a wonderful surprise.

[1] *Profile of SAT and Achievement Test Takers.* The College Board, compiled by Music Educators National Conference, 2001.
[2] Peter H. Wood, "The Comparative Academic Abilities of Students in Education and in Other Areas of a Multifocus University," ERIC Document ED327480 (1990).
[3] *U.S. Gallup Poll.* 2008 Music USA NAMM Global Report (August, 2008): 139.

- **She enjoys *playing her favorite songs*.** Nancy always dreamed of learning her two favorite Beatles tunes. Now, she's thrilled to play these and many other classic hits for friends and family.

- **Her *mind and spirit are enlivened*.** The process of learning something completely new has been intellectually and emotionally stimulating for Nancy. She enjoys a sense of adventure when exploring new musical concepts and genres with her classmates. Playing the piano has made her feel more fully alive.

Studies have shown that recreational group music-making can significantly improve the quality of life and personal well-being among those who embrace it. So even when you're playing the piano just for fun, *practice makes prosperous* in meaningful ways that far exceed the balance in your 401(k).

To give the piano a whirl, contact a local music store or independent piano teacher to find out about recreational piano classes in your area. Whether you're young or old, striving for success or just playing for fun, the prodigious power of playing the piano can change your life.

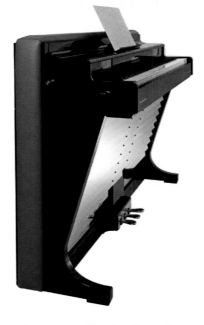

ACOUSTIC OR DIGITAL
What's Best For Me?

Alden Skinner and Larry Fine

SHOULD YOU BUY an acoustic (traditional) piano or a digital (electronic) piano? For many, there will be no easy answer to this question. Many factors play into this seemingly simple decision, some practical, some not. Ideally, perhaps, the answer should be "Both"—take advantage of the "organic" qualities and connection with tradition of the acoustic piano, as well as the extreme flexibility of the digital. But assuming that, for a variety of reasons, "Both" isn't an option, careful consideration of the advantages and disadvantages of each will probably quickly reveal which will be best for you.

The advantages of the acoustic piano start with the fact that it's the "real thing," inherently capable of nuances that are difficult for the digital piano to emulate. The experience of playing an acoustic piano—the harmonics, the vibrations, the touch, the visual appeal, the interaction with the room, the connection with tradition—is so complex that digitals cannot reproduce it all. And, provided that it's a decent instrument and properly maintained, the acoustic will continue to serve you or a subsequent owner for several generations, after which it might be rebuilt and continue to make music.

If you're a beginner, the tone and touch of a good-quality digital piano should not interfere with the elementary learning process for a while, but is likely to become less satisfactory as you advance. If your aspiration is to play classical piano literature, the choice is clear: A digital may serve as a temporary or quiet-time practice instrument (some well-known classical pianists request that a digital piano be placed in their hotel rooms for practice and warmup), but the first time you play an acoustic piano that stirs your soul, there will be no turning back. Although digitals continue to draw closer to the ideal, there is, as

yet, nothing like the total experience of playing a fine acoustic instrument.

The downside of an acoustic piano? Initial cost is generally higher, they're harder to move, the best ones take up a lot of space, and tuning and maintaining them adds several hundred dollars a year to their cost. And—most important—*all they will ever be or sound like is a piano.*

So why do sales of digital pianos outnumber sales of acoustics by more than two to one? Because, in addition to making a piano sound, digitals can also sound like any other instrument imaginable. State-of-the-art digital pianos can allow a player with even the most basic keyboard skills to sound like an entire orchestra. Many models have features that will produce an entire band or orchestra accompanying you as the soloist. Digital pianos can also be used as player pianos. They can enhance learning with educational software. They can be attached to a computer, and you can have an entire recording studio at your fingertips, with the computer printing the sheet music for anything you play. Many fine players whose main piano is a quality acoustic also have a digital, providing the technology for

band and/or orchestral compositions, transcriptions, and fun!

Add to all that the advantages of lower cost, convenience, lack of maintenance expense, the ability to play silently with headphones, meeting the needs of multiple family members, the obvious advantages for piano classes, and computer connectivity, and you have a powerful argument for the digital.

While digital pianos have a lot of advantages, it's important to also consider the disadvantages. In addition to those related to learning and playing classical music, mentioned above, the life expectancy of a good digital piano is limited, primarily by obsolescence (digitals haven't been around long enough to know how long they will physically last), while the life expectancy of a good acoustic piano is upward of 50 years. Acoustic pianos hold their value rather well, while digitals, like other electronics, quickly drop in value. Obviously, then, if you're buying a starter instrument and plan to upgrade later, from a financial perspective you would do better to start with an acoustic piano.

Both variations have places in our musical lives. Now, which is right for you?

(If you're still unsure, you might want to consider a hybrid piano—see our article on the subject elsewhere in this volume.)

PIANO BUYING BASICS

Larry Fine

Introduction

The purpose of this article is to provide an overview of the process of buying an acoustic (traditional) piano, with an emphasis on the decisions you'll have to make along the way, and on the factors that will affect any purchase of an acoustic piano. References are given to other articles in this publication, or to *The Piano Book*, for further information on selected topics. For an overview of the process of buying a digital (electronic) piano, please read our **article** on that subject.

Why Is Buying a Piano So Hard?

An acoustic (traditional) piano can be one of the most expensive—and difficult—purchases most households will ever make. Why so difficult?

Lack of qualified advice. A person who sets out to buy a piano is unlikely to have a social support network of family and friends who are knowledgeable about pianos to serve as advisors, as they might if buying a car, house, or kitchen appliance. A "modern" piano is essentially a 19th-century creation about which few people know very much, and about which much of what they *think* they know may not be accurate or current. Even music teachers and experienced players often know little about piano construction or the rapidly changing state of piano manufacturing, often relying on their past experience with certain brands, most of which have changed significantly over the years.

Confusing array of choices. Acoustic pianos are marketed nationally in the United States under some 70 different brand names from a dozen countries (plus dozens of additional names marketed locally), with thousands of models available in dozens of furniture styles and finishes—and that's just new

pianos! Add in more than a century's worth of used pianos under thousands of brand names in an almost infinite variety of conditions of disrepair and restoration. Just thinking about it can make one dizzy.

Value for the money unclear. New pianos vary in price from $2,000 to $200,000. But unlike many other consumer items, whose differences can be measured or are readily apparent, most pianos, regardless of price, look very similar and do pretty much the same thing: they're shiny and black (or a wood color), play 88 notes, and have three pedals. The features advertised are often abstract, misleading, or difficult to see or understand. For this reason, it's often not clear just what you're getting for your money. This can lead to decision-making paralysis.

Confusing sales practices. While many piano salespeople do an honest and admirable job of guiding their customers through this maze, a significant minority—using lies, tricky pricing games, and false accusations against competing dealers and brands—make the proverbial used-car salesman look like a saint. And once you get through haggling over price—the norm in the piano business—you may be ready for a trip to a Middle East bazaar.

Dealing With Technical Issues

As you shop for a piano, you'll likely be bombarded with a great deal of technical jargon—after all, the piano is a complicated instrument. But don't allow yourself to be confused or intimidated. Although some technical information can be useful and interesting, extensive familiarity with technical issues usually isn't essential to a successful piano-shopping experience, especially when buying a new piano. (A little greater familiarity may be advisable when buying a used or restored instrument.)

Most technical information you'll come across relates to how the manufacturer designed the instrument. You should focus on how the instrument sounds, feels, and looks, not how it got that way. In addition, technical features are often taken out of context and manipulated by advertising and salespeople—the real differences in quality are often in subtleties of design and construction that don't make good ad copy. For those readers who love reading about the finer technical details, we recommend the author's earlier work, *The Piano Book*.

Vertical or Grand?

Probably the most basic decision to make when buying a piano—and one you may have made already—is whether to buy a vertical or a grand. The following describes some of the advantages and disadvantages of each.

Vertical Advantages

- Takes up less space, can fit into corners
- Lower cost
- Easier to move

Vertical Disadvantages

- Sound tends to bounce back into player's face, making subtle control of musical expression more difficult.
- Action is not as advanced as in grand; repetition of notes is slower and less reliable in most cases, and damping is sometimes less efficient.
- Keys are shorter than on grands, making subtle control of musical expression more difficult.

- Cabinetwork is usually less elegant and less impressive.

Vertical pianos are suitable for those with simpler musical needs, or where budget and space constraints preclude buying a grand. Despite the disadvantages noted above, some of the larger, more expensive verticals do musically rival smaller, less expensive grands. They may be a good choice when a more subtle control of musical expression is desired, but where space is at a premium.

Grand Advantages

- Sound develops in a more aesthetically pleasing manner by bouncing off nearby surfaces and blending before reaching player's ears, making it easier to control musical expression.
- More sophisticated action than in a vertical. Grand action has a repetition lever to aid in the speed and reliability of repetition of notes, and is gravity-assisted, rather than dependent on artificial contrivances (springs, straps) to return hammers to rest.
- Longer keys provide better leverage, allowing for significantly greater control of musical expression.
- Casework is usually more elegant and aesthetically pleasing.

Grand Disadvantages

- Takes up more space
- Higher cost
- Harder to move

What Size?

Both verticals and grands come in a wide variety of sizes. The important thing to know here is that size is directly related to musical quality. Although many other factors also contribute to tonal quality, *all else being equal*, the longer strings of larger pianos, especially in the bass and midrange sections, give off a deeper, truer, more consonant tonal quality than the strings of smaller pianos. The treble and bass blend better and the result is more pleasing to the ear. Also, longer grands usually have longer keys that generally allow superior control of musical expression than shorter grands. Therefore, it's best to buy the largest piano you can afford and have space for. Small differences in size between models are more significant

A Little Bit of the Technical

A little bit (but not too much) of technical information about the piano is useful to have while shopping for one. Important words are in **boldface**.

A piano can be thought of as comprising four elements: mechanical, acoustical, structural, and cabinetry.

Mechanical: When you press a piano **key** (usually 88 in number), the motion of your finger is transmitted through a series of levers and springs to a felt-covered wooden **hammer** that strikes the strings to set them vibrating. This complex system of keys, hammers, levers, and springs is known as the **action**. Also, when you press a key, a felt **damper** resting against each string lifts off, allowing the string to vibrate. When you let the key up, the damper returns to its resting place, stopping the string's vibration. **Pedals**, usually three in number and connected to the action and dampers, serve specialized functions such as sustaining and softening the sound. The right-foot pedal is called the **damper** or **sustain pedal**; it lifts all the dampers off all the strings, allowing the strings to ring sympathetically. The left-foot, **soft pedal** (on a grand piano, the **una corda pedal**) softens the sound. The function of the middle pedal varies depending on the type and price level of the piano. As a **sostenuto pedal**, it selectively sustains notes or groups of notes, a function required only rarely in a small percentage of classical compositions. Other possible functions for the middle pedal include a damper pedal for the bass notes only (**bass sustain**), and a mute or **practice pedal** that reduces the sound volume by about half.

Acoustical: Piano **strings** are made of steel wire for the higher-sounding notes (**treble**), and steel wire wrapped with copper for the lower-sounding notes (**bass**). They are graduated in thickness, length, and tension, and strung tightly across the structural framework of the piano. Each note has one, two, or three strings associated with it. Each such set of strings is known as a **unison** because all the strings in a set sound the same note. The strings lie across narrow hardwood **bridges** that transmit their vibrations to a wooden **soundboard**, usually made of spruce. The relatively large area of the soundboard amplifies what would otherwise be a rather weak sound and broadcasts the sound to the ears. The dimensions, arrangement, and positioning of all the acoustical elements in a piano is known as the piano's **scale design**.

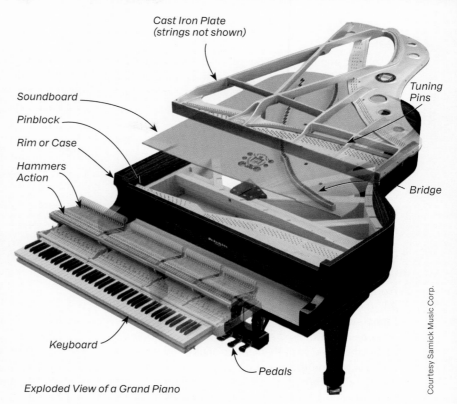

Cast Iron Plate (strings not shown)

Soundboard

Pinblock

Rim or Case

Hammers

Action

Keyboard

Tuning Pins

Bridge

Pedals

Exploded View of a Grand Piano

Courtesy Samick Music Corp.

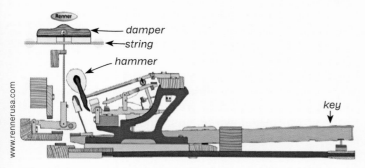

damper

string

hammer

key

www.rennerusa.com

The key and action parts of a single note from a grand piano

The scale design varies with the model and is a major determinant of the piano's tone.

Structural: The strings are strung across a gold- or bronze-colored **plate** (sometimes called a **frame** or **harp**) of cast iron, which is bolted to a substantial wooden framework. This heavy-duty structure is necessary to support the many tons of tension exerted by all the taut strings. A **vertical**, or upright, piano is one in which this structure stands vertically, and is most commonly placed against a wall. A **grand** piano is one in which this structure lies horizontally. In a vertical piano, the wooden framework consists of vertical **back posts** and connecting cross beams; in a grand, wooden beams and the familiar curved **rim** comprise the framework. One end of each string is anchored to the plate toward the rear of a grand or the bottom of a vertical piano. The other end is coiled around a **tuning pin** embedded in a laminated hardwood **pinblock** hidden under the plate at the front (grand) or top (vertical). A piano is **tuned** by turning each tuning pin with a special tool to make very slight adjustments in the tension of its string, and thus to the string's frequency of vibration, or **pitch**.

Cabinetry: The piano's **cabinet** (vertical) or **case** (grand) provides aesthetic beauty and some additional structural support. A grand piano's rim is part of both the wooden structural framework and the case. Accessory parts, such as the music desk and lid, are both functional and aesthetic in purpose.

Although the acoustical and structural elements have been described separately, in fact the plate, wooden framework, soundboard, bridges, and strings form a single integrated unit called the **strung back**. A piano, then, consists of a strung back, an action (including keyboard), and a cabinet or case.

in smaller pianos than in larger ones. However, a difference in size of only an inch or so is not generally significant, as it could be merely due to a larger cabinet or case.

Verticals

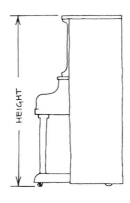

Vertical pianos are measured from the floor to the top of the piano. Verticals less than 40" tall are known as spinets. They were very popular in the post–World War II period, but in recent years have died out. Verticals from 40" to about 43" or 44" tall are called consoles. Spinet and console actions must be compromised somewhat in size or placement within the piano to fit them into pianos of this size. The tone is also compromised by the shorter strings and smaller soundboard. For this reason, manufacturers concentrate on the furniture component of small verticals and make them in a variety of decorator styles. They are suitable for buyers whose piano needs are casual, or for beginning students, and for those who simply want a nice-looking piece of furniture in the home. Once students progress to an intermediate or advanced stage, they are likely to need a larger instrument.

Studio pianos, from about 44" to 47" tall, are more serious instruments. They are called studios because they are commonly found in the practice rooms of music schools. Manufacturers make them in both attractive furniture styles for the home and in functional, durable, but aesthetically bland styles for school and other institutional use. If you don't require attractive furniture, you may save money by buying the school style. In fact, many buyers prefer the simple lines of these models.

Verticals about 48" and taller, called uprights, are the best musically. New ones top out at about 52", but in the early part of the 20th century they were made even taller. The tallest verticals take up no more floor space than the shortest ones, but some buyers may find the taller models too massive for their taste. Most uprights are made in an attractive black, traditional or institutional style, but are also available with exotic veneers, inlays, and other touches of elegance.

The width of a vertical piano is usually a little under five feet and the depth around two feet; however, these dimensions are not significantly related to musical quality.

Grands

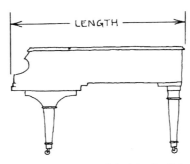

Grand pianos are measured (with the lid closed) in a straight line from the very front of the piano (keyboard end) to the very back (the tail). Lengths begin at 4' 6" and go to over 10' (or even longer in some experimental models). Widths are usually around 5' and heights around 3', but only the length has a significant bearing on musical quality.

Grands less than 5' long are usually somewhat musically compromised and are mainly sold as pieces of furniture. Grands between about 5' and 5½' are very popular. Although slightly compromised, they can reasonably serve both musical and furniture functions and are available in many furniture styles. (By the way, piano professionals prefer the term *small grand* to *baby grand*. Although there is no exact definition, a small grand is generally one less than about 5½' long.) Above 5½', pianos rapidly improve, potentially becoming professional quality at about 6'. Pianos intended for the home or serious professional top out at about 7' or 7½'. These sizes may also satisfy the needs of smaller concert venues. Larger venues require concert grands, usually about 9' long.

When considering what size of piano is right for your home, don't forget to add two to three feet to the length of a grand or the depth of a vertical for the piano bench and pianist. Shoppers tend to underestimate what will fit and buy smaller pianos than necessary. Sometimes, the next-size-larger instrument can give you a great deal of tonal improvement at little additional cost. Dealers can usually lend you templates corresponding to different piano sizes to lay down on your floor so you can measure what will fit.

The subject of used pianos is vast. *The Piano Book* has a chapter devoted to it, including how to do your own preliminary technical examination of a piano. A summary of the most important information, including a description of the most common types of used pianos, where to find them, and how much to pay, can be found in the article "**Buying a Used or Restored Piano**" elsewhere in this volume. See also other articles on used or restored pianos in this volume, as well as our archive of past feature articles at **www.pianobuyer.com**.

The Piano Dealer

The piano dealer is a very important part of the piano-buying experience, for several reasons:

- A knowledgeable and helpful salesperson can help you sort through the myriad possibilities and quickly home in on the piano that's right for you.
- A dealership with a good selection of instruments can provide you with enough options to choose from that you don't end up settling for less than what you really want (although you can make up for this to some extent by shopping among a number of dealers).
- All pianos arrive from the factory needing some kind of pre-sale adjustment to compensate for changes that occur during shipment, or for musical finishing work left uncompleted at the factory. Dealers vary a great deal in their willingness to perform this work. There's nothing worse than trying to shop for a piano, and finding them out of tune or with obvious defects. It's understandable that the dealer will put the most work into the more expensive pianos, but a good dealer will make sure that even the lower-cost instruments are reasonably playable.
- A good dealer will provide prompt, courteous, skilled service to correct any small problems that occur after the sale, and act as your intermediary with the factory in the rare event that warranty service is needed.

Knowledge, experience, helpfulness, selection, and service—that's what you're looking for in a dealer.

Shopping Long-Distance via the Internet

The question often arises as to whether one should shop for a piano long-distance via the Internet. It turns out that this is really two different questions. The first is whether one should locate a dealer via the Internet, possibly far away, then visit that dealer to buy a piano. The second is whether one should buy a piano sight unseen over the Internet.

If you're shopping for a new piano, you'll probably have to visit a dealer. This is because dealers are generally prohibited by their agreements with manufacturers from quoting prices over the phone or via the Internet, or from soliciting business from customers outside their "market territory," the definition of which differs from brand to brand. But once you set foot in the dealer's place of business, regardless of where you came from, you're considered a legitimate customer and all restrictions are off, even after you return home. There are no such restrictions for advertising or selling used pianos. (Exception: If a brand of new piano is one that the dealer owns or controls—known as a *house brand*—you may be able to purchase it without ever visiting the dealer.)

Customers, of course, don't care about "market territories." They just want to get the best deal. Given the ease of comparison shopping via the Internet, and the frequency with which people travel for business or pleasure, dealers are increasingly testing the limits of their territorial restrictions, and more and more sales are taking place at dealerships outside the customer's area. This is a delicate subject in the industry, and the practice is officially discouraged by dealers and manufacturers alike. In private, however, dealers are often happy when the extra business walks in the door (though they hate like heck to lose a sale to a dealer outside their area), and some manufacturers are choosing to look the other way.

There are obvious advantages to shopping locally, and it would be foolish not to at least begin there. Shopping, delivery, and after-sale service are all much easier, and there can be pleasure in forging a relationship with a local merchant. That said, every person's lifestyle and priorities are different. A New Yorker who frequently does business in San Francisco may find it more "local" to visit a piano dealer in downtown San Francisco, near his or her business meeting, than to drive all over the New York metropolitan area with spouse and children on a Saturday morning. In the marketplace, the customer is king. As people become more and more at ease with doing business of all kinds long-distance with the aid of the Internet, it's likely that piano shopping will migrate in that direction as well.

Buying a piano sight unseen (which, in view of the above discussion, is likely to involve used pianos, not new) is something entirely different. Obviously, if you're at all musically sensitive, buying a piano without trying it out first is just plain nuts. But, as much as I hate to admit it, it may make sense for some people, particularly beginners or non-players. In the piano business, we like to say—and I say it a lot—that a piano is not a commodity; that is, a product of

which one example is more or less interchangeable with another. Each piano is unique, etc., etc., and must be individually chosen. But for someone who is buying a piano for a beginner, who has no preference in touch and tone, and who just wants a piano that's reasonably priced, reliable, and looks nice, a piano may, in fact, actually be a "commodity." I might wish it were otherwise, just as an audiophile might wish that I wouldn't buy a stereo system off the shelf of a discount department store, but we're all aficionados of some things and indifferent about others, and that's our choice. Furthermore, just as people who buy electronic keyboards frequently graduate to acoustic pianos, the person who today buys a piano over the Internet may tomorrow be shopping at a local dealer for a better piano with a particular touch and tone. Although it isn't something I'd advise as a general rule, the fact is that many people have bought pianos via the Internet without first trying them out and are pleased with their purchase (and some people, probably, are not so pleased).

If you're thinking of making a long-distance purchase, however, please take some precautions (not

all of these precautions will apply to every purchase). First, consider whether it's really worth it once you've taken into account the cost of long-distance shipping. Find out as much as you can about the dealer. Get references. Get pictures of the piano. Hire a piano technician in the dealer's area to inspect the piano (to find a technician, use the Piano Technicians Guild website, **www.ptg.org**) and ask the technician about the dealer's reputation. Make sure the dealer is experienced with arranging long-distance piano moves, and uses a mover that specializes in pianos. Find out who is responsible for tuning and adjusting the piano in your home, and for repairing any defects or dings in the finish. Get the details of the warranty, especially who is responsible for paying the return freight if the piano is defective. Find out how payment is to be made in a way that protects both parties. And if, after all this, you still want to buy long-distance, my best wishes for a successful purchase.

It bears emphasizing that the above discussion was about buying a piano over the Internet from a *commercial dealer*, against whom you have at least some possibility of recourse if something goes wrong in the transaction. If buying long-distance from a *private individual*, in addition to the above advice, consider use of an escrow service, such as that provided by **Piano Buyer Classifieds** and **Pianomart.com**. The escrow service will hold your funds and not release them to the seller until you've had an opportunity to make sure that the piano you received is in the condition you expected.

Negotiating Price and Trade-Ins

The prices of new pianos are nearly always negotiable. Only a handful of dealers have non-negotiable prices. If in doubt, just ask—you'll be able to tell. Some dealers carry this bargaining to extremes, whereas others start pretty close to the final price. Many dealers don't like to display a piano's price because not doing so gives them more latitude in deciding on a starting price for negotiation. This makes shopping more difficult. Use the price information in the "**Model & Pricing Guide**" of the current issue of *Acoustic & Digital Piano Buyer* to determine the likely range within which a given model will sell. Don't give in too quickly. It's quite common for the salesperson to call a day or two later and offer a lower price. If there's an alternative piano at another dealership that will suit your needs just as well, it will help your negotiating position to let the salesperson know that.

Due to the high cost of advertising and conducting piano megasales (such as college sales, truckload sales, etc.), prices at these events are often actually *higher* than the price you could negotiate any day of the week, and the pressure to buy can be substantial. Shop at these sales only after you've shopped elsewhere, and look for the real bargains that can occasionally be found there.

If you're buying a new piano to replace one that's no longer satisfactory, you'll probably want to trade in the old one. Dealers will usually take a trade-in, no matter how bad it is, just to be able to facilitate the sale. In fact, in many cases the dealer will offer you what seems like a king's ransom for the old one. The downside is that when a generous trade-in allowance is given on the old piano, the dealer is then likely to offer you a less-generous price on the new one. To see if you're being offered a good deal, you'll have to carefully analyze the fair-market value of the old piano and what would be a likely price for the new one without a trade-in. Sometimes it will be to your advantage to sell the old piano privately, though in that case you'll need to take into account the hassle factor as well.

For more information about new-piano prices and negotiating, see the article "About New-Piano Pricing," elsewhere in this volume, as well as in *The Piano Book.*

Used-piano prices may or may not be negotiable. If the used piano is being sold by a dealer who primarily sells new pianos at negotiable prices, then the used-piano prices are probably also negotiable. Prices of restored pianos sold by the restorer are less likely to be negotiable, as technical people are usually less comfortable with bargaining. Prices of pianos for sale by private-party sellers are usually negotiable, in part because the seller often has little idea of what the piano should sell for and has made up a price based only on wishful thinking. But even knowledgeable sellers will usually leave a little wiggle room in their price.

Electronic Player-Piano Systems

Prior to the Great Depression, most pianos were outfitted with player-piano mechanisms—the kind that ran on pneumatic pressure and paper rolls. Today's player pianos are all electronic; they run on smartphones, iPads and other tablets, notebooks and laptops, MP3s, CDs, or electronic downloads from the Internet, and are far more versatile and sophisticated than their pneumatic ancestors. Now you don't have to wait until Junior grows up to hear something interesting from the piano! A substantial percentage of

The control box for some electronic player-piano systems is attached to the underside of the keybed.

new pianos, especially grands, are being outfitted with these systems. In fact, many pianos are being purchased as home-entertainment centers by buyers who have no intention of ever playing the piano themselves.

Several companies make these systems. Yamaha's Disklavier and Steinway's Spirio are built into select Yamaha, Steinway, and Bösendorfer models at these companies' factories. PianoDisc and QRS PNOmation, the two major aftermarket systems, can be installed in almost any piano, new or used, typically by the dealer or at an intermediate distribution point. Properly installed by a trained and authorized installer, none of these systems will harm the piano or void its warranty. However, such installations are complicated and messy and must be done in a shop, not in your home.

The most basic system will play your piano and accompany it with synthesized orchestration or actual recorded accompaniment played through speakers hidden underneath the piano. The aftermarket systems generally add $5,500 to $7,000 to the price of the piano. Add another $1,500 to $2,000 to enable the piano to record your own playing for future playback. For a little bit more, you can mute the piano (stop the hammers from hitting the strings), turn on a digital piano sound, and listen through headphones—a great alternative for late-night practicing. The range of prices reflects the variety of configurations and options available, including what music source you use (smartphone, iPad, CD, MP3 player, etc.). Higher-level systems that reproduce music in audiophile quality cost $15,000 or more. For more information, see the article **"Buying an Electronic Player-Piano System,"** elsewhere in this volume.

Furniture Style and Finish

Although for most buyers the qualities of performance and construction are of greatest importance in selecting a piano, a piano is also a large piece of furniture that tends to become the focal point of whatever

Continental Style

Institutional or
Professional Style

Samick Music Corp.

School Style

Pramberger Piano Co.

Hybrid Style

Wyman/Orla

Decorator Style:
French Provincial Cherry

Pramberger Piano Co.

Decorator Style:
Mediterranean Oak

Samick Music Corp.

Decorator Style:
Traditional Mahogany

Pramberger Piano Co.

room it is placed in. This is especially true of grands. Add to that the fact that you'll be looking at it for many years to come, and it becomes obvious that appearance can be an important consideration. For some buyers, it may be the most important consideration.

Vertical pianos without front legs are known as *Continental* style (also called *contemporary, European contemporary,* or *Euro style*). They are usually the smallest (42" to 43" high) and least expensive pianos in a manufacturer's product line.

Pianos with legs supported by *toe blocks* (struts that connect the body of the piano to the front legs) are sometimes known as *institutional* or *professional* style, particularly when the cabinet also has little in the way of decoration or embellishment.

School pianos are a subset of the institutional-style category. Generally 45" to 47" in height, these are institutional-style pianos made specifically for use in school practice rooms and classrooms. They usually come equipped with long music racks for holding multiple sheets of music, locks for both the lid and the fallboard, and heavy-duty casters for easier moving. They are generally available in ebony or satin wood finishes. Sturdy and sometimes plain-looking, they are also often purchased for home use for less furniture-conscious locations. (If you're buying a piano for an institution, please read "**Buying Pianos for an Institution**," elsewhere in this volume.)

Vertical pianos with free-standing legs not reinforced by toe blocks are generally known as *decorator* style. Common decorator styles are Queen Anne and French Provincial, generally in cherry (or Country French in oak), all with curved legs; Italian Provincial, typically in walnut with square legs; Mediterranean, usually in oak with hexagonal legs; and Traditional, most often in mahogany or walnut, with round or hexagonal legs. Matching music racks and cabinet decoration are common furniture embellishments. Furniture-style preference is an entirely personal matter. A practical consideration,

Straight Leg

Spade Leg

Queen Anne Style

Victorian Style
with Ice-Cream Cone legs

Yamaha Corp.

Samick Music Corp.

Petrof

however, is that front legs not supported by toe blocks have a tendency to break if the piano is moved frequently or carelessly.

Hybrid styles, containing features of both institutional and decorator styles, are common, especially in Asian pianos.

Grand pianos come in far fewer styles than verticals. As you shop, it's likely you'll see only a few different styles, in a number of woods and finishes.

The traditional grand piano case is likely familiar to everyone. It has rather straight or slightly tapered legs, often flaring slightly just above the floor (called a *spade* leg), and usually a rather plain, solid music rack.

Victorian style (sometimes called *classic* style) is an imitation of a style in fashion in the late 1800s, with large, round, fluted legs and a fancy, carved music desk. Variations of the Victorian style have "ice-cream cone" or other types of round-ish legs.

As with verticals, grands also come in Queen Anne and French Provincial styles, with curved legs, and in other period styles. In addition to the leg style, these usually differ in the treatment of the music rack and cabinet embellishment as well.

Pianos come in a variety of woods, most commonly ebony (sometimes called ebonized), which is not actual ebony wood, but an inexpensive, sturdy veneer that has been finished in black; as well as mahogany, cherry, walnut, and oak. Exotic woods include bubinga, rosewood, and many others, available on higher-priced uprights and grands. In pianos of lesser quality, sometimes a less expensive wood will be stained to look like a more expensive one. Pianos are also available in ivory or white, and it's often possible to special-order a piano in red, blue, or other colors.

In addition to the wood itself, the way the wood is finished also varies. Piano finishes come in either high polish (high gloss) or satin finishes. Satin reflects light but not images, whereas high polish is nearly mirror-like. Variations on satin include matte, which is completely flat (i.e., reflects no light), and open-pore finishes, common on European pianos, in which the grain is not filled in before finishing, leaving a slightly grainier texture. A few finishes are semigloss, which is partway between satin and high polish. As with furniture style, the finish is an entirely personal matter, though it should be noted that satin finishes tend to show fingerprints more than do high-polish finishes.

Most piano finishes are either lacquer or polyester. Lacquer was the finish on most pianos made in the first three-quarters of the 20th century, but it is gradually being supplanted by polyester. In my opinion, lacquer finishes—especially high-gloss lacquer—are more beautiful than polyester, but they scratch quite easily, whereas polyester is very durable. (Lacquer finishes can be repaired more easily.) Hand-rubbed satin lacquer is particularly elegant.

Touch and Tone

Touch, in its simplest form, refers to the effort required to press the piano keys. Unfortunately, the specifications provided by the manufacturers, expressed in grams, don't do justice to this complicated subject. The apparent touch can be very different when the piano is played quickly and loudly than when it is played softly and slowly, and this difference is not captured in the numbers—if you're a player, be sure to try it out both ways.

Advanced pianists tend to prefer a touch that is moderately firm because it provides better control than a very light touch, and strengthens the muscles. Too light a touch, even for a beginner, can cause laziness, but too firm a touch can be physically harmful over time. The touch of most new pianos today is within a reasonable range for their intended audience, but the touch of older pianos can vary a lot, depending on condition. A piano teacher may be able to assist in evaluating the touch of a piano for a beginner, particularly if considering an entry-level or used piano.

Piano *tone* is also very complex. The most basic aspect of tone, and the one most easily changed, is its brightness or mellowness. A *bright* tone, sometimes described by purchasers as *sharp* or *loud*, is one in which higher-pitched overtones predominate. A *mellow* tone, sometimes described as *warm*, *dull*, or *soft*, is one in which lower-pitched overtones are dominant. Most pianos are somewhere in between, and vary from one part of the keyboard to another, or depending on how hard one plays. The key to satisfaction is to make sure that the tone is right for the music you most often play or listen to. For example, jazz pianists will often prefer a brighter tone, whereas classical pianists will often prefer one that is mellower, or that can be varied easily from soft to loud; i.e., that has a broad dynamic range. However, there is no accounting for taste, and there are as many exceptions to these generalizations as there are followers. A piano technician can adjust the brightness or mellowness of the tone to a limited degree through a process known as *voicing*.

Another aspect of tone to pay attention to is *sustain*, which is how long the sound of a note continues at an audible level while its key is depressed before disappearing. Practically speaking, this determines the ability of a melodic line to "sing" above an accompaniment, especially when played in the critical mid-treble section.

Most pianos will play loudly quite reliably, but providing good expression when played softly is considerably more challenging. When trying out a piano, be sure to play at a variety of dynamic levels. Test the action with your most technically demanding passages. Don't forget to test the pedals for a sensitivity commensurate with your musical needs.

The Piano Warranty

Most pianos never generate a warranty claim. That said, few people would sleep well if worrying about potential problems arising in such a major purchase. Key warranty issues are: what is covered, for how long, and who stands behind the warranty.

The overwhelming majority of new-piano warranties cover the cost of parts and labor necessary to correct any defect in materials or workmanship. The warrantor (usually the manufacturer or distributor) also generally reserves the right to replace the piano should it choose to in lieu of repair. The warrantee (the customer) generally makes warranty claims to the dealer who, upon approval of the warrantor, makes the necessary repairs or replaces the instrument, as applicable. If the dealer has gone out of business, or if the customer has moved, warranty claims are made to the new local dealer of that brand, if any, or directly to the warrantor.

Warranties are in effect from the date of purchase and generally run between five and fifteen years, depending on the manufacturer. Note that there is little correlation between the length of the warranty and the quality of the piano, as decisions on warranty terms are often made based on marketing factors. For example, a new manufacturer might well offer a longer warranty to help bolster sales.

The Magnuson-Moss Warranty Act mandates that warranties be either *full* or *limited*. In the piano industry, the only significant difference is that full warranties remain in effect for the entire stated term, regardless of piano ownership, whereas limited warranties cover only the original purchaser. If you plan on possibly selling or trading up within a few years, a full warranty offers protection to the new owner, increasing the piano's value to them, and may justify a little higher selling price or trade-in value.

The final key issue about piano warranties concerns who stands behind the warranty. In most cases the warranty is backed by the actual manufacturer. This is advantageous, as the manufacturer has a major capital investment in its factory and has probably been in business for many years. The likelihood is that it will be around for the entire five- to fifteen-year period of your warranty. In today's piano market, however, many brands are manufactured under contract for a distributor, and the warranty is backed only by that distributor. Often, the distributor's only investment is a small rented office/warehouse and a few dozen pianos. Pianos are also often made to order for a particular dealership under a private brand name and are sold—and warranted—only by that dealership and/or its affiliates. In those cases, the warranty is further limited by the financial strength of the distributor or dealership, which can be difficult for the shopper to evaluate. In these situations, caution is called for.

When purchasing a used or restored piano, there is no warranty from a private, non-commercial seller, but a commercial seller will usually provide some kind of warranty, even if for only a few months. Pianos that have been completely restored typically come with a warranty with terms similar to that of a new piano, though of course it is backed by only the restorer.

Miscellaneous Practical Considerations

Bench

In all likelihood, your purchase of a new piano will include a matching bench. Benches for consumer-grade pianos are usually made by or for the piano manufacturer and come with the piano. Benches for performance-grade pianos are more often provided separately by the dealer.

Benches come in two basic types: fixed-height and adjustable, and in single and "duet" widths. Consumer-grade pianos usually come with fixed-height duet benches that have either a solid top that matches the piano's finish, or a padded top with sides and legs finished to match the piano. The legs of most benches will be miniatures of the piano's legs, particularly for decorative models. Most piano benches have music-storage compartments. School and institutional-type vertical pianos often come with so-called "stretcher" benches—the legs are connected with wooden reinforcing struts to better endure heavy use.

Adjustable benches are preferred by serious players, and by children and adults who are shorter or taller than average. The deeply tufted tops come in a heavy-duty vinyl and look like leather; tops of actual leather are available at additional cost. Adjustable benches vary considerably in quality. The best ones are expensive ($500 to $750) but are built to last a lifetime.

Finally, if the piano you want doesn't come with the bench you desire, talk to your dealer. It's common for dealers to swap benches or bench tops to accommodate your preference, or to offer an upgrade to a better bench in lieu of a discount on the piano.

For more information, see "**Benches, Lamps, Accessories, and Problem Solvers**," elsewhere in this volume.

Middle Pedal

As I mentioned near the beginning of this article, the function of the middle pedal varies. In some circumstances, you may need to consider whether the function of the middle pedal on a particular instrument will meet your musical needs.

On most new vertical pianos, the middle pedal operates a mute that reduces the sound volume by about 50%, a feature often appreciated by family members of beginning students. If your piano lacks this feature, after-market mute mechanisms are available for grands and verticals through piano technicians or dealers. On older verticals and a few new ones, the middle pedal, if not a mute, usually operates a bass sustain, although occasionally it's a "dummy" pedal that does nothing at all. I've never known anyone to actually use a bass-sustain pedal, so it might as well be a dummy.

On most grands and a few expensive uprights, the middle pedal operates a sostenuto mechanism that selectively sustains only those notes whose keys are down at the moment the pedal is pressed. This mechanism is called into action for only a relatively few pieces of classical music, yet it is generally considered obligatory for any "serious" instrument. Only inexpensive new and used grands omit the

1988–2018

The 30th Anniversary

KINGSBURG
QUALITY | RELIABILITY | VALUE

KINGSBURG
YANTAI KINGSBURG
PIANO CO.,LTD.

sostenuto, usually in favor of a bass sustain. (The obligatory nature of the sostenuto pedal—or any middle pedal—on a grand piano is a largely American phenomenon. Until fairly recently, many "serious" European pianos made for the European market had only two pedals.)

Fallboard *(Keyboard Cover)*

Vertical pianos use one of three basic fallboard designs: the Boston fallboard, a sliding fallboard (both of which disappear when open), or a one-piece "drop" fallboard with integrated music shelf.

The Boston fallboard is found on most furniture-style pianos and characteristically is a two-piece, double-hinged assembly. It is easily removed for service, and the rigidity provided by the hinges keeps the fallboard and the piano's side arms from being scratched when the fallboard is opened or closed.

The sliding fallboard, a one-piece cover that slides out from under the music desk to cover the keys, is considerably less expensive. However, if it is pulled unevenly and/or upwardly, it can scratch the fallboard or the inside of the piano's side arms.

The one-piece "drop" fallboard is commonly found on larger uprights. It is simply hinged at the back and lifts up to just past vertical, where it lies against the upper front panel of the piano. Attached to its underside is a small music shelf that is exposed when the fallboard is opened, then manually unfolded.

Grand pianos have a smaller, one-piece "drop" fallboard that opens under the music desk. Fallboards on most newer grands (and some newer verticals) are hydraulically damped to close slowly over the keys, eliminating the possibility of harming the player's or a young child's fingers. Aftermarket kits are available for pianos that lack this feature.

Slow-Close Grand Piano Lid

A relatively new device, called Magic Lid, adds hydraulic damping to a grand piano lid, substantially reducing the effort needed to raise and lower this extremely heavy part of the piano, and reducing the chance of injury when doing so. This is a standard feature of a few piano brands, but can also be retrofitted to most grand pianos. For more information, see our review in the archive of past feature articles at **www.pianobuyer.com**.

THE NEW-PIANO MARKET TODAY

Larry Fine

WHEN I BEGAN servicing pianos during the 1970s, most pianos sold in the U.S. (with the important exception of the growing number of pianos from Japan) were made in the U.S. by about a dozen different makers, which together turned out hundreds of thousands of pianos annually. By current standards, many were not particularly well made. Today, only three companies make pianos in the U.S. in any real quantities, which combined amount to no more than a few thousand instruments per year. However, over 30,000 new acoustic pianos are sold here annually under some 70 different brand names, made by more than 30 companies in a dozen countries. The quality is the best it's ever been. Here are the highlights of what's happened:

- The Japanese "invasion" of the 1960s onward was followed by a wave of pianos from Korea in the 1980s and '90s. Together, these imports put most low- and mid-priced American makers out of business.
- Rising wages in Korea in the 1990s caused much of that country's piano production to move to Indonesia and China.
- The economic emergence of China during the 2000s resulted in a new wave of low-priced, low-quality pianos appearing in the U.S. and globally.
- Foreign firms and investors have combined low-cost Chinese and Indonesian labor with high-quality design and manufacturing expertise, parts, and materials from Western countries to greatly increase the quality of low-priced Chinese and Indonesian pianos.
- Cheaper equipment for computer-aided design and manufacturing has allowed for their more widespread use by small and large firms alike, with a consequent increase in precision of manufacturing at all price levels.
- Since the 1990s, a dozen or more European makers of high-quality pianos have been aggressively marketing their pianos in the U.S., challenging entrenched interests and creating more choice and higher quality in the high end of the piano market.
- To better survive in a global economy, high-end companies have diversified their product lines to include low- and mid-priced pianos, setting up factories or forming alliances with companies in parts of the world where labor is cheaper. At the same time, makers of low- and mid-priced pianos are creating higher-priced models using parts and expertise usually associated with the high-end companies, thus blurring the line between the high and low ends of the piano market.

China

Pianos made in China now dominate the North American market, constituting more than a third of all new pianos sold in the U.S. A decade ago, most were just barely acceptable technically, and musically undesirable. Over the years, however, both the technical and musical qualities have taken big leaps forward. While some remain at the entry level, others rival the performance of more expensive pianos from other parts of the world. Reports sometimes suggest less consistency than with pianos from other countries, and a continuing need for thorough pre-sale preparation by the dealer, but otherwise few major problems. The prices of the better models are rising, but for entry- and mid-level buyers, many Chinese brands are still good value.

The first piano factory in China is said to have been established in 1895, in Shanghai (perhaps by the British?). During the 1950s, the Communists consolidated the country's piano manufacturing into four government-owned factories: Shanghai, Beijing, and Dongbei (means "northeast") in the northern part of the country, and Guangzhou Pearl River in the south. Piano making, though industrial, remained primitive well into the 1990s. In that decade, the government of China began to open the country's economy to foreign investment, first only to partnerships with the government, and later to completely private concerns.

As China's economy has opened up, the nation's rising middle and upper classes have created a sharp increase in demand for pianos. Tempted by the enormous potential of the Chinese domestic market, as well as by the lure of cheap goods manufactured for the West, foreign interests have built new piano factories in China, bought existing factories, or contracted with existing factories for the manufacture of pianos. The government has also poured money into its own factories to make them more quality competitive and to accommodate the growing demand.

From about 2000 to 2005, most sales of Chinese pianos in the U.S. were based on the idea of luring customers into the store to buy the least expensive piano possible. Dealers that staked their business on this approach often lost it. A growing trend now is to manufacture and sell somewhat higher-priced pianos that have added value in the form of better components, often imported to China from Europe and the U.S., but still taking advantage of the low cost of Chinese labor. The best ones are not just a collection of parts, however, but also have improved designs developed with foreign technical assistance, and sufficient oversight to make sure the designs are properly executed.

Except for the government involvement, the piano-making scene in China today is reminiscent of that in the U.S. a century ago: Hundreds of small firms assemble pianos from parts or subassemblies obtained from dozens of suppliers and sell them on a mostly regional basis. The government factories and a few large foreign ones sell nationally. Many of the brands sold in the Chinese domestic market are still primitive by Western standards. Primarily, the quality has markedly improved where foreign technical assistance or investment has been involved; only those pianos are good enough to be sold in the West.

Although in China the government factories have long had a monopoly on sales through piano dealers, that hold is gradually being eroded, and the government entities are experiencing great competitive pressure. Already, one of its factories, Dongbei, has been privatized through its sale to Gibson Guitar Corporation, parent of Baldwin Piano Company; and another, Guangzhou Pearl River, has successfully completed an initial public offering to become a public company.

Besides Baldwin, Pearl River, and the government-owned factories, other large makers in China for the North American market are Parsons Music (Hong Kong), Yamaha (Japan), Young Chang (Korea), and, for the Canadian market, Kawai (Japan)—all of whom own factories in China. Other foreign-owned companies that own factories in China or contract with Chinese manufacturers to make pianos for the U.S. market include AXL (Palatino brand), Bechstein (W. Hoffmann Vision brand), Blüthner (Irmler Studio brand), Brodmann, Cunningham, Heintzman, Perzina, Schulze Pollmann, and Wilh. Steinberg. Many American distributors and dealers contract with Beijing, Pearl River, and other makers, selling pianos in the U.S. under a multitude of names. Steinway & Sons markets the Essex brand, designed by Steinway and manufactured by Pearl River.

And one company, Hailun, is owned and operated by a Chinese entrepreneur, Chen Hailun.

Indonesia

Indonesia is China's closest competitor in terms of price and quality. But unlike China, in which

PRAMBERGER

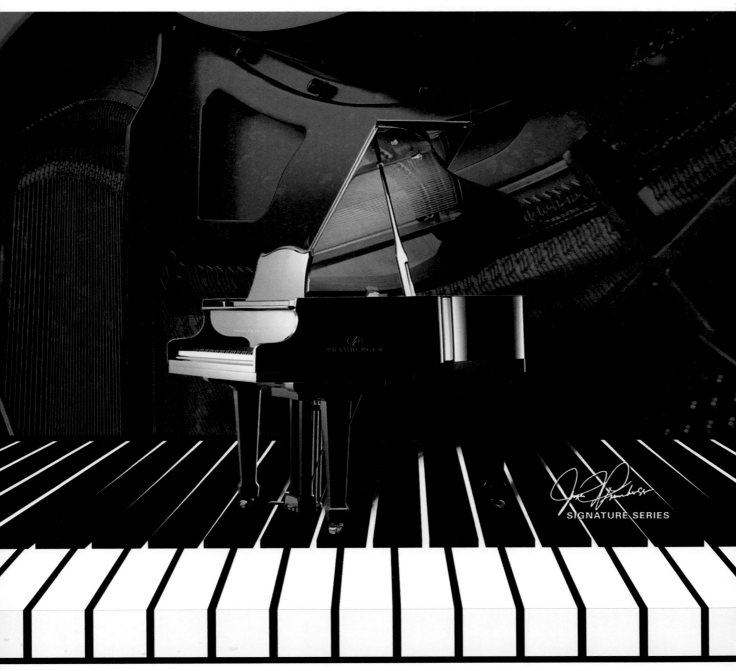

SIGNATURE SERIES

Building on **Seven Generations**
of **Piano Artistry**

www.prambergerpianoco.com

many small and large companies, domestic and foreign, are involved in piano manufacturing, virtually all pianos made in Indonesia are the products of three large, foreign players: Yamaha, Kawai, and Samick. For the U.S. market, Yamaha makes an entry-level grand and most of their smaller verticals in Indonesia; Kawai makes all its small and medium-sized verticals there, and one entry-level grand; and Samick makes all its pianos for sale in North America there, both grand and vertical.

Overall, the manufacturing quality is similar to China's, but Indonesia got to this level of quality more rapidly and is perhaps more consistent. This may have been due to the smaller number and, on average, larger size of Indonesia's piano manufacturers, as well as to cultural and political differences between the countries. Development of manufacturing in Indonesia was aided by the fact that the country was already a democratic (more or less), capitalist nation with strong ties to the West, and accustomed to Western ways of working and doing business, with English widely spoken. The government does not own or manage the factories.

One of the big challenges in Indonesia, as in the rest of tropical Asia (which includes southern China), is climate control inside the factories, and the proper handling of wood to avoid problems later on when the instruments are shipped to drier countries and the wood dries out. All three companies, as well as Pearl River in southern China, have done a good job of meeting this challenge, but caution and proper climate control by the consumer are especially advised when these pianos are to be used in very difficult, dry indoor climates.

Korea

The Korean piano industry has had a tumultuous history, from its beginnings in the war-torn 1950s through its meteoric global rise in the 1980s; through labor unrest, the Asian economic crisis, and the abrupt collapse of the country's piano industry in the 1990s; and most recently through bankruptcies, reorganizations, aborted takeovers, and more bankruptcies. Today, both Samick and Young Chang seem to be on relatively stable financial footing, the latter having just emerged from bankruptcy after being purchased by Hyundai Development Company. As mentioned earlier, due to high labor costs in Korea, both companies have moved most of their manufacturing

elsewhere, limiting production at home to the more expensive models.

Quality control in the Korean models is now nearly as good as in pianos from Japan, but getting there has taken 30 years of two steps forward, one step back. The reasons for the slow development are probably numerous, but undoubtedly some are cultural in nature: Western piano-company personnel have often reported that their Korean counterparts can be proud people, reluctant to take advice from Americans (not that they necessarily should—unless they're trying to sell products to Americans).

Musically, the two companies' pianos have never really gained clear, aesthetic identities of their own, other than as very acceptable musical products. Periodic redesigns by German engineers, or American engineers with Germanic names (always sought by piano makers), have brought some progress, but never as much as was hoped for. Part of the reason for the lack of identity may be that there have been such a multitude of product lines made in different factories to constantly changing specifications that nothing has settled down long enough to stick. Internal politics and dealing with quality-control problems have also taken up much energy over the years.

Things are settling down now for both companies. Samick, in its upper- and mid-level lines, is producing some of its nicest pianos ever. Young Chang is playing catch-up, but also has some good designs, with new ones in the pipeline. Both companies' top-level products have much to offer at good prices.

Japan

Japan's two major piano manufacturers, Yamaha and Kawai, began making pianos around 1900 and 1927, respectively, with export to the United States beginning in earnest in the early 1960s. The first few years of export were spent learning to season the wood to the demands of the North American climate, but since then the quality control has been impressive, to say the least, and the standard to which other piano manufacturers aspire. Both companies also have outstanding warranty service, so customers are never left hanging with unsatisfactory instruments. As in Korea, labor costs in Japan have risen to the point where both companies have been forced to move much of their manufacturing elsewhere, making only their more expensive models in Japan. With some exceptions, their grands and tallest uprights are made in Japan, small and mid-sized verticals in other Asian countries.

The tone of Japanese pianos tends to be a little on the bright and percussive side (Yamaha more than Kawai), though less so than in previous years, and pleasing in their own way. In addition to their regular lines, both companies make high-end lines with more "classical" qualities, as well as entry-level lines that reflect a compromise between price and quality. The pianos are very popular with institutions and are real workhorses. Although more expensive than most other Asian pianos, a Japanese-made Yamaha or Kawai piano is hard to beat for reliability. Kawai also manufactures the Boston brand, designed by Steinway and sold through Steinway dealers.

United States

Only three companies manufacture pianos here in any numbers: Steinway & Sons, Mason & Hamlin, and Charles R. Walter. A few boutique makers, such as Ravenscroft, build high-end pianos to order. Baldwin, for a century one of the largest American producers, finally ceased production at its American factory in 2009, having moved all piano production to its plants in China.

Steinway & Sons has been making high-quality pianos in New York City since its founding in 1853 by German immigrants. For most of the past century, the company has had little competition in the U.S.: when one desired to buy a piano of the highest quality, it was simply understood that one meant a Steinway. The last few decades have seen some erosion of that status by more than a dozen European and Japanese firms and our own Mason & Hamlin. Although each by itself is too small to make a dent in Steinway's business, their combined effect has been to claim a significant share of the market for high-end pianos in the home. (Steinway still completely dominates the concert-grand market and, to a lesser extent, the institutional market.) This was made easier by the fact that in certain respects the European-made pianos were visibly and audibly of higher quality than American-made Steinways (to be distinguished from Steinways made at the company's branch factory in Hamburg, Germany, which have always been of the highest quality). Steinways have classic designs and use proven materials and methods of construction, but for much of the last fifty years, the musical and aesthetic finishing of the American-made pianos

has too often been left uncompleted at the factory in the expectation, frequently unmet, that the dealers would finish it off. Fortunately, the past ten years have seen a reversal of this trend in the form of many improvements at the factory, as well as perhaps better performance by dealers. The ratio of compliments to complaints, in my experience, has become much more favorable.

Mason & Hamlin, Steinway's principal competitor in the early part of the 20th century, went into a long period of decline after the Great Depression. After a series of bankruptcies and reorganizations in the 1980s and '90s, Mason & Hamlin was purchased in 1996 by the Burgett brothers, owners of PianoDisc, a leading manufacturer of player-piano systems. Since then, from an old brick factory building in Haverhill, Massachusetts, the Burgetts have completely restored the company to its former excellence, and then some. They and their staff have designed or redesigned a complete line of grand pianos and modernized century-old equipment. Rather than compete with Steinway on Steinway's terms, Mason & Hamlin has repositioned itself as an innovator, seeking out or developing high-quality but lower-cost parts and materials from around the world, and combining them with traditional craftsmanship to produce a great piano at a somewhat lower price.

Charles R. Walter, a piano design engineer by profession, has been making high-quality vertical pianos in Elkhart, Indiana, since the 1970s, and grands for over ten years. The factory is staffed in large part by members of his extended family. The instruments are built using the best traditional materials and construction practices. Right now, times are tough for small companies such as this, which produce an excellent product but are neither the high-priced celebrated names nor the low-cost mass producers. If you're looking to "buy American," you can't get any more American than Charles R. Walter.

Europe

European makers that regularly sell in the U.S. include: Bechstein, Blüthner, August Förster, Grotrian, Sauter, Schimmel, Seiler, Steingraeber, and Wilh. Steinberg (Germany); Bösendorfer (Austria); Fazioli and Schulze Pollmann (Italy); Estonia (Estonia); and Petrof (Czech Republic). Most are of

WILH. STEINBERG

WST

Fine pianos. Made in Germany.
Since 1877.

Keep the legacy   Continue the history

Extraordinary German Craft and Quality

Exceptional Touch & Tonal Response

WILH. STEINBERG, established in Eisenberg where the
art of piano making in Germany originated.
Its highly skilled artisans and modern factories have
made Eisenberg famous over the world for piano building.
The result of 140 years of experience and tradition in
piano manufacturing.
WILH. STEINBERG pianos comprise a unique blend of
tonal quality and exquisite cabinet design.

P-121

Thüringer Pianoforte GmbH   Mozartstr. 3, 07607 Eisenberg, Germany

extremely high quality; even the least of them is very good. Until two decades ago, most of these brands were virtually unknown or unavailable in the U.S., but as the European demand for pianos contracted, many of the companies found that Americans, with their large homes and incomes, would buy all the grand pianos they could produce. The liberation of Eastern Europe resulted in an increase in the quality of such venerable brands as Estonia and Petrof, which had suffered under Communist rule, and these brands, too, became available and accepted here.

The rush to sell to Americans has caused some European companies to reconsider the tonal designs of their instruments and to redesign them for better sound projection, tonal color, and sustain—that is, to sound more like American Steinways. Considering that some of these companies are five or six generations old and have redesigned their pianos about that many times in 150 years, this degree of activity is unusual. Some of the redesigns have been great musical successes; nevertheless, the loss of diversity in piano sound is to be mourned.

Several German companies have started or acquired second-tier lines to diversify their product lines, and have gradually shifted much of their production to former Soviet-bloc countries with lower labor costs, producing brands such as W. Hoffmann (by Bechstein) in the Czech Republic, and Wilhelm Schimmel, formerly Vogel (by Schimmel), in Poland. Today, there is enough commonality in business practices, laws, and attitudes toward quality among the countries of Europe that the distinction between Eastern and Western Europe carries little meaning—except for labor costs, where the savings can be great.

Globalization, Quality, and Value

The worldwide changes in the piano industry are making it more difficult to advise piano shoppers. For many years, the paradigm for piano quality has been an international pecking order: pianos from Russia, China, and Indonesia at the bottom; followed by Korea, Japan, and Eastern Europe; and, finally, Western Europe at the top, with pianos from the U.S. scattered here and there, depending on the brand. This pecking order has never been foolproof, but it has served a generation of piano buyers well enough as a rule of thumb.

Now this order is being disturbed by globalization. High-end and low-end makers are, to some extent, adopting each other's methods and narrowing the differences between them. On the one hand, some Western European and American makers of high-end pianos are partially computerizing the manufacture of their "hand-built" pianos, quietly sourcing parts and subassemblies from China, and developing less expensive product lines in Eastern Europe and Asia. On the other hand, some Korean and Chinese makers are importing parts and technology from Germany, Japan, and the U.S., producing pianos that sometimes rival the performance of more expensive pianos from the West. Global alliances are bringing new products to market that are more hybridized than anything we've seen before. Although the old pecking order still has some validity, the number of exceptions is increasing, causing temporary confusion in the marketplace until a new order emerges.

At the same time that the range of quality differences is narrowing, the range of prices is widening, bringing into greater prominence issues of "value." Eastern European brands have emerged as "value" alternatives to Western European brands, the latter becoming frightfully expensive due to high labor costs and the rapid appreciation of the euro against the dollar. Some of the better pianos from China, Korea, and Indonesia have become value alternatives to Japanese pianos. Brands that don't scream "value" are being squeezed out of the market.

As mentioned above, one of the consequences of globalization is that parts and materials formerly available only to high-end makers are now for sale to any company, anywhere, that's willing to pay for them. Thus, you'll see a number of Asian firms marketing their pianos with a list of well-regarded brand-name components from Germany and North America, such as Renner, Röslau, Mapes, and Bolduc. The question then naturally arises: Given that high-end pianos are so expensive, and that today one can buy for so little a Chinese-made piano with German design, German parts, and perhaps even a German name, is it still worth buying a performance-grade piano made in the West? Are there any differences worth paying for?

There's no question that high-end components, such as Renner hammers and Bolduc soundboards, add to the quality and value of consumer-grade pianos in which they're used. But in terms of quality, components such as these are only the tip of the

iceberg. Although the difference between performance- and consumer-grade pianos has narrowed, in many ways the two types of manufacturers still live in different worlds. Differences are manifested in such things as the selection, drying, and use of wood; final regulation and voicing; and attention to technical and cosmetic details.

Makers of performance-grade pianos use higher grades of wood, selected for finer grain, more even color, or greater hardness, strength, and/or acoustical properties, as the use requires. Wood is seasoned more carefully and for longer periods of time, resulting in greater dimensional stability and a longer-lasting product. Veneers are more carefully matched, and finishes polished to a greater smoothness. Action assemblies purchased from suppliers may be taken apart and put back together to more exacting tolerances than originally supplied. The workspace is set up to allow workers more time to complete their tasks and a greater opportunity to catch and correct errors. Much more time is spent on final regulation and voicing, with an instrument not leaving the factory, in some cases, until a musician has had an opportunity to play it and be satisfied. Of course, the degree to which these manifestations of quality, and many others not mentioned, are present will vary by brand and circumstance, but underlying them all is this philosophical difference: with performance-grade pianos, the driving force behind decision-making tends to be the quality of the product; with consumer-grade pianos, cost is a greater factor.

A MAP OF THE MARKET FOR NEW PIANOS

Larry Fine

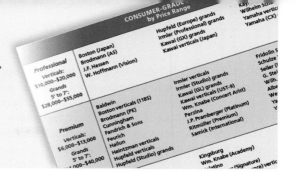

THE CHART AND COMMENTARY that follow are intended to provide the newcomer to the piano market with a simple summary of how this market is organized. This summary is not, strictly speaking, a ranking of quality; rather, it is intended as a description of how manufacturers and dealers position their products in the marketplace. That is, if a dealer carried every brand, how would he or she position those brands, in terms of relative quality, when presenting them to prospective purchasers?

For pianos intended for consumer use, this positioning is usually done along lines of price; for high-end and luxury instruments—where price is less likely to be a buyer's primary concern—there is a rough pecking order based on reputation. As will be discussed later, while price and reputation are often associated with quality, that association is far from perfectly consistent. Nevertheless, in the larger picture and speaking very generally, price and reputation are associated with quality closely enough that this chart can be used as a *rough* guide to the quality of today's new pianos, though not as a precise or authoritative one.

The key to proper use of this chart, then, is not to follow it religiously, but to understand that, given its nature, it should be used only as a learning tool. In addition, use common sense when comparing one brand with another. Compare verticals with other verticals of similar size, and grands with similarly sized grands, or models whose selling prices fall within the same range. Don't get hung up on small differences between one group and the next—the distinctions can be quite subtle. Furthermore, the preparation of the piano by the dealer can be at least as important to the quality of the product you receive as some of the distinctions listed in the chart. Note that there may be quality differences within a single product line that, for the sake of simplicity, we do

not indicate here; and a few brands have been omitted due solely to lack of sufficient information about them. **Within each group, the brands are listed in alphabetical order. No judgment of these brands' relative quality should be inferred from this order.**

Prices shown for each group represent, in round numbers, a typical range of Suggested Maximum Prices (SMP) of new pianos in the least expensive styles and finishes—smaller models toward the low end of each range, larger models toward the high end. (Significant discounts from these prices are likely—see the article "About New-Piano Pricing," elsewhere in this volume.)

Performance-Grade Pianos

Performance-grade pianos generally have several of the following attributes:

- They are built to a single high standard, almost without regard to cost, and the price charged reflects whatever it takes to build such a piano and bring it to market.
- A greater proportion of the labor required to build them is in the handwork involved in making custom refinements to individual instruments, often with fanatical attention to detail.

- Most are made in relatively small quantities by firms that have been in business for generations, often under the ownership of the same family. As a result, many have achieved almost legendary status, and are often purchased as much for their prestige value as for their performance.
- These are the instruments most likely to be called into service when the highest performance level is required, particularly for classical music.
- Most performance-grade pianos are made in Europe or the United States; a few are now made in Japan.

Performance-grade pianos are divided here into four groups, based on our perception of their reputation in both the musical and technical spheres of the piano business. (Of course, our perceptions are ultimately subjective, and reasonable people, especially outside the U.S., may disagree with our rankings to varying degrees.) The first two groups are reserved for those brands whose prestige figures prominently in their value. Brands labeled *Iconic* are those that seem, by general agreement, to be the ones that would be the flagship line of any dealer that carried them—they are, so to speak, the Maseratis and Lamborghinis of the piano industry. Those labeled *Venerable* are not quite Iconic, but have a virtually uninterrupted period of 150 years or more of very high quality, and some have been owned by the same family for generations. (The word *venerable* carries a connotation of respect due in part to age.) Of course, the prestige of these two groups is based in large part on their extremely high quality, but marketing success and historical accident also play important roles in the reputations of these and other high-end brands.

The brands in the third group, *Distinguished*, are also of very high quality, but are either fairly recent arrivals to the Performance-Grade category, or have returned to very high quality in the last 20 years or so after a period of decline. Though not Iconic or Venerable, they are nonetheless excellent in every way. Preferences among performance-grade pianos in general are greatly dependent on musical taste in tone and touch. For these reasons, a number of brands in the third group have devoted followings and, practically speaking, may be just as good despite not having as much prestige associated with their names.

The last group in this category, *Notable*, consists of a few brands that are less often thought of as Performance Grade, but by price and reputation should

PERFORMANCE-GRADE PIANOS
by Reputation (see text)

Iconic *Verticals:* $30,000–$70,000 *Grands* 5' to 7': $75,000–$150,000+	C. Bechstein Blüthner Bösendorfer Fazioli Steingraeber & Söhne Steinway & Sons (Hamburg)
Venerable *Verticals:* $20,000–$50,000 *Grands* 5' to 7': $60,000–$105,000	August Förster Grotrian Sauter Steinway & Sons (New York)
Distinguished *Verticals:* $20,000–$40,000 *Grands* 5' to 7': $50,000–$90,000	C. Bechstein (Academy) Estonia Haessler Shigeru Kawai Mason & Hamlin Petrof Schimmel (Konzert/Classic) Seiler (Germany) Yamaha (CF)
Notable *Verticals:* $18,000–$27,000 *Grands* 5' to 7': $45,000–$80,000	W. Hoffmann (Tradition/ Professional) Rönisch Schulze Pollmann (Masterpiece) Wilh. Steinberg (Signature) Charles R. Walter Yamaha (SX)

Notes: Unless otherwise stated, brand names refer to both grand and vertical models. Prices are Suggested Maximum Prices (SMP) of vertical models, and of grand models from 5' to 7' in length, regular style, lowest-price finish (usually polished ebony). Substantial discounts from these prices are common—see "About New-Piano Pricing," elsewhere in this volume, for further explanation. The prices shown for a category reflect, in round numbers, the approximate range into which most of the brands and models in that category fall, but a few models may fall outside the range. Also, keep in mind that an individual brand's price range may be narrower than that of the category it is listed under.

CONSUMER-GRADE PIANOS
by Price Range

Professional *Verticals:* $10,000–$20,000 *Grands* 5' to 7': $28,000–$55,000	Boston (Japan) Brodmann (AS) Wilhelm Grotrian grands W. Hoffmann (Vision) Hupfeld (Europe) grands	Irmler (Professional) grands Kawai (GX) grands Kawai verticals (Japan) Kayserburg (Artist)	Wilhelm Schimmel Wertheim (Fandrich) Yamaha verticals (Japan) Yamaha (CX) grands
Premium *Verticals:* $6,000–$13,000 *Grands* 5' to 7': $14,000–$40,000	Baldwin Boston verticals (118S) Brodmann (PE) Cunningham Fandrich & Sons Feurich Wilhelm Grotrian verticals Hailun Heintzman verticals Hupfeld verticals	Hupfeld (Studio) grands Irmler verticals Irmler (Studio) grands Kawai (GL) grands Kawai verticals (UST-9) Wm. Knabe (Concert Arist) Perzina J.P. Pramberger (Platinum) Ritmüller (Premium) Samick (International)	Fridolin Schimmel Schulze Pollmann (Studio) Seiler (ED) G. Steinberg Wilh. Steinberg (P) Story & Clark grands Albert Weber Wertheim (Euro/Platinum) Yamaha (GC) grands Yamaha verticals (P22)
Mid-Range *Verticals:* $5,000–$8,000 *Grands* 5' to 7': $11,000–$21,000	Brodmann (CE) Cline Essex Heintzman grands Gerhard Heintzman verticals Kawai verticals (Indonesia) Kingsburg	Wm. Knabe (Academy) Palatino Pramberger (Signature) Ritmüller (Performance) verticals Schumann verticals Johannes Seiler	Weber Wertheim (Gold) Yamaha verticals (Indonesia) Yamaha (GB) grands Young Chang
Economy *Verticals:* $4,000–$6,500 *Grands* 5' to 7': $9,500–$15,000	Cristofori/Paul A. Schmitt A. Geyer Hallet, Davis & Co. Hardman, Peck Gerhard Heintzman grands	Wm. Knabe (Baltimore) Pearl River Pramberger (Legacy) Ritmüller (Classic)	Ritmüller (Performance) grands Schumann grands Story & Clark verticals

> **Note: This chart is *not*, strictly speaking, a rating of pianos by quality. Consumer-grade pianos are listed here by price range, performance-grade pianos are listed by general reputation. For explanation, see the accompanying article.**

probably be separated from the Consumer-Grade category. Most of these are also considerably less expensive than those in the other groups, and may be a better value when the highest levels of quality or prestige are not needed.

Consumer-Grade Pianos

Consumer-grade pianos are built to be sold at a particular price, and adjustments to (i.e., compromises in) materials, workmanship, and method and location

Why don't we strictly judge piano quality in **Piano Buyer**? During the last half of the 20th century, a great many pianos, especially low-end instruments manufactured in the U.S. and in developing countries, had significant defects that made separating good instruments from bad relatively easy. That is no longer the case. Due to globalization and the computerization of manufacturing, virtually all pianos now sold in the West are competently made and without major defects, and the differences between them are increasingly subtle and subjective. While it's still clear that high-end pianos are better than entry-level ones, comparisons of instruments that are closer in price are less conclusive, and much more subject to the whims of personal preference, how well the pianos have been prepared for sale, room acoustics, and so forth.

In addition, the definition of *quality* itself is extremely vague. Depending on the buyer's priorities, *quality* could refer, among other things, to a piano's musical performance, to the aesthetics of its furniture, to its ability to hold up under the demands of heavy use in a school, or to its ability to survive in difficult climates. If *quality* refers to its musical performance, is that in a concert venue, a teaching studio, or a living room? If in a concert venue, solo or with an orchestra? For playing Mozart, Debussy, Rachmaninoff, or Gershwin? And whose preferences in tone and touch should we enshrine as the standard by which all pianos should be measured? Each answer to those questions will produce a different ordering of pianos by quality. Furthermore, even those responsible for the technical design of pianos often can't agree on which features and specifications produce the best instruments.

In such a context of extreme subjectivity, varying priorities, and contradictory expert opinions, making too fine a distinction among brands based on their quality tends to give a false impression of scientific objectivity, and inhibits shoppers from making their own judgments and possibly discovering something wonderful for themselves. For these reasons, we have chosen to take a less active but, we think, more honest approach to giving piano-buying advice, by providing newcomers to the market with a simple frame of reference and a few personal recommendations (see our "**Staff Picks**" section online), and otherwise letting them explore and discover for themselves what appeals to them.

of manufacture are made to meet that price. Most are mass-produced in Asia, with less in the way of custom refinement of individual instruments.

Consumer-grade pianos are grouped here by price range. As mentioned earlier, in the larger picture, price is a reasonably good guide to quality. But as one focuses more closely on smaller areas of the market, the association of price with quality breaks down somewhat. For example, some brands may offer a better value than others because they are reduced in price to gain a larger market share, or because they are made in a country with lower labor costs. Some brands or models, especially those that are new to the market, may be mispriced because their manufacturers haven't yet learned from experience what the public is actually willing to pay for them. Two brands that are roughly equal in price and overall quality may have different blends of strengths and weaknesses. In fact, some lower-priced models may appeal to you more than some higher-priced ones because of their particular characteristics or features.

As can be expected, upper-level consumer-grade pianos generally have premium components and better performance than lower-level instruments. The best of them are made in Japan or Europe, or are partly made in China or Indonesia and then shipped to Europe for completion. Some have become so advanced in their designs, materials, and manufacturing technologies that they now rival some performance-grade pianos in musicality, and are sometimes recommended as substitutes for them, often at considerably lower prices. The economy models, on the other hand, are basic, no-frills pianos suitable for beginners and casual users, but which a conscientious student may outgrow in a few years.

In my view, the brands in the Premium group tend to offer the best ratio of price to performance (i.e., the best value) among consumer-grade pianos. However, shoppers on a limited budget, or those looking for something a little more upscale, may benefit from the other groups shown.

PLEYEL

Depuis 1807 à Paris

PLEYEL ET COMP

Chopin's Piano for eternity

Frédéric Chopin and hundreds of legendary pianists have made the famous Pleyel romantical sound a myth all over the world. Building on more than two centuries of innovation and tradition, the French historical brand comes back to life.

www.pleyel.com

CH Series

Model:CH-1
47″
Straight Leg
Ebony Polish
MSRP:11,200

Model:CH-2
47.5″
Straight Leg
Walunt Polish
MSRP:12,400

Model:CH-3
48.5″
Straight Leg
Ebony Polish
MSRP:11,900

Model:CH-4
48.5″
Cabriole Leg
White Polish
MSRP:13,600

Model:CH-5
49″
Straight Leg
Cherry Satin
MSRP:13,900

Model:CH-6
49″
Cabriole Leg
White Satin
MSRP:13,900

WH Series

Model:WH-1
48.5″
Straight Leg
Ebony Polish
MSRP:15,000

Model:WH-1BS
48.5″
Straight Leg
Mahogany Satin
MSRP:20,000

Model:WH-2
49″
Straight Leg
Ebony Polish
MSRP:22,800

NY Series

Model:NY-123
48.5″
Straight Leg
Cocobolo Polish
MSRP:15,600

Model:NY-125
49″
Straight Leg
Padouk Polish
MSRP:23,500

HZ Series

Model:HZ-125
49″
Straight Leg
Ebony Polish
MSRP:13,000

Since 2015, Bush & Gerts Piano Company has resumed its mass production and global sales. Prior to that, they accepted orders of high-end, private, hand-built pianos only. Renowned as one of eight world-class piano brands at the top-ranking concerts, Bush & Gerts pianos stand at par with those of top-tier musical instruments in the world today. The models available for export to the U.S. are the White House, New York, Horowitz, and Chicago collections, which commemorate the company's early days. Components are sourced from the German first-rate companies.

You will have to play a Bush & Gerts piano to discover the rich, full, and heavenly sound that this piano gives to every player.

ABOUT NEW-PIANO PRICING

Larry Fine

ABOUT PRICES

The subject of piano pricing is difficult, complicated, and controversial. One of the major problems is that piano dealers tend to prefer that list prices be as high as possible so they can still make a profit while appearing to give very generous discounts. Honesty about pricing is resisted. But even knowing what is "honest" is a slippery business because many factors can have a dramatic effect on piano pricing.

For one thing, different dealerships can pay very different wholesale prices for the same merchandise, depending on:

- the size of the dealership and how many pianos it agrees to purchase at one time or over a period of time
- whether the dealer pays cash or finances the purchase
- the degree to which the dealer buys manufacturer overstocks at bargain prices
- any special terms the dealership negotiates with the manufacturer or distributor.

In addition to these variations at the wholesale level, retail conditions also vary from dealer to dealer or from one geographic area to another, including:

- the general cost of doing business in the dealer's area
- the level of pre- and post-sale service the dealer provides
- the level of professionalism of the sales staff and the degree to which they are trained and compensated
- the ease of local comparison shopping by the consumer for a particular type of piano or at a particular price level.

Besides the variations between dealerships, the circumstances of each sale at any particular dealership can vary tremendously due to such things as:

- how long a particular piano has been sitting around unsold, racking up finance charges for the dealer
- the dealer's financial condition and need for cash at the moment
- competing sales events going on at other dealerships in the area
- whether or not the customer is trading in a used piano.

As difficult as it might be to come up with accurate price information, confusion and ignorance about pricing for such a high-ticket item is intolerable to the consumer, and can cause decision-making paralysis. I strongly believe that a reasonable amount of price information actually greases the wheels of commerce by giving the customer the peace of mind that allows him or her to make a purchase. In this guide I've tried to give a level of information about price that reasonably respects the interests of both buyer and seller, given the range of prices that can exist for any particular model.

Prices include a bench except where noted. (Even where a price doesn't include a bench, the dealer will almost always provide one and quote a price that includes it.) Most dealers will also include delivery and one or two tunings in the home, but these are optional and a matter of agreement between you and the dealer. Prices do not include sales tax.

In the online Model & Pricing Guide at **www.pianobuyer.com**, two prices are given for each model: Manufacturer's Suggested Retail Price (MSRP) and Suggested Maximum Price (SMP).

Manufacturer's Suggested Retail Price (MSRP)

The MSRP is a price provided by the manufacturer or distributor and designed as a starting point from which dealers are expected to discount. I include it here for reference purposes—only rarely does a customer pay this price. The MSRP is usually figured as a multiple of the wholesale price, but the specific multiple used differs from company to company. **For that reason, it's fruitless to compare prices of different brands by comparing discounts from the MSRP.** To see why, consider the following scenario:

Manufacturer A sells brand A through its dealer A. The wholesale price to the dealer is $1,000, but for the purpose of setting the MSRP, the manufacturer doubles the wholesale price and sets the MSRP at $2,000. Dealer A offers a 25 percent discount off the MSRP, for a "street price" of $1,500.

Manufacturer B sells brand B through its dealer B. The wholesale price to the dealer is also $1,000, but manufacturer B triples the wholesale price and sets the MSRP at $3,000. Dealer B offers a generous 50 percent discount, for a street price of, again, $1,500.

Although the street price is the same for both pianos, a customer shopping at both stores and knowing nothing about the wholesale price or how the MSRPs are computed, is likely to come away with the impression that brand B, with a discount of 50 percent off $3,000, is a more "valuable" piano and a better deal than brand A, with a discount of 25 percent off $2,000. Other factors aside, which dealer do you think will get the sale? It's important to note that there is nothing about brand B that makes it deserving of a higher MSRP than brand A—how to compute the MSRP is essentially a marketing decision on the part of the manufacturer.

Because of the deceptive manner in which MSRPs are so often used, some manufacturers no longer provide them. In those cases, I've left the MSRP column blank.

Suggested Maximum Price (SMP)

The Suggested Maximum Price (SMP) is a price I've created, based on a profit margin that I've uniformly applied to published wholesale prices. (Where the published wholesale price is unavailable, or is believed to be bogus, as is sometimes the case, I've made a reasonable attempt to estimate the SMP from other sources.) Because in the SMP, unlike in the MSRP, the same profit margin is applied to all brands, the SMP can be used as a "benchmark" price for the purpose of comparing brands and offers. The specific profit margin I've chosen for the SMP is one that dealers often try—but rarely manage—to attain. Also included in the SMP, in most cases, are allowances for duty (where applicable), freight charges, and a minimal amount of make-ready by the dealer. Although the SMP is my creation, it's a reasonable estimate of the **maximum** price you should realistically expect to pay. However, **most sales actually take place at a discount to the SMP**, as discussed below.

Actual Selling or "Street" Price

As you should know by now from reading this publication, most dealers of new pianos are willing—and expect—to negotiate. Only a handful of dealers have non-negotiable prices. For more information on negotiating, please see **"Negotiating Price and Trade-Ins"** in the article "Piano Buying Basics." *The Piano Book* also gives advice about negotiating tactics.

How good a deal you can negotiate will vary, depending on the many factors listed earlier. But in order to make a budget, or to know which pianos are within your budget, or just to feel comfortable enough to actually make a purchase, you need some idea of what is considered normal in the industry. In most cases, discounts from the Suggested Maximum Price range from 15 to 25 percent. This does *not* mean that if you try hard enough, you can talk the salesperson into giving you a 25 percent discount. Rather, it reflects the wide range of prices possible in the marketplace due to the many factors discussed earlier. For budgeting purposes only, I suggest figuring a discount of about 20 percent. This will probably bring you within about 5 percent, one way or the

other, of the final negotiated price. Important exception: Discounts on Steinway pianos generally range from 0 to 10 percent. For your convenience in figuring the effects of various discounts, a discount calculator is included in the model and price database, accessible through the electronic edition of this publication.

There is no single "fair" or "right" price that can be applied to every purchase. The only fair price is that which the buyer and seller agree on. It's understandable that you would like to pay as little as possible, but remember that piano shopping is not just about chasing the lowest price. Be sure you are getting the instrument that best suits your needs and preferences, and that the dealer is committed to providing the appropriate level of pre- and post-sale service.

For more information about shopping for a new piano and how to save money, please see pages 60–75 in *The Piano Book, Fourth Edition.*

VAUGHAN
◆— LEIPZIG 1876 —◆

Vaughan piano is originated from Leipzig, Germany, also known as "the city of music". Tim Vaughan founded Vaughan in 1876, when he already became the third successor of Vaughan piano manufacturing, as his grandfather started to make piano as early as in 1780, which was named after his grandfather`s name "Vaughan". Back at that time, the Vaughan piano is made by hand by Vaughan family members, who produced it in limited numbers to secure great touch experience and best sounding, making Vaughan piano all the more precious. In 1880, Vaughan was in mass production, and gained great reputation in music colleges, opera houses and concert halls across the world.

Office Add: Str. des 18. Juni 11, 0610 Leipzig, Germany.
Web:www.en.vaughanpiano.com
E-mail:vaughan@hotmail.com

In 2015, a production base was authorized by Vaughan Piano to be built in Hangzhou city, China, marking that Vaughan Piano is making its way to Chinese market. The Chinese factory remains committed to its time-honored piano manufacturing technique, bringing in advanced equipment and components to make excellent products. Among others, it introduces tungsten steel tuning pins from Germany to secure sounding stability, brings in FFW/ABEL hammers to create exquisite and fine tunes, and utilizes top-off-line ROASUL strings. All the manufacturing process keeps to that of Germany and the piano`s standards, sounding and touching experience and all others come from German traditional manufacturing techniques. In the same year, Vaughan Piano made its presence in Shanghai international musical instrument exhibition and Guangzhou international musical instrument exhibition. It has made its way to Chinese market with its cutting-edge equipment and German time-honored techniques. The pianos made in China`s factory are recognized by the German company, and start to export some models back to German.

VN-123
Size 48"
MSRP(USS)* 9,125

WN-03T
Size 49.2 "
MSRP(USS)* 11,975

VN-132
Size 51.9"
MSRP(USS)* 11,650

SALES TALK

Larry Fine

CERTAIN TECHNICAL FEATURES of pianos are frequently the subject of sales talk, either to persuade you to buy a particular piano, to upgrade to a more costly model, or to not buy a competitor's piano. Untangling the truth from the salesmanship can be difficult, sometimes even for professionals in the business. The important differences in quality between brands are more often in subtleties of design and attention to detail than in advertised features, and even where meaningful features are involved, they are easily manipulated by advertising. *The Piano Book* explains in some detail many popular piano features and how they are sometimes misused in sales talk. Here I discuss just three examples: laminated versus solid soundboards, wet-sand-cast versus vacuum-cast plates, and issues related to the wood used in grand piano rims.

At the heart of some of these discussions is the fact that the piano industry—particularly the high end of the business—is very consertive, in large part because consumers are spending a lot of money to buy something they know little about and thus are easily scared away from anything that departs from the "old-fashioned" way of doing things. In addition, the purchase of a high-end piano is often the expression of a conservative part of one's nature—the desire to invest in something enduring and traditional, not cheap or trendy.

Because the design and construction practices used in making the best pianos have evolved over a long period of time, a certain wisdom is embodied in them that should not be too quickly tossed aside. But it must also be remembered that most of these practices are a century old and evolved under certain technological and economic constraints, some of which no longer exist. In other words, there may be

better ways of doing things now that are not being pursued for reasons that have no basis in logic. The low end of the piano market is less constrained by this conservatism, but is still influenced by it.

Soundboards

One of the choices you may need to make among consumer-grade pianos is that between a solid spruce soundboard and a laminated soundboard. First, it must be said about this and any other tone-related technical issue that if the piano sounds good, you needn't question why—just enjoy it! However, since the technical issue may be raised by the salesperson (usually in the context of steering you toward or away from a piano with a laminated soundboard), you may want to know more.

Traditionally, the soundboards in all pianos have been made in the form of a solid sheet of vertical-grain (quartersawn) spruce. This solid spruce soundboard, as it is called, is made by gluing many narrow planks of spruce together, edge to edge. The soundboards of all performance-grade and many upper-level and mid-range consumer-grade pianos are still made this way. The soundboard is bent into a slightly convex shape, called crown, to better resist the downward pressure of the strings and to enhance the tone. Over many years' time, the wood gradually dries and shrinks, causing the crown to flatten or disappear and cracks to form. Although sometimes the problem is primarily cosmetic, if severe enough it can and often does affect the instrument's tone. Usually it takes decades for this to happen, but in very dry indoor climates, problems of this sort can occur even within the warranty period.

It was in large part to lessen warranty costs from prematurely cracking soundboards that, in the 1960s, several manufacturers developed laminated soundboards. These soundboards were essentially sheets of plywood. The sandwich of wood and glue prevented the soundboard from cracking or losing crown. The problems with these soundboards were three-fold: First, the pianos into which they were installed were usually the cheapest, and deficient in a variety of ways unrelated to the soundboard. Second, engineers failed to take into account in its design that a plywood soundboard would have different vibrating characteristics from a solid one. Third, although sometimes spruce was used in the plywood, often cheap, inappropriate woods such as basswood or lauan were used, disguised by an outer veneer of spruce. As a result of these three factors, these pianos usually sounded poor, giving the term "laminated soundboard" a bad name. Laminated soundboards of the plywood type are still used by a few manufacturers.

Over the past couple of decades better laminated soundboards have been developed, and the pianos into which they've been installed are more advanced, too. The principal new type, known as a "veneer-laminated" or "surface-tension" soundboard, consists of a core of solid spruce (essentially a solid spruce soundboard) covered on both sides by a very thin veneer of spruce. This type of soundboard vibrates much more like a solid one than a plywood one, but still retains the benefit of protection against cracking and loss of crown. Pianos with these soundboards usually sound reasonably good, and occasionally very good. Although solid spruce soundboards may still have a tonal advantage, the laminated feature can be an advantage in durability, particularly in challenging climates, and may contribute to better tuning stability through the annual cycle of seasonal climate changes.

Despite the improvement, you'll generally find these new laminated soundboards primarily in entry-level or lower mid-range pianos. But the reason for this has less to do with their quality than with marketing: Laminated soundboards are a feature still sometimes used by manufacturers to differentiate a lower-cost instrument from a higher-cost one for marketing purposes, even when the laminated one might arguably be better. If you're shopping in the entry-level price range and a piano with a laminated soundboard meets your musical and other expectations, there's no reason not to purchase it.

Plates

The piano's cast-iron plate is the gold or bronze-colored metal framework across which the strings are strung. For well over 100 years, plates have been made using the wet-sand method of casting, which works something like this: Wooden molds are made in the image of the front and back of the plate. Each mold is pressed into a tray of moist sand, thus transferring the shape of the plate to the sand. The moisture enables the sand particles to stick together to retain the impression. The two trays of sand representing the front and back of the plate are clamped together, and molten iron of a carefully controlled chemical composition is poured into the cavity created between the two impressions. When the iron cools, the trays are unclamped and removed, revealing a cast-iron plate identical in shape and appearance to the wooden molds. Although factory engineers have largely perfected this method over the years, the plates produced in this manner are quite rough, requiring a lot of sanding and finishing work, and vary slightly in dimension from plate to plate, which is less than ideal for highly automated factories that depend on uniformity.

In the 1960s, to manufacture plates that were more uniform, and faster and less costly to make and finish, Yamaha developed the Vacuum Shield Mold Process, or V-Pro. In this method, fine dry sand is used, and a thin plastic film and vacuum pressure keep the sand in place to retain the mold shape. This process produces plates that are not only more uniform, but also show decorative detail much more clearly while requiring less finishing work.

The V-Pro method is used by a number of large Asian manufacturers, where it fits in well with their rapid, highly automated production. All smaller manufacturers, including those of the highest quality, use the traditional wet-sand method. From this it might be assumed that the wet-sand plates are superior in quality, and companies that use this method often make a point of mentioning it in their advertising. However, the reason for the difference is more likely to be one of economics than of quality—the capital costs for starting up a V-Pro plate foundry are very high, and there is not enough advantage to most piano makers to undertake this. For some large Chinese manufacturers that still use the wet-sand method, the low cost of labor to finish the rough plates outweighs the cost of building a new plate foundry. For smaller, high-end makers that might in theory employ the services of an independent V-Pro plate foundry, there is little advantage because these companies finish their plates to very high standards anyway, and the labor saved by starting with plates a little less rough is not significant. In addition, due to the aura of superiority surrounding wet-sand plates, the switch by a high-end maker to V-Pro plates might engender negative publicity that would hurt sales.

There is some talk that plates made by the wet-sand method may be less likely to steal energy from the strings, or that V-Pro plates may add some unwanted metallic sound to the piano tone, but the truth is more complicated. According to the experts I consulted, when plates are made by the wet-sand method, the moisture in the sand, when contacted by the molten iron, produces a large amount of steam. To counter the invasive effects of the steam, the plates, to retain their strength, must be made thicker than would otherwise be the case. The V-Pro method, using dry sand—and thus producing no steam—allows plates to be made thinner *if desired*, as might be the case with an inexpensive piano. Rather than remain inert, as it's supposed to, a plate with less mass will have a greater tendency to ring in sympathy with the vibrating strings, thus causing a loss of tonal energy and creating a metallic distortion to the tone. However, if a plate is made just as massive by the V-Pro method as it would have been by the wet-sand method, these negative effects do not occur, and the V-Pro plate works just as well as the wet-sand one. Therefore, any differences between the two types of plates are more likely to be related to the price and quality of the pianos in which they're used than with the casting method per se.

Grand Piano Rims

The wooden rim of a grand piano serves two functions: structural and acoustical. Structurally, it's the foundation to which the cast-iron plate is bolted, and as such it assists the plate in supporting the tremendous tension exerted by the taut strings. The acoustical function is less well understood. The soundboard is glued along its perimeter to a shelf formed by the inner rim of the piano case. The vibrational energy in the soundboard thus contacts the rim, and is either reflected back into the soundboard or is siphoned off into the rim, depending on the density of the wood used in the rim's construction, and on the stiffness and total mass of the rim. Dense woods and a stiff, massive rim will reflect sound energy to a greater degree, causing the sound to sustain longer, whereas softer woods and a thinner, more flexible rim will tend to absorb more energy, causing the sound to disappear sooner. This is why most of the best grand pianos have very thick rims made of dense woods such as maple and beech. (Bösendorfer, a high-end piano, has a relatively soft, spruce rim and so may seem an exception to this rule. But spruce transmits sound well, so the tonal energy is not so much lost as spread throughout the structure, which then becomes an extension of the soundboard.) Less expensive grands may use softer woods like lauan (sometimes known as Philippine mahogany, though lighter and more flexible than true mahogany), or alternating layers of harder and softer woods.

Two things are important to note here. First, the hardness or density of the wood in the rim has nothing to do with the rim's ability to fulfill its function of structural support. A rim made with a less-dense wood like lauan won't "fall apart" or cause the piano to go out of tune faster; the issue is strictly one of how the rim affects the tone. Second, the words *hardwood* and *softwood* are botanical terms that have little to do with how hard or soft the woods actually are. So when a piano ad touts a "hardwood rim," or a rim made from "select hardwoods," chances are that the woods involved are not very hard at all; if they were, the ad would likely name the actual species of wood instead of hiding behind such general and potentially deceptive terms.

BUYING A USED OR RESTORED PIANO

Larry Fine

What to Buy: A Historical Overview

1700–1880

The piano was invented about 1700 by Bartolomeo Cristofori, a harpsichord maker in Padua, Italy. Cristofori replaced the plucking-quill action of the harpsichord, which can pluck only with unvarying force and hence unvarying volume of sound, with a newly designed striking-hammer action, whose force could be precisely controlled by the player. Thus was born the *gravicembalo col piano e forte* (keyboard instrument with soft and loud). This name was later shortened to *pianoforte*, then *fortepiano*, and finally just *piano*. In the 1700s the new instrument, made mostly by craftsmen in their shops, spread quietly through upper-class Europe. A number of different forms of piano action and structure were invented, such as the Viennese action, the English action, the square piano, and so on. Replicas of early fortepianos are popular among certain musicians who prefer to play the music of that period on the original instruments for which that music was written.

In the 1800s the piano spread more quickly through the middle classes, and across the ocean to North America. Riding along with the Industrial Revolution, piano-making evolved from a craft into an industry. Many important changes took place during the 19th century: The upright piano was invented; the modern grand piano action was invented, incorporating the best aspects of the previous rival actions; the cast-iron plate was invented, vastly strengthening the structure and allowing the strings to be stretched at a higher tension, thus increasing the power and

Cristofori Piano, circa 1720

(This article is adapted from Chapter 5, "Buying a Used Piano," of The Piano Book, Fourth Edition, by Larry Fine. Before reading this article, be sure to read "**Piano Buying Basics**"—especially the section "New or Used?"—elsewhere in this publication.)

volume of sound; the range of the instrument was extended from about five octaves to the present seven-plus octaves; and, toward the end of the century, the square piano died out, leaving just grands of various sizes and the full-size upright. By 1880, most of these changes were in place; the pianos made today are not very different from those of a hundred or more years ago.

In your search for a piano, you're unlikely to run across instruments made before 1880, with two exceptions. The square piano, or square grand, as it is sometimes called, looks like a rectangular box on legs (see illustration), and was very popular as a home piano during the 19th century. Its ornate Victorian case makes very pretty furniture—but it also makes a terrible musical instrument for 21st-century playing and practicing. Tuning, servicing, and repair are difficult and expensive, very few piano technicians know how to do it, and parts are hard to come by. Even at their best, these instruments are unsuitable to practice on, even for beginners.

Another piano to avoid is a type of upright made primarily in Europe from the middle to the end of the 19th century. The dampers on these piano are positioned *above* the hammers and actuated by wires in *front* of the action—the

Buying a Used or Restored Piano

reverse of a modern-day upright. This over-damper system has been nicknamed the "birdcage action" because the damper wires form an enclosure that resembles a bird cage. Besides being very difficult to tune and service through the "bird cage," these pianos are usually so worn out that they won't hold a tuning longer than about ten seconds, and their actions work erratically at best. Many of these pianos were cheaply made to begin with, but they often have ornate cabinets and fancy features, such as candlestick holders, that make them attractive to antique collectors.

Square Grand, 19th Century

Although most pianos you'll come across made prior to 1880 will have little practical or financial value, the few that have historical value are best left to specialists and collectors who can properly conserve them.

1880–1900

The years from 1880 to about 1900 were a transition period, as some old styles were slow to fade. But some pianos from this period may be suitable for you. A piano with only 85 instead of 88 notes may be perfectly satisfactory if you don't anticipate ever needing the highest three notes. The resale value of such a piano may be slightly lower than its modern equivalent, but so should be the price you pay for it. A piano with an old-style cast-iron plate that, while extending the full length of the piano, leaves the pinblock exposed to view is, for all practical purposes, just as structurally sound as one in which the plate covers the pinblock. Avoid, however, the so-called "three-quarter-plate" piano, in which the plate ends just short of the pinblock. These pianos have a high rate of structural failure. Pianos with actions that are only very slight variations on modern actions are fine as long as the parts are not obsolete and absolutely unobtainable.

Most pianos this old will need a considerable amount of repair and restoration to be fully usable, so the best candidates from this period will be those instruments that justify the expense involved, such as Steinway, Mason & Hamlin, Bechstein, and Blüthner grands, or, in rare instances, a more ordinary brand that has been exceptionally well preserved. With occasional exceptions, the vast majority of uprights and cheaper grands that survive from this period are not worth repairing, unless for historical or sentimental reasons.

1900–1930

The period from about 1900 to 1930 was the heyday of piano manufacturing in America. The piano held an important place in the national economy and as a symbol of culture and social status. Hundreds of small firms turned out millions of pianos during this time; in fact, far more pianos were made annually then than are made today. If you're shopping for a used full-size upright or a grand, some of the pianos you'll see will probably be from this period. Smaller pianos weren't introduced until later. Although some well-preserved instruments from this period may be usable as is, most will need rebuilding, or at least reconditioning.

Those in the market for a used piano often ask for recommendations of specific brands from this period. This is a problem, because the present condition of the piano, the kind of use you'll be giving it, and the cost of the piano and repairs are far more important factors than the brand when considering the purchase of an old piano. Even a piano of the best brand, if poorly maintained or badly repaired, can be an unwise purchase. Time and wear are great levelers, and a piano of only average quality that has not been used much may be a much better buy. Nevertheless, since that answer never satisfies anyone, I offer a list (see box) of some of the brand names of the period that were most highly regarded. Please note that this list, which is by no means complete—or universally agreed on—applies only to pianos made before about 1930, since in many cases the same names were later applied to entirely different, usually lower, quality standards.

During this period, a large percentage of the pianos made were outfitted with pneumatically driven player-piano systems. When these mechanisms eventually fell into disrepair, they were often removed. Although there is still a small group of technicians and hobbyists dedicated to restoring these fascinating relics of the past, in most cases it is not economically practical to do so except for historical or sentimental reasons.

1930–1960

The rise of radio and talking pictures in the 1920s competed with pianos for the public's attention and weakened the piano industry, and the Great Depression decimated it. During the Depression, many piano makers, both good and bad, went bankrupt, and their names were bought up by the surviving companies. Sometimes the defunct company's designs continued to be used, but often only the name lived on. Still, piano making in the 1930s, though reduced in quantity from earlier years, was in most cases of a similar quality.

To revive the depressed piano market in the mid-1930s, piano makers came up with a new idea: the small piano. Despite the fact that small pianos, both vertical and grand, are musically inferior to larger ones, the public decided that spinets, consoles, and small grands were preferable because they looked better in the smaller homes and apartments of the day. There has always been a furniture aspect to the piano, but the degree to which piano makers catered to that aspect from the mid-'30s onward marked a revolution in piano marketing.

During World War II, many piano factories were commandeered to make airplane wings and other wartime products, and what piano making there was fell somewhat in quality because of a lack of good raw materials and skilled labor. Things changed for the better in the postwar period, and you'll sometimes find used pianos from this period, still in reasonably good condition or needing some reconditioning, from such brands as Steinway, Baldwin, Mason & Hamlin, Sohmer, Everett, Knabe, and Wurlitzer.

1960–Present

In the 1960s, the Japanese began exporting pianos to the U.S. in large numbers. Although at first they had some difficulty building pianos to the demands of our climate, by the mid- to late-'60s their quality was so high and their prices so low that they threatened to put all U.S. makers out of business. In response, most of the mid-priced American makers cheapened their product to compete. As a result, the 20 years from about 1965 to 1985 are considered, from a quality standpoint, to be a low point in U.S. piano manufacturing. In any case, the Americans were unable to compete. The international takeover of the U.S. piano market accelerated in the 1980s as the Koreans began to export here, and by 1985 all but a few U.S. piano makers had gone out of business. As in an earlier period, some of their brand names were purchased and later used by others.

Please see the article "**The New-Piano Market Today**" for more information on the post-1960 period. See also the article "**Advice About Used Pianos for Parents of Young Beginning Piano Students**" for a list of specific brands of this period to avoid.

A used piano made within the past few decades can often be a very good deal, as these

An old-fashioned, pneumatically-driven player piano with punched-paper music roll and pumping pedals

www.antiqueplayerpiano.com

If you're looking for a piano made within the last few decades, there is usually a plentiful supply of used Yamaha and Kawai pianos originally made for the Japanese market. However, there has been some controversy about them. Sometimes called "gray-market" pianos, these instruments were originally sold to families and schools in Japan, and some years later were discarded in favor of new pianos. There being little market for these used pianos in Japan—the Japanese are said to have a cultural bias against buying any used goods—enterprising businesspeople buy them up, restore them to varying degrees, and export them to the U.S. and other countries, where they are sold by dealers of used pianos at prices significantly lower than those of new Yamahas or Kawais. Used Korean pianos are available under similar circumstances. (Note: The term "gray market" is used somewhat erroneously to describe these pianos. They are used instruments, not new, and there is nothing illegal about buying and selling them.)

Yamaha has taken a public stand warning against the purchase of a used Yamaha piano made for the Japanese market. When Yamaha first began exporting pianos to the United States, the company found that some pianos sent to areas of the U.S. with very dry indoor climates, such as parts of the desert Southwest and places that were bitterly cold in the winter, would develop problems in a short period of time: tuning pins would become loose, soundboards and bridges would crack, and glue joints would come apart. To protect against this happening, Yamaha began to season the wood for destination: a low moisture content for pianos bound for the U.S., which has the greatest extremes of dryness; a higher moisture content for Europe; and the highest moisture content for Japan, which is relatively humid. The gray-market pianos, Yamaha says, having been seasoned for the relatively humid Japanese climate, will not stand up to our dryness. The company claims to have received many calls from dissatisfied owners of these pianos, but cannot help them because the warranty, in addition to having expired, is effective only in the country in which the piano was originally sold when new.

My own research has led me to believe that while there is some basis for Yamaha's concerns, their warnings are somewhat exaggerated. There probably is a greater chance, statistically, that these pianos will develop problems in conditions of extreme dryness than will Yamahas seasoned for and sold in the U.S. However, thousands of gray-market pianos have been sold by hundreds of dealers throughout the country, in all types of climates, for many years, and, while there have been problems, particularly in sections of the country with temperature and humidity extremes, I haven't found evidence of anything close to an epidemic. In mild and moderate climates, reported problems are rare. There are, however, some precautions that should be taken.

These pianos are available to dealers in a wide variety of ages and conditions. The better dealers will sell only those in good condition made since about the mid-1980s. In some cases, the dealers or their suppliers will recondition or partially rebuild the pianos before offering them for sale. Make sure to get a warranty that runs for at least five years, as any problems will usually show up within that period if they are going to show up at all. **Finally, be sure to use some kind of humidity-control system in situations of unusual dryness.** Remember that air-conditioning, as well as heating, can cause indoor dryness.

It's not always possible to determine visually whether a particular instrument was made for the U.S. or the Japanese market, as some original differences may have been altered by the supplier. The dealer may know, and Yamaha has a utility on its website (**www.yamaha.com/ussub/pianos/SerialNumberlookup.aspx**) that will look up the origin of a particular Yamaha piano by serial number.

instruments may still show very few signs of age and wear, but with a price far below that of a new piano. The most recently made used pianos may even come with a warranty that is still in effect. Also, the influx of new, low-priced, Chinese- and Indonesian-made pianos has driven down the price of used pianos, in some cases rather substantially, as the imports offer the opportunity to buy a new piano for a price only a little higher than a decent used one previously commanded. If you're considering a piano from this period, you may wish to read applicable articles in this publication about new pianos, as well as current and

Find the serial number of the piano so you can look up its year of manufacture in the *Pierce Piano Atlas*. Usually four to eight digits, the serial number is most often located near the tuning pins, either printed directly on the plate or engraved in the wooden pinblock and showing through a cut-away portion of the plate. Or the number may be printed somewhere else on the plate or soundboard, printed or engraved on the top or back of a vertical piano back, or printed or engraved on the front edge of a grand piano key frame (Figure 1). (Sometimes a three- or four-digit number used in the manufacturing process also appears on various case parts; don't confuse this with the serial number.) When no serial number can be found or if the year of manufacture isn't listed in *Pierce*, sometimes a technician can estimate the age within about ten years just by looking at the case styling or technical details.

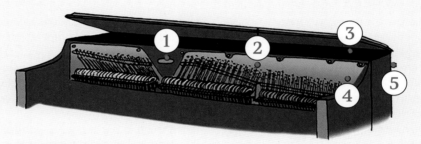

FIGURE 1a. The serial number of a ***vertical piano*** can usually be found in #1, either stamped on the plate or engraved in the pinblock and showing through a cut-away portion of the plate. #2 and #4, also on the plate, are other possibilities. On newer pianos, the serial number is sometimes on the top of the piano back (#3) or stamped on the back of the piano (#5).

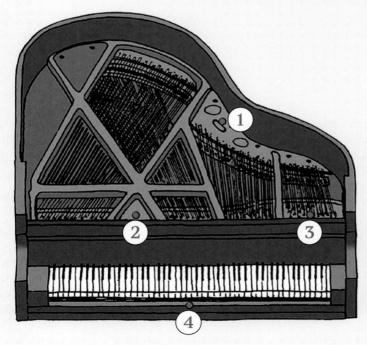

FIGURE 1b. The serial number of a ***grand piano*** is usually in position 2, stamped on the plate or engraved in the pinblock; elsewhere on the plate or soundboard (such as #1 and #3); or stamped on the front of the key frame (#4). Access to the key frame is gained by removing the keyslip.

Solid spruce soundboards swell and shrink with seasonal changes in humidity and, over time, can develop cracks. One of the problems that comes up most frequently in buying a used piano is judging the significance of a cracked soundboard.

Contrary to popular belief, cracks in the soundboard, while often unattractive, are not necessarily important, as long as the tone is acceptable. Very extensive cracking, however, can indicate that the piano has suffered great climatic extremes, and that its life expectancy may be short. In such a case, other symptoms of this will usually be evident elsewhere in the piano. If the cracks have been filled with wooden shims, this means that, at some point, the piano was rebuilt and the cracks repaired.

The ribs run perpendicular to the grain of the soundboard, and therefore perpendicular to any cracks. Any separation of a rib from the soundboard at a crack is a potential source of buzzing noises. A piano with a cracked soundboard should be carefully checked for rib separations before purchase. Repair of rib separations can usually be done at reasonable cost without rebuilding the piano.

When manufactured, the soundboard has built into it a curvature or *crown*. In a traditionally made, solid spruce soundboard, the crown is maintained by the compression of the wood fibers, whose elasticity causes the crowned soundboard to push back against the downbearing pressure of the strings on the bridges. Together, these two opposing forces enhance the tone of the piano. Over many years, because of the drying out of the wood and the loss of the wood's elasticity, the soundboard loses some or all of its crown, a condition that can be accompanied by the appearance of cracks.

A related condition is that of *compression ridges*. When a soundboard's compression exceeds the elastic limit of the wood fibers, those fibers may become crushed, producing slightly raised ridges in the soundboard's surface. This can happen, for example, in humid climates, or due to conditions related to the soundboard's manufacture. Compression ridges are quite common, and do not necessarily affect the piano's tone. However, when crushed, wood fibers lose their elastic properties, so the compression ridges are likely to turn into cracks as the soundboard's crown diminishes over time.

Although, in theory, cracks and a loss of crown should result in a deterioration of tonal quality, the actual results vary greatly from piano to piano; therefore, the tone quality of each such instrument must be evaluated on its own merits. In addition, your tolerance for such imperfections will depend on how expensive the piano is, and on your use of and expectations for it.

For more information on this subject, see *The Piano Book*.

---

past editions of *The Piano Book*. See also the accompanying sidebar about so-called gray-market pianos.

Though in each decade both good and bad pianos have been produced, and each piano must be judged on its own merits, this brief historical overview may give you some idea of what to expect to see as you shop for a used piano. You can determine the age of a piano by finding its serial number (see sidebar) and looking it up in the *Pierce Piano Atlas* (**www. piercepianoatlas.com**), or perhaps by asking a piano dealer or technician to look it up for you.

How to Find a Used Piano

Finding a used piano essentially involves networking, a concept very much in vogue these days. Some networking can be done by computer, and some with old-fashioned phone calls and shoe leather. Here are some of your options—you may be able to think of others.

- **Contact piano technicians, rebuilders, and used-piano dealers**

People who service pianos often have customers who want to sell their instruments. Some technicians also restore pianos for sale in their shops. Contacting these technicians or visiting their shops is a good way to acquaint yourself with local market conditions, to better understand what's involved in piano restoration, and to see an interesting slice of life in your community you might not otherwise encounter. If you decide to buy from a technician, you may pay more than you would a private party, but you'll have the peace of mind of knowing that the piano has been checked over, repaired, and comes with a warranty. Even though you trust the seller, it's a good idea to hire an independent technician to inspect the piano before purchase, just as you would if the piano were being sold by a private party, because even the best technicians can differ in their professional abilities and opinions.

www.cunninghampiano.com

Restoring the piano case to like-new condition

■ *Visit dealers of new pianos*

New-piano dealers take used pianos in trade for new ones all the time, and need to dispose of them to recoup the trade-in allowance they gave on the new piano. Although many of the trade-ins will be older pianos, it's quite common for a customer to trade in a piano purchased only a few years earlier for a bigger or better model, leaving a nearly new piano for you to buy at a substantial discount on its price when new. Again, you may pay more than you would from a private party—usually 20 to 30 percent more—but it may be difficult to find something like this from a private party, and the dealer will likely also give some sort of warranty. Some of the best deals I've seen have been acquired this way. If you're also considering the option of buying a new piano, then you'll be able to explore both options with a single visit. On the other hand, sometimes dealers advertise used pianos just to get customers into the store, where they can be sold on a new piano. The used piano advertised may be overpriced, or may no longer be available. When you have a used piano inspected, make sure the technician you hire owes no favors to the dealer who's selling it.

■ *Shopping via the Internet*

The best way to use the Internet to shop for a used piano is to look for sellers, both commercial and non-commercial, within driving distance of your home. That way, you can more easily try out the piano, develop a face-to-face relationship with the seller, and get a better sense of whether or not you want to do business

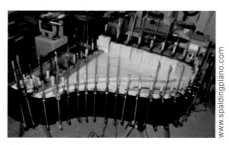

www.spaldingpiano.com

Gluing a new soundboard into the rim of a grand piano

with them. Craigslist (**www.craigslist.org**), though not a piano-specific site, seems to have become the preferred classified-ad site for this purpose, as it's both free and is organized by city. If you travel frequently, you should check out sellers in other cities, too—easy to do on Craigslist. Other popular piano classified-ad sites include **www.pianoworld.com** (which also has extensive forums for exchanging information and getting answers to your questions), **www.pianomart.com** (smartly organized for easy searching), and our own Piano Buyer Classifieds (**www.pianobuyer.com**), which uses the Pianomart database and search engine. These sites either charge a monthly fee to list or a small commission upon sale, but are free to buyers.

You'll also find pianos for sale on the Internet auction site **eBay**. Search on a variety of keywords, as each keyword will bring up a different group of pianos for sale. This can be frustrating, as either too broad or too specific a search term may yield unsatisfactory results. The bidding process generally provides a window of time during which you can contact the seller for more information, see the piano, and have it inspected before placing a bid. This is definitely not a good way to buy a piano unless you have the opportunity to first try out the piano and have it inspected. On both eBay and the classified-ad sites mentioned above, many listings that appear to be non-commercial will actually turn out to have been placed by commercial sellers, who may have many more pianos for sale than the one in the ad you answered.

The website of the Piano Technicians Guild (**www.ptg.org**) has a listing of dealer websites and other resources that may be useful in locating used or restored pianos. If your situation is such that finding a local source of used pianos is unlikely, one reliable source that ships nationwide is Rick Jones Pianos in Beltsville, Maryland (**www.rickjonespianos.com**).

If you're thinking of making a long-distance purchase, the precautions mentioned in the section **"Shopping Long-Distance via the Internet,"** in the article "Piano Buying Basics," bear repeating: First, take into account the cost of long-distance shipping and consider whether it's really worth it. If buying from a commercial source, find out as much as you can about the dealer. Get references. If you haven't actually seen the piano, get pictures of it. Hire a technician in the seller's area to inspect the piano and ask the technician about a commercial seller's reputation. Make sure the dealer has experience in arranging long-distance moves, and uses a mover that specializes in pianos. Find out who will be responsible for tuning and adjusting the piano in your home, and for repairing any defects or dings in the finish. Get the details of any warranty, especially who is responsible for paying the return freight if the piano is defective. Find out how payment is to be made in a way that protects both parties.

■ *Non-Internet Techniques*

In this age of the Internet, it's important not to forget older, more conventional methods of networking that still work, such as placing and answering classified print ads in local newspapers and want-ad booklets; and posting and answering notices on bulletin boards anywhere people congregate, such as houses of worship, community centers, laundromats, etc. Other, more aggressive, techniques include contacting movers and storage warehouses to see if they have any pianos abandoned by their owners; attending auctions; contacting attorneys and others who handle the disposition of estates; and just plain old asking around among coworkers, friends, and acquaintances.

■ *Obtaining a Piano from a Friend or Relative*

It's nice when pianos remain in the family. I got my piano that way. But pianos purchased from friends and relatives or received as gifts are as likely as any others to have expensive problems you should know about. It's very hard to refuse a gift, and perhaps embarrassing to hire a piano technician to inspect it before you accept it, but for your own protection you should insist on doing so. Otherwise you may spend a lot of money to move a "gift" you could have done without.

Which of these routes to finding a used piano you end up following will depend on your situation and what you're looking for. If you have a lot of time and transportation is no problem, you may get the best deal by shopping around among private owners or in out-of-the-way places. If you're busy or without a car but have money to spend, it may be more convenient to shop among piano technicians, rebuilders, or dealers, who may be able to show you several pianos at the same time and spare you from worrying about future repair costs and problems. If you travel a lot to other cities or have few piano resources in your local area, the Internet can be a big help in locating an appropriate commercial or non-commercial source far away. (See the ads in this publication for movers that specialize in long-distance piano moving.) The best route also depends on where you live, as some communities may have a brisk trade in used pianos among private owners but few rebuilding shops, or vice versa, or have an abundance of old uprights but few grands.

Buying a Restored Piano

Three terms are often used in discussions of piano restoration work: *repair, reconditioning,* and *rebuilding.* There are no precise definitions of these terms, and any particular job may contain elements of more than one of them. It's therefore very important, when having restoration work done on your piano or when buying a piano on which such work has been done, to find out exactly what jobs have been, or will be, carried out. "This piano has been reconditioned" or "I'll rebuild this piano" are not sufficient answers. One technician's rebuilding may be another's reconditioning.

Repair jobs generally involve fixing isolated broken parts, such as a broken hammer, a missing string, or an improperly working pedal. That is, a repair does not necessarily involve upgrading the condition of the instrument as a whole, but addresses only specific broken or improperly adjusted parts.

The following is a list of the tasks that might comprise a fairly complete rebuilding of a grand piano. Any particular job may be either more or less extensive than shown here, depending on the needs and value of the instrument and other factors, but this list can serve as a guide. See also *The Piano Book* for information about specific rebuilding issues pertaining to Steinway and Mason & Hamlin pianos.

Notice that the restoration can be divided into three main parts: the soundbox or resonating unit, the action, and the cabinet. The *soundbox* (also known as the *strung back* or *belly*) includes the soundboard, ribs, bridges, strings, pinblock, tuning pins, plate, and the structural parts of the case; the *action* includes the keyframe and action frame, keys and keytops, hammers, dampers, trapwork, and all other moving action parts; the *cabinet* includes cosmetic repair and refinishing of the case and of the nonstructural cabinet parts and hardware. Note that the damper parts that contact the strings are restored with the soundbox, whereas the damper underlever action is treated with the rest of the action.

There is very little overlap among the three types of work; each of the three parts could be performed alone or at different times, as technical conditions permit and/or financial considerations require. In a typical complete rebuilding job, restoration of the soundbox might comprise 45 percent of the cost, the action 30 percent, and the cabinet 25 percent, though these percentages will vary according to the particulars of the job.

Soundbox or resonating unit

- Replace or repair soundboard, refinish, install new soundboard decal (if not replacing soundboard: shim soundboard cracks, reglue ribs as necessary, refinish, install new soundboard decal)

- Replace pinblock
- Replace bridges or bridge caps
- Replace or ream agraffes, restore capo-bar bearing surface
- Refinish plate, paint lettering, replace understring felts
- Replace strings and tuning pins, tune to pitch
- Replace damper felts, refinish damper heads, regulate dampers

Action

- Replace hammers, shanks, and flanges
- Replace or overhaul wippen/repetition assemblies
- Replace backchecks
- Replace front-rail key bushings
- Replace balance-rail key bushings or key buttons
- Replace or clean keytops
- Replace key-end felts
- Clean keys
- Clean and refelt keyframe
- Replace let-off felts or buttons
- Clean and, if necessary, repair action frame

- Regulate action, voice
- Overhaul or replace damper underlever action and damper guide rail
- Overhaul pedal lyre and trapwork, regulate

Cabinet

- Repair music desk, legs, other cabinet parts, as needed
- Repair loose or missing veneer
- Strip and refinish exterior; refinish bench to match piano
- Buff and lacquer solid-brass hardware, replate plated hardware

Reconditioning always involves a general upgrading of the entire piano, but with as little actual replacement of parts as possible. For instance, reconditioning an old upright might include resurfacing the hammer felt (instead of replacing the hammers) and twisting (instead of replacing) the bass strings to improve their tone. However, definitions of *reconditioning* can vary widely: Many technicians would consider the replacement of hammers, tuning pins, and strings to be part of a reconditioning job in which more extensive work is either not needed or not cost-effective; others would call such work a partial rebuild.

Rebuilding is the most complete of the three levels of restoration. Ideally, *rebuilding* means putting the piano into "like new" condition. In practice, however, it may involve much less, depending on the needs and value of the particular instrument, the amount of money available, and the scrupulousness of the rebuilder. Restringing the piano and replacing the pinblock in a grand, as well as repairing or replacing the soundboard, would typically be parts of a rebuilding job. In the action, rebuilding would include replacing the hammer heads, damper felts, and key bushings, and replacing or completely overhauling other sets of parts as well. Refinishing the piano case is also generally part of the rebuilding process. Because of the confusion over the definitions of these terms, sometimes the term *remanufacturing* is used to distinguish the most complete rebuilding job possible—including replacement of the soundboard—from a lesser "rebuilding." However, there is no substitute for requesting from the technician an itemization of the work performed.

When considering buying a rebuilt piano, or having a piano rebuilt, particularly an expensive one, the rebuilder's experience level should count heavily in your decision. The complete rebuilding of a piano requires many dissimilar skills. The skills required for installing a soundboard, for example, are very different from those required for installing a new set of hammers or for regulating the action. Mastering all of these skills can take a very long time. In a sense, you should be shopping for the rebuilder as much as for the piano.

Many rebuilders contract out portions of the job, particularly the refinishing of the piano's case, to others who have special expertise. Although this has always been so, more recently groups of technicians, each with his or her own business and shop, have been openly advertising their close, long-term collaboration with one another on rebuilding jobs. In a typical collaboration of this type, one person might rebuild the strung back or soundbox (soundboard, bridges, pinblock, strings, tuning pins, cast-iron plate); another would rebuild the action and do the final musical finishing, such as regulating and voicing; and the third would refinish the case. Collaboration of this kind is a positive development, as it means that each technician does only what he or she does best, resulting in a better job for the customer. But make sure you know with whom you are contracting or from whom you are buying, and which technician is responsible for making things right if problems arise.

It may occur to you that you could save a lot of money by buying an unrestored piano and having a technician completely restore it, rather than buying the completely restored piano from the technician. This is often true. But the results of a rebuilding job tend to be musically uncertain. That is, if you are particular in your taste for tone and touch, you may or may not care for how the instrument ultimately turns out. For that reason, especially if a lot of money is involved, you might be better off letting the technician make the extra profit in return for taking the risk.

"Vintage" . . . or New?

"Vintage" pianos are those made during the golden years of piano-making in the United States—roughly,

from 1880 to World War II. More specifically, the term usually refers to the Steinway and Mason & Hamlin pianos made during that period, though it's occasionally applied to other great American makes as well. In the last few decades the demand for these pianos, and consequently their prices, has mushroomed due to a (until recently) strong economy, increased entrepreneurial activity on the part of rebuilders and piano brokers, allegations by rebuilders and others that today's new pianos are not as well made as the older ones were, and the purchase of many older Steinways by Steinway & Sons itself for rebuilding in its factory.

What makes these vintage pianos so alluring? Many musicians and technicians believe that these instruments, when rebuilt, sound and play better than new pianos. However, no one knows for sure why this should be so, since most of the components in the piano are replaced during rebuilding. Some point to the fact that Steinway operated its own plate foundry until about World War II, afterward using a commercial plate foundry (which it now owns). Because this radical change in the manufacture of such an important component roughly corresponds with the end of the vintage era, and because the plate is one of the few original parts to survive the rebuilding process, some speculate that it holds the key to the difference. Others say it has to do with changes in the quality of the wood available to Steinway and other

companies. Still others say it wasn't any single thing, but rather a combination of many fortuitous factors, including extremely skilled and talented craftsmen, that enabled these companies to make such special pianos during that period, but allegedly not afterward (though that doesn't explain why the rebuilt ones from that period should be better).

Steinway & Sons, for its part, disputes the entire idea that older Steinways are better, dismissing it as a romantic notion spread by purveyors of those pianos in their own financial interest. The company says it has done extensive testing of both plates and woods, and the idea that the older plates and woods were better has no scientific basis. It says it has also carefully inspected hundreds of older Steinways at its factory rebuilding facility, which is the largest Steinway rebuilding facility in the world, and finds no evidence that the older pianos were built better than today's—in fact, it believes that just the opposite is true. Steinway acknowledges that some pianists may prefer the sound of specific older pianos for subjective artistic reasons, but says that those considering the purchase of a restored, older instrument should do so to save money, not to seek better quality.

For more discussion of this topic, and of specific technical issues applicable to the rebuilding of a Steinway or Mason & Hamlin, please see *The Piano Book*.

a considerable amount of editorial discretion to produce price ranges that were not so broad as to be useless as guidelines, and to retain at least a modicum of internal consistency in the chart. For that reason, you should expect to find some markets or situations in which prices higher or lower than those given here are normal or appropriate.

The prices given here for pianos that are not reconditioned or rebuilt (those labeled Worse, Average, Better) are the price ranges you might expect to find when buying pianos *from private owners*. The Reconditioned and Rebuilt categories represent prices you might encounter when shopping for such pianos *at piano stores or from piano technicians*, with a warranty given. In some cases we have omitted the Rebuilt price because we would not expect rebuilding to be cost-effective for pianos of that general age and type. In every case, prices assume the least expensive style and finish; prices for pianos with fancier cabinets, exotic veneers, inlays, and so forth, could be much higher.

Quality

"Best brands" include Steinway, Mason & Hamlin, and the very best European makes, such as Bechstein, Blüthner, and Bösendorfer. "Better brands" include the well-regarded older names mentioned in the accompanying article for the pre–1930 period, such as Knabe and Chickering; and names such as Baldwin, Everett, Kawai, Sohmer, Yamaha, and others of similar quality for the 1950–1985 period. "Average brands" are pretty much everything else.

Condition

Worse, Average, and Better refer to the condition of the piano in comparison to the amount of wear and tear one would expect from the piano's age. However, even Worse pianos should be playable and serviceable. Note that because many buyers are quite conscious of a piano's appearance, pianos that are in good shape musically but in poor shape cosmetically will often sell at a price more consistent with the Worse range than with a higher one. This offers an opportunity for the less furniture-conscious buyer to obtain a bargain.

For a discussion of the definitions of *reconditioned* and *rebuilt*, please see the section "**Buying a Restored Piano**" in this article. **For the purposes of this chart, however, we have adopted the**

requirement that a piano has not been *rebuilt* unless its pinblock has been replaced, and that a piano that has been restrung, but without a new pinblock, is considered to have been *reconditioned*. Note that these definitions are not precise, and that both the quality and the quantity of the work can vary greatly, depending on the needs of the instrument and the capabilities of the restorer. These variations should be taken into account when determining the piano's value.

Depreciation

The *depreciation* method of determining fair market value is based on the fact that many types of consumer goods lose value over time at a more or less predictable rate. A *depreciation schedule*, such as the one here, shows how much an unrestored used piano

DEPRECIATION SCHEDULE			
Age in Years	Percent of New Value		
	Worse	Average	Better
5 or less	70	75	80
10	60	65	70
15	45	50	55
20	35	40	45
25	25	30	35
30	20	25	30
Verticals only			
50	5	10	15
70	0	5	10
Grands only			
50	10	15	20
70	5	10	15
Steinways			
5 or less	70	75	80
10	60	65	70
15	50	55	60
20	40	45	50
25	30	35	40
30	25	30	35
Verticals only			
50	5	10	15
70	5	10	15
Grands only			
50	15	20	25
70	10	15	20

is worth as a percentage of the actual selling price of a new piano of comparable quality. The problem here is that so many older brands are now made by companies different from the original, in different factories and parts of the world, and to different standards, that it can be difficult or impossible to determine what constitutes a "comparable" new piano. Thus, this method of figuring value is best used for pianos of relatively recent make when the model is still in production, or for older pianos whose makers have remained under relatively constant ownership, location, and standards, and for which, therefore, a comparable model can reasonably be determined.

Note that depreciation is from the *current* price of the model, not the original price, because the current price takes into account inflation and, if applicable, changes in the value of foreign currencies. The values are meant to reflect what the piano would sell for between *private, non-commercial parties*. I suggest adding 20 to 30 percent to the computed value when the piano is being sold *by a dealer,* unrestored, but with a warranty. These figures are intended only as guidelines, reflecting our general observation of the market. "Worse," "Average," and "Better" refer to the condition of the used piano for its age. A separate chart is given for Steinway pianos. Other fine pianos, such as Mason & Hamlin, or some of the best European brands, may command prices between the regular and Steinway figures.

Idealized Value Minus the Cost of Restoration

This is the difference between the cost of a rebuilt piano and the cost to restore the unrebuilt one to like-new condition. For example, if a piano, rebuilt, would be worth $50,000, and it would cost $30,000 to restore the unrebuilt one to like-new condition, then according to this method the unrebuilt piano would be worth $20,000. This method can be used when a piano needs extensive, quantifiable repair work. It's not appropriate to use this method for an instrument that is relatively new or in good condition.

Other Types of Valuation

Several other types of valuation are sometimes called for:

Replacement value is what it would cost to replace the used piano with a brand-new one. This value is often sought when someone has purchased an insurance policy with a rider that guarantees replacement of a lost or damaged piano with a new one instead of paying the fair market value of the used one. The problem here, again, is what brand and model of new piano to consider "comparable" if the original brand and model are no longer being made, or are not being made to the same standards.

Here it may be helpful to consult the chart in the article "A Map of the Market For New Pianos." Choose a brand whose relationship to today's piano market is similar to that the original brand bore to the piano market of its day. Whatever brand and model you choose, depending on how high a replacement value you seek, you can use either the manufacturer's suggested retail price (highest), the approximate street price (lowest), or something in between. These prices, or how to estimate them, can be found in the online "**Model & Pricing Guide**" at **www .pianobuyer.com**.

Trade-in value is what a commercial seller would pay for the used piano, usually in trade (or partial trade) for a new one. This is discounted from the fair market value, typically by at least 20 to 30 percent, to allow the commercial seller to make a profit when reselling the instrument. (In practice, the commercial seller will often pay the fair market value for the used piano, but to compensate, will increase the price of the new piano to the consumer.)

Salvage value is what a dealer, technician, or rebuilder would pay for a piano that is essentially unplayable or unserviceable and in need of restoration. It can be determined using the idealized-value-minus-cost-of-restoration method, but discounted, like trade-in value, to allow the commercial seller to make a profit.

Inspect, Inspect, Inspect

In closing, I'd like to remind you that your best protection against buyer's remorse is having the piano inspected by a piano technician prior to purchasing it, particularly if the piano is more than ten years old. Sometimes it will be sufficient to speak to the seller's technician about the piano, if he or she has serviced it regularly and has reason to believe that he or she will continue servicing it under your

ownership. However, in most situations, you'll be better off hiring your own technician. You can find a list of Registered Piano Technicians in your area on the website of the Piano Technicians Guild, **www.ptg.org**.

More Information

If you're serious about buying a used piano, additional information in *The Piano Book* may be useful to you, including:

- How to remove the outer cabinet parts to look inside the piano
- How to do a preliminary inspection of a piano to rule out those that are not worth hiring a technician to inspect, including an extensive checklist of potential problem areas
- A discussion of issues that frequently come up in regard to the rebuilding of Steinway pianos
- A complete list of older Steinway models, from 1853 to the present
- How to locate the serial number of a piano
- A list of manufacturing dates and serial numbers for Steinway pianos.

ADVICE ABOUT USED PIANOS
For Parents of Young Beginning Piano Students

SALLY PHILLIPS

THERE ARE MANY common misconceptions about buying pianos for young students, and one of them is that a suitable piano can be had for only a few hundred dollars. The truth is that, to progress, young students need *better* pianos, not worse.

Parents may not want to invest a lot of money in a piano—after all, the child may lose interest—so an older, cheaper piano may seem the logical place to start. However, a bad purchasing decision at this point in a student's learning tends to be a self-fulfilling prophecy. In many cases a piano that is too old, too small, or simply not good enough will soon become useless to the student. Students don't have enough experience to distinguish between a bad piano and their own lack of ability. When a piano's action can't be regulated to the correct touch, or its strings tuned to a harmonious sound, the student, unable to duplicate what was taught in a lesson, will become frustrated and discouraged, and will lose interest. *No amount of practice on such an instrument can overcome its shortcomings.* And when you include other factors—the costs of moving, tuning, and repairs; an older piano's shorter remaining life; lack of warranty protection; the need to hire experts to make repeated trips to evaluate the conditions of various older pianos—a new or more recently made instrument may start to look like a bargain in the long run.

For these reasons, I would encourage the financially able family to look at good-quality new pianos, or better used pianos no more than 15 years old. And with a young talented student, moving up to a quality grand is never a mistake. If an older piano is chosen, it should be one that was of good quality to begin with, and has been restored to like-new condition. If you're concerned about a child's continuing interest,

I suggest renting a new instrument now, with an option to purchase it later. Most reputable piano dealers offer month-to-month rental programs.

Although good *and* bad pianos have been made in every decade, and every used piano must be evaluated on its own merits, certain decades or categories of piano frequently found in today's used-piano market should raise red flags:

Old uprights

These are usually 48" to 60" high and somewhere around 100 years old. Many buyers will purchase an old upright with the idea that it might have antique value, then quickly find out that it doesn't. In some instances, buyers fascinated by old uprights see them as an opportunity to tinker with and learn something about pianos. There's nothing wrong with this—as long as a young student is not saddled with it.

Most pianos that are a century old and have not been discarded will need extensive restoration before they can be useful to the student, but few are worth enough to have such work performed on them. Many have difficulty holding a tuning, and/or desperately need new strings, hammers, dampers, or pedal repairs—or all of the above. Parents who purchase these deteriorating instruments as practice pianos for beginners will probably face a constant stream of complaints and subsequent repairs. In most cases, this category of used piano should be avoided for use in serious practice.

Here are some brand names from the 1960s, '70s, and '80s—and others from a little earlier and later—that are probably best avoided by students, though some may be acceptable for casual use if carefully serviced or reconditioned.

Aeolian

The following were some of the many brand names owned and made by the Aeolian Corporation, which went out of business in 1985. Many of these, and other names not listed, were "stencil pianos"—essentially identical instruments with different names applied to them, to meet dealers' needs. Note that this list applies to the use of these names only during the mid to late 1900s. Some of these names were used in earlier periods on fine pianos, and several are still being used today, but on pianos that have no connection to the ones warned about here.

Bradbury	J. & C. Fischer
Cable	Kranich & Bach
Duo Art	Melodigrand
George Steck	Pianola
Hallet, Davis & Co.	Poole
Hardman, Peck & Co.	Vose & Sons
Henry F. Miller	Winter & Co.
Ivers & Pond	

Other U.S.-made brands of the period

Betsy Ross (by Lester)	Kincaid (by Grand)
Brambach (by Kohler & Campbell)	La Petite (by Kimball)
Currier	Lester
Estey	Marantz (by Grand/ Marantz)
Grand	Rudolf Wurlitzer (by Wurlitzer)
Gulbransen	Westbrook (by Currier)
Hobart M. Cable (by Story & Clark)	Whitney (by Kimball)
Jesse French (by Grand)	

Foreign-made brands of the period

Belarus (Belarus)	Sojin (Korea)
Daewoo (Korea)	Suzuki (China)
Horugel (Korea)	Tokai (Japan)
J. Strauss (various countries)	

Small, cheap, American-made pianos from the 1960s, '70s, and '80s

During this period, American companies started feeling the competition from Japanese (and, later, Korean) makers who could undercut their prices. The result was that the few remaining American makers of inexpensive pianos began to cut as much cost as they could from their production. In addition, small pianos, especially spinets, were heavily promoted for their cabinet styling at the expense of their musical qualities.

Spinets, which are 36" to 40" high, have a recessed, or "drop," action that is connected to the keys with long "stickers" of wood or metal. These actions are difficult—and thus expensive—to repair. Also, during the 1950s and early '60s, many spinet actions were manufactured with connecting parts, called "elbows," made of plastic—a technology then in its infancy—which eventually deteriorated and broke off. Installing a set of replacement elbows can cost hundreds of dollars.

Spinets were usually the least expensive entry-level pianos a company would manufacture, and most are not worth repairing. Many of these small, cheap pianos were so poorly designed and constructed that, even when new, and regulated and tuned as well as possible, they played poorly and sounded terrible.

The first wave of pianos from this era began to enter the used-piano market in the 1980s, as the people who originally purchased them began to retire. But many others were passed on to this generation's children, and now, as those children retire, a second wave of these instruments is entering the market. Even pianos from this period that were well made—and there were some—are now 30 to 50 years old, and so are likely to need some restoration before they will be suitable for the student. Caution should be used to separate those that have potential as good student instruments from those that don't. (See sidebar for some of the names from this period to be avoided.)

Early offerings from Korean and Chinese makers

Korean pianos made before the early 1990s, and Chinese pianos from before the early 2000s, often exhibit unpredictable, idiosyncratic problems. Quality control was erratic, and wood was often not properly seasoned, resulting in sticking keys and binding cabinet parts. Replacement parts can be difficult to obtain. Especially problematic were the small console pianos without legs (continental furniture style). These pianos tend to be plagued with sticking keys that repeat too slowly due to poor action design, a problem that can't be inexpensively corrected.

Of course, the used-piano market also offers many well-made pianos from the past, including some with famous names, that are of potential value to a student, but these can also present pitfalls for the unwary. Don't buy, without professional guidance, a piano that is not thoroughly playable and tunable, with the idea that you can simply have a few inexpensive repairs done once you get the piano home. Get repair estimates *before* you commit to purchasing any used piano. Every piano technician with any experience has stories of arriving at a tuning appointment to work on a newly acquired piano, only to find an unserviceable instrument. The fact that the instrument may have been rebuilt sometime in the past is not necessarily an advantage. A piano that was rebuilt 40 years ago is no better than a 40-year-old piano that has never been rebuilt, and if the rebuilding job was not competently done, it could be worse—it's more difficult to properly restore an instrument when certain critical design specifications have been modified due to a past restorer's mistakes.

Finally, don't rely on a private seller for important information about the piano you're thinking of buying. Even the best-intentioned sellers—including ones who play well—tend not to be knowledgeable about piano construction and mechanics, and may have absorbed erroneous information about the instrument, or forgotten important things about its history. Hire a piano technician to inspect any piano you're seriously considering buying. Sometimes, just a phone call to a technician will be enough to verify whether or not a particular instrument should be considered a serious candidate; if it is, the next step is an inspection by that technician.

HOW TO SELL OR DONATE YOUR PIANO

Steve Cohen and *Piano Buyer* staff

SELLING A USED PIANO can be a challenge: Since the Recession, used pianos at all price levels have plummeted in value. Used pianos for sale far outnumber shoppers to buy them, making it a buyer's market. Several conditions—some inherent to used-piano sales and some specific to current times—have tended to increase supply and/or drive down the prices of used pianos:

- Globalization and the computerization of manufacturing have made inexpensive, new, high-quality consumer-grade pianos from China and Indonesia abundantly available, leaving lower-quality used instruments from previous eras with little value.
- Digital pianos have become so advanced in tone and touch, and so competitive in price, that for many on a limited budget, a new digital piano may be a better buy than a used acoustic.
- Baby boomers, retiring and downsizing, are flooding the market with the pianos their kids took lessons on. In many cases, these instruments were inherited from the boomers' own parents and are now 50 or more years old.
- The Internet, especially websites such as Craigslist and eBay, makes it easier than ever for sellers to advertise at little or no cost.
- Because people tend to sell when moving, time pressure is involved—as the moving date approaches, often the asking price must be cut drastically.

For buyers on a limited budget, the costs involved in moving a piano to its new location and getting it in good playing condition after the move are relatively high, leaving them with less to pay you for the piano itself. Typical buyer costs include:

- $200–$500 to move an upright piano, or $300–$600 to move a grand, within a 25-mile radius and to a home with no more than three or four steps. Costs can double for shipping over greater distances and/or to more challenging destinations, such as a building with many steps, or to an upper floor.
- $200–$300 to pitch-raise and tune the piano. For most pianos offered for sale, a pitch raise is necessary to compensate for years of tuning neglect.
- $200–$400 for necessary repairs, regulating the action, and voicing of a console or upright, and twice that for a decent-quality grand piano. Almost all pianos over 10 years old will need this work to play well and sound good.

Thus, even when the seller is willing to give away the piano, it still can cost a recipient $1,000–$2,000 to accept it. This expense alone can approach or exceed the budget of a shopper looking for a low-cost option, and means that instruments of lower quality, low brand-name recognition, and less-than-stellar reputation tend to attract little or no sales interest.

Is My Piano Saleable?

To determine if your piano is suitable for resale, there are three basic things to consider: appearance, brand, and age/condition.

Appearance: People who buy decent-quality pianos usually have well-decorated environments for them to go into. This means that, in a buyer's market, many pianos that play well may nevertheless not be saleable at any price if they don't look as good as they play. This is true of most vertical pianos with badly scarred or damaged cases, as well as older, off-brand pianos in plain cabinets. If the piano looks worn, it's less likely to sell.

Brand: Well-known brands with good reputations will generally generate more interest and be valued more than brands that lack name and/or quality recognition. The brands today that are most saleable are Baldwin, Kawai, Steinway & Sons, and Yamaha. Performance-quality, handmade brands—such as Bechstein, Blüthner, Bösendorfer, Fazioli, Grotrian, Mason & Hamlin, and Schimmel—though without wide name recognition among the general public, have great reputations among those who know them, and so are also eminently saleable. On the other hand, some well-known piano brands from the past, such as Wurlitzer and Kimball, may be difficult to sell because their reputations are not particularly good.

Age/Condition: Many piano owners mistakenly believe that pianos made over 100 years ago are valued as "antiques." They aren't, with the occasional exceptions of instruments with unusually decorated cases in fine condition—and even these can have difficulty finding a home. Most pianos are made with a life expectancy of 40 to 60 years, and, contrary to popular belief, do not get better with age.

Pianos that do not sell well due to age (among other factors) include:

- Vertical pianos over 40 years old of little-known brand
- Most pianos, grand or vertical, over 60 years old. Exceptions include: a few top-notch performance-quality brands such as Bechstein, Blüthner, Mason & Hamlin, and Steinway & Sons; pianos that have been completely rebuilt; and occasional instruments that, due to low use and favorable environmental conditions, are still in exceptional condition.

- Pianos with player-piano systems made before about 2000, as their player-piano technology is now obsolete.

Keep in mind that while a piano might sound and feel fine to you, it may have significant problems of which you are unaware. It takes an experienced piano technician to know with certainty that a piano is in good condition. Often sellers who know little about pianos will claim that the piano is in excellent condition based simply on the fact that all the keys make a sound when played, and that the cabinet isn't in rough shape. In many cases, neither a serious piano player nor his or her piano technician would agree.

You can determine your piano's age by looking up its serial number in the *Pierce Piano Atlas*, available from piano dealers, technicians, libraries, and **piercepianoatlas.com**—or have us look it up for you when you use *Piano Buyer*'s **Seller Advisory Service.** On vertical pianos, the serial number is usually found on the metal plate, or harp, just inside the lid. On grands, it's usually on the plate, under the music desk. For more detailed instructions on finding the serial number, read "How to Locate the Serial Number of a Piano" in the article "Buying a Used or Restored Piano," elsewhere in this volume, or watch our video on the subject at **www.pianobuyer.com/ Resources/Videos**.

Determining the Fair Market Value of Your Piano

The fair market value (FMV) is the price an informed buyer and seller are likely to agree on, where both parties are private, noncommercial entities (not piano dealers), and neither is under a compulsion to buy or sell. (An example of a compulsion to sell is when a seller is moving and must get rid of the piano by the end of the month, before the moving van leaves.)

Although, in today's information age, researching the reasonable price range in which a particular piano should sell is becoming easier, it can still be difficult, and will rarely yield a single figure that you can use with great certainty—except, perhaps, with nearly new examples of a few very well-known brands. Unlike real estate or cars, piano sales are not regulated, and there is no major service that tracks the actual sale prices of used pianos. Even if there were, pianos can vary so much in age and condition that finding one or more instruments that are exact matches to yours would be unlikely. Therefore, you'll have to settle on a range of possible selling prices, and be prepared to lower your asking price as you gauge the response (or lack of response) to your initial asking price, and as whatever deadline you're working toward approaches.

The FMV is best determined by using several sources and methods, including the classified-ad services on which you'll probably end up listing your piano, articles in this volume, and online appraisal services such as *Piano Buyer*'s **Seller Advisory Service** (SAS). The SAS provides a solid estimate of FMV by experts, as well as tips, customized to your situation, on how and where to sell, information on donations, selling to dealers, and appraisals for insurance purposes. The piano technician who has been servicing your piano, or another technician, may also be able to provide a value. However, many technicians do not keep up with changes in the used-piano market.

The section **"How Much Is It Worth?,"** in the article "Buying a Used or Restored Piano," provides a depreciation schedule for pianos in current production, and a chart of estimated ranges of FMV for other categories of piano based on their quality, age, and condition. After reading the article and referencing the tables, you may be able to place the value of your piano within a reasonable range.

Follow this up by checking a number of classified-ad websites (see next section). Just keep in mind that the prices there are *asking* prices, which may be far higher than the actual amounts buyers end up paying. Still, if your piano is a common model, and the comparables you find all have similar prices, this gives an indication that the asking prices are probably close to the actual selling prices. On the other hand, if you're selling a little-known brand, you may have trouble determining what a comparable brand and model might be, and may require professional assistance to determine a market value.

Everyone wants to feel that he or she has gotten a good deal, so be prepared to adjust your asking price in a negotiation. We suggest setting your initial asking price about 10–15% higher than the FMV, and accept any offer within 15–20% of the FMV.

Note that checking prices of used pianos at local dealerships is likely to be of limited value in determining FMV because the dealership usually adds significant value to an instrument, resulting in a much higher price. Usually the piano dealer has:

- tuned, regulated, and voiced the piano to perform well;
- cleaned it thoroughly;
- touched up the cabinet and polished the hardware;
- offered a warranty, backing up the purchase with the security of a business (a buyer thus risks less when buying from a business than from a private party, who, more than likely, is moving away); and
- will provide a free tuning after delivery.

Where to Advertise Your Piano

Before trying to sell to strangers, consider mentioning to family, friends, neighbors, and coworkers that you'd like to sell your piano. Word of mouth among people you know results in stronger and safer contacts than those obtained from commercial listings. Also, print out and post notices where people congregate: houses of worship, schools, your workplace, etc. Send out a text or e-mail to your contact list, and post on social-media sites, such as Facebook. Be sure to include photos of your piano.

Ask your piano technician if he or she knows of anyone who might be interested in your piano. Also ask about advertising with the local chapter of the Piano Technicians Guild (PTG). Chapters often have an e-mail list of members to whom they send a chapter newsletter. Sometimes, members or their clients may advertise pianos for sale, either for free or for a small charge. You can find a list of PTG members in your area at **www.ptg.org**, where you can search by zip code or PTG chapter.

Classified-ad sites on which you should consider advertising include:

- **Craigslist.com**, localized for your geographic area, under "Musical Instruments by Owner," then search on "pianos."
- **PianoBuyer.com/classifieds** has an international audience with search capabilities by location. **PianoMart.com** is a related site with all the same listings as **PianoBuyer.com**. When a piano is listed on one of these sites, it automatically appears on both. A basic listing is free; premium listings, including a custom-designed banner ad on **PianoBuyer.com**, are available for an extra fee. You pay a 3% commission on sale if you sell through the site.
- Other major online classified-ad sites include **PianoWorld.com**, **eBay.com**, and **Klaviano.com**.

Tips for Selling Your Piano

There are two keys to ensuring that your piano sells: creating a sales presentation to prospective buyers, and properly preparing your piano for sale.

First, if the company that made your piano is still in business, learn the features, advantages, and benefits of your piano brand and model when compared to other pianos the shopper may be considering. The "Brand and Company Profiles" section of this volume, and the more complete online version at **www.pianobuyer.com**, have descriptions of currently manufactured pianos that usually include their features, advantages, and benefits, as well as the history of the manufacturer. **"A Map of the Market for New Pianos,"** also in this volume, will help you determine the quality of your piano relative to other brands in the marketplace. If your piano has outlasted its manufacturer, you can research the brand's history online. Weave this information, along with the history of your particular instrument and your experience of it, into a narrative that presents the facts about your piano in a persuasive context. You can use the checklist below to help you form answers to the questions potential buyers will ask, and determine how best to articulate those answers in a way that will place your piano in its best light.

- Make: The brand name is found on the fallboard (keyboard cover) and/or on the cast-iron plate.
- Model: The model designation or number is usually found just inside the lid or on the back of an upright (vertical) piano, and usually under the music desk of a grand.
- Serial number and age: See earlier discussion.
- Relative quality of brand and model: See earlier discussion.
- Cosmetic condition: Look the piano over closely with a flashlight and note any visible wear or damage.
- Performance condition: If you play, how would you describe your piano's performance to a shopper? If you don't play, ask your piano technician how he or she would describe it.
- Date of last tuning or other service.
- Why you're selling the piano.

Here's a checklist of what to do to prepare your piano for sale:

- If you expect to sell your piano for over $1,500, we strongly suggest that you have the piano tuned and its condition inspected before putting it up for sale. (An exception would be a piano that you know to be untunable and unplayable, and offered for sale only to someone who intends to restore it.) We realize that you may not want to put any more money into an instrument you're selling, but spending a few hundred dollars and a couple of hours can produce a good return in both the selling price of the piano and in the ease of sale. Keep in mind that when a piano is significantly out of tune, has notes that don't work properly, or has other obvious defects—even small ones—the chance of being able to sell it is dramatically reduced. Most potential buyers, knowing little or nothing about piano mechanics, will be concerned that the defects they see or hear are symptoms of more serious problems. By presenting the piano in its best condition, you can remove doubts and unnecessary obstacles to the sale.
- Clean the piano's case thoroughly and, if possible, touch up any cosmetic blemishes. Your local hardware store will likely have touch-up felt-tip markers that match the finish of your piano, and a brass cleaner for the pedals. For grand pianos, have your piano technician clean under the strings and inside the piano. With vertical pianos, vacuum the piano's back, and inside the bottom cavity where the pedals are attached.
- Clear everything off the lid of the piano so that potential buyers can look inside. Raise the lid of a grand piano so that potential buyers don't have to (it can be dangerously heavy).
- Clear access to the piano so that potential buyers can see the entire cabinet.
- If necessary, clean the room the piano is in, and be sure it is well lit.

Selling a High-End Piano

"You've got to spend money to make money." You've probably heard that expression, and it especially applies to selling a performance-quality piano. The potential buyer of such an instrument will probably be an experienced player who, in a buyer's market, will have a lot of options. It bears repeating that in order for you to get anything close to fair market value, you should have your piano thoroughly tuned, regulated, voiced, and cleaned—and touch up the cabinet and polish the brass hardware. Failure to invest in this work can keep a shopper from buying, as potential buyers will often avoid buying a good instrument with even minor problems out of a concern, sometimes subconscious, that more serious problems lurk beneath the piano's lid.

Ask your piano technician (or rebuilder, if the piano was recently rebuilt) to provide a written, detailed report of the condition of the piano, and an appraisal of its value. If possible, obtain several such reports and appraisals. A good report and appraisal based on an onsite inspection of the instrument might cost $150 or more, but is well worth the expense for the peace of mind it can bring to the potential buyer of a high-end piano.

High-end pianos may sell to, among others, professional musicians, such as the music faculty of colleges and private piano teachers in your area. The college's website may have profiles of the faculty that include their e-mail addresses. You may wish to contact the faculty, offering to send them the piano's report and appraisal. Buyers willing to pay tens of thousands of dollars for a piano will usually read everything they can about a high-quality used piano before buying it.

If all else fails, check to see what local dealers will pay for your piano, which is generally no more than half the FMV. If the dealer has been in business a long time and is well known to schools and music teachers, ask if the dealer would be willing to take your piano on consignment. This means that the dealer takes physical possession of your piano, but doesn't pay you until it's been sold. You can expect to pay the dealer a commission of 33–50% of the selling price when selling a piano on consignment, but the resulting loss may not be as great as it seems—the dealer may be able to get a higher price for it than you could on your own.

The Donation Option

If you have a piano of decent quality but all of your efforts to sell it fail, you may want to consider donating it to an organization in need. Keep in mind, though, that if your piano is unsaleable because of poor quality or condition, it is *not* a candidate for donation!

PERIOD PIANO CENTER

www.periodpianos.org
Conservation, Historical Study, Collection

www.historicalpianosociety.org
Online Piano Database

(See the *Piano Buyer* article "**Piano Purgatory: The Donated Piano.**")

Note that a well-performing instrument might provide a significant tax deduction. Check with your accountant or tax advisor about what the IRS will require to consider the donation tax-deductible. This is discussed in the *Piano Buyer* article "**Taking a Tax Deduction When Donating a Piano.**"

Our favorite donations are to aspiring piano students who are not in a position to purchase a piano commensurate with their talent. Receiving such a donation can be life changing; however, it is generally not tax-deductible to the donor. For help in finding such a student, contact your local music-teacher association, the local chapter of the **Piano Technicians Guild**, or local piano dealers.

Here is a list of some organizations that facilitate piano donations:

- Piano Finders: **pianofinders.com**
- Piano Adoption: **www.pianoadoption.com**
- Pianos for Education: **www.pianosforeducation .org**
- Society of Unique Artists: **www.suartists.org**
- Keys 4/4 Kids: **www.keys44kids.org**

The Final Curtain

If all else fails, it may be time for—brace yourself—the last rites: disposing of the piano at a local landfill. If it comes to that, you should have professional piano movers do the job—pianos are simply too heavy, bulky, and dangerous to move to subject family

members or friends to the task of lugging it to the dump. Give up, too, any thoughts of salvaging the piano's parts; they have little salvage value, and disassembly is time-consuming and difficult. Burning the wood salvaged from the case can give off toxic fumes, due to the chemicals used in the finish. Even the ivory keys have no value.

Think of it this way: The piano likely brought the gift of music to many during its long life. It's time to let it go.

DONATING, CONVERTING, OR RECYCLING YOUR PIANO

Karen Lile

IN MY 31 YEARS of experience as a piano appraiser and broker, and as a partner in a piano-rebuilding business, I have daily encountered people who are considering donating or otherwise disposing of their pianos. In this article, I outline some of the options available to those who have a piano they don't want to keep or sell, but would like to see it go somewhere other than the dump or local landfill.

Because of the diversity of my clients—piano dealers, piano owners, antique-store owners, collectors, investors, banks, insurance companies, estate appraisers, courts, probate trustees, and nonprofit organizations—I have found it important to establish an effective framework for discussing and advising people about the transfer of a piano from one ownership and/or use to another. In particular, I have learned to separate discussions of the current condition and potential of a piano from the needs and desires of the people and organizations involved. This makes it possible for me to discuss with each party what is in its or their best interest.

Donating a Piano

Say, for example, someone wants to donate a piano to a nonprofit organization that can either use it or resell it for their tax-exempt purposes. The person making the donation may need the piano to be removed from its present location by a specific time, and have specific criteria as to which worthy causes they are willing to contribute. The nonprofit receiving the piano, however, may have specific criteria about how, when, and where they will receive a donated piano, as well as specific restrictions about its condition, quality of construction, durability, and appearance. This is because a piano is a big item that requires storage in a protected environment and access to skilled people to tune and repair it. Also, musicians have specific artistic requirements, and the piano will simply take up space and other resources if it can't fulfill those requirements. The two parties' criteria may or may not be a good match, and the nonprofit might turn down the donation. If the donor has waited until the last minute to decide to donate a piano, then his or her options will be much more limited than if time had been allowed for a nonprofit to consider the offer and, if appropriate, make arrangements for receiving the piano.

In order to make a good decision about where to donate the piano, it is recommended that you know its current condition and fair market value. A piano technician hired to inspect the piano can tell you its condition and value, and advise you on its potential uses, taking into account its quality of design and construction and its present condition. There are also some online services available for obtaining a ballpark estimate of its value, such as on **PianoBuyer.com**.

Although it's beyond the scope of this article to discuss which types and sizes of piano are appropriate for institutions and other nonprofits (see other articles in this volume), if your piano can hold a tune, and has a consistent, uniform, and predictable response from key to key, then it is more likely to be a good instrument for students and musicians to practice and perform on, and a donation can be made either directly to the nonprofit that needs the piano, or to a nonprofit that can sell it and apply the money to a good cause that you want to support.

The types of organizations that might be interested in a donation of a good working piano are schools, social groups, clubs, senior centers, preschools, retirement homes, service clubs, after-school programs, recreation centers—any venue that has some type of formal or informal entertainment, or where groups meet for social occasions. (Note: Spinets and consoles with freestanding legs should be limited to use where they will not be moved frequently, as the legs are prone to breaking if the piano is moved often.)

If you would like to donate the piano to an organization that provides a valuable service to the public but lacks the tax-exempt status that would allow you to take a tax deduction for the donation, you might be able to find another organization, with tax-exempt status and a similar or complementary mission, that can give you the tax deduction while legally passing along the donation to your preferred group.

Although piano dealers usually have more than enough used pianos on hand, taken in trade for new ones, occasionally they may be able to find a new home for your older piano with a student or family who can't afford to pay for one, or with a nonprofit organization.

You might also check to see if your city has an organization devoted to using donated pianos for public art purposes. An example is the Sing for Hope Foundation, which each year places 88 donated, repaired, and painted pianos in parks and public spaces throughout New York City for the public to play and enjoy. After their two-week display, the pianos are donated to underserved local schools, healthcare facilities, and community organizations. See their website at **www.singforhope.org**.

If your piano has not been well maintained, needs major repairs, and/or its cabinet does not look good, then it will be more difficult to find a nonprofit organization that will take the piano as a donation. The rest of this article discusses options for this type of piano.

The Piano Donation Project

Many pianos can have their touch and tone improved by a piano technician or be restored by a piano rebuilder. If the instrument was of high quality when manufactured, then repair or rebuilding are viable options that can result in superior looks, sound, feel, quality, and resale value. This is especially true of many vintage pianos of American and German origin; they were often built to last, and were constructed with high-quality woods that are scarce and expensive today.

My company, Piano Finders, has a Piano Donation Project that helps place pianos with nonprofit organizations. We don't charge for the service, but offer it as a benefit to our clients, who have often paid us for an appraisal or consultation and are considering what to do with their pianos. This project helps save and restore pianos that are well built and still have market value, but are in need of minor to major repairs or rebuilding. If you have a piano that has not been tuned or maintained, or needs some work, but is a good instrument with value and potential, then we may be able to find a sponsor who will bring the condition of the instrument up to a state where it can be used or resold by a nonprofit to benefit its programs. A sponsor can be a piano rebuilder who performs the repair work, or an individual or organization that cares about music and pianos and pays to have the work done. From pianos offered for donation, Piano Finders selects those we feel will be good investments for the nonprofit organizations we work with. Once the work is completed, the piano is either sold to raise funds for the nonprofit organization or is put to use in the nonprofit's programs. If sold, the piano receives a new life in the home of a family or individual who plays and appreciates the piano, or within a deserving organization. Piano Finders works with nonprofits across the country.

Converting a Piano to Furniture or Art

Even when the piano's innards may be ready for disposal, its cabinet might be a beautiful piece of craftsmanship, with carvings and high-quality woods. If you think that parts of your piano's case would make a beautiful piece of furniture, such as a desk, cabinet, or coffee table, you could hire a furniture builder or piano rebuilder to convert those parts into something that will be useful and a work of art. Included here are photos of some examples from the portfolio of craftsman Frank Bidinger, who has converted old uprights and square grands into beautiful works of furniture art. (Bidinger, a former employee of Piano Finders, now runs his own rebuilding business in

Frank Bidinger's coffee table (above) made from a grand lid and various core parts of vintage uprights.

Frank Bidinger's cabinet made from the sides and core parts of a vintage upright. The cherry is new wood; the cabinet has shelves and a drawer in it.

San Ramon, California. He can be contacted through Piano Finders.)

Sometimes, the opposite is true: The cabinet may not be worth much, but the piano's parts—hammers, keys, legs, strings, hardware—can be turned into imaginative pieces of art and sculpture. See **www.pianoasart.com** for impressive examples of this new art form.

Recycling

A piano can be recycled by removing and breaking down its parts—wood, steel wire, screws, cast iron, etc.—for reuse. Recycling is usually done locally, as the cost of transporting a complete piano can be prohibitive; check to see if someone in your area recycles pianos. Sometimes, electronics recyclers also take pianos.

If your local recyclers don't take pianos but will accept their disassembled parts, then you can take the piano apart yourself or, better yet, pay an expert to do it. (Piano parts can be heavy and strings are under high tension; unless you know what you're doing, some danger is involved.) Companies that do building demolition and work with construction sites usually know who can take the cast-iron frame, the heaviest part of the piano. Wood can go to a piano shop or high school wood shop, to be used for making new things. Ivories can go to a piano technician or piano-rebuilding shop. Steel wire, copper, and hardware can often be recycled. However, finding out where to send the various parts of the piano for recycling can be time consuming.

You could also ask a local service club—Rotary, Kiwanis, Lions, etc.—if they'd be willing to do this as a service project. Advertise to the public a weekend of piano recycling, rent a workspace, and hire a piano rebuilder to work with the club's volunteers to disassemble pianos. It often costs more to recycle than to send something to the trash—but if people care about the wood, ivory, and cast iron that went into a piano's construction, and the many memories that a piano contributed to over its life, why not have a big party to celebrate its passage from life as a piano to a new life of helping to make other things of value? Local dealers, teachers, and technicians might decide to be sponsors of the event, which could be connected to a sale of new pianos, a concert by a local symphony, or another musical event happening in the community. The event could also be partnered with the city or county recycling programs, to promote the concept of recycling.

TAKING A TAX DEDUCTION WHEN DONATING A PIANO

Larry Fine

THERE WAS ONCE a time when, for tax-deduction purposes, if you needed to know the value of a piano you were donating to an institution or charity, you would just contact your piano technician or dealer. He or she would search memory for a recent transaction involving a similar instrument, and would settle on a figure that "felt" right. Because each piano is, to some extent, unique, and comparable sales are therefore hard to find, this valuation process would sometimes more closely resemble the seeking of divine revelation than it would hard science. The technician or dealer would then write a brief memo that included the piano's brand name, serial number, and value; you would enter that figure on your tax return; and you could be more or less assured that this "expert" opinion would not be challenged by the Internal Revenue Service.

While such a process is still acceptable for some kinds of transactions, it can no longer be used to value noncash, tax-deductible contributions when the value claimed is over $5,000. If the piano being donated is not in at least good used condition, this threshold drops to only $500. This has actually been the case for some time, but the IRS is getting stricter about enforcing its rules, and some piano technicians and donors are finding their "appraisals" rejected by the IRS—and also by insurance companies, which are increasingly adopting the IRS standards.

As part of the Pension Protection Act of 2006, Congress tightened the valuation and reporting rules for noncash charitable contributions. Exactly what the IRS considers a *Qualified Appraisal* for tax purposes, and whom it considers to be a *Qualified Appraiser*, are spelled out in detail in IRS Publication 561, *Determining the Value of Donated Property*.

According to Publication 561, a Qualified Appraisal must be done according to generally accepted appraisal standards, and no earlier than 60 days before the donation is made. In most cases, the appraisal fee must be a flat or hourly fee, not one based on a percentage of the appraised value. The appraisal must be of the item's *Fair Market Value*, which the IRS defines as "the price at which property would change hands between a willing buyer and a willing seller, when neither is forced to buy or sell, and when both have reasonable knowledge of all relevant facts." This value, generally based on comparable sales, could also be the piano's *salvage value* when the instrument needs complete rebuilding, and could include aspects of *intangible value* when the piano has significant historical value or was owned or used by a celebrity.

The IRS-Qualified Appraisal report must include, among other information:

- A description of the piano (including photos) in enough detail that a person not generally familiar with pianos could determine that the appraised property and the donated property were one and the same.
- The date, or expected date, of contribution, as well as the appraisal date.
- The fair market value on the date of contribution
- The method of valuation used (e.g., comparable sales), and the specific basis of the valuation, such as specific comparable sales transactions.
- The qualifications of the appraiser, including the appraiser's background, experience, education, and membership in any professional appraiser organizations.

Appraisers must also complete IRS Form 8283, to be filed with the donor's tax return, certifying that the appraiser is competent and qualified to do the appraisal, and aware of the penalties for over-stating the value of the donated item. An appraiser who knows that an appraisal will be used with a tax return can be fined by the IRS if he or she substantially overvalues an item and the appraisal results in a substantial underpayment of tax. The donee organization must also provide the donor with a dated letter acknowledging acceptance of the gift, and must sign Form 8283.

An IRS-Qualified Appraiser must either have earned an appraisal designation from a recognized appraiser organization; or must have met certain minimum education and experience requirements, including college- or professional-level coursework relevant to the property being valued, and at least two years of experience in the trade or business of buying, selling, or valuing the type of property being valued. He or she must also regularly prepare appraisals for which he or she is paid. The appraiser must be a disinterested third party, and therefore cannot be the donor, the donee, the person claiming the tax deduction, a party to the transaction in which the donor acquired the property being appraised (in

most cases), or anyone employed by or related to any of these people.

Piano technicians and piano dealers usually have greater technical knowledge about pianos than do professional appraisers, and may also know more about piano sales, but they rarely meet the legal qualifications to be IRS-Qualified Appraisers. For that reason, it may be advantageous for technicians and dealers to form partnerships with professional appraisers, in which the technician or dealer examines the piano on-site and writes an inspection report, then the appraiser performs the valuation research and writes the appraisal report according to established appraisal standards. A professional appraisal cannot be done via the Internet without an on-site inspection of the piano.

An IRS-Qualified Appraisal is also required for the valuation of items of personal property for tax purposes related to the settlement of estates and the dissolution of marriages. However, a person buying or selling a piano is not legally required to have an IRS-Qualified or other professional appraisal. Many piano-technician and piano-dealer appraisers may wish to continue writing less formal appraisal documents in these situations. That said, there are some instances in which a buyer or seller might be well advised to hire a professional appraiser, such as when a piano has special historic or artistic value, or when the ownership or signature of a celebrity has added intangible value to the instrument. These are areas in which professional appraisers have had special training, and piano technicians and dealers usually have not. Another instance is when buyer and seller are related to one another or are friends, and wish to be especially certain that the value is accurately set without bias to either side.

This article is intended to be only a brief overview of the subject, not personal tax advice. Please see IRS Publication 561 for more details, and your tax advisor for advice on your personal situation.

EVERYTHING OLD IS NEW AGAIN

Stuart Isacoff

IS OLDER BETTER? Archeologists, antique dealers, and even aging writers will tell you so. And many pianists agree, especially when one finds a certain special instrument with which he or she can form the musical partnership of a lifetime. But even legendary wines can turn to vinegar. So when dealing with the acquisition—or restoration—of a vintage piano, it's important to get the advice of experts.

There are reasons to favor an older instrument over a new one, and one of the strongest is purely sentimental. "To the extent this was grandma's piano, there is a certain attraction," says Bill Youse, who heads Steinway & Sons' restoration center in Long Island City, New York. "We've had people come in and cry at seeing their restored pianos. One time we asked a technician to play something on it as the customer entered the room to see the results, and she nearly fainted. It turned out that the piece he was playing was the one her husband had last played on the instrument before he passed away. The coincidence was amazing. But the point is, when you bring a piano back to life, you get the family history, the love, the memories. You can't get that with a new instrument."

It's also rare to get the sound in new pianos that vintage instruments produce, say Sara and Irving Faust, of Faust Harrison Pianos in New York City, a dealership renowned for high-level restorations. "The old Steinways, produced in the late 1800s and early 1900s, have never been surpassed," says Sara. "They have warmth, soul, what I would call a sort of 'three-dimensionality' and color in the sound that you can't find in a modern instrument. And each era seems to have its own special quality. Starting in the 1920s, the Steinway sound became more extroverted. Steinways of the 1940s are both lush and bold. Most importantly, in the hands of a top piano restorer the special rich,

mellow, colorful tones of the older instruments are retained. They may look, feel, and smell like new pianos, but they sound like wonderful old pianos.

"You have to have a very large sample to appreciate this fully," Faust continues. "I'm making these judgments based on working with thousands of pianos." The exact reasons why the old Steinways sound different from today's instruments remain a mystery; one theory attributes it to changes in the manufacture of the cast-iron plate that sits at the heart of the instrument.

At Cunningham Piano Co. in Philadelphia, founded in 1891, co-owner Rich Galassini agrees that there are differences among Steinway pianos made at different times. "The final product depends on choices made in materials, design, and the execution of these designs in manufacturing. Any change, intentional or unintentional, in any of these categories will result in a difference in performance.

"But I wouldn't single out just one brand," adds Galassini. "There are a number of beautifully made instruments that historically have had their own voice and, restored, have wonderful performance potential." Galassini would include in this list such venerable brands as Mason & Hamlin, Bösendorfer, Blüthner, and Bechstein, as well as the slightly lesser-known Chickering and Knabe, among others. "There is a very wide palette of tone and touch available to a

This 1915 Steinway advertisement reflects the prevailing
sentiment of the time—that developing her musical skills
would increase a young woman's chance of a good
marriage.

Source: NW Ayers Advertising Agency Records, Archives
Center, National Museum of American History, Smithsonian
Institution

pianist who wishes to seek out an older instrument
that speaks to him or her personally."

Steinway's Bill Youse has a somewhat different perspective. There may be differences in quality between
older instruments and today's, he says, but it's difficult
to render an opinion because, "by the time I get them,
they are in demise." More likely, the perceived differences have to do with changing aesthetics, he adds:
"The tonal requirements today—the sounds people
are looking for—are different than they were years
ago. Today we juice the hammers to produce a brighter
sound. We tune at a higher pitch. Sometimes it's too
harsh for my senses. I like pianos voiced in a mellow

way. But the entire piano industry has developed that
trend toward brightness."

Perhaps because of these different outlooks, the
three firms have different approaches to restoration.
"We replace rather than repair," reports Youse. "We
retain original parts only in a museum-type restoration, as we did for the White House piano, and the
'Peace Piano'—the one with gold stars all around
that had been in Congress and that now resides at
the Smithsonian Institution. When we worked on the
'King of Sweden' piano, which arrived with envoys and
armed guards, we of course had to use the original types
of glue and varnish. But in most cases, we believe that
newer is better.

"There is a perception that the old craftsmen did
it better," Youse continues. "Yet the materials we use,
and the ways we have of testing things, have gotten
better. We replace hardware, to avoid sympathetic
vibrations that develop as things wear. The modern
action is an improvement over older ones.

And our wood technologist tells me that after
about 60 years the cellular structure of spruce breaks
down, and the soundboard just won't have the same
resilience. The newer ones are superior."

At Faust Harrison Pianos, standardizing parts is
not always considered the right way to go. Indeed,
their technicians often mix replacement parts—
combining elements of Renner and Steinway, for
example— to achieve the desired results. Rather than
replacing items wholesale, they may design individual
solutions for each area of the instrument being serviced, in order to accommodate the original dimensions and materials, or to maintain the look of an
earlier design.

Cunningham, too, takes a more customized
approach to restoration. "All manufacturers change
the design of their pianos over time," says Galassini,
"in part to improve their instruments, but also in an
attempt to appeal to the fashionable tone of the time."
Because of this, rebuilders must decide if they wish to
be faithful to the originally intended design, or if they
wish to make the piano sound more modern. "For
instance," says Galassini, "a well-educated rebuilder,
if he wanted to, could reproduce the tone and touch
of the Mason & Hamlin that so moved Ravel."

Of course, all of these companies employ expert
workers. One particular Steinway restorer, brags
Bill Youse, can make anything seem new again: he
once repaired a mummy that had lost a leg in tran-
sit. Another, he claims, "can duplicate any painting

Installing new hammers on a Steinway grand

A.C. Pianocraft, Inc.

you show him." That comes in handy when the piano to be worked on is an "art case" instrument: one of those exquisitely designed models, often decorated with paintings or built with rare woods, that emerged in the 19th century—a piano-building tradition recently resurrected at Steinway. These pianos, with their highly artistic cabinetry, can be extraordinarily attractive—and valuable.

That touches on a third reason to seek historic instruments: their monetary value. Older instruments may be of a rare vintage, or possess an unusual pedigree. In any case, as remnants of a more genteel age, when pianos held a prominent place in nearly every home, they nearly always carry an aura of romance.

In fact, good Victorian families set aside a formal area for piano entertaining, which was once the best way to demonstrate a flair for stylish living. The evidence can still be found in the preserved dwellings of important figures from the past, including Mark Twain, whose home in Hartford, Connecticut, featured a Steinway & Sons baby grand used for recitals organized by his wife, Livy; and Louisa May Alcott, who, when not walking to Walden Pond for boat rides with Henry David Thoreau, played a Chickering square piano in her parlor. Emily Dickinson kept a Wilkinson piano in her Amherst house, and Edna St.

Vincent Millay had two Steinways. Eugene O'Neill loved his player piano—a coin-operated instrument with stained-glass panels—and named it "Rosie."

Surprisingly, the piano wasn't instantly popular. Though its official birth date is generally agreed to be 1700, in many ways the piano was still in its infancy at the end of the 18th century. In London, the instrument's public debut as a solo instrument didn't take place until 1768 (Johann Christian Bach had the honor). Leading craftsmen in the decades that followed produced no more than 30 to 50 instruments a year. But a great wave was coming. By 1798, English piano maker James Shudi Broadwood could not keep up with demand. "Would to God we could make them like muffins!" he wrote to a wholesaler. Five decades later, the desire for pianos had exploded: England was suddenly the center of the piano world, with some 200 manufacturers. And, with increased production, large segments of the population could now afford to purchase one.

No wonder George Bernard Shaw wrote that, in the late 19th century, piano playing had become a "religion." The instrument served every musical and social need, making it possible to learn and perform great works, strengthen family ties, and impress the neighbors.

Replacing a pinblock in a grand piano

Keyboards have enjoyed a long history as symbols of prosperity. The piano art case, in fact, had its origins in the 16th and 17th centuries, when harpsichords were adorned with paintings, often of Orpheus charming the animals or battles on horseback. Sometimes they were also inscribed with mottos: "I was once an ordinary tree," read one, "although living I was silent; now, though dead, if I am well played I sound sweetly."

The instruments then were intended primarily for the women of the household, and the piano boom was similarly helped along by young ladies of a certain social status who were taught that developing their musical skills would increase their chances of a good marriage. As late as 1847, critic Henri Blanchard, in France, reported that "Cultivating the piano is something that has become as essential, as necessary, to social harmony as the cultivation of

the potato is to the existence of the people. . . . The piano provokes meetings between people, hospitality, gentle contacts, associations of all kinds, even matrimonial ones . . . and if our young men so full of assurance tell their friends that they have married twelve or fifteen thousand francs of income, they at least add as a corrective: 'My dear, my wife plays piano like an angel.'"

The attractiveness of the instrument as a piece of furniture was also important. The wood, ivory, and artistic detail of a fine instrument lent elegance to a home. And, as a center of attention, it cried out for special enhancements. England's Mrs. Jane Ellen Panton pointed out, in her authoritative *From Kitchen to Garret* (1888), a bestseller of the era, that it was a good idea to decorate one's piano with material "edged with an appropriate fringe," and to place a big palm in a brass pot into the bend of the instrument, to give it "a finished look." Victorian prudishness also sometimes came into play, with suggestions that coverlets be put over the piano's legs for the sake of modesty.

Some piano makers even designed special models with the homeowner in mind. An "upright grand Pianoforte in the form of a bookcase" was patented by William Stodart in 1795 (there is evidence that Haydn visited Stodart's shop and approved of the device); and the early 19th century saw the introduction of a square piano in the form of a sewing table. Highly decorated upright pianos featured giant lyres, arabesques, and flutings; one extant sample includes a medallion bust of Beethoven.

It didn't take long for the piano to gain a foothold in the New World as well, where it reached beyond the big cities into America's western territories. "'Tis wonderful," wrote Ralph Waldo Emerson in *Civilization* (1870), "how soon a piano gets into a log-hut on the frontier." We can glimpse the results in diaries kept by American homesteaders. Living in the mining town of Aurora, Nevada in the 1860s, a Mrs. Rachel Haskell recorded that in the evening, after dinner, her husband would come into the sitting room and place himself near the piano as their daughter, Ella, accompanied the entire family in song. Rachel's daytime regime included instructing Ella at the piano, along with practicing the multiplication tables with her sons, making dinner, and visiting friends.

This trend caught the attention of W.W. Kimball, who settled in Chicago in 1857 and announced that he wanted to sell pianos "within the reach of the farmer on his prairie, the miner in his cabin, the fisherman in his hut, the cultivated mechanic in his neat cottage in the thriving town." He based his new business on the installment plan—as did D.H. Baldwin, a Cincinnati dealer who, in 1872, hired an army of sewing-machine salesmen to recruit new customers.

The piano in America continued to be seen as a tool to regulate the life of the tender sex, just as it had across the ocean. The critic of the *New York World*, A.C. Wheeler, laid out the argument in 1875: "[It] may be looked upon as furniture by dull observers or accepted as a fashion by shallow thinkers, but it is in reality the artificial nervous system, ingeniously made of steel and silver, which civilization in its poetic justice provides for our young women. Here it is, in this parlor with closed doors, that the daughter of our day comes stealthily and pours out the torrent of her emotions through her finger-ends, directs the forces of her youth and romanticism into the obedient metal

and lets it say in its own mystic way what she dare not confess or hope in articulate language." Through the early decades of the 20th century, pianos continued to be built—and to be played—in this cultural atmosphere of naïveté and old-world charm. We live in a very different world now: one filled with iPods, interactive games, and—for pouring out torrents of emotion—talk therapy. But the gracefulness and enchantment of that earlier time still imbue many of the instruments it produced.

Restoring those pianos to their full beauty can be a painstaking process, as one quickly discovers when touring the sprawling restoration facility of Faust Harrison Pianos in Dobbs Ferry, New York, where each aspect of piano rebuilding warrants its own room. There is a lot to consider. "Take the hammers," explains Sara Faust; "they each have to hit the strings at the optimum point for sound production. Yet if they are placed optimally, you may not see a perfectly straight hammer line, but something that resembles a gentle roller coaster, particularly in the third register. Sometimes technicians try to compensate for a weak sound by putting extra lacquer on the hammers, but the right answer is often not lacquer at all, but to make an adjustment to the strike point. Indeed, minimally lacquered Steinway hammers have a special beauty that should be preserved whenever possible. A new hammer may start out like a closed rosebud, but as it is played it hardens naturally from compression, and the sound opens up and blossoms.

"And new hammers have more wood than old ones," she continues, "so we sometimes remove some wood, changing the mass and shape of the hammers, to clarify the sound. Why do we drive ourselves crazy in this way? Because when you have a well-crafted hammer, the piano can sound both more beautiful and more powerful at the same time."

In the "rubbing room," a series of sandings, using finer and finer materials, ensures a beautiful cabinet surface. But there are dangers here as well: in the wrong hands, important cabinet details in a vintage artcase instrument can be lost. A good restorer will bring them back.

It all has to be done with a light touch, inside and out. At A.C. Pianocraft, in New York City, owner Alexander Kostakis explains that "The instrument will tell me what to do. I have to keep everything in perspective. Each instrument has a personality, or 'soul.' We have restored all the American and European brands of yesteryear—Steinways, Mason & Hamlins,

IT'S A
MATERIAL WORLD

Twentieth-century innovations brought us the first man on the moon, the split atom and colossal advances in technology, medicine and science — but there was a profound lack of progress in piano design ... **until now.**

What's in your piano?

WNG
Wessell, Nickel & Gross

High Performance Action Parts
www.wessellnickelandgross.com

Bechsteins, Blüthners, Pleyels, Knabes, Chickerings. Each one is different, and the experience has made us better mechanics, more versatile.

"For example, old pianos had a flat inner rim where the soundboard was attached. But sometimes, when restoring the piano, we've added a pitch to the rim to give the soundboard more resonance. As for replacing parts, you always have to remember that the perishable items within an instrument have a certain lifespan. But we also try to maintain the authentic character of the instrument, and sometimes choose to repair rather than replace."

In a business driven mostly by a love of the instrument, piano restorers sometimes seem to work miracles. Even so, there are limits to what can be accomplished. "Some brands you'll restore once, but never again," says Kostakis—"every time you touch something, something else breaks. But we've also had amazing successes. I advised a customer not to restore a family heirloom: a Kranich & Bach Louis XV model in walnut. It was a beautiful piece of furniture, but it looked like restoring the action would be impossible because no one makes the right parts anymore. But the customer was adamant about restoring the instrument, so we agreed to repair the action parts rather than replace them. Working on the piano, however, I realized that the old action parts, even repaired, would never be good enough, and might give trouble later on. It was a Herculean task, but in order to do the right thing for the piano and for the customer—and, frankly, to sleep well at night—I actually reproduced brand-new parts in the exact style of the old ones."

Steinway, too, has seen its share of horror stories. "There was a church down in Georgia," remembers Bill Youse; "they had a Model O that had been badly damaged by a fire, and they wanted it restored. I asked for a photo. All that was left was the harp and a bunch of burnt strings sticking up. They were essentially asking us to build a piano around the old harp—an impossible task."

Still, had the assignment been humanly possible, he would have tried. "I love my job," he says. "I'm third generation here at Steinway. My grandfather was a blind tuner back in the late '40s. My father started here in 1955. I've been here 37 years. For me, this is an honor. My first bicycle was a beat-up model I had to restore. My first car was a beatup old Chevy I had to restore. This was a natural progression. It's what I was meant to do."

SHOULD I HAVE MY PIANO REBUILT?

Sally Phillips

TECHNICIANS OFTEN GET calls from piano owners interested in having their pianos rebuilt. Given the high cost of rebuilding, most technicians will screen the call by asking about the brand and age of the piano, and its intended use, in order to determine whether a visit to inspect the piano is worth the customer's time and money. This article discusses some of the factors that go into that determination.

Why do pianos need to be rebuilt?

Depending on how you count them, a piano has as many as 12,000 parts. Over time, many of these parts are affected by wear and environmental changes to the point of being unrepairable without completely rebuilding the piano. A piano that sees constant use in a school or performance venue with poor climate control might need partial rebuilding in as little as 10 years. On the other hand, a seldom-used piano in a living room in a mild climate may go 100 years before being rebuilt. As a rule of thumb, most pianos become ready for rebuilding somewhere between 40 and 60 years of age.

Rebuilding a piano is a large, time-consuming project that can take almost as much time as the construction of a new instrument by the original manufacturer. Quality rebuilding work is very expensive, easily ranging from $25,000 to $40,000, or even more, for a first-class restoration of a high-quality instrument. Most aspects of the rebuilding process fall into three main areas:

- The *action*, including the keyframe and action frame, keys and keytops, hammers, damper underlevers, trapwork, and all other moving action parts. These parts get worn with use, causing noisy movement and poor touch and tone. As many as 8,000 of a piano's parts are in its action. Restoring the action also includes the regulation or adjustment of those parts.
- The *soundbox*, also known as the strung back or belly, including the soundboard, ribs, bridges, strings, pinblock, tuning pins, plate; the damper felts, heads, and wires; and the structural parts of the case. Soundboards dry out, crack, lose their crown, and no longer transmit tone well. Bridges crack from the pressure of the strings on the bridge pins. The pinblock, a plank of laminated wood in which the tuning pins are embedded, often becomes cracked or worn, and can no longer hold the tuning pins tightly enough to keep the strings in tune. Although this is the most common reason for restringing a piano, the strings themselves can become compromised with rust, pitting, or metal fatigue. In better pianos that must be tuned accurately for professional use, even though the tuning pins are still tight, the strings may require replacing simply to restore the instrument's tone or its ability to be accurately tuned.
- The *cabinet*, including cosmetic repair and refinishing of the case and of the nonstructural cabinet parts and hardware. Refinishing the cabinet is a very expensive part of the restoration

process—in some cases as much as a third of the cost.[1]

Technicians refer to instruments that are candidates for rebuilding as "core pianos." This means that the only possible use for the piano is to rebuild it. For the reasons mentioned above, these instruments are usually untunable and/or unplayable, and thus unusable as is. If you own what is essentially a core piano, and intend to use it other than as a piece of furniture, you'll have to have it rebuilt or replaced.

Why Most Pianos Are Not Good Candidates for Rebuilding

The main reason a piano may not be a good candidate for rebuilding is that it simply is not a good enough instrument, something that's usually indicated by the potential resale value of the instrument after rebuilding. If the cost of rebuilding the piano exceeds its potential resale value when rebuilt, then rebuilding is usually not a wise investment—for less money, the owner could buy a better-quality instrument. Although an inspection by a qualified technician or rebuilder is necessary to confirm the cost of repairs and the potential value of your instrument when rebuilt, the most important factors in determining its potential value after restoration are its brand and model. Before contacting a technician for an estimate, an Internet search for examples of your model of instrument for sale, restored or unrestored, will likely give you a good dose of reality. You may immediately find that pianos like yours sell for premium prices—or that similar models are being given away cheap or for free on Craigslist.

It turns out that, from a financial point of view, except for premium-quality instruments, most pianos are not worth a private owner's investment in their rebuilding. Putting thousands of dollars into a low-quality instrument won't increase its value by much, and there's no guarantee that any of the cost of rebuilding can be recouped in resale. Piano dealers who sell rebuilt pianos choose candidates very carefully in order to get a return from their investment in parts and labor, and the private owner should be just as wary. In my experience, if the client expects

to recoup rebuilding costs should there be a need to liquidate, the least-expensive instruments that should be considered as candidates for rebuilding are models that currently retail new for over $60,000. The mistake I usually see is that a piano with sentimental value but very marginal quality has been rebuilt, and the family is now trying to sell it and recoup the cost of the work. There's nothing wrong with having a piano restored for sentimental reasons—but you should be clear that the return on your investment will not be a financial one.

On a case-by-case basis, older instruments with poor resale value may be worth the value of the repairs to the owner, but to no one else. I once had a client—a piano teacher—who'd been given an older piano that, although well built, would have had little resale value. In her situation, a more modest, partial rebuilding without cosmetic work, costing about $15,000, resulted in a usable, decent piano for her teaching studio. Partial rebuilding may also make sense for some newer used pianos that have not yet reached core-piano status. For example, a medium- to high-quality instrument less than 50 years old whose pinblock and soundboard are still in acceptable condition may benefit from restringing and action rebuilding (two procedures that are often considered normal maintenance on performance instruments), which can significantly extend the piano's useful life until the time its other elements require restoration. But such situations make sense only if—taking into account the remaining life expectancy of its *un*restored parts—the resulting instrument exceeds the quality of a new piano costing the same as the rebuilding. The higher the rebuilding cost, the more expensive is the new piano to which the rebuilt one needs to favorably compare.

Older, inherited pianos that have been in a family for many years often acquire mythologies of value and provenance that decidedly deviate from reality. Earlier technicians may have unwittingly contributed to this because they were reluctant to tell the truth. Often, a new technician called in to examine an older piano is met with an heir's lofty impressions of it: "Mr. Binkie [the deceased] said that this was the best piano he'd ever seen." Even though the new technician knows that the tuning will not be very successful, he or she is reluctant to tell the owner, and so just does his or her best and heads to the next appointment. When the day comes that the technician must tell the owner that, due to structural failure, the instrument can no

---

[1] For a more complete list of what the complete rebuilding of a piano entails, see the **Grand Piano Rebuilding Checklist** in the *Piano Buyer* article "Buying a Used or Restored Piano."

Quality Class	Example	Unrestored Value*	Cost to Restore	Potential Retail Price of Restored Piano	Realistic Private-Party Resale Price
High	Steinway B c.1920 (core piano)	$5,000–$10,000	$25,000–$40,000 (full rebuild)	$65,000–$75,000	$42,000
High	Steinway B c.1990 (still functional)	$28,000	$15,000 (partial rebuild)	$65,000	$42,000
Medium to High	Baldwin L c.1950 (core piano)	$1,000–$2,000	$25,000 (full rebuild)	$22,000	$8,000
Medium to High	Baldwin L c.1990 (still functional)	$5,000	$9,600 (partial rebuild)	$16,000	$12,000
Medium	Sohmer Grand c.1918 (core piano)	$100–$500	$25,000 (full rebuild)	$8,000	$3,500
Low to Medium	Brambach Grand c.1925 (core piano)	$0	$25,000 (full rebuild)	$3,500	$1,500

*Even if the owner didn't pay for the piano, it still has a value that must be considered in the calculation.

longer be tuned, the harsh reality must be faced. "But can't you repair it?" the customer asks. At that point, the technician must explain that the repairs will cost thousands more than the value of the instrument.

"But isn't my piano an antique?" Most older pianos do *not* qualify as antiques. American pianos from the late 19th and early 20th centuries have no real antique value unless they have very unusual or heavily carved, ornate casework utilizing expensive cabinet woods and/or marquetry. Ivory keys do not add value, and, given new laws regarding the sale of ivory, may even be a detriment in some cases. Even with very fancy casework, few dealers or rebuilders will invest in rebuilding for resale if the core-piano value is minimal. I recommend asking any technicians who examine the piano what they would do if it were *their* piano. Be open to the professional's opinion—don't shoot the messenger. If dealing directly with rebuilders, ask if they'd be interested in buying the piano unrestored. If they decline, that might tell you something about its core-piano value.

Having a Premium-Quality Piano Rebuilt

Even with a premium-quality instrument, the $25,000 to $40,000 cost of a first-class restoration may be hard to recover by a private owner selling out of the home. A fully rebuilt piano selling from a retail store is generally thought of as a like-new instrument, and thus is sold at a retail price that includes a warranty or implied warranty, providing valuable peace of mind. However, a piano sold from a home is considered—legally and in terms of buyers' perceptions—as merely a used piano. It generally does not come with a warranty, and is likely to bring a much lower price (similar to wholesale) because of the concerns that buyers may have about potential technical problems and longevity. To alleviate the client's reservations about spending a huge sum of money to rebuild a piano, a restorer will sometimes exaggerate the value of the rebuilding work to imply that, post-restoration, the client can expect to make a profit on the sale of the piano. However, this is rarely the case because while the client has paid a retail price for the restoration, he or she can realistically expect only a wholesale return when selling.

For this reason, the customer who's thinking of spending money to rebuild a piano should seriously consider the length of time they want to retain ownership. If the rebuilding is to be a long-term investment in which the payoff is primarily many years of pleasure at the piano, it may well make financial sense. But if you expect to sell soon after rebuilding, don't expect to make a profit—and it may be necessary to take a small loss.

Here, an important factor is the piano's end user. If the piano is being restored for professional use by a pianist, or for any owner with specific tastes in tone and touch, the outcome of the restoration work is

POOR OR PROBLEMATIC CANDIDATES FOR REBUILDING

Here is a partial list of pianos that are unlikely to be candidates for rebuilding, or that may have problems that reduce their desirability for rebuilding:

Older grands from manufacturers of low-quality pianos that are no longer in business: These pianos are much more difficult to restore because parts—especially action parts—are not readily available. Technicians can use generic parts with some success, but may have to re-engineer or modify the entire action in order to do so, which makes these instruments even more costly to properly restore.

Spinets, consoles, and old uprights: None of these—even old Steinway uprights—will sell for as much as the cost of a quality restoration.

Steinway 85-note grands and six-legged player grands: Most customers would assume that any Steinway grand would be a good prospect for rebuilding, and for the most part that's true—but the 85-note, older, 19th-century models will not bring as much in the marketplace from knowledgeable buyers. Modern pianos have 88 notes, the change from 85 having occurred mostly in the 1880s and '90s. This doesn't mean that an 85-note instrument can't be restored, but such pianos are usually not desirable for the professional pianist because of the musical limitations caused by the omission of the three highest notes in the treble. For casual use in the home, however, an 85-note piano is entirely acceptable. The older player-piano Steinway grands with six legs (two at each of the three leg positions) have extremely long keys that are very difficult to regulate so that the touch feels right. The sound can be restored, but the function of the action will never match the performance and feel of a new piano.

Previously rebuilt pianos: Pianos that have already been rebuilt are sometimes poor candidates for a second rebuilding. The quality of the prior work may have actually reduced or ruined the value, due to the rebuilder's failure to properly replicate the original instrument's design. Also, in the 1950s, many old pianos, when rebuilt, had their ornate legs, lyres, and music desks replaced with more modern, plain-looking case parts. There are companies that make replacements, but the cost of a set of these ornate parts can exceed $5,000.

more critical than if it is going into the parlor of a family home for light, casual use. More than new pianos, rebuilt instruments vary unpredictably in their musical qualities even when restored by experienced rebuilders, and there's no guarantee that the musical outcome of even a high-quality rebuilding job will be to a discerning owner's satisfaction. If the rebuilt instrument is not what you hoped it to be, you may need to sell it, which could lead to an unanticipated loss. To avoid this scenario, it may be preferable for this type of owner to instead sell or trade in the core piano to a rebuilder, then purchase a new or rebuilt instrument whose musical qualities can be ascertained beforehand.[2]

A few examples that illustrate the concepts discussed so far are shown in the accompanying table.

---

[2] If the owner plans to donate the rebuilt instrument, additional considerations apply. See my article "Piano Purgatory: The Donated Piano" elsewhere in this volume.

Shopping for Rebuilding

If you decide to take the restoration plunge, visit rebuilding shops, ask to see examples of their work, and get references and more than one estimate. If you're going through a dealer, find out who will actually do the work. Many dealers send work out to subcontractors, and you need to find out who is actually responsible for the final product. Don't forget to calculate the round-trip transportation of the piano to the rebuilder's shop, especially for out-of-state transport; often, this is not included in estimates.

Keep in mind that the quality and scope of the rebuilding services offered differ from shop to shop. Some specialize in performance instruments, whereas others deal more frequently with the family piano, or are more interested in the cosmetic elements. Also, there is no licensing in the U.S. piano trade, and certification by trade groups and/or schools does not guarantee the level of experience or competence required.

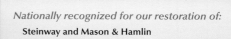

In considering ways to save money, know that, most of the time, a reduction in the price of the work will be reflected in reduced performance of the rebuilt piano. However, omitting the piano's cosmetic elements (e.g., refinishing the case) from the restoration can greatly reduce the cost without sacrificing the instrument's musical functionality. Even if refinishing is not entirely omitted, money can be saved by having a less-expensive finish applied. For example, a satin finish applied with a spray gun, but not hand-rubbed, costs less than a hand-rubbed or high-polish finish.

When considering reductions in the scope of the work in order to save money, however, the rebuilder's skill and experience are even more vital to success. The better the rebuilder, the more likely they are to turn down work that will not, in their opinion, result in a successful job. Sadly, that also means that the less-experienced rebuilders will often tackle jobs that are either well beyond their abilities, or unlikely to result in satisfactory instruments.

Last, before making a final decision, also shop around for new pianos, or for rebuilt or better-quality used ones, and compare their prices with the cost of restoring your current piano. Today's new pianos, in particular, are of much higher quality than the new instruments of 20 or 30 years ago. I find that, in some cases, clients who haven't looked at new instruments in years are making the decision to rebuild based on out-of-date impressions or opinions. Before investing in repairs, be sure that your comparisons are fresh and reflect the current market.

THREE APPROACHES TO PIANO RESTORATION

Bill Shull, David G. Hughes, Delwin D. Fandrich

WHEN REBUILDING A PIANO, the restorer is presented at every turn with questions concerning the extent to which the piano's original design, parts, and materials should be preserved or, conversely, altered or replaced. The philosophies that guide these decisions fall, roughly, into three camps, which might be called, respectively, Conservative, Modern, and Innovative. Of course, this division is, to some degree, a generalization; a particular restorer may combine elements of more than one approach in his or her work.

With the conservative approach, the restorer places a high priority on preserving as much of the original instrument as possible, even, if necessary, sacrificing some degree of performance in the interest of maintaining historical authenticity (not just to save money). So with this approach, for example, rather than replace a cracked soundboard, a restorer would shim the cracks with wood (if possible, with old wood); and rather than discard and replace old wooden action parts, the restorer would replace only their worn leather and cloth surfaces. Design changes, even minor ones, are unthinkable.

With the modern approach, the restorer places a higher priority on the instrument's performance, and so replaces as many parts as possible with new ones. But the restorer attempts to make the piano only as good as it was when new, closely maintaining the original design. Sometimes minor design changes will be made to correct known defects, especially ones the manufacturer itself corrected in later instruments.

With the innovative approach, the restorer not only replaces worn parts with new, but also feels free to modify the design of the instrument in any way that, in the restorer's judgment, would make it perform better—even in ways the manufacturer never contemplated and might not approve of. So the thickness and taper of the soundboard might be changed, the bridges moved, the stringing scale altered, even new holes made in the cast-iron plate and pinblock to accommodate new strings—anything that can be done within the confines of the original case and plate is on the table for consideration.

In this article, several well-respected piano restorers, each approximately representing one of the above positions, explain their approaches to restoration in general and, specifically, how they might be applied to various eras of Steinway grands.

— *Editor*

Conservation-Informed Piano Rebuilding

Bill Shull, RPT, M. Mus.

Twenty-two years ago, the purchase of an 1878 Style 2 (7' 2") Steinway grand piano led me down the road to a different approach to piano restoration. This piano was one of the last examples of antique piano building, and one of the last bridges to the modern era. It was a strange instrument, very unlike a modern Steinway and difficult to rebuild, and I learned that there were few existing protocols for restoring it. As a result, I was inspired to study these earlier Steinways—and earlier pianos from other makers—more thoroughly, and sought to learn more about the field of conservation in general. Since then, my research and teaching have brought me in contact with leading conservators and their work, and in my presentations and classes I have begun to encourage my colleagues to be more careful in modifying older pianos, and to become familiar enough with conservation to give responsible counsel when retained to assess and appraise older instruments.

What has cemented these convictions has been my experience in locating early Steinway pianos for my study. As I examined rebuilt examples of early Steinways, I found, among rebuilders, a widespread disregard for these pianos as objects of conservation, and nearly equal disregard for restoring them to their original structural, mechanical, or musical design. Permanent alterations routinely include replacement of soundboards, bridge caps, and action parts, and the use of near-permanent polyester or polyurethane finishes. Some alterations include experimental designs. If the piano is antique or historically important—things not always easy to know—its historical value, and probable future value as an antique piano, can be lost forever in the rebuilding shop.

This lack of respect for early Steinways can be shown even by conservators and early-piano specialists, who may recognize the emergence of modern design elements but can have insufficient regard for these instruments as historical documents. Steinways from 1853 to 1892 represent an era of transition: from flat-strung to cross-strung; and from antique soundboards with long cutoff bars and grain parallel to the spine, to the modern crowned soundboard supported by angled ribs and grain. Before 1860, pianos were, to a great extent, built by hand, but by 1880, construction techniques had been mechanized and standardized. So while early Steinways tend to be ignored by students of the early piano, these instruments are critical to an understanding of piano history, and deserve respect as objects of conservation. Even "modern" Steinways from the 1880s to as late as the 1930s can contain design nuances that are often glossed over and discarded by the modern rebuilder.

This attitude follows the lead of Steinway & Sons' own Restoration Center, which usually treats antique Steinways like their modern counterparts, and in restoring them seems to follow no consistent policy of conservation. There is a certain irony to Steinway's relative lack of interest in its own early instruments, for the stories these pianos tell are of some of the company's best, most enduring innovations. Indeed, it was the antique, 1860s design of my Style

Angled mid-treble or mid-tenor string terminations in some vintage Steinways are believed to improve sustain by slightly de-tuning the unisons. Conservative restorers are likely to retain this element; modern restorers usually re-cap the bridge and square off the terminations perpendicular to the strings. This photo of an unrestored bridge from an 1887 Steinway D shows several angled mid-tenor terminations and a perpendicular one.

2 Steinway that catapulted the company to industry leader in 1867!

While it is generally thought, among piano restorers, that conservation is for only museum objects, consumers increasingly seek competence in restoring antiques from professional piano restorers. Not only is the general public becoming more aware of the value of conserving antiques, but pianists are increasingly interested in performing music on instruments from the period in which the music was composed. This development in piano performance practice relies on the availability of well-restored original instruments and good replicas.

Leading conservators, curators, and early-piano experts have had a profound influence on my rebuilding and have helped me to define my work. Especially important has been Robert Barclay's seminal book, *The Preservation and Use of Historic Musical Instruments: Display Case and Concert Hall* (Earthscan from Routledge, 2005). Barclay explains that, among the options for conservators of musical instruments, none satisfactorily permits both continued use ("currency") *and* historical preservation ("conservation"), and the "restoration" option invasively alters the historical document. Barclay defines a mediating alternative that he calls "restorative conservation": careful application of conservation principles and techniques in a manner that permits those who wish to play and hear the instrument to do so. It is this philosophy of restorative conservation that I attempt to follow in my shop.

Applying restorative conservation to piano rebuilding requires making many difficult and nuanced decisions. A few examples:

Bridge modification or careful wire selection. Modern rebuilders solve wire-matching problems by adding wound strings, or by moving or adding bridges. For example, the top two octaves of early Steinways had shorter string lengths and more flexible music wire than modern Steinways. Today's stiffer wire requires longer strings, so rebuilders often move the treble bridge to increase the effective string length. However, to maintain the historical integrity of the original instrument, I no longer move the bridge, but instead seek out the best available replacement music wire intended for period instruments, several types of which have recently become available. I also document the original scale and archive the old music wire.

Early damper actions. Early Steinway damper actions used a damper wire that threaded into the wooden damper-lever flange, or a setscrew threaded into wood. These systems did not age well, and sometimes cannot be successfully restored. Since most Steinways can be retrofitted with a complete, new damper action without any compromise of design, I often take advantage of that alternative, saving the original parts (or representative samples) for future study. Options also exist for partial replacement of the damper action where that would suffice.

Bass strings. Even with modern restoration techniques, old iron-wound bass strings rarely approach the tonal palette of properly designed new ones. If the owner wants to return the instrument to its highest possible performance level, the original strings will be replaced and saved for future study. Depending on the owner's use and preference, for greater authenticity, I may replace old iron-wound strings with new ones of the same material, or, for greater longevity, with modern copper-wound strings.

Hammers. It's a cause for celebration when I find a completely original piano, including the hammers. (The hammers and finish are usually the first things to be replaced, followed by the strings.) No solution for hammer replacement satisfies everyone. Technicians will usually reshape the hammers to eliminate the grooves. Conservators prefer to send the original hammers to Europe to have their wooden moldings recovered with new felt, retaining as much as possible the weight and resilience of the originals; however, this still destroys the original hammer as a historical document. I prefer to replace the entire action so that the original action can be saved intact for historical study. More often than not, however, the client cannot afford this, in which case I prefer to replace the hammers with new ones of similar weight and density, along with the shanks and flanges, and save the originals for the historical record.

Steinways built between 1864 and 1880 usually have actions that appear modern, but have a much higher action ratio (leverage). These are cumbersome to play with the heavier hammers of the modern era, including modern New York Steinway hammers, so I encourage the use of lighter hammers and higher gearing on Steinways (and other makes) originally designed that way. I also retain original rocker-style capstans instead of retrofitting with new screw capstans and new-style wippens.

Soundboard and bridge caps. The soundboards of most pianos built through the 1860s last far longer than is commonly believed, because they are not of the "crowned and loaded" design of the modern piano, in which the stress applied to the soundboard tends to shorten its useful life. Even the more modern crowned soundboards may still be viable, as the modern soundboard design always has a significant functional stiffness, even if there is no crown. If I must replace the soundboard, I copy the original design, extensively document my findings, and retain the original soundboard as an artifact. I also prefer to retain any unique design elements, such as the angled mid-treble unison terminations used on Steinway Cs and Ds from 1884 through the 1930s, and faithfully replicate them if a bridge must be recapped. This unusual element adds sustain and projection power to the treble by slightly de-tuning the unisons. Squaring the termination to tame the resulting slight false-beating "wildness" of sound neutralizes the designer's intent for the treble tone (see illustration).

The Steinway piano has dominated the field of piano restoration, resulting in the mass disposal of many other venerable brands of high quality. Surviving examples of these other brands, however, are often in near-original condition. I'm especially joyful to find pianos in this state of benign neglect, as they represent a variety of tonal and performance ideas that could still have a voice through responsible, conservation-informed rebuilding: the articulate, Érard-like sound of the 19th-century Weber; the warm sustain of the three-bridge Knabe; the distinctive registrations of the flat-strung Chickering; the easy touch of the Edwin Brown action often found in Chickerings and other makes; and the sweet, warm sound of the Viennese piano.

Today, when restoring pianos, most rebuilders routinely replace parts, and many extensively redesign the instruments. While these approaches have their place in the piano rebuilder's repertoire, indiscriminately applying them to vintage or antique instruments risks changing the unique historical, tonal, and performance character of the restored piano. Our rebuilding shop seeks to reveal the unique musical personalities of historical instruments while respecting their function as historical documents. It is not always possible to do both, and we are always leaning one way or the other, but it's a fascinating and rewarding journey.

A Modern Approach to Piano Restoration

David G. Hughes, RPT

In the undertaking of any task, prudence dictates establishing a list of goals and standards, and the art of piano restoration is no exception. I take a modern approach to piano rebuilding. I grant myself liberty to make those mechanical and structural changes that result in lengthening the instrument's working life, and in restoring the classic tone and touch it once possessed, but no more: in my shop, a vintage Steinway remains a Steinway.

I like to divide a piano and its rebuilding into three main areas of concern: the vibrating system or belly, the action, and the case. Three qualities must be present in the belly: immediacy of sound, projection, and sustain (the harmonic content and brightness of the tone are refined later in the process, when the hammers are installed and voiced). The belly should possess an abundance of horsepower—controlling an excess of sound is preferable to grasping for something that isn't there. The keyboard and action should be capable of any demand. The touchweight should be 54 grams at the lowest note, tapering off to 47 grams in the top octave; the speed of repetition should be such that no performer can outplay it; and player fatigue must never be an issue. The rim and its associated structural components must be rock solid, the cosmetic veneer and case parts absent of defect, and the reapplied finish showroom-new in appearance.

In the belly, my approach is to build everything new within the capability of a small shop. This means the rim and plate are retained, and everything else discarded. Specifically, the ribs, soundboard panel, bridge caps, trim moldings, pinblock, tuning pins, and strings are replaced. As well, the plate receives a gleaming new finish with hand lettering, nickel-plated hardware, and new agraffes, hitch pins, and felts. I always retain Steinway's original string scale. However, I modernize the skewed treble-bridge notching of older models B, C, and D with modern perpendicular terminations, as Steinway does in its own factory restorations.

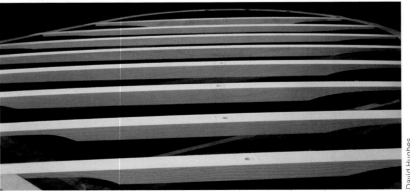

Pre-crowned ribs are fitted to the inner rim of a grand piano in David Hughes' shop prior to being glued to a new soundboard panel.

David Hughes

I honor the piano's original rib locations and lengths. I have created my own ideal rib depths (thicknesses) for all the Steinway and Mason & Hamlin models, loosely resembling the original dimensions—which, in any case, varied slightly from instrument to instrument, even of the same model. Where I part ways with tradition is in how I crown the soundboard. Unlike Steinway's compression crowning, in which straight ribs are forced into a curved shape by bending them during the crowning process, I choose to cut the curved shape into the ribs by machining them. A compression-crowned soundboard is indeed lively at first, but, in my experience, can prematurely lose its aural luster. In my approach, the ribs are cut to the intended radius of crown, then glued to the back of the soundboard. Done this way, there is virtually no stress at the rib-to-panel glue joint, and the cross-grain pressure on the soundboard (so-called compression crushing) is greatly reduced, virtually eliminating the possibility of damage to wood fibers. When the soundboard is judiciously loaded with the string plane's downbearing, decades of musical sparkle will result. Improved tuning stability is a fringe benefit, as this stiffer soundboard is not as easily influenced by swings in humidity.

So what should all this techno-talk mean to the discerning rebuilding client? Of the three desirable belly attributes cited earlier, immediacy and projection are instantly appreciated when heard, if difficult to quantify. Sustain, however, is easily expressed: A mezzo forte blow on D in the fifth octave should linger nicely for at least 12 seconds without enhancement by the sustain pedal. Melody-range notes one octave higher should sustain about two-thirds as long. A seven-finger fortissimo chord spread across several octaves while employing the sustain pedal should dwell considerably longer than is musically necessary.

The only original elements of the keys and action I retain and restore are the keyframe, tubular metallic action frame, and damper heads. Eighty-eight new keylevers are designed and fit to the rebuilt keyframe, with top priority given to convergence (the interaction of the moving parts in a manner that minimizes friction) and optimal action leverage ratio (ratio of hammer movement to key travel). When the vintage (pre–World War II) Steinways were built, these critical requirements fell prey to small variations in plate location that occurred while fitting the pinblock. This defect can be rectified by a custom rebuilder. The keyframe is fitted with anodized-aluminum keypins that are virtually frictionless, and the keys receive capstans of the same material.

The action frame receives a fresh gold-colored finish, new letoff screws and buttons, hammershanks, wippens, and hammers. I insist on using Steinway hammers in Steinway pianos; I have found them essential to achieving the classic Steinway tone. A raw set of hammers from Steinway's Parts Department requires nearly two days of prep work in my shop to achieve the ideal shape and weight. Final voicing efforts are equally meticulous.

I endorse Steinway's Accelerated Action concept, placing the lead required to counterbalance the weight of the hammer action as close as possible to the balance point of the key. One cannot argue with the physics of inertia and momentum: If lead is installed near the front end of the key, angular momentum is increased and repetition is rendered substandard. The closer to the balance point this weight is located, the less it is noticed by the player.

With the keyboard and action complete, I install a new damper tray and damper underlevers. However, unlike Steinway's procedure, I locate the pivot point for the tray in line with that of the underlevers, resulting in identical performance and regulation for both key lift and sustain-pedal engagement. To minimize noise and friction, I also modernize the vintage-style connection between the sustain-pedal trap lever and the damper tray, as Steinway has recently begun to do. Further, I install lift capstans for the underlevers on the damper tray to perfect the uniformity of damper engagement by the pedal, a result not truly attainable with Steinway's factory setup. The damper heads receive a fresh ebony finish and new damper felts, and the damper guide rail is rebushed to guarantee snug damping. After assembly and initial adjustment of all parts, the keyboard and action spend eight hours on a pounding machine to settle the regulation and voicing.

Old pedal lyres typically come unglued vertically. As the discovery of a spreading pedal lyre three months after a restored piano is delivered to the client is no joyful revelation, during the restoration process I routinely coax apart all glue joints and renew the entire structure. The pedals receive new bushings and felts, as does the trapwork on the underside of the keybed. With all due respect, Steinway's system of limiting the throw of all three pedals is archaic. I install heavy-duty, infinitely adjustable stop mechanisms in the trap levers to introduce precision and ease of regulation for decades to come. Finally, I repaint the undercarriage the original factory color so that the instrument appears completely new from any angle as it is rolled into the customer's home.

The instrument's case receive a hand-rubbed, closed-pore, satin finish. New furniture parts are fitted and applied as necessary, with particular attention paid to the lid and legs, which tend to split with age. All of the piano's hardware is either replated in nickel or polished in brass, as appropriate.

With this recipe complete, only the instrument's reapplied serial number reveals its age.

Value-Added Rebuilding

Delwin D. Fandrich, RPT

Over the past 35 years, I have developed the concept of redesigning pianos while rebuilding them because the results of conventional restoration and/or rebuilding were no longer satisfying. For lack of a better term, I call this concept "value-added" rebuilding.

Assuming competent work, conventional rebuilding—i.e., replicating and restoring the instrument's original design and construction—will return a piano's performance to its original level, but that will include the original design's weaknesses as well as its strengths. Though I began as a conventional rebuilder, increasingly those weaknesses bothered me. I began searching for ways to keep the best parts of each piano's intrinsic voice—its natural timbral character—while improving or eliminating weaknesses in its original design.

For the value-added rebuilder, the piano's brand name and year of manufacture are not important considerations. It is important that the original instrument be structurally well made, but many brands with essentially similar designs and construction provide the value-added rebuilder with equal potential. For example, a 1970s Kimball 5' 8" grand—not usually well regarded—shares enough core design and construction details with the Steinway Model M grand that, for the value-added rebuilder, its potential is essentially the same. Major components of the original—such as the stringing scale, the soundboard and rib set, and the bridges—are going to be redesigned and replaced anyway. At the end of the process I would expect the same level of performance from both, with the design weaknesses of both pianos being improved, and the tonal qualities of the Kimball becoming much more like those of the Steinway.

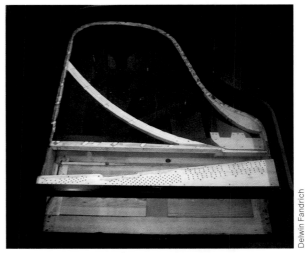

In Del Fandrich's shop, a Baldwin model L has a soundboard cutoff bar and treble soundboard filler added during rebuilding to decrease the size of the soundboard and increase its efficiency; and two treble belly braces and a bellyrail stiffener added (with extensions for two additional plate nosebolts) to reduce energy loss in the treble. These are some of the tools available to the innovative restorer.

By subtly changing the design, it becomes possible to tailor a piano's performance more closely to the owner's personal preferences. With my own pianos, I can suit my personal taste. I want the overall warmth and dynamics of the wonderful American pianos of the early 20th century without their common weaknesses—an indistinct lower bass, uneven bass/tenor break, and choppy or percussive tone in the upper tenor and low treble. With appropriate redesign, I can achieve a clear and distinct bass, a musically transparent bass-to-tenor transition, and a clear and sustaining voice through the upper tenor and low treble. I can have a common timbre across the compass of the scale—a piano that sounds "all of a piece," with a unifying tonal quality throughout all sections.

Because the basis for the overall timbre, or tone character, of any piano is its stringing scale, that is where I start. Both the relative lengths and tensions of the original scale are considered, in an examination that reveals the range of tonal options I have with any given piano. A piano originally designed with a low-tension scale will be limited to a low-tension scale. For example, the smaller Steinways have scales that are relatively low-tensioned but erratic;

to raise the string tensions on these instruments is structurally and tonally unwise. The beauty of these pianos is the warm, dynamic sound characteristic of low-tensioned scaling. I will give them a more balanced and consistent tone across the keyboard, and improve the quality of voice in the low bass, but their basic character will remain.

A piano originally built with a high-tension scale, such as a larger concert grand, presents a wider range of options. For example, because many pianists love the clarity and extended sustain characteristic of the concert grand's low bass, more of these instruments are now being found in private homes. But the percussive power of the concert grand is so overwhelming in a small space that it can mask a great deal of musical subtlety. With appropriate redesign, the acoustical palette can be matched to the smaller space. The bass retains that wonderful, long-string clarity and sustain, but the whole instrument becomes more balanced and controllable.

Another option with redesign is to adapt the tonal palette to better suit a particular musical style. Many pianists find the percussive power of even the more lightly-strung modern pianos inappropriate for works by the early classical composers. For these players, the piano's design can be altered to give a more subtle and delicate voice, to emulate the sound of the pianoforte of the mid-19th century. The action can be given a lighter, quicker touch and feel, while retaining the reliability and consistency of a modern action.

Achieving acoustical balance is a common goal of the value-added rebuilder. Most of the stringing scales found on vintage pianos—and more than a few new ones—are very uneven. New stringing scales that meet the new acoustical goals set for the instrument are designed, and new bridges are built to suit. Particular care is taken to blend the piano's voice across the bass-to-tenor transition; by its nature this transition should be imperceptible to the musician and should not require extensive hammer voicing to mask any inherent shortcomings of the fundamental design. In recent years, low-tensile–strength music wire has become available. This wire is more flexible than traditional music wire. Its selective use in certain parts of the scale—a technique called hybrid scaling—can make achieving a musically transparent bass-to-tenor transition much easier.

It's critical that the vibrating characteristics of the soundboard match the character of the stringing scale. Until the 1970s, the design and function of the modern piano's soundboard was shrouded in mythology. Since then, the hundreds of hours and thousands of dollars invested by many rebuilders in study and experimental work have given them a whole new set of design tools to work with that allow them to accurately predict the acoustical performance of a new soundboard design. The effects of soundboard thickness, grain orientation, and ribs are better understood, so rather than simply duplicating the original soundboard—which may or may not have worked all that well—new soundboards can now be designed and built to work predictably in synergy with the stringing scale. Ribs are usually crowned to a precise radius, and are cut to a calculated thickness and height to carry a known string-downbearing load. Rib locations can be moved to better distribute the vibrating energy of the strings, and to control unwanted resonances and give the piano a smoother voice. Soundboard shaping devices such as cutoff bars are used to reduce the size of the soundboard and make the system more efficient.

Today's rebuilder also has a wide selection of actions from which to choose. These range from simply replacing the wippens and hammershanks with new wood components from Renner or Tokiwa, to fitting a completely new composite action stack made by Wessel, Nickel & Gross. The range of options for tailoring action characteristics to suit the individual performer has never been greater.

With the proper balance between the stringing scale and the soundboard system, hammer selection becomes relatively easy. The value-added rebuilder will have a good understanding of the physical characteristics of the aftermarket hammers available—and today the choices are excellent—and will know which hammers will best suit the particular piano he or she is working on. Ideally, the hammers will require a minimal amount of voicing. Indeed, excessive hammer voicing is always an indication that something is out of balance: either the stringing scale and the soundboard system are not well matched, or the wrong replacement hammers have been selected.

Rebuilding a piano in this fashion costs very little more than conventional rebuilding, and supplies the pianist, amateur or professional, with an instrument specifically tailored to his or her personal taste, and that will provide a supremely satisfying musical experience.

THE UNCOMPROMISING WORLD OF HIGH-END PIANOS

Sally Phillips

THOSE WHO'VE FOUND themselves in a showroom full of beautifully crafted, prestige and high-performance pianos know that the experience can be both impressive and unnerving—impressive for obvious reasons, unnerving because of the extraordinary prices these instruments command—from \$50,000 to \$150,000 or more. Sometimes, novice buyers question whether the prices are justified—or are just the result of the clever marketing of well-known brand names. In this article, I explain what sets high-end pianos apart from less costly ones that might, at least superficially, look the same, and why the higher price can be justified. This discussion should be considered general in nature, however; actual differences will depend on the specific brands and models compared, and the differences in their prices.

The Definition of Quality

In the manufacture of medium-grade pianos, the term *quality* typically refers, in large part, to *quality control*; that is, that each example of a particular model is exactly like every other example. So, in theory, a model could have a satisfactory but unexceptional tonal design, and use satisfactory materials that meet structural specifications, and if all the pianos of that model are made to the same standards, the model could be considered to be of good quality.

In the manufacture of high-end pianos, however, *quality* means something more: Each instrument is judged not on its similarities to other examples of the same model, but on its excellence as a unique musical instrument. In fact, because the natural materials that pianos are made from are never completely uniform, and because the craftspeople who make these instruments are trained to maximize the musical potential of each instrument, any particular model of high-end piano is likely to exhibit small variations in performance characteristics from instrument to instrument.

■ ■ ■

So what do serious pianists, piano owners, piano technicians, and administrators of institutional music programs look for and expect in a high-end piano?

Tonal Quality

A piano with a singing tone, long sustain, and a wide dynamic range gives the pianist more latitude in creating musically expressive performances. The length of an instrument's sustain is essential to the pianist's ability to make it "sing" in passages that require one note to connect with the next. In addition, the ability of a concert instrument to project to the back of today's large halls is critical to its success. Although a piano's tonal color (harmonic content) will vary depending on the tonal philosophy of the manufacturer, it should be consistent from note to note within each register, and transition smoothly from register to register across the instrument's entire range. Playing with different levels of force should produce predictable variations of tonal color and volume (see "Action Control," below). Professional pianos excel in these regards, and the technician's ability to artistically voice an instrument to bring out these elements of tone depends on the excellence of the soundboard wood, the rim stock, and the hammers.

At first, customers may feel they can't hear the difference between fine instruments and less-expensive models, but this is easily remedied with more exposure to the better instruments. Listen carefully to recordings, live concerts, and fine instruments at educational institutions, and your ear will begin to hear the difference.

Action Control

There are many opinions about the extent to which a pianist can affect the tone of a piano while playing, but it is a fact that, with the more sensitive actions of high-quality instruments, the skilled pianist is able to more reliably control the speed of the hammers' attack on the strings, and thus create a wider tonal palette, giving the audience a better and more nuanced musical experience. This is readily apparent at international piano competitions, at which many pianists, playing the same works on the same piano, can nonetheless bring forth very different tonal qualities from it. The ultimate experience of action control for the artist, possible with only the finest instruments, occurs when the piano becomes a seamless extension of the pianist's thoughts and feelings—the action seems to disappear, the music seeming to rise effortlessly from the instrument without the presence of an intervening mechanism.

Amateurs also benefit by discovering that many concepts discussed by more advanced pianists, such as phrasing, legato playing, and fast and reliable repetition, are now achievable when playing actions of more sophisticated design, longer keys, and parts that can be regulated more accurately.

Service and Maintenance

Because high-end pianos are more musically sensitive than less costly ones, they may require more frequent servicing if they are to be kept at peak performance levels. But this doesn't necessarily mean that they're delicate and finicky. Most of these expensive instruments are built to be taken down, moved, and set up constantly; played with vigor for many hours a day; and tuned and serviced regularly. In my experience, after an initial settling-in period, and a good regulation and tuning, high-end pianos are actually easier to maintain than less costly ones, requiring only slight touch-up adjustments on a regular basis. This comes as a surprise to many shoppers who are concerned that the maintenance of these instruments will be costly.

The reason is that high-end pianos usually have designs and materials that make their tuning and servicing easier, more accurate, and more stable. The woods used are more carefully chosen and processed with consideration for their ability to resist environmental changes, and more robust and careful construction of the piano's structural elements result in greater tuning stability and longevity. The action regulation and voicing are more likely to be stable because of better musical preparation at the factory, and higher qualities of cloth and felt in the action and hammers. More careful design and detailing of the piano at the factory mean fewer annoying problems to deal with later on.

■ ■ ■

High-performance pianos are much more expensive than consumer-oriented models because they are so much more costly to build. Moreover, when these higher costs, along with overhead and profit, are spread over the smaller demand for this type of piano, the cost difference per instrument is greatly magnified. In the manufacture of the best pianos, few economies of scale are available.

Materials

Many of the woods used in making high-end pianos—e.g., spruce, sugar pine, hard rock maple, beech, hornbeam, ebony, poplar, and rosewood—are chosen for specific properties: ability to transmit sound, strength-to-weight ratio, density, straightness of grain, etc. Woods used for components that will be visible to the buyer, such as soundboards and case veneers, must be visually flawless as well. High-end piano hammers will have tighter specifications for the wool used in their felt, as well as for their construction, to more predictably produce the tonal goals of that manufacturer. In less-expensive instruments, substitutions of less costly materials can often be

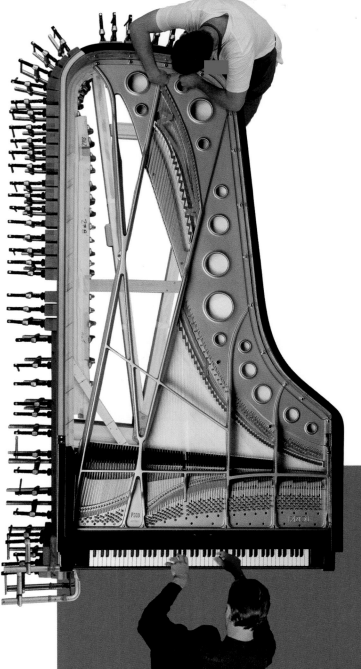

SEILER

— Family of Pianos —

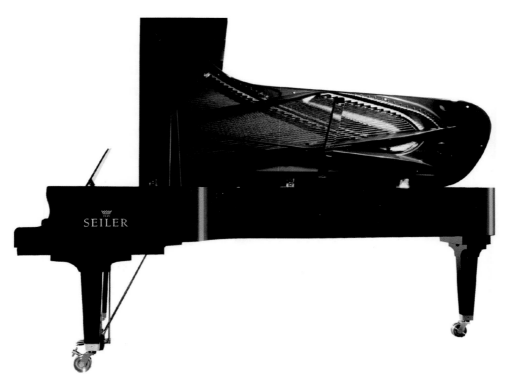

MASTERING THE ART OF PIANO BUILDING SINCE 1849

"The Seiler Concert is a new piano to the Nashville Opera. We love its elegant tone,
crisp action and impressive durability through the rigors of long hours of Verdian opera."

- Amy Tate Williams, Nashville Opera Chorus Master & Accompanist

Enrico Caruso, Arthur Nikisch, Ruggiero Leoncavallo

www.seilerpianousa.com

Seiler Piano USA   /   1329 Gateway Drive Gallatin, TN 37066   /   Tel : 615-206-0077

made that will still result in instruments that are satisfactory for their less-demanding, intended use. But in a premium instrument, any such substitution that would compromise the piano's tone, stability, longevity, or appearance cannot be tolerated. Because makers of high-end pianos demand only the very best from their suppliers of parts and materials, but do not buy in large volume, they have little leverage over prices, which continue to rise as the choicest natural materials become more scarce.

The refinements of seasoning and quartersawing wood add more cost, but are necessary for maximum stability and longevity. Logs must be air dried for years, then kiln dried to a specific moisture content, so that the wood won't warp, twist, and crack later on, after installation in a piano. Quartersawing is a method of cutting boards from logs such that the grain is oriented in a direction that results in greater dimensional stability. However, it is a very inefficient use of the log, much of which cannot be used and thus is wasted. While all piano makers season and quartersaw wood to some extent, high-end makers are more fastidious in their selection and use of lumber. This contributes to pianos whose tunings and action regulations are more stable, even when in constant use in practice rooms, teaching studios, and recital halls, and under varying climatic conditions. Less-expensive pianos made primarily for home use won't survive such conditions nearly as well.

High-end companies use the same materials in all sizes of piano they make, with no compromises on the smaller pianos. This results in very expensive smaller grands and verticals.

Some less-costly brands claim that they use the same parts or materials that high-end brands do. Even when this is technically true, there can be a world of difference in how those materials are processed and/or the parts installed. For example, some less-costly brands advertise that they use the same Renner parts in their actions as are found in some high-end brands. But the high-end companies usually disassemble the parts and reassemble them to their own, stricter specifications, then custom-install them in the pianos, taking into account slight variations in the instruments that require slight repositioning of the parts. This process is too time-consuming and expensive for lesser brands, and may call for expertise that their workers simply don't have; they're more likely to use the parts just as they come from Renner, and install them according to a general formula. While this results in instruments that are good enough for most purposes, and perhaps better than those that use lesser-quality parts, it may not allow the actions to be regulated accurately enough for the most musically demanding uses. This example also highlights the error consumers make when comparing brands solely on the basis of features, specifications, and/or lists of parts and materials.

Design and Construction

In the interest of achieving better performance, appearance, or longevity, high-end piano makers are more likely to incorporate in their instruments unique or unusual construction methods or components, even though these may be more labor intensive and thus more expensive. Pianos that are more mass-produced, on the other hand, tend to include design compromises that enable faster or more efficient manufacturing. For example, the soundboards of most mass-produced pianos are shaped according to a design that is applied uniformly to every instrument of that model, whereas some high-end brands thin their soundboards by hand for best tonal quality, to compensate for slight variations in the wood.

Other examples of more expensive designs include unusual methods of bending or building up the rim, the use of multiple species of wood in rims or bridge caps, unique patented components for enhancing the tone, and more keys and/or strings than are found in a standard piano. Some of these design elements are present in part for reasons related to a brand's history, others purely for reasons of quality, but each is there because it serves the performance objectives of the manufacturer and is part of what makes each brand unique. All such idiosyncratic variations add considerably to the time and cost of manufacture.

Settling-in Time

A very necessary but expensive part of building a piano is the time it takes the components to settle between stages of construction, and these periods will generally be longer in a factory making high-performance instruments. On any visit to a piano factory, one may be puzzled by the sight of many pianos and components sitting around in various states of completion, not being worked on. This seems counterintuitive to anyone from an industry in which the main measure of efficiency is getting as many products out the door in as short a time as possible.

But in piano manufacturing, patience is crucial to getting good results. Grand-piano rims may have to sit for months after being bent, in order to stabilize before they can be worked on further. In between action regulations, pounding machines are used to compress the action cloth. The pianos must be tuned numerous times to stretch the strings, with settling time between tunings. Hammers must be voiced to perfection by hand. In the long run, the time it takes to let the 12,000 or so parts of a piano get used to each other pays off handsomely in the form of greater longevity and stability of action, tuning, and tone.

Custom Musical Preparation

To maximize each instrument's potential once basic construction has been completed, high-end pianos are given much greater musical preparation—tuning, action regulating, and voicing—in the factory. This highly skilled, exacting work requires years of training. Performing extensive musical prep at the factory ensures that by the time the piano reaches the customer, its tuning will be stable, and the cloth and felt used throughout the action will have settled; as a result, the piano will need less initial servicing by the customer. Because the skill and experience of the craftspeople in a high-end factory are almost certainly greater than what is available to dealers or customers, this also ensures that every step in the piano's musical preparation has been performed, at least this first time, to a high standard, and that the instrument leaves the factory having fulfilled the manufacturer's performance objectives. In my experience, a piano that has been stabilized in this manner will wear more evenly, have fewer and less idiosyncratic problems, and will be easier and thus less expensive to service throughout its working life.

Worker Training, Experience, and Autonomy

The craftspeople in companies that produce high-end pianos are highly trained, and because of the enormous investment made in that training, companies are willing to pay a lot to employ these people over many years. It can take years of experience, for instance, to become a skilled voicer. The better

companies have extensive programs that gradually move employees into areas of greater responsibility, so that skilled replacements are readily available when needed. This greatly increases the cost of labor over companies that make less-costly instruments, where workers need not be so highly skilled.

In the making of high-performance instruments, more autonomy is given to individual craftspeople to make changes or corrections as needed. For example, in a high-end factory, a voicer unhappy with the tone from a particular set of hammers has permission to replace them. This is in contrast with high-production factories, in which workers may pay less attention to mistakes or unsatisfactory results, and flawed instruments may go far down the assembly line before being caught (if they're caught at all), by which time making the correction may be too time consuming, and thus too expensive, to bother with.

Cabinet Detailing and Appearance

Between high-end and mass-produced pianos, there can be great differences in the quality of hardware (casters, hinges, pedals, screws), the thickness and surface preparation of the cabinet and plate finishes, the felt and cloth used in the case parts, and in the thickness and fit of the legs, lyre, and lid. Consumers may rarely notice these details, but they're important to the instrument's longevity, and affect the appearance and noiseless operation of all case parts.

■ ■ ■

Whether for a concert or for home, a professional pianist's choice of high-end piano is primarily based on the instrument's tone and touch: Does it sustain, to enable a singing line? Does it project the tone? Does it offer a wide range of dynamics and tonal color? Does the action repeat quickly and reliably, transfer power efficiently, and remain well within the player's control? For the amateur pianist, high-end pianos open up a wider world of sound and performance than is otherwise achievable—and having that range of expression literally at one's fingertips can lead to a tremendous joy in making music that is rarely experienced with lesser instruments.

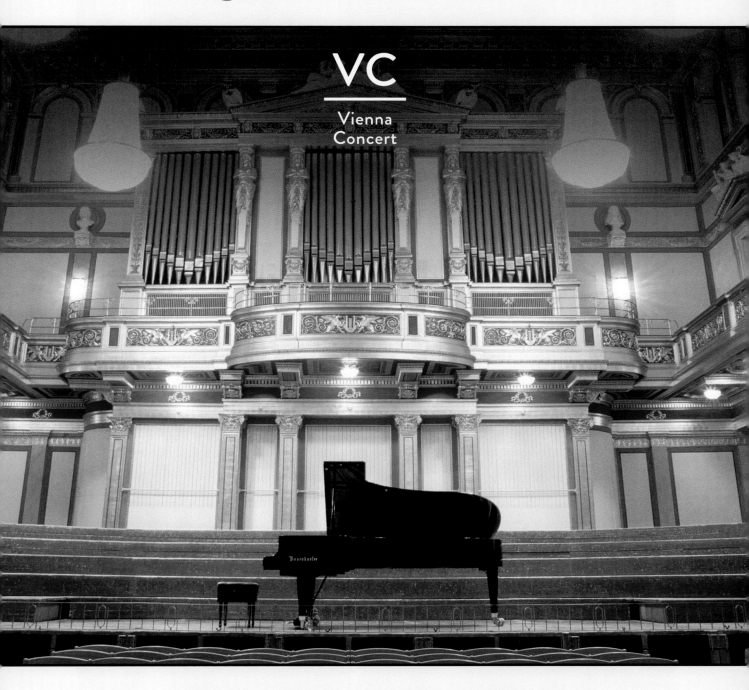

THE BEST PIANO
A Story

Ori Bukai

SINCE THE PIANO'S INVENTION by Bartolomeo Cristofori in 1700, its evolution has been driven by the desire to meet the changing musical needs of the times, by advances in technology, and by the business and marketing requirements of the piano manufacturers. High-end pianos exemplify this evolutionary process.

Early pianos were limited by the technology of the day to a lightweight structure, and a design that produced a tone—bright and intimate, but with short sustain and low volume—that evolved from the sound of the harpsichord. This complemented both the musical styles favored by the Classical period, especially chamber music, and the smaller, more intimate venues in which music was then customarily performed. As technology advanced, it became possible—using cast-iron plates, stronger strings, and higher-tension scale designs—to produce more robust instruments capable of filling a large hall with sound. This suited the composer-virtuosos of the Romantic period, such as Liszt and Brahms, whose works for the piano demanded from the instrument greater power, and the ability to be heard above the larger orchestras of the day. However, this louder, more overtone-filled sound could also conflict with and overpower other chamber instruments and their performance settings.

The great American pianos, having come of age during the Romantic era, tend toward the Romantic tonal tradition. The great European piano makers, however, embedded in a culture steeped in centuries of musical tradition, have long had to satisfy the conflicting tonal styles of different ages, and this has resulted in a wide variety of instruments with different musical qualities. As the American market for European pianos grows, the European companies are further having to reconcile remaining true to their own traditions with evolving to please the American ear. While all brands make full use of technological advances and are capable of satisfying diverse musical needs, some tend toward a more pristine tone, with plush but low-volume harmonics, perfect for chamber music or solo performances in small rooms; others are bright and powerful enough to hold their own above the largest symphony orchestras; and many are in between.

The good news is that the best way to find the right piano for you is to play as many as you can—a simply wonderful experience!

What follows is a story with a valuable perspective from a well-respected dealer of performance-quality instruments.

—Editor

"I'm tone deaf," declared the husband. "I can't tell the difference between one piano and another."

His wife nodded in agreement. "He *is* tone deaf. And while I can hear some differences, it's all so confusing. All we want is a piano that our kids can learn to play on. We don't need a *great* piano."

A short conversation ensued in which I learned, among other things, that this couple had three children, ranging in age from seven years to six months.

"Our daughter just turned seven," the wife said. "She's interested in piano lessons, but we're not sure how committed she'll be."

"You know kids," the husband shrugged. "She may want piano lessons now, but in a few months' time . . . ?"

"You're right," I said. "Kids change their minds all the time. I started piano lessons at the age of six, and stopped only a few months later. But the piano stayed in our home, and at the age of 12 I was drawn back to it. I played a few tunes by ear, and after a while I started lessons again. But . . . would you like your youngest child to play the piano as well?"

They looked at each other. It seemed that the possibility of their six-month-old baby taking lessons sometime in the future was something they hadn't considered.

"This means that whatever instrument we choose, it will probably stay in our home for a very long time," the woman said to her husband. "Perhaps we should look at a greater range of instruments than just the few we had in mind . . . ?"

"But still," he said, turning to me, "is there enough difference in the tone of the pianos to justify a greater investment, and a possible increase in our budget?"

Such conversations are not rare. Some people feel they won't be able to hear the differences between pianos, or that a high-end piano will be wasted on them. Others try to accommodate only what they perceive their needs to be at the time of purchase, rather than over the many years they may end up owning a piano.

Often, piano buyers form an idea of what they want and how much to spend, and consider only a few brands, without ever sufficiently researching the differences in manufacturers' philosophies and how these might affect the tone, touch, musicality, and price of the instrument. However, such information can help the consumer clarify his or her true needs and preferences. Many shopping for a piano all but ignore higher-end models, considering them beyond their needs or means. But for more than a few of these buyers, a better-quality piano may prove the better fit and value.

There are significant differences in manufacturing methods between performance-oriented instruments, which are often referred to as "handmade," and mass-produced instruments, in which some musical qualities are sacrificed to meet a lower retail price.

Performance-oriented manufacturers, especially at the highest level, are looking to capture a wide range of tonal characteristics. Some of these qualities, such as sustain, tonal variation, and dynamic range, are universally accepted as helping the playing of pianists of all levels sound more musical. All makers of high-end pianos strive to make pianos that excel in these areas. Other tonal characteristics, however, such as tonal color—the specific harmonic structure of the tone—can reflect a particular manufacturer's philosophy of what the best piano should sound like, and are the elements that separate one high-end make from another. A piano maker's decision to emphasize certain musical qualities over others is manifested through differences in the instrument's design, in the instrument's resulting tone and touch, and in its appeal to a particular player or listener.

"Would you like to hear some higher-end instruments as well, just to compare?" I asked the couple.

"Yes, please," replied the woman.

And so we went on a tour of Piano Land, playing, listening to, and assessing the tone of a variety of instruments. "Ooohhh," said the wife in response to one particular make. "Aaahhh," sighed her husband, as the realization struck him: He actually *could* hear the differences between these pianos; not only that, he had some rather clear preferences.

"But which is the *best* piano?" he asked. There are quite a few instruments here, all so beautiful, but so different from each other. Which *is* the best?

This is a question customers ask me again and again when visiting our showroom—we represent most of the high-end makers, and side-by-side comparisons are always possible. And while, time after time, our customers do find the absolute "best," for each of those customers the "best" is represented by a different make, according to his or her preferences. The combination of musical qualities emphasized by one piano maker may speak to one customer while leaving another indifferent—who, in turn responds enthusiastically to an instrument made by another manufacturer that has left the first customer cold. Some people prefer a bold, outgoing, and powerful sound; others want a more delicate, clear, and melodic tone. Some like focused, defined, and pure tonal characteristics, while others look for instruments whose sound is more robust, deep, and dark.

At the top end of piano manufacturing, each instrument should have a high level of design, parts, materials, execution, workmanship, and attention to detail. However, it is personal preference—the buyer's response to the various manufacturers' interpretations of the "perfect sound"—that determines the answer to the question of "But which is the *best* piano?" The answer is different for every customer.

But which piano is the "best" is also a matter of other factors. Some high-end instruments might be considered the "best" in one setting, but not

quite the best in another. A piano that sounds its best in a large concert hall with hundreds of people may not necessarily be the right fit for the typical living room.

"The best instrument," I replied to the couple, "is the one that you'll most enjoy listening to as your children—and perhaps, before you know it, your grandchildren—play and develop their musical skills. The 'best' piano is the one you'll be happy with over the many years it will live in your home, and that one day, when you have the time, perhaps may tempt you to take lessons yourself. The best piano is the one that will deliver to you and your family the joy of music, now and over the long run."

EACH NOTE
A CONCERT
EXPERIENCE

Since 1885, it has been our passion to employ our artistic craftsmanship and knowledge to enable uncounted people, famous, well-known and unknown, to achieve their keys to happiness. Because of this, most quality pianos out of German production are made by Schimmel.

BUYING PIANOS FOR AN INSTITUTION

George F. Litterst

Institutional Basics

Institutions vary so widely in size, makeup, and needs that it is impossible to cover in a single article all the variables that might apply. For example, the studio of a graduate-school piano professor might be 12 feet square, carpeted, and cluttered with bookshelves, desk, and chairs, but still needs a performance-grade instrument. A church sanctuary—often a carpeted, irregularly shaped room with a raised dais and filled with pews, glass windows, and lots of sound-absorbing people—needs a piano that can accompany the choir, be heard throughout a huge room, and also be used as a solo instrument for visiting artists. A school may need dozens of pianos for everything from tiny practice cubicles to a concert hall.

However, regardless of whether you're purchasing a piano for a church, school, performance space, or another institutional location, you need to start with some basic questions that will help identify the piano (or pianos) that are appropriate for your situation.

For example:

- Who will use the piano—beginners, advanced players, or concert artists?
- How often will the piano be played—in the occasional concert, or for 18 hours per day of intense student practice?
- How will the piano be used—lessons for graduate students? church services? recordings?
- Will the piano's location be fixed, or will it be moved often?
- In what size room will it primarily be used?

After answering these questions, this article will help you establish some basic parameters, including:

- Grand vs. Vertical
- Size
- New vs. Used

This article assumes you are already familiar with the basics of piano-shopping (see "**Piano Buying Basics**" and other appropriate articles in this publication), and treats only those aspects of the subject that are specific to the institutional setting.—Ed.

- Digital vs. Acoustic
- Traditional Acoustic vs. Acoustic with Record/Playback/Computer Features

Budget

Once you've narrowed down the parameters of your ideal instrument or group of instruments, you need to consider your budget. In doing so, it's best to remember that quality instruments properly maintained will last a long time. Accordingly, it's best to view the cost of each instrument not as a one-time expense, but as a total expense amortized over the life of the instrument.

When figuring out the true annual cost of an instrument:

- Spread out the instrument's purchase price over the span of its working life
- Factor in the cost of money, that is, the interest you would pay if you were to finance the purchase (even if you don't actually plan to finance it)

Include costs of tuning (typically three to four times a year, but far more often for performance instruments), regulation, and repairs

When you figure the cost of an instrument this way, you may even discover that certain more expensive instruments are more affordable than you thought.

The 21st-century classroom is quite different from its predecessors. Wall charts have been replaced by projectors and screens or flat-panel monitors. Chalkboards and whiteboards have given way to "smart," interactive whiteboards. Phonographs, CD players, and DVD players have been made obsolete by mobile devices that wirelessly send sound to speakers and visual information to large display devices. In some classrooms, professors can even transmit visual information directly to students' iPads in real time.

The potential benefit of all this technology is better communication between teacher and students. Today, there is general recognition that any class of students comprises people who embody a variety of learning styles: visual, aural, kinesthetic, cerebral, and more. The teacher is tasked with the responsibility of reaching all of them simultaneously.

How does a piano fit into this new educational scene?

In addition to being used for piano lessons, pianos are traditionally used to play musical examples in classes (music history, theory, composition), accompany the choir, facilitate instrumental and vocal lessons, and more. Technology-equipped acoustic and digital pianos can be used in all of these ways, yet potentially offer so much more.

Imagine a music theory class. Of course, the teacher can show prepared examples using an app such as PowerPoint—but what about addressing educational issues on the fly?

With a technology-equipped piano and an appropriate app, the professor can sit at the keyboard and play a musical example, and on the classroom's large display screen the class will instantly see the result, beautifully notated, even analyzed. By doing nothing more than just playing the piano, the professor can now address multiple learning styles in real time by putting sound into the air, graphics on the display, and creating an instant analysis.

These kinds of scenarios are made possible by a form of electronic musical communication known as Musical Instrument Digital Interface (MIDI). Virtually all pianos and keyboards that include any kind of electronics offer MIDI communication with music apps running on laptops and mobile devices. As you might expect, the computing device can be connected to the audio-visual resources in the room. You can even modernize a traditional acoustic piano by installing a MIDI strip under its keys.

Many kinds of applications are available when a technology-equipped piano is brought into the equation. Imagine:

- a piano that can be connected to another piano via the Internet for the purpose of long-distance lessons, concerts, and master classes
- an instrument that can record and play back a student's performance, or play selections from a library of pre-recorded performances for study purposes
- an instrument that can accompany vocalists, string players, or wind players as they practice— even when a pianist is unavailable
- a piano that functions as an interactive composition tool
- a piano that can be used with score-following software to rehearse a concerto with a virtual orchestra that follows the soloist

The piano has a history of more than 300 years of technological change and innovation, and new technologies are rapidly becoming integral parts of our musical landscape. You can expect that any piano you buy today will last for a long time; in making your selection, be sure to consider the many educational opportunities that can arise when you take advantage of modern advances in piano technology.

Once you've determined your budget, and the size and other features of the instruments you desire, you can use the **online searchable database** at **www.pianobuyer.com** to assist you in finding the specific brands and models that will fulfill your needs.

Grand vs. Vertical

Many situations are adequately served by vertical pianos, including:

- Practice rooms where the piano is used primarily by, or to accompany, non-pianist musicians
- Places where there is no room for a grand
- Instruments that are not used for intense playing or difficult literature

A number of features of vertical pianos are commonly sought by institutional buyers:

- Locks on fallboard and tops
- A music desk long enough to hold multiple sheets of music or a score

- Toe-block leg construction with double-wheel casters—particularly important if the piano will be moved often
- Heavy-duty back-post and plate assembly for better tuning stability
- Climate-control systems
- Protective covers

Grand pianos, however, have keys, actions, and tonal qualities that are more appropriate for practicing and performing advanced literature, and are therefore preferred in situations where they are largely used by piano majors or performing pianists. Grands are preferred by piano majors even for small practice rooms, because the students use these instruments primarily to develop advanced technical facility, something that's almost impossible to do on vertical pianos. Commonly sought features of grands are:

- Mounting on a piano *truck* (a specialized platform on wheels) for moving the piano easily and safely
- Protective covers to avoid damage to the finish
- Climate-control systems
- Lid and fallboard locks

Size

Carefully consider the size of your space. You can easily spend too much on a piano if it's larger than the space requires, and you can easily waste your money if you purchase an undersized instrument. For more information about how room acoustics might affect the size of instrument you should purchase, see "**Ten Ways to Voice a Room**," elsewhere in this volume.

Of course, the tonal quality and touch of the instrument are related, in large part, to its size. If you're purchasing pianos for teaching studios in which artist faculty are instructing graduate piano majors, or for practice rooms used primarily by piano majors, there may be musical reasons for choosing larger grands despite the fact that the spaces are small. You'll be able to capture most of the advantages of a larger grand's longer keys with an instrument six to six-and-a-half feet long. Any longer will be overkill for a small teaching studio or practice room. A larger teaching studio may be able to accommodate and make good use of a seven-foot grand. The size of the piano is much less important in the training of beginning pianists or non-pianist musicians. There, other factors, such as the size of the room, will be the dominant considerations.

Vertical pianos made for institutions are almost always at least 45 inches tall. Smaller verticals may have inferior actions and tone, and cabinetry that is more prone to breakage. Verticals taller than about 48 inches are probably unnecessary for most small studio and practice rooms, but may be appropriate in larger spaces where a larger sound is needed but a grand is out of the question.

Yamaha

A special problem often occurs when a house of worship or small recital venue with limited funds tries to make do with a grand piano that's too small for the space. The pianist will tend to play much harder than normal, and overuse the sustain pedal, in an effort to make the piano heard at the back of the sanctuary or hall, causing strings and hammers to break and pedal systems to wear out prematurely. Generally, a small- to medium-size sanctuary will require a grand six to seven feet long to adequately fill the hall with sound, but this can vary greatly depending on the size of the hall, its acoustics, how large an audience is typically present, whether the piano is being used as a solo instrument or to accompany others, and whether the sound is amplified. A piano dealer can help sort out these issues and recommend an appropriate instrument.

New vs. Used

Excellent acoustic pianos that are well maintained should last for decades. Given this fact, should your institution consider purchasing used instruments and thus save some money? If this is something you're considering, read "**Buying a Used or Restored Piano**" in this publication before continuing. When comparing a used piano to a new one, consult a trusted piano technician to get a sense of the used instrument's condition and remaining useful life. Then amortize the cost of the pianos, including expected repair costs, over their expected lifetimes to determine which is the better value.

If considering a used acoustic piano with embedded electronics, such as an electronic player piano, be careful to avoid purchasing an instrument whose technology is so obsolete that you can't use it productively. On the other hand, if your intention is to use a player piano's MIDI features mostly in conjunction with a computer, you do have one protection against obsolescence on your side: Although MIDI has been around since 1982, it's still an industry standard that works well and shows no sign of disappearing in the near future. Accordingly, you can continue to upgrade the features of an older MIDI piano merely by upgrading the software you use on your computer.

Acoustic vs. Digital

Digital pianos continue to improve every year, and the benefits realized for every dollar spent on a digital piano continue to grow with advances in technology.

Here are some examples of institutional situations in which a digital piano is generally the preferred instrument:

- Class piano, where students and teachers wear headsets and the teacher controls the flow of sound in the room with a lab controller
- Multipurpose computer/keyboard labs where students need to work independently on theory, composition, and performance projects without disturbing others in the room
- A church that features a so-called "contemporary service" in which the keyboard player needs an instrument with lots of on-board sounds, registrations, and automatic accompaniments

In other situations, the preferred choice may not be so obvious. For example, if a school has a practice room largely used by singers and instrumentalists (not pianists), should you supply a digital piano or a vertical?

When weighing these and similar questions, keep in mind:

- In an institutional setting, a typical, wellmaintained acoustic piano has a life expectancy of 20 to 40 years; a higher-quality instrument might last 30 to 50 years. Because the digital piano is a relatively recent invention, we can't be as certain how long they will last in an institutional setting.

A reasonable estimate for a good-quality digital instrument might be 10 to 20 years. However, digital instruments are subject to a rapid rate of technological advance that may eventually limit the instrument's usefulness, even though it still functions. On the other hand, the digital piano won't need tuning, and may go for years before it needs any other maintenance.

- Some digital pianos are simply a substitute for the acoustic equivalent. Others have additional features that may be highly desirable, such as connectivity to a computer, orchestral voices, and record and playback features.
- Some acoustic pianos are also available with digital-piano–like features, such as record and playback, and Internet and computer connectivity. If your choice comes down to an acoustic piano (for its traditional piano features of touch and tone) and a digital piano (for its embedded technologies), you may need to consider a hybrid digital/acoustic instrument. (See the article on **hybrid pianos** elsewhere in this volume.)

Assessing Pianos Before Purchase

Assessing digital pianos is a relatively straightforward matter. You simply play and compare the features of various makes and models and make your selection. If you choose Model X, it doesn't matter if you take possession of the actual floor model that you tried: All Model X digital pianos will be the same.

Acoustic pianos are a different animal. There is more variation among pianos of the same model from a given manufacturer. However, it is important to note that some manufacturers have a reputation for producing uniformly similar instruments, while others have a reputation for producing more individually distinctive instruments.

If you're purchasing a single acoustic piano or a small number of acoustic pianos, you can and should take the opportunity to audition each one of them and make your selection carefully. If you're purchasing a concert or other very large grand, you may need to travel to the manufacturer's national showroom in order to make your selection. If so, factor the cost of the trip into your budget. In some situations it may be possible to audition a large grand in the space in which you intend to use it. This will give you an opportunity to know for sure that you're making the right decision. On the other hand, if you're purchasing a dozen practice room upright pianos, or are completely replacing your inventory of instruments, it's more practical to audition just a sample of each model and make your purchase decision on that basis.

Keep in mind that any fine acoustic piano can be adjusted within certain parameters by a concert-quality technician. If a piano sounds too bright when it is uncrated, skilled needling of the hammers can result in a noticeable mellowing of the sound. Similarly, a new action may require some additional adjustment (called *regulation*) to provide you with a keyboard that is optimally responsive.

Preparation, Tuning, and Maintenance

All pianos require maintenance, and acoustic pianos more than digitals. New acoustic pianos need to be properly prepared before they're deployed. All acoustic pianos should be tuned regularly, and regulated as needed. Acoustic pianos with record and play-back systems also may need periodic calibration of their embedded systems. See the **accompanying article** for more information on the maintenance of acoustic pianos in institutions.

Who Should Make the Purchase Decision?

As the foregoing discussion suggests, there are many intersecting practical, artistic, and financial factors to be considered when making an institutional purchase of a piano or group of pianos. This raises the question: Who should make the purchase decision?

No single answer fits all situations. By tradition, a church's decision-making process may be handled by the music director, the pastor or priest, or perhaps by a lay committee. In a school of music, decisions may be delegated to the chair of the piano department, the chair of the music department, the dean of fine arts, or some other individual or faculty committee.

In many instances, well-intentioned individuals with no knowledge of pianos find themselves having to make a final decision. It is important that those involved in the process commit themselves to understanding the intersecting issues, and bring into the decision-making process appropriate people from the artistic, technical, and/or financial sides. At a minimum, that means the piano technician, and the most advanced, or most frequent, professional users. If a digital-technology–based instrument is being considered, someone should be involved who can speak to those technical issues as well. A department chair who has not actually used the technology in question may or may not be in a position to evaluate it.

Negotiating a Purchase

Before negotiating a price or sending a proposal out to bid, it's usually a good idea to do some price research. This can be tricky, however.

For example, if you or someone you know simply calls up a dealer and asks for a price, you're unlikely to be told the lower "institutional price" that you might ultimately get. Some dealers are reluctant to quote prices over the phone, or are prohibited by their suppliers from doing so. Others will refuse to quote a price if they know that the purchase will ultimately go out to bid.

Your institutional purchase may benefit the dealer or manufacturer in ways other than the profit from the sale. Therefore, when discussing your possible purchase, don't hesitate to mention:

- How prominently positioned the instruments will be in your institution or in the community
- How many students or audience members will come in contact with the instruments on a regular basis
- How often you or your institution is asked for purchase recommendations
- How musically influential your institution is in the surrounding community

The bottom line is this: You won't know what the final price will be until an official representative of your institution actually sits down with the dealer principal or until bids are awarded. Before you reach that point, however, and for planning purposes, you can make discreet inquiries and put together some estimates. As a rule of thumb, and only for the purposes of budgeting, if you subtract 10% to 15% from

LOAN PROGRAMS: *AN ALTERNATIVE TO PURCHASING*

Often, institutions find themselves needing to acquire a number of pianos at one time. Perhaps the institution needs to replace a large number of aging instruments or to furnish a newly expanded facility or program—or a school may want to acquire a number of new instruments each year to demonstrate to prospective students that it has a music program of high quality. Such situations can pose a budgetary dilemma—the simultaneous purchase of even a few pianos can cause fiscal stress. Fortunately, relief is sometimes available in the form of a school loan program.

On the surface, a school loan program may seem too good to be true: free pianos, loaned for an academic year. At the end of the year, the pianos are sold. More free pianos the next year.

In truth, a school loan program can work only when it makes sense for both the school and the local dealer. (Although the manufacturer may be a participant in the program, the contract is normally with the local dealer.) Both sides of the agreement have obligations to the other.

For example, a school *may* receive any of the following, depending on the structure of the program:

- Free or very-low-cost use of a significant number of pianos
- Free delivery
- Free tuning and maintenance
- Name association with a prestigious manufacturer

A school may also have any of these obligations:

- Liability for damage
- Delivery charges
- Tuning and maintenance costs
- Requirement to purchase a certain percentage of the instruments
- Requirement to supply an alumni mailing list to the dealer for advertising purposes
- Requirement to provide space for an end-of-year piano sale

When evaluating a loan program, it's generally a good idea to consider:

- The quality of the dealership that stands behind the program
- The appropriateness of the mix of pianos offered
- The school's vulnerability if the program were to be discontinued by the dealership after the current year

That last point is a key issue. What happens if you replace your inventory of old pianos with loaned instruments and the loan program becomes unavailable the next year? Suddenly and unexpectedly, you are faced with having to buy replacement instruments.

Generally speaking, it is a good idea to include with your loan program a purchase component so that you are building your inventory of quality instruments over the course of the loan.

the dealer's "sale" price, you will likely come close to the institutional price.

If you represent a school that's required to send purchase requests out to bid, you may not have much of a role to play in negotiating a price. However, the way in which you word your bid will have a lot to do with the bids that you receive and the instruments that the bidding rules will compel you to purchase.

For example, if you really want Brand X with features A, B, and C, be sure to write your bid description so that it describes—within acceptable guidelines—the instrument that you wish to purchase, and rules out instruments that don't fit your needs. If your bid description is loosely written, you may receive low bids for instruments that don't meet your requirements.

Because pianos can last a very long time, any piano-buying decisions you make today for your institution can have consequences for a generation or more. Therefore, it pays to take the time to think carefully about your institution's present and future needs, to budget sufficient funds for purchase and maintenance, and to consult with individuals both within and outside your institution who may have special expertise or be affected by your decision. If you take the time to do this properly, then your constituents—be they students, faculty, worshippers, or concert-goers—will enjoy the fruits of your work for years to come.

Avoid A Sour Note

- Honest, Ethical Advice <u>Before</u> You Buy.
- Professional, Quality Piano Service After.

Find a Registered Piano Technician at

www.ptg.org

PIANO MAINTENANCE IN INSTITUTIONS

Chris Solliday, RPT

THE ADEQUATE AND EFFECTIVE MAINTENANCE of pianos in institutional settings differs from the typical service needs of the home environment in two major ways. Pianos in schools, churches, and colleges are, first of all, usually subjected to heavy use, and second, are very often situated in difficult climatic environments. These pianos will require more frequent service by technicians with special skills, and greater attention to climate control.

In college and university settings, pianos are frequently used eight to twelve hours a day by many different players. Some students have practice habits that involve a great deal of repetition, which causes greater wear to the actions and keys of the instrument in a way that reflects the patterns of their practice. This can easily be ten times more patterned repetition than a piano normally receives in your home. The parts of piano keys and actions that will show the greatest wear are made of felt, leather, and wood, and there are thousands of them in each piano. These materials are chosen, designed, and treated by manufacturers to maximize their working life, and considering the repetitive nature of their use, it's a wonder they last as long as they do.

No matter how well made, however, the nature of these materials dictates that when the piano is used for many hours, day after day, week after week, the wear and deterioration can be extensive. To maximize their longevity, it is very important to keep these pianos in good regulation so that the wear proceeds more evenly. Along with tuning, regular regulation of the action, pedals, and tone should be basic parts of any effective plan of piano maintenance. Without this, neglected instruments in such environments will quickly become impossible to regulate without extensive overhaul or replacement of parts.

At some point, of course, parts *will* have to be replaced, worthy instruments rebuilt, and unworthy ones replaced. But there is no need to hasten the inevitable by subjecting pianos to the worst form of abuse: neglect. Frequent and regular servicing of pianos is a requirement for any institution that hopes to maintain an adequate performance or learning situation that will not only meet the needs of its members, but serve as a vehicle for the recruitment of new students.

Depending on the security and rules established for using the pianos, abuse can also come in the form of vandalism or simple carelessness. Rules should be established that keep food and liquids away from pianos. Procedures for the safe moving of pianos should be established and strictly enforced to protect the instruments as well as those who do the moving. Untrained personnel should never move a piano anywhere.

The single largest factor affecting the need for piano maintenance, however, is a fluctuating climate. While an environment that is always too hot or too cold, or too wet or too dry, can cause deterioration, pianos can usually (within reason) be regulated to reliably perform in such an environment. However, many institutions provide interior climates of constant change. It's not unusual to find a school or church whose HVAC system produces 80°F and 8% relative humidity during the winter heating season, but 76°F and 80% relative humidity in the summer. These systems' air-exchange devices can also create drafts that blow directly on the piano, further varying the temperature and relative humidity by a great deal. Often, the temperature settings on these systems are changed during vacation periods. A good target for any piano's environment is 68° F and 42% relative humidity. Installation of inconspicuously-located climate-control systems for the pianos is almost always necessary in institutional environments. A plan for the regular monitoring and servicing of these systems should also be considered. [*See the article,* "**Caring For Your Piano**," *for more information on climate-control systems for pianos.—Ed.*]

The most important factor in maintaining the utility and longevity of any institution's pianos is the choice of piano technician. An institutional technician should possess the advanced skills and experience required to prepare pianos for public concerts, organize and manage a large inventory of instruments, deal daily with high-level pianists and educators, and be familiar with the techniques necessary for the time-efficient maintenance of practice-room pianos. An underqualified technician can contribute to an accelerated rate of deterioration and shorten the lives of the instruments under his or her care. Some fully qualified technicians, mostly manufacturer-trained, have no formal credentials. However, hiring a Registered Piano Technician (RPT) member of the Piano Technicians Guild (PTG) ensures that at least a minimum standard of expertise has been tested for and achieved. A good way to begin planning any institution's piano-maintenance program is to read PTG's *Guidelines for Effective Institutional Piano Maintenance*, available in printed form or as a free download from **www.ptg.org**.

PIANO PURGATORY
The Donated Piano

Sally Phillips

PIANO TECHNICIANS will tell you that the worst pianos they are asked to service are usually found in houses of worship or other institutions that accept pianos as donations. How do such institutions become populated with so many inappropriate instruments?

Pianos make their way into the purgatory of institutional use in several ways:

The pastor gets a call from a member of the congregation who wants to donate to the church Aunt Matilda's prized 1952 spinet piano. Neither the donor—most likely, Aunt Matilda's heir—nor the pastor knows anything about pianos, their condition, or value, and the donor is unaware that, 20 years ago, the piano technician told Aunt Matilda that the piano was untunable due to major structural and mechanical defects. Stuck in the limbo between being too compromised to use and having been donated by too prominent a member to be given the last rites, the piano sinks lower and lower in the church's graces, from choir room to nursery and, finally, into the basement, where it marks the entrance to the boiler room. All the while, the music director is hoping that the relic will somehow be forgotten so that the church can buy a new, functional instrument.

Or: A member of the congregation or other institution wants to buy and donate an inexpensive new 4'11" grand. The music director is horrified by the suggestion; unlike the 7' professional grand he or she had in mind, a 4'11" piano, being built for light home use, is not designed to be a performance-quality instrument. Facing a fate worse than Aunt Matilda's spinet, the director must find a way to turn down a shiny, new, but very modestly built piano that can't be serviced to professional levels, has a disappointing tone, and demonstrates its shortcomings even before the brass plate engraved with the donor's name has begun to tarnish.

How does the savvy administrator avoid having to accept such gifts? How does she or he turn down offers of nearly useless instruments, and instead get the professional equipment the school or church really needs?

Develop a Plan

First, identify your institution's piano-related needs, goals, and budget. Without a plan, you're a sitting duck for well-intended but useless donations that, due to poor condition or inappropriate construction or both, eventually become nuisances. Convene a committee—be sure to include the music director—to answer these questions:

- **Who will play the piano, and what is its purpose?** Will it be used only to accompany the children's choir in a church where the organ is the main instrument, or will it be the primary instrument? Other than the accompaniment of singers, what type of repertoire do you envision? In addition to services, will it be used as a tool for outreach, drawing interest from local piano teachers for recitals and concerts? If so, the piano needs to hold up under heavy use, and perform well enough to attract the better musicians. Will it be used in recordings?
- **Where will the piano go?** In how large a space will the instrument be used? Will it go into a large sanctuary or auditorium, or will it spend most of its time in a choral or band rehearsal space? Will the space have limited heat and

air-conditioning during the week, when no services are held? Will the piano be moved around a lot?

- **What is your budget**, not only for a new piano, but also to maintain it at a professional level?

With the answers to these questions, develop a wish list of target instruments for every space that needs a piano, so that you're prepared for those calls from would-be donors.

Establishing a Target Instrument

The music director and committee members will need to make sure that the pianos being considered are actually of professional quality and size. Entry-level and many mid-range consumer-grade pianos are designed to appeal to the home market, but won't meet the needs of institutions. Small (under 5' 6") grands, regardless of quality, are unsuitable for use in sanctuaries, concert halls, and auditoriums. The most common misconception about small grands is that if you have sound amplification, then size doesn't matter. But these pianos are usually designed for home use and do not hold up well in institutional venues. Their strings will start to break, they can't be tuned and serviced to exacting professional standards, and their case parts and hardware won't stand up to heavy use or frequent moving.

Pianos designed for professional institutional use are more expensive because their sound quality is closely tied to the acoustically favorable woods of which they're made, and to the sophistication of their design and construction. Prices rise with each step up in size and/or quality, as manufacturers include more expensive materials, better design, and more attention to detail. This results in the performance quality and durability needed in institutional settings.

If you consult piano technicians and/or teachers about what sort of piano is appropriate, make sure that they are specific about which models they recommend. Many manufacturers make a large number of models; some are home pianos and others are professional, and the price differences can be huge. And if you're buying a new piano, be sure that the dealer's salespeople know what demands will be placed on the instrument.

Large Sanctuary or Auditorium Pianos

If the piano is to be used as a solo instrument or to accompany vocalists in a large space, I recommend nothing smaller than a 6' grand of Performance Grade or Professional-level Consumer Grade. (For definitions of these terms, see "**A Map of the Market for New Pianos**," elsewhere in this volume.) If you also expect it to serve for professional piano recitals, recording, or chamber music, you'll need a grand of 7' to 9'. If you choose a vertical piano for your main performance space, you'll need an upright at least 50" tall for adequate projection of sound to the rear of the hall. But be aware that the choice of a vertical eliminates the use of the space for serious piano recitals or chamber music. Institutions that have a great acoustic environment and a professional piano have become well known as recording venues. If this describes your hall, you might consider what needs your community has in this regard; your building could generate some income from its use as a recording space.

Choir Rooms and Rehearsal Spaces

A grand of 5' 6" to 6' is appropriate for these smaller spaces and less critical uses. In the smallest spaces, a large professional upright will do. In general, a grand is more desirable than a vertical because of the better musical control a grand action provides. In addition, unlike with an upright, the pianist can see over the lid of a grand while accompanying a choral group. However, a better-quality vertical 46" or taller can be musically superior to many grands under 5' 6".

Examples of Suitable Models

- **School Studio Verticals 45" to 47":** These durable pianos are sold to schools as practice-room instruments. They usually have an angled upper panel with a wide music rack capable of holding many music books, hymnals, or heavy scores. Their cabinets are functional and simple in styling, with toe blocks and large casters for safe, easy moving. Prices for new ones range from $6,000 to $26,000. Use: Practice room, small choir room, Sunday-school room, teaching, very small chapel, accompaniment.
- **Professional Verticals 48" to 49":** Instruments this size, built for professional use, have larger soundboards, longer strings, and heavier hammers. They are louder and project better. Prices of new ones range from $8,000 to $30,000. Use: Choir room, small sanctuary, accompaniment.

- **Large Verticals 50" and taller:** These are usually examples of the high end of each maker's vertical-piano line, and can sometimes sound like a grand piano of the same brand. They have much better projection and, usually, such features as a larger music rack and longer keys, as well as better-quality sound-producing materials. Prices of new ones start in the $10,000–15,000 range, but elite models can easily reach $50,000 or more. Such pianos are expensive, but can be a better choice than a very small grand when space limitations are severe.
- **Grands 5' 6" to 6' 4":** These mid-size grands have similar actions to their larger counterparts, though sometimes with shorter keys. This, their smaller soundboards, and shorter strings make them too small for professional solo work in large spaces, but fine for rehearsal, accompaniment, smaller spaces, and other less- or mid-critical uses. New performance-quality grands start at around $25,000 and go up to $85,000.
- **Semi-Concert Grands 6' 5" to 7' 11":** These pianos are usually built for heavy professional use. I especially recommend the larger Japanese, American, and European models. These will do in a smaller hall for solo and chamber music, as well as for more routine accompaniment work. New ones start at around $40,000 and go up to well over $100,000 for the highest quality.
- **Concert Grands 8' to 9' (or longer):** In large halls, the concert grand is the gold standard. If your institution plans to host professional piano recitals, chamber music, or orchestra concerts, a larger piano is a must. New concert grands start at about $100,000.

New Pianos: Setting Goals and Budget

Create a realistic budget for a new purchase by identifying several models that fit your needs and noting their prices. You'll need time to raise the money, so when you ask for bids, be sure to give the dealer a timetable for your purchase so that price increases can be taken into account.

Establish a budget just prior to announcing the need for a new instrument, so that offers of less expensive, inappropriate pianos can be turned into gifts toward the goal instrument. This will avoid a situation in which, for example, someone gives $10,000 toward a grand for the sanctuary, and that amount then becomes the budget. If someone offers less than the full amount, be sure to inform the donor of the full budget for the instrument, to give the donor the opportunity to make a donation covering the entire amount. Most donors simply have no idea how much a professional piano costs. It always amazes me that a congregation won't blink at spending hundreds of thousands of dollars to restore a pipe organ, but will be horrified that a new piano can cost over $50,000.

Avoid allowing one donor to make the decisions regarding the purchase of a new piano, especially if that person has no musical background. The steep learning curve in choosing a piano is made much more difficult when the donor doesn't play. That said, in my experience, when a church committee visits a piano store to hear a selection of pianos, even though some members may express ignorance, they can readily hear the difference when pianos of varying quality are played for them.

Make sure that you make an appointment to see the pianos. Piano dealers cannot be expected to always have every instrument in tune. Given advance notice, most dealers will put their best foot forward by preparing for your consideration several of the most likely candidates.

Used Pianos: Myths and Reality

Other than in the first year or two, when some pianos may slightly improve as they stabilize and their actions get played in, pianos really do not get better with age. A piano's life is a long, downhill slope toward a complete rebuilding job, assuming the piano is worth it (and very few verticals are worth rebuilding), and sale or disposal if it's not. The myth that older pianos are automatically better is an idea that does not hold up under scrutiny. Some older pianos were built well, and some were not. Some new pianos are cheaply built, and some are better than pianos have ever been. Real strides in piano manufacturing have been made in the last 20 years, making the continued reverence for older instruments insupportable.

Be aware that when the donor, who probably has no technical knowledge of pianos, says that the piano needs only tuning, he or she may not understand that pianos of a certain age and compromised condition can no longer be tuned. The tuning pins may be too

The hammers are the parts of a piano that change the most, wear out fastest, and as much as possible should be eliminated from your initial impression of an instrument. Like tires on a car, they're part of a performance piano for only a relatively short period in that instrument's life. The timbre of a set of hammers can change dramatically with the humidity, and any wear or maintenance of the hammers will change the piano's voicing. To maintain the tone of a concert piano, hammers must be maintained as often as the piano is tuned. Hammer wear is directly related to the number of hours a piano is played and the intensity of that playing. Hammers can last for many years if the piano is played only three or four times a year, but concert instruments in constant use can require new hammers after only five concert seasons.

Hammers can be voiced using an arsenal of techniques, including needling, ironing, hardening, or filing the hammer felt, and fitting the hammers to the strings. A good voicer can make a piano sound more mellow without reducing its volume, or can make it sound brighter but without harshness. Even when selecting among different instruments of the same make and model, you will encounter pianos with a variety of timbres. Try not to be swayed by this; to judge an instrument, keep returning to the basic tonal capacity of its belly for sustain and volume, and thus for power and projection.

That said, hammers that are voiced too bright will make the piano sound thin in the treble, and may obscure what might otherwise be a beautiful-sounding instrument. If, during selection, a piano sounds a bit bright, you might ask the technician to quickly voice it down, or at least address the notes that appear to you to stick out above the others. If the piano sounds too mellow but has a long sustain, you can be assured that it will be very easy later on to brighten it. But I want to stress that any voicing changes made during the selection process should be minor—for best results, the piano must be fine-voiced in the hall in which it's to be used.

The Action

Of course, any process of selecting among several pianos should include playing them—after all, that's why a pianist has been given the task. If high-level playing weren't a necessary part of the process, a technician alone could do the job.

However, a concert piano should never be chosen solely on the basis of how its action feels. Why? Actions can be changed, and they will change on their own anyway. The action of a new piano will change as soon as it is played in and settled: the felt and leather pack down, altering the regulation dimensions. I can't tell you how many times I've heard pianists say that they chose a piano for its action, only to complain, several weeks after delivery, that the action doesn't feel like it used to. But such changes are normal, and easily reversed with a minor touch-up regulation.

In addition, actions are very malleable, and can be adjusted in many ways to accommodate the player. If you love the sound of a piano but don't like its feel, ask the attending technician if he or she can correct whatever you find objectionable. Some typical action-related complaints—all of which, within limits, can be corrected or changed—include unevenness (requires some touch-up regulation to compensate for uneven compression of felt and leather), difficulty playing pianissimo (let-off needs adjusting), and key travel too shallow or too deep (set by manufacturer, but slight adjustment is possible). In most situations, assuming the pianos have already been well prepped, these fine adjustments can be made in a short amount of time while you're trying another piano. In my experience, however, if the piano has been regulated consistently from note to note and is within a reasonable range of touchweight, a pianist of high caliber will usually have no problem adjusting to its action. Just remember that what is most important is the instrument's sound. Trying to separate that sound from your response to the instrument's action is perhaps the hardest part of selecting a piano.

Playing Tests

Dynamic Range. Starting very softly, play a note in each section, repeating it with increasing loudness, and count how many discrete levels of volume you can produce. The more levels you can produce, the more expressively you will be able to play.

Play fortissimo and listen to what happens. Does the sound "top out"—that is, do you want the sound to get louder but can't get the instrument to give you any more? Does the sound "break up," getting ugly and harsh when loudest? Or can you play as loudly as you like without harshness?

Touchweight and Repetition. The touchweight of a concert grand action should be between 48 and 55 grams, and most modern grands easily fall into this range. If you like a piano's tone, its action can always be made a bit lighter or heavier. If an action is too light, however, problems can occur with rapidly repeated notes. Many good technicians can't play fast enough to make an action fail in fast repetition, and so have developed action measurements and tests to ensure that these problems never occur when a good pianist plays demanding repertoire. But now, in the selection process, is the time to test repetition with some really fast passages.

After the Instrument Arrives

After you receive your new performance piano, you'll need to play it in for a while and let it acclimate to the hall. Your selected piano may need no adjustments on arrival, but any new piano will sooner or later need some touch-up regulation, and that can be done after a few weeks of playing. In my opinion, however, voicing should be delayed until the piano has been played extensively, so that everyone involved can agree on which direction the voicing should take.

After I have done the preliminary regulation touch-up, and made minor adjustments to even out the voicing without changing its character or volume, I usually invite two pianists to the final voicing: one to play, and the other to join me out in the hall, walking about and listening. I then make whatever voicing changes are needed, the pianists trade places, and we repeat the entire procedure until everyone is happy.

A piano will always sound a little different in the concert hall from how it sounded in the selection room. Halls that have been acoustically optimized for sound-reinforcement systems rather than for acoustic instruments can be especially challenging in the area of sound projection. However, I caution institutions not to jump to the conclusion that a piano's sound must be brightened if at first it seems a bit mellow. Not only will playing automatically brighten it over time, but most concert grands will blossom after a few months or several changes of season, and the piano will suddenly sound bigger and more robust. Indeed, if a piano is delivered in the summer and has been subjected to slightly higher humidity in shipment, it will take a few weeks in an air-conditioned hall before it sounds as it did at the selection. Patience in this regard is paramount. A good set of hammers can easily be ruined by overbrightening in response to initial complaints about a new piano's dullness of tone. Any changes in voicing should be made conservatively.

Special Considerations for Pianos in the Home

As mentioned at the beginning, even if a concert grand is being chosen for a home, it would be wise to choose one with plenty of power and projection, so that it can later be sold to an institution if desired. However, the issue of power and volume will obviously not be quite as important in the home as in the concert hall, and if the instrument is of less than concert-grand size, it will be less important still. In that case, more emphasis should be placed on the sustain tests than on the volume tests.

Institutional buyers are likely to buy a well-known brand based on its reputation, and its instruments' ability to be used for a wide range of concert repertoire. A purchaser for the home, on the other hand, is more likely to have narrowed down the selection to one particular brand after considering many, based on that buyer's desire for a particular tonal quality and the type of music he or she most often plays. Similarly, whereas institutional buyers must be primarily concerned with satisfying an audience with the sound of the piano rather than with its action, a buyer for the home is the audience, and thus, when shopping for an instrument, has more leeway to consider the action as part of his or her total musical experience.

Just as a concert piano will sound different in the concert hall than in the selection room, so will it sound different in the home. The home piano is usually easier to voice because projection is not a factor. However, the quality of sound will be substantially affected by carpeting, drapes, upholstered furniture, wall hangings, etc. A technician or acoustical expert may be able to help you adjust the acoustics of the room, and the piano's placement in it, for optimal results. In a home, owners often solve the problem of excess volume by closing the piano's lid. I encourage customers to let me voice the instrument to the room with the lid open. This way the piano can be played with the lid left open, and without excess volume, without stifling the piano's true tone.

If the brand chosen has a significantly idiosyncratic tonal palette, it's best to find, for follow-up service, a technician who has experience with that brand, and is familiar with its unique tonal characteristics.

The Premier Piano of Japan.

REGULATION & VOICING
What Buyers of Performance-Quality Pianos Should Know

Sally Phillips

REGULATION AND VOICING—the work of preparing a piano so that its touch and tone are even and beautiful—require a combination of painstaking technical adjustments and artistic considerations. Without this preparation, even the finest instrument is reduced to little more than a collection of parts, almost certain to disappoint. As a purchaser of a performance-quality piano, you have a much better chance of finding a suitable instrument if you have a basic understanding of these subjects.

Many pianists believe a piano's action or tone can't be changed, or that the performance quality of a piano or action is determined solely by its brand. But *any* piano's action can go out of regulation, become dirty and worn, suffer from neglect, or merely vary within a normal range—top-rated brands are no exceptions. Many wonderful instruments, new and used, are rejected by buyers because a lack of recent or competent service—or both—is disguising their true potential. Many a hidden gem is available to the buyer who asks the right questions, and can find the right technician to solve an instrument's problems.

Steinway & Sons pianos made in Hamburg, Germany, are considered among the finest instruments in the world. In the past several months, however, I have worked on three Hamburg Steinways, each of which had different problems that made it unsatisfactory to its owner. The solutions to their problems reveal much about action regulation and voicing in performance-quality instruments in general—but before introducing the pianos, I'll discuss the analysis and procedures used to solve these kinds of problems.

Analysis and Procedures

The technician must first assess what the piano needs, and then, taking into account the customer's goals and budget, make recommendations. The solution can range from a touchup regulation to a complete replacement of the action. If the owner's budget is slim, I try to first perform the least expensive and most effective steps, to mitigate the most serious problems. Usually I will regulate a sample key or section to show the customer what the results are likely to be, installing samples of new action parts where appropriate.

In explaining to clients how I address problems in piano regulation and voicing, I divide the subject into several sections:

Friction

Unless friction problems are solved prior to regulation, little real progress will be made. A piano's

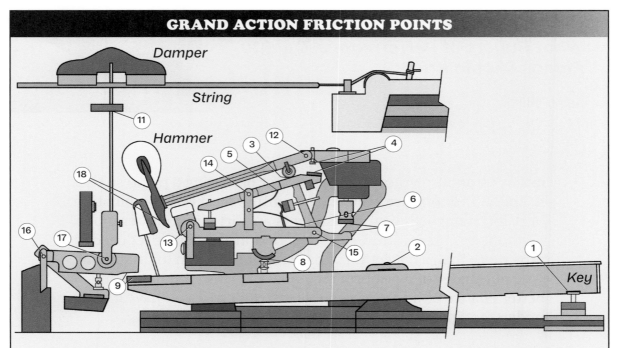

GRAND ACTION FRICTION POINTS

Shown here, in a single note of a grand piano action, are the many points where friction needs to be minimized or controlled through the cleaning, polishing, lubricating, replacing, resurfacing, repinning, and/or positioning of parts.

1. Front key pin and key bushing
2. Balance key pin and key bushing
3. Jack top, repetition lever, and knuckle
4. Drop screw and leather pad
5. Repetition spring and slot
6. Jack spring and hole
7. Letoff button and jack tender
8. Capstan screw and wippen cushion
9. Damper underlever (or spoon, in some actions) and key end felt
10. Damper underlever spring and slot (in older actions) (not shown here)
11. Damper guide rail and damper wire
12. Hammershank center
13. Wippen center
14. Repetition lever center
15. Jack center
16. Damper underlever center
17. Damper post center
18. Hammer tail and backcheck

action contains thousands of friction points, mostly in places where pieces of cloth, felt, or leather serve as buffers between metal pins and wood. Too much friction can slow the working of the action and create what feels like extra weight in the key. The main culprits are dirty friction points, which make the action sluggish; the solution is to clean or replace the dirty parts and lubricate friction points. Knowing what to lubricate and which lubricants to use takes experience. Lubricants such as WD-40, oil, and wax can ruin a piano action, so don't try to do this yourself.

As part of the friction-control process, action centers—the points around which action parts pivot—must be repinned where necessary to correct inconsistencies in action-center friction. In very old pianos, especially New York Steinways of certain eras, buildups of verdigris—a greenish corrosion of the metal center pins in the action centers—can greatly stiffen the action parts, making them unplayable. In most such cases, these parts will need to be replaced.

Geometry

A piano's action is an assemblage of levers that move in intersecting arcs of motion, and these parts must be installed in correct relationship to each other in order to operate optimally. These relationships are known as the action's geometry. Even in fine pianos, many reasons for geometry problems can arise. Some new pianos leave the factory with these problems, but most often they result from rebuilds done over the last 40 years, a period during which replacement parts in the original dimensions were often unavailable. In some cases, a piano born with poor action geometry has been rebuilt, and the problems have become even worse.

In the last 15 years, better parts have become available, and action manufacturers are now much more astute in anticipating the problems that can arise in replacing action parts. Piano technicians, too, have developed more sophisticated methods of addressing geometry issues, including: changing the locations of specific action parts, resetting the position of the entire action stack relative to the keyboard and strings, adding or removing action cloth, rehanging hammers, or installing a completely new action. Most important is that the proper analysis be made of the extent to which poor action geometry is contributing to the problems reported by the player.

Action Regulation

As keys are played, pads of cloth, leather, and other materials serve to silence the action parts as they move. As these materials pack down and wear with use, the positions of the parts change slightly over time, and periodically need to be brought back to their original positions in order for the instrument to play properly, a procedure known as action regulation.

How often this needs to be done depends on how much the piano is used and the level of performance expected from it. Changes in action regulation occur so slowly that pianists generally remain unaware of them until they suddenly realize that their playing has become difficult to control. It may be years before the average amateur musician playing a piano in the home realizes this, but working concert instruments are regulated (and voiced) almost as often as they are tuned, and a fine piano in the home is no different if a professional level of performance is expected from it. The regulation will remain much more stable if very fine adjustments are made frequently, rather than infrequent wholesale changes made only in response to emergencies.

Piano actions have many points of adjustment that control the positions of the parts. The regulation procedure involves adjusting these so that each key feels the same when depressed. That may sound simple, but with keys being of different lengths, the hammers graded in size from bass to treble, hammer

and action wear varying from section to section, and other variables, action regulation can be a daunting task involving thousands of steps. Most manufacturers provide regulation specifications for the actions of their current models; but for older instruments, when parts have been replaced, or when the pianist requests a particular touch, these specifications may no longer work and must be modified, which only increases the difficulty of the job.

Sometimes pianists' complaints about the tone, such as a lack of dynamic range or power, or the inability to play softly, are best remedied with fine action regulation instead of voicing. In particular, power in the action is the result of accurate and close regulation, not simply the hardening of the hammers (a voicing technique).

Touchweight

The touchweight, or downweight, is the amount of force needed to depress a key to the point of escapement with the damper pedal depressed. Most manufacturers today aim for a consistent touchweight across the keyboard of 47 to 52 grams, with slightly more weight acceptable in the bass than in the treble, due to the heavier bass hammers.

In weighing off a keyboard, gram weights are experimentally placed on each key to measure its downweight; other, permanent weights, of lead, are inserted in or removed from holes drilled in the side of the key, to bring it to its proper downweight. A keyboard can be weighed off only after the action's friction and geometry have been checked and corrected, and the action regulated. Frequently, after the fine regulating is finished, only minor weight changes are necessary to even out the touchweight.

Many touchweight problems are the result of installing replacement hammers that are heavier than the originals. Heavier hammers can be used, but the added weight must be offset by changes in action geometry, which will often necessitate replacing other action parts as well. Simply adding lead weights to the keys to counterbalance heavier hammers, even when this results in nominally correct touchweight, may make the action sluggish during rapid playing due to increased inertia in the action system.

Voicing, or Tone Regulation

When the action regulation and weighoff have been completed, the tone regulation can proceed.

However, if the strings have worn deep grooves in the hammers, the hammers must be filed *before* action regulation and weighoff, because removal of so much felt reduces a hammer's size and weight. Deep string grooves cause the tone to suffer, both from slight damping of the strings and because the hard, crusted felt creates noise on the attack.

After filing, the hammers must be fitted to the strings, a painstaking process that must be done before any needling of the hammer felt. Due to slight inconsistencies in the heights of the strings, the hammer angles, and/or any previous filing, tiny amounts of felt must be filed off the top surfaces of the hammers so that each hammer strikes both or all three of the strings assigned to it at precisely the same time. This ensures that all that hammer's strings are put in motion simultaneously, which will greatly improve the tone. Some technicians might initially address this problem on a new or newly rebuilt piano by leveling the strings, but eventually this fitting must also be done by minutely filing or ironing the felt.

Once the hammers are filed and fitted to the strings, the actual work of setting the tonal level and evenness can begin. This is the part of the job most likely to require and benefit from customer input, to ensure that the customer's tonal preferences are satisfied. If radical changes to tone are desired, I prefer to do several voicing sessions, gradually changing the sound each time. Between visits, it's important that the pianist have an opportunity to listen carefully to what I've done, and to play-in the hammers to settle the felt.

Harder hammers produce a brighter sound, softer hammers a mellower sound, but many other shades of tone are possible between bright and mellow. Needling the hammers evens out the consistency of the hammer felt so that each hammer has the same amount of compression and tension and, therefore, should sound the same. Needling different areas of a single hammer will give different results; here, an experienced voicer can make all the difference.

Adding a hardening lacquer to the hammers can add body and depth to the tone. Some pianists prefer the brighter, more complicated sound of lacquered hammers, while others prefer a cleaner sound, without lacquer. Over the years, tastes in tone have changed significantly; in recent years, I have had fewer requests for a bright tone.

Three Hamburg Steinways: Problems and Solutions

1935 Steinway D (8' 11¾")

This piano, which is in the private residence of a professional pianist who plays major repertoire, was rebuilt in the 1990s. The pianist complained that the repetition was too slow, and that the piano lacked good tonal presence in the treble. Another technician had added lead weights to the rear section of the keys in an attempt to make the action repeat faster, but this only made it more sluggish.

When inspected, the instrument turned out to have friction and geometry problems that had to be addressed before the action could be regulated and weighed off. When the piano was rebuilt, new action parts were installed, but they had become compressed and dirty in the 17 years since, and friction had become a major problem. In addition, the replacement action parts available when the piano was rebuilt had not been of the size originally installed, which created the geometry problems. Finally, the plate—and therefore the strings—had been reinstalled a bit too high, making regulation even more challenging and creating repetition problems. However, there was almost no hammer wear.

Given the good condition of the hammers and the high cost of replacing parts, I decided that in this case it would be more cost-effective to modify the existing parts than to replace them. First, I filed the hammers, repinned most of the action centers, cleaned and polished most other friction points and contact surfaces, and removed the extra lead weights from the keys. Then, to correct the geometry problems and compensate for the excess string height, I raised the action stack and made small changes to the contours, heights, and positions of some of the action parts. Finally, I regulated the action and corrected the touchweight.

After the problems of friction, geometry, regulation, and touchweight had been solved, I slightly repositioned the action relative to the treble strings, to get a more optimal treble tone. At the same time, the owner removed a rug from under the piano, which gave me more volume to work with. Interestingly, in addition to the above, the solution to getting more treble tone was to needle the hammers. This counterintuitive approach increased the flexibility of the hammer shoulders, which produced a rounder tone and boosted the body of the sound. The result was a more singing treble, a much more colorful tenor and bass, and greater dynamic range.

1984 Steinway O (5' 10½")

This Model O had had a succession of technical changes made by a series of technicians in attempts to address action problems that were primarily the results of age and heavy use. The main complaints were that the action was very uncontrollable and heavy, and the sound harsh.

Originally, the owner had complained about the action to Technician A, who replaced the hammers, shanks, and flanges with parts made by another manufacturer that were not suitable matches to the original. This technician had noticed that the hammers were worn, and ascribed the customer's complaints to that, even though the customer had at first had no complaint about the tone—he was concerned about the *feel* of the action, which, it turned out, was dirty, worn, and had not been regulated in 28 years. But Technician A never addressed the friction or action-regulation problems, so, despite the new parts, the initial problem persisted. The customer, still not happy, called Technician B.

Technician B reinstalled the original parts (which the customer had kept), but, like Technician A, did not address the friction and regulation issues. When the customer complained to a third technician of an inability to control the piano's volume, Technician C tried to remedy that by hardening the original, 28-year-old hammers. I then arrived to find the worn, original hammers, shanks, and flanges screwed back onto the action, the action far out of regulation, and the hammers hardened beyond retrieval.

The primary source of the problems was friction in the action—so much friction that the piano was very difficult to play at all—and the customer's inability to control the volume was aggravated by uneven regulation. I salvaged many of the original action parts by minimizing the friction, but had to replace the hammers, shanks, and flanges because the hammers were now too hard to be voiced and the hammershank knuckles were worn.

This incident highlights the need for good communication between technician and customer, and the need for the technician to investigate beyond the customer's initial complaint, in order to find the ultimate sources of the problems.

2010 Steinway D (8' 11¾")

This nearly new piano belongs to a university. The very astute pianists there wanted a bigger sound in a portion of the tenor area, and complained that the piano was a bit unresponsive, its action sluggish, its tone too mellow.

It turned out that this lovely instrument was just fine. What had happened was that it had experienced the normal settling of new action parts that occurs with every new instrument, and needed only the very minor regulation touchup that is entirely normal and predictable for a new piano that has had little use. The hall in which it was kept was a bit humid, which not only made the hammers swell slightly, muting their sound, but had slightly unseated the keyframe. Remedying what had been described as a lack of power in the tenor section required only a very minor reseating of the keyframe.

Following a thorough regulation in which I made only minuscule adjustments, I lubricated the key pins to reduce friction, and ironed the hammers to tighten their surfaces enough to restore the tone. With the tone and power restored, it was easier for the pianists to produce the sound they wanted, which had the psychological effect of eliminating the action's perceived sluggish lack of response. What had been presented as a complaint about the voicing of a small section of the tenor had turned out to be, for the most part, problems of regulation and humidity. After I'd touched up the fit of hammers to strings, evening out the tone in the first treble section required the very slight needling of only a few hammers.

In Conclusion

When pianists praise a piano for being even and smooth, with effortless control, these qualities are the results not only of a quality action correctly installed, but also of hours, days, or weeks of technical attention paid, in both the factory (or rebuilding shop) and in the field, to realize the instrument's potential. As the above examples illustrate, the real problems and the true potential of a fine instrument are not always obvious, and even the best pianos can play poorly when badly maintained or rebuilt, or when their problems are misdiagnosed. A purchaser armed with this understanding, and with the support of an experienced piano technician, is in a position to recognize otherwise excellent instruments with correctable problems that others might pass up. As an informed

owner, you can communicate your complaints about action and tone more clearly, and you'll be in a better position to evaluate whether or not your technician can satisfy your piano's technical needs.

As the owner of the 1935 Steinway D wrote to me after several weeks and many visits to correct its problems:

"I think many pianists live with the frustration of never quite playing the way they really hear the music, never realizing that things can be better. You really *can* sing at the piano, and the instrument can be truly miraculous if you don't have to fight it. As a result of our collaboration over the past few months, I have been able to develop my tonal palette considerably."

CARING FOR YOUR PIANO

Larry Fine

A PIANO MAY LOOK large and imposing, but there is a great deal inside it that is delicate, and sensitive to both use and environmental changes. You have made a considerable investment in the instrument and now should protect that investment, as well as maximize your enjoyment of it, by properly caring for it. For most pianos in good condition receiving moderate use in the home, a budget of $300 to $500 per year should suffice for normal service.

If you bought the piano from a commercial seller, your first service will probably be a few weeks after delivery, by a technician associated with the seller. If you bought a used piano from a private seller and do not have a trustworthy recommendation to a technician, you can find the names of Registered Piano Technicians (RPT) in your area from the website of the Piano Technicians Guild (PTG), **www.ptg.org**. To become an RPT, one must pass a series of exams, assuring at least a minimum level of competence in piano servicing.

The following are the major types of service a piano needs on a regular or semi-regular basis. More information can be found in *The Piano Book*.

Tuning

Pianos go out of tune mostly because of seasonal changes in humidity that cause the soundboard and other parts to alternately swell and shrink. This happens regardless of whether or not the piano is played. Pianos vary in their responsiveness

A piano has over 200 strings, each of which must be individually tuned.

to fluctuations in humidity, but the variance is not always related to the quality of the instrument. People also differ in their sensitivity to tuning changes. New or newly restored pianos should be tuned three or four times the first year, until the strings are fully stretched out. After that, most pianos should be tuned between one and three times per year, depending on seasonal humidity changes, the player's sensitivity, and the amount of use. Pianos that receive professional levels of use (teaching, performance) are typically tuned more often, and major concert instruments are tuned before each performance. A regular home piano tuning typically costs between $100 and $200. However, if the piano has not been tuned regularly, or if it has undergone a large change in pitch, additional tuning work may be required at additional cost.

Regulation

Pianos also need other kinds of service. Due to settling and compacting of numerous cloth and felt parts, as well as seasonal changes in humidity, the piano's

action (key and hammer mechanism) requires periodic adjustments to bring it back to the manufacturer's specifications. This process is called *regulation*. This should especially be done during the first six months to two years of a piano's life, depending on use. If it is not done, the piano may wear poorly for the rest of its life. After that, small amounts of regulating every few years will probably suffice for most pianos in home situations. Professional instruments need more complete service at more frequent intervals.

Voicing

Within limited parameters, the tone of a piano can be adjusted by hardening or softening the hammers, a process called *voicing*. Voicing is performed to compensate for the compacting and wear of hammer felt (which causes the tone to become too bright and harsh), or to accommodate the musical tastes of the player. Voicing should be done whenever the piano's tone is no longer to your liking. However, most piano owners will find that simply tuning the piano will

greatly improve the tone, and that voicing may not be needed very often.

Cleaning and Polishing

The best way to clean dust and finger marks off the piano is with a soft, clean, lintless cloth, such as cheesecloth, slightly dampened with water and wrung out. Fold the cloth into a pad and rub lightly in the direction of the grain, or in the direction in which the wood was originally polished (obvious in the case of hand-rubbed finishes). Where this direction is not obvious, as might be the case with high-polish polyester finishes, rub in any one direction only, using long, straight strokes. Do not rub in a circular motion, as this will eventually make the finish lose its luster. Most piano manufacturers recommend against the use of commercially available furniture polish or wax. Polish specially made for pianos is available from some manufacturers, dealers, and technicians.

To clean the keys, use the same kind of soft, clean cloth as for the finish. Dampen the cloth slightly with water or a mild white soap solution, but don't let water run down the sides of the keys. If the keytops are made of ivory, be sure to dry them off right after cleaning—because ivory absorbs water, the keytops will curl up and fall off if water is allowed to stand on them. If the black keys are made of wood, use a separate cloth to clean them, in case any black stain comes off (not necessary for plastic keys).

Dust inevitably collects inside a piano no matter how good a housekeeper one is. A piano technician can safely vacuum up the dust or otherwise clean the interior of the piano when he or she comes to tune it.

Humidity Control

Because pianos are made primarily of wood, proper control of humidity will greatly increase both the life span of the piano and your enjoyment of it. A relative humidity of 42% is sometimes cited as ideal for a piano, but any humidity level that is relatively constant and moderate will suffice. Here are some common steps to take to protect your piano from fluctuations and extremes of humidity:

- Don't place the piano too near radiators, heating and cooling ducts, fireplaces, direct sunlight, and open windows.
- Avoid overheating the house during cold weather.
- Use air-conditioning during hot, humid weather.

Dampp-Chaser Corporation

- Dehumidifier
- Humidifier
- Easy-Fill Watering Tube
- Humidistat
- Light Panel
  (can be installed out of view)

- Dehumidifier
- Humidifier
- Easy-Fill Watering Tube
- Humidistat
- Light Panel
  (can be installed out of view)

■ Add humidity to the air during dry weather with either a whole-house humidifier attached to a central air system or with a room humidifier. Room humidifiers, however, have to be cleaned and refilled frequently, and some make a lot of noise. If you use a room humidifier, don't place it too near the piano.

Instead of the above, or in addition to it, have a climate-control system installed in the piano. They make no noise, require very little maintenance, and cost $350 to $500 for a vertical piano or $400 to $600 for a grand, ordered and installed through your piano technician or piano dealer. The illustrations on the previous page of the Dampp-Chaser climate-control system show how the system's components are discreetly hidden inside the piano. For more information about these systems, see **www.pianolifesaver.com**.

Another solution to the humidity-control problem is **Music Sorb**, a non-toxic silica gel that naturally attracts moisture from the air when humidity rises above 50%, and releases that same moisture when the humidity drops below 50%. It comes in cassettes or pouches sold through piano technicians or from the website **www.musicsorbonline.com**. A supply sufficient for a single piano costs about $125 and may need replacing once a year, depending on local humidity variations.

WHEN SHOULD I HAVE MY PIANO TUNED?

When to tune your piano depends on your local climate. You should avoid times of rapid humidity change and seek times when the humidity will be stable for a reasonable length of time. Turning the heat on in the house in the fall, and then off again in the spring, causes major indoor humidity changes, and in each case it may take several months before the piano's soundboard fully restabilizes at the new humidity level.

In Boston, for example, the tuning cycle goes something like that shown in the graph. A piano tuned in April or May, when the heat is turned off, will probably be out of tune by late June. If it is tuned in late June or July, it may well hold its tune until October or later, depending on when the heat is turned on for the winter. If the piano is tuned right after the heat is turned on, however, say in October or November, it will almost certainly be out of tune by Christmas. But if you wait until after the holidays (and, of course, everyone wants it tuned for the holidays), it will probably hold pretty well until April or even May. In my experience, most problems with pianos in good condition that "don't hold their tune" are caused by poor timing of the tuning with the seasonal changes.

Note that those who live in a climate like Boston's and have their piano tuned twice a year will probably also notice two times during the year when the piano sounds out of tune but when, for the above reason, it should probably not be tuned. The only remedies for this dilemma are to have the piano tuned more frequently, or to more closely control the humidity.

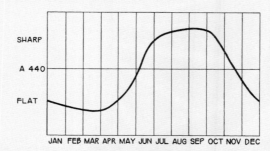

The pitch of the piano in the tenor and low treble ranges closely follows the annual cycle of indoor humidity. The graph shows how a typical piano in Boston might behave. Most areas of the country that have cold winters will show a similar pattern.

PIANO TUNING
An Introduction

Sally Phillips

WHAT IS TUNING?

Tuning a piano is the process of adjusting the tension of its strings, thereby altering their *pitch*, or frequency of vibration, by slightly turning the tuning pins to which they're attached, so that each string sounds pleasingly in harmony with every other string. This harmony is achieved by tuning the piano according to certain known acoustical laws and aesthetic rules and customs.

How Is a Piano Tuned? Is It Difficult?

To the uninitiated, tuning a piano may seem a simple, straightforward procedure, but it isn't. The process is complicated by the sheer number of strings and tuning pins (more than 200 of each, the exact number varying with the model), by the high tension under which the strings are stretched, by the tightness with which the tuning pins are anchored in the pinblock, and by the friction points over which the taut strings must slide as they're being tuned. All of these factors are obstacles not only to tuning, but also to creating a tuning that will be stable for a reasonable length of time, given the piano's use and environment.

Tuning is also potentially made more difficult by the design element of modern pianos known as *loop stringing*. In loop stringing, each length of steel music wire in the treble actually forms two strings, which are separated by a sharp bend in the wire where the strings are anchored to the piano's cast-iron frame. Sometimes these two strings sound the same note and are tuned to the same pitch. Other times, they are parts of adjacent notes, with one half of the wire tuned a half step higher or lower than the other half, the two halves necessarily held at distinctly different tensions. Because all parts of a single wire have a tendency to seek the same tension, loop stringing is a more challenging environment in which to learn how to create a stable tuning.

In addition to physical obstacles, there are acoustical obstacles to tuning. A paradox common to all fixed-pitch instruments, first discovered by the ancient Greeks, is that it's impossible for *all* the intervals— thirds, fourths, fifths, sixths, etc.—within a perfect octave to themselves be perfect. This problem is dealt with by slightly expanding or contracting—*tempering*—each of these intervals so that, together, they will add up to a perfect octave. The tuner creates a *temperament*—a single octave of 13 notes at the center of the keyboard in which every note is tuned in its correctly tempered relationships to all other notes in that octave—and then copies those relationships to all remaining sections of the keyboard by tuning each note to be a perfect octave (or octaves) above or below the corresponding note in the temperament octave.

But even the phrase *perfect octave* is a bit of a misnomer. Vibrating strings give off *harmonics*—fainter tones whose frequencies are in a specific mathematical relationship to that of the *fundamental*, or principal frequency at which the string is vibrating. For a piano to sound right, the tuner must tune each string so that its harmonic *and* fundamental frequencies are all in tune with those of the other strings. Due to the stiffness of steel strings, the frequencies of their harmonics are somewhat higher than the theoretical ideal, a property called *inharmonicity*. In addition, the human ear tends to hear the higher pitches as a little flatter than they actually are. To compensate for these effects, the tuner must tune (*stretch*) the octaves a bit sharper in the treble and a bit flatter in the bass than would be the case were the octaves actually perfect. How *much* sharper or flatter is both an art and a science, which is one of the reasons why some astute musicians may prefer one tuner over another.

To tune each note, and then to confirm its accuracy, the tuner performs certain listening tests. These tests require listening to faint, regularly undulating interference patterns in the soundwave, called *beats*, that occur when two notes that form an interval are played together, and harmonics of the two notes are at almost but not quite the same frequency. The tuner tunes one of the notes so that the beats are either eliminated (*beatless*) or occur at a certain precise rate of speed, depending on the particular test and the interval being tested. In addition, most notes on a piano are sounded by sets of two or three strings each, called *unisons*; to sound in tune, every string in a unison must be tuned at precisely the same pitch—that is, they must be beatless relative to each other.

When you combine tuning's physical and acoustical obstacles, you can see why it takes years of training and practice to become an accomplished piano tuner.

What Tuning Does *Not* Include

Tuners often arrive at a service call to find a piano with sticking keys, hanging dampers, and/or broken parts. However, *tuning* involves only correcting the pitches of the strings. It does not cover cleaning, adjustment, or repairs to the mechanical, structural, or cosmetic parts of the piano, or *voicing* (tone adjustment). The tuner and client should discuss these other needs so that both clearly understand the work to be done and how much it will cost. That said, if a piano problem is caused by something accidentally dropped inside the piano, such as a pencil or hair ornament, and it can be removed with no more than a few minutes' work, the tuner will often include that service in the tuning fee.

When contacting a tuner, be sure to let him or her know the piano's brand and model, whether it is a vertical or a grand, when it was last tuned, and any repairs or adjustments you believe need to be made.

This will allow the tuner to allot sufficient time, and to be prepared with the proper tools and materials for the job.

How Often Should a Piano Be Tuned?

This is the question most frequently asked by customers. The answer depends, first, on the piano's use. In the most critical situations, such as in a recording studio, where the accuracy of the tuning will live in perpetuity in a recording, the answer is probably every day, or even several times a day. In concert halls and other performance situations, the piano is tuned before every rehearsal and every performance, and sometimes the tuning is even touched up at intermission.

For a piano used in the typical home, tuners usually state the recommendation in terms of so many tunings per year. Because a piano is *always* going out of tune, beginning as soon as the tuner has finished the job, the frequency of tuning will depend on the tolerance of the pianist to changes in pitch, the piano owner's budget, the ability of that piano to hold its tuning, the consistency of the temperature and humidity in the room the piano is kept in, and in how skillful the tuner is in creating stable tunings. For most home pianos, the owner will be satisfied if the piano is tuned two or three times a year. For professional use or fussier owners, four to six tunings a year, or even more, may be appropriate.

Why Won't My Piano Hold Its Tune?

First, we consider the physical condition of the piano, something of which many owners will not be aware—the instrument could be faulty due to age and wear. Various conditions, some described in terms of "cracked" parts and often confused by customers, may or may not be affecting the ability of the piano to hold its tune:

Pinblock The pinblock is a plank of laminated hardwood, located beneath the cast-iron plate at the front of a grand or at the top of a vertical, into which holes are drilled for the tuning pins, and into which the pins are driven and tightly held. Over time, these holes can expand slightly from wear, age, and dryness, causing the tuning pins to loosen and no longer be able to hold the strings at their correct tensions. Cracks can also appear around the holes or between laminations (thus the term *cracked pinblock*). A worn or cracked pinblock is the most common structural cause of a piano's inability to hold a tune.

Plate The cast-iron *plate* or *frame*, along with the piano's wooden case, is the primary structural support for the tension of the strings. On rare occasions, the plate will crack, usually rendering the piano untunable, and possibly unrepairable. This can happen due to a design flaw or a flaw in the casting, or due to extreme mishandling of the instrument during moving, such as dropping the piano from a height. Cracked plates are very rare; most technicians will see only a few in an entire career.

Soundboard The soundboard is a thin wooden board, usually of spruce, that is partly covered by the cast-iron plate. The soundboard is made to resonate by the vibrating strings, thus amplifying their sound and transmitting it to our ears. Just about everyone has heard of a *cracked soundboard*. However, soundboard cracks have no effect on a piano's ability to hold its tune.

Bridges Bridges are strips of hardwood, glued to the soundboard, that transmit the strings' vibrations to the soundboard. The strings are stretched over the top of the bridges and bear against them, held in place by bridge pins. Age, dryness, and the pressure of the strings against the bridge pins can, over time, cause cracks to form around the pins, which then loosen. Except in extreme cases in which a bridge is virtually falling apart, the principal effect of loose bridge pins is not on the ability of the piano to hold its tune. Rather, loose bridge pins provide insecure termination points for the vibrating strings, causing tonal irregularities called *false beats* that, when excessive, make the affected strings sound out of tune even when they've been tuned as well as possible.

Strings Metal fatigue, rust, corrosion, pitting, and any history of liquid spilled into a piano can cause false beats and other irregularities, making tuning more difficult and less accurate. Due to the effects of metal fatigue, concert instruments may require restringing in as few as 10 years. Pianos in the home may benefit from restringing after about 25 years of use, though few receive that treatment.

Daily and, especially, seasonal variations in humidity are the most common cause of pianos without structural flaws going out of tune. The soundboard swells and shrinks slightly with changes in humidity, altering the tension on the strings. Wide swings of humidity can keep a piano's pitch in a constant state of flux, forcing the tuner to radically change the pitch with each tuning. The further out of tune the piano gets between tunings, the less stable its tuning will be when it does get tuned. When making a large pitch correction, the tuner may tell the customer that the piano is too flat or too sharp for a stable tuning to be done in a single session, and that after getting the tuning close to accurate, he or she will have to return in a few weeks to retune the piano. If the customer fails to have the piano tuned regularly, it will seem to be always out of tune. I have many customers who, in order to keep their pianos as close to pitch as possible, have them tuned once a month. It's not uncommon for pianos kept in the faculty and practice studios of conservatories to be tuned two or three times a month; concert pianos, even when not in use, are usually tuned once a week just to keep them close to pitch. Tuning stability can be greatly increased by use of a humidity-control system—for the entire home, for just the piano room, or inside the piano itself.

Counterintuitively, frequent service is particularly important with *new* pianos. Brand-new instruments can be very unstable as their new strings and soundboard continue to settle, and in their first year usually must be tuned four to six times. Most dealers will tune a new piano before delivery, and once or twice after delivery, often at no additional cost to the customer. Depending on how many times it was tuned on the dealer's floor, and before that in the factory, this may or may not be enough to stabilize the piano so that the frequency of tuning can return to whatever the customer considers normal. Failure to ensure that the recommended post-sale service is actually done can substantially lengthen a new piano's break-in period and make its tuning seem unstable.

A piano's tunability is also a factor of its quality and price—when offering a piano at a particular price point, manufacturers take into account the sophistication and expectations of prospective purchasers. More expensive pianos can be tuned more accurately, and, given equivalent conditions of use, will usually hold a tune better than less expensive ones because of their superior designs, better materials, more robust construction, better workmanship, and more extensive preparation in the factory. Due to globalization and the increasing computerization of manufacturing, these differences are less pronounced than in former eras, but are still obvious in comparisons of high-end with entry-level instruments.

Lastly, the mechanical skill of the tuner is very important to the stability of the tuning. One of the greatest obstacles to tuning stability is the unequal tension that occurs between the vibrating and non-vibrating sections of a string as, during tuning, the wire is drawn over the friction points that separate those sections near the string's two ends. As soon as the note is forcefully played, the tension will equalize and the string will go out of tune. To prevent this from happening during a performance or shortly after the tuner leaves, tuners use *test blows*—striking the keys at least as forcefully as any pianist would—to settle the strings so that they can be immediately retuned, if necessary, and stabilized. Another important mechanical skill is the ability to turn very tight tuning pins by minute amounts and without bending them—a bent pin will quickly unbend, and throw its string out of tune.

A highly skilled tuner working on a good instrument can tune so stably that when the humidity changes, most of the notes on the piano will seem to move sharp or flat together, and the tuning will continue to sound good for some time. In most cases, a skilled tuner can do a terrific job in 1½ to 2½ hours, sometimes less. Inexperienced tuners who take all day to tune a piano will move and bend the pins much more than necessary, producing an unstable tuning and possibly damaging the pinblock.

Electronic Tuning Devices vs. Tuning by Ear

Electronic tuning devices (ETDs) are now used by many piano tuners, even by some who can tune by ear.

Unlike the *aural* (by ear) tuner, ETDs can "hear" only one note at a time; they don't listen to intervals or beats, or tune the strings of a unison to one another. When using an ETD, it isn't necessary to first tune a temperament. In theory, one could tune a piano with an ETD by starting at the lowest note on the piano and working upward to the highest.

A skilled tuner who has trained as an aural tuner can use an ETD to great advantage. The use of an ETD doesn't eliminate the need for the tuner to develop superior listening skills, but it does allow the already skilled tuner to perform such tasks as pitch raising faster and more accurately, reducing the need to retune sections that have already been tuned. Use of an ETD also allows the tuner to tune for longer periods of time with less fatigue, and makes it possible to tune in noisy environments that would be difficult for an aural-only tuner.

For concert and recording work, an ETD is a more accurate pitch reference than a tuning fork, which can vary in pitch with temperature. This is particularly important when tuning a piano that will be accompanied by an orchestra, as many professional orchestras tune to a pitch of from A–441 to A–443, both of which are slightly higher than the traditional A–440 to which most pianos are tuned. (The numbers refer to the frequency, in cycles per second, of the A above middle C.) In an institutional setting in which two or more pianos must be tuned together, an ETD makes it easy to synchronize not only the overall pitch, but also the stretching of the octaves in the upper and lower sections of the keyboard.

Problems occur, however, when novice tuners without aural skills are entirely dependent on ETDs. They can't hear when they make a mistake, or when they need to override the judgment of the machine to get the best results. Also, an ETD cannot, by itself, create a stable tuning. The tuner must still know how to manipulate the tuning pins and strings so that the piano will stay in tune when the job is done.

VOICING AND TONE
What Piano Buyers and Owners Should Know

Sally Phillips

TO MOST PIANO BUYERS and owners, a piano's tone is probably its most important aspect, but also the most difficult to quantify or describe. Likewise, the shaping of the tone by the technician through the procedure known as voicing involves unfamiliar terminology, and techniques that are difficult for technicians to communicate to the customer. The purpose of this article, then, is to provide information about tone, voicing, and definitions of some commonly used terms so that piano owners and technicians can better communicate with each other, and piano shoppers can make more informed buying decisions.

Voicing, or tone regulation, comprises a variety of techniques that technicians use to change a piano's tone. Most involve adjusting the hardness, density, tension, and surface of the hammer felt to produce a spectrum of tonal qualities ranging from bright to mellow. Slight repositioning of the strings may also be part of this process.

Voicing differs from tuning, which is the adjustment of the strings' tensions to produce the proper pitches. In voicing, it is the *timbre* of each note, not its pitch, that is addressed. Voicing must also be distinguished from action regulation, i.e., the mechanical adjustment of the keys and action for evenness of touch and response. However, a piano needs to be tuned and its keys and action regulated *before* being voiced because these procedures themselves clear up many tonal problems. For example, a piano can sound tinny simply because it is out of tune—something that no amount of voicing can correct. An inability to play softly may be caused by a poorly regulated action, which can make the touch difficult to control.

Why Pianos Need to Be Voiced

Any piano's sound will gradually brighten over time, as its hammer felts are repeatedly packed down by the impact of the hammers on the strings; it will need regular voicing to maintain good tone. Since hammer felt absorbs moisture, the tone can become mellower in more humid weather, brighter in drier weather. The voicing can become uneven when some notes are played more often than others. Heavy use of the una corda pedal in grands also causes the voicing to become uneven. I usually do some voicing during each tuning. If this is done consistently, the tone of the hammers will remain good until wear demands that they be changed.

Alexander Kobrin, the 2005 Van Cliburn International Piano Competition Gold Medalist, explains how an uneven tone can affect the performer. According to Kobrin, when the pianist can be distracted by notes that stick out or are weak in the scale, he or she has to remember which notes don't perform like the others. This inhibits the performance, and ultimately, the audience doesn't get the full benefit of the artist's interpretation of a piece. The student practicing on instruments with this problem will have much more difficulty performing on other instruments. Kobrin also states the need for young pianists to have a properly prepared piano for practice, because that is where they develop an appreciation for the quality of tone that, as future professionals or advanced amateurs, they will be responsible for producing.

Describing Tone

Here are some terms commonly used by piano technicians, in the voicing context, to describe tone:

Timbre is the particular blend of harmonics in a piano's tone, or in the tone of a single note. The timbre is said to have *color* when it contains a blend of harmonics that is pleasing to the ear. The piano is said to have a *broad spectrum of tonal color* when the hammers are voiced in such a way that the timbre changes with minor differences in touch by the pianist, making accessible a broad range of timbres over the instrument's full range of volume. This is achieved by using hammers of very high quality that have been carefully voiced so that very slight increases in the speed of the hammer increase not only the sound's volume, but also, slightly, its brightness. Pianos with a broad spectrum of tonal color provide the pianist with a larger expressive range. However, producing the same degree of change in timbre for each hammer so that the voicing is even across the keyboard and throughout the piano's range of volume requires that the voicer be very skilled.

Bright describes tone with a concentration of higher harmonics. Bright pianos that have been properly voiced have a clear, clean, brilliant brightness that still has lots of tonal color, whereas pianos whose bright sound is a result of the hammers needing reshaping and voicing tend to lack such color. This latter, unpleasant brightness is described by terms such as *brassy*, *metallic*, *glassy*, and *tinny*. (Note that the word *sharp* is not used because it refers to pitch, not tone.) Making a piano brighter is referred to by technicians as *voicing up*.

A *mellow* tone has a stronger fundamental frequency and fewer upper harmonics. Pianos that sound mellow, but that still have articulation and color, are described as sounding *sweet*, *round*, *dark*, or *rich*; those whose mellowness is without these redeeming qualities can be described as *dead*, *dull*,

weak, or *without power*. The latter kind of mellowness is the result of the instrument needing voicing or new hammers, or lacking in tone-producing capability for other reasons—such as worn bass strings, loss of soundboard crown, or poor scale design. Voicing pianos to be mellower is referred to as *voicing down*.

Hammers in European pianos, or by European hammer makers such as Renner and Abel, and those in Asian pianos, are generally harder than American hammers; e.g., those in older American pianos from the early 20th century, in current Steinway (New York) instruments, and from American hammer-maker Ronsen. European and Asian hammers are traditionally voiced by voicing down, American hammers by voicing up.

Even and *uneven* describe how similar or different the timbre is from note to note on the same piano. The process of evening out the timbre is usually a much faster one than making a wholesale change in the instrument's tone.

Big describes a piano sound with greater-than-average volume and projection (power)—the qualities needed, for example, for the sound to reach the rear of an auditorium. These factors are not usually problematic in pianos in the home, but are of critical importance in a concert setting. Power is primarily a function of the instrument's size and ability to sustain, the latter being dependent on the piano's design, and the composition of its rim and soundboard. But the choice of hammer can also greatly influence sustain and therefore power, and voicing can be used to improve these characteristics in a high-quality instrument with very good hammers. With instruments and hammers of lesser quality, sustain, power, and projection should be considered inherent in the design of the instrument, and amenable to little change through voicing.

It's important to distinguish brightness from power, but they overlap, especially in the concert setting. Concert instruments must usually be voiced brighter than home instruments in order to cut through the sound of an orchestra. Brightness can also partially substitute for power when the latter is lacking. But an overly bright instrument will lack color, and attempts to voice it down could sacrifice its power. Eric Schandall, an American technician living and working in Europe, describes the newer Hamburg Steinways as generally having a bigger sound than those of even ten years ago: "There is a wider envelope of sound and more variety of timbre. This allows more room to voice the piano less bright and still have a big sound, not relying on brightness in place of a big sound."

Similarly, Alexander Kobrin speaks about the larger spectrum of tonal color available in a piano with a big sound, and how that affects the choice of concert instrument. In comparing two concert grands, Kobrin says he would choose the one with the bigger sound and greater tonal color for Romantic works, but one with a clean attack and less color for Classical compositions.

Voicing Techniques

Here are some of the techniques used to change a piano's tone:

Hammer shaping, filing, and sanding—This is the process of removing with sandpaper the grooves in the top of the hammer made by the impact of the hammer on the strings, and restoring the hammer's elliptical shape so that only the very small area of the crown at the top of the hammer strikes the string. When the grooves are very deep and wide, they not only damp the sound but also produce a louder impact noise, commonly characterized as *metallic*, *brassy*, or even *woody*.

Mating the strings and hammers—When a tenor or treble hammer doesn't strike its three strings simultaneously, the result can be buzzing or other odd sounds, as well as a loss of power. Mating the strings and hammers can be achieved by a combination of leveling the strings and sanding very small amounts of felt off the hammer crowns.

Needling the hammers—Careful insertion of needles into the hammer felt releases tension in the hammer and makes it softer, resulting in a mellower tone. Many techniques can be applied, with varying results. For example, needling the lower shoulder area can actually increase the volume of sound, while needling lightly into the crown of the hammer can make the sound sweeter on a soft blow. With older hammers that have hardened, lost tension and compression, or are excessively worn, the technician must be more cautious about making changes. Older hammers react more radically to needling, and could be very difficult to maintain at optimal levels if there is not enough felt left to work with, hastening the need for replacement.

Hardening the hammers—Lacquer solutions, typically thinned with solvent, can be applied to the hammer felt to increase its hardness and brighten the

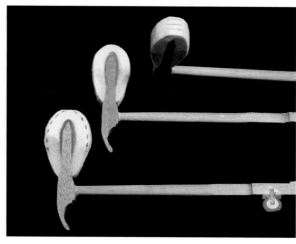

The impact of the hammers on the strings causes the hammers' striking points, over time, to become broadened, flattened, and grooved. Reshaping the hammers to restore the striking points to their original size, shape, and surface quality is an important part of the voicing process.

tone. Needling to even out the tone after the lacquer dries is then necessary. Applying lacquer is a highly skilled job for an experienced technician, who must make an informed judgment about the mixture, amount, and placement of lacquer for best results. One reason experience is called for is that using lacquer to increase a piano's power and sustain can actually make the tone worse if the tonal problem actually is in the soundboard and strings. Technicians call the adding of lacquer "building the tone"; for some manufacturers, such as Steinway, the use of lacquer is necessary to achieve the brand's traditional sound.

Ironing the surface of the hammer compresses the fuzzy surface and makes the hammer produce a cleaner sound. Though less common in North America, ironing of hammers is still done extensively in Europe, and can add moderate brightness without the use of chemical hardeners. In some cases, ironing hammers in very humid conditions will dry them out, making the action feel lighter and restoring the tone.

Voicing an older piano in which a new set of hammers has been installed is quite different from voicing a brand-new instrument. The pre-voicing and prep of a fine new piano at the factory by a skilled voicer can take days, and the technician servicing the piano in the field encounters hammers that have already been

Until the mid-20th century, it was commonly accepted that pianos began life as relatively mellow instruments, brightening with playing over time. Early in the 1960s, however, there was a sea change in the perception of tone. Pianos began being made brighter in response to changing tastes and larger concert halls. Dealers found that the piano-buying public was easily impressed with the very bright-sounding pianos they were starting to import from Japan. Individual tastes always come into play, but in general, the pianos desired for concert work were getting brighter, too.

"There is a limit to how bright a piano can be and still be controllable and musically beautiful," says piano technician Eric Schandall, "and we've gotten to that point over the last 40 years. Although there are still differences in tonal tastes, the pendulum has swung toward a more moderate brightness in the way hammers are made, and in how they are voiced, too."

Ed Foote, piano technician at Vanderbilt University, has had years of experience in the Nashville recording industry. He feels that the tonal palette has been narrowed by overly bright pianos. (Foote recalls adding lacquer to the hammers of a brand-new, already-bright Yamaha C7 grand to get a colorful, aggressively bright sound that "sold a million records.") He sees the current trend as slowly moving away from excessive brightness, with pianists finding that a piano can have a bigger sound, a wider range of dynamics, and more colorful tone without sounding too harsh.

Ron Coners, Steinway's Chief Concert Technician, notes that in the last several years the density of the hammer felt in Steinway models B (7') and D (9') has been increased, resulting in more robust power without increasing the impact sound. He says that this change has allowed the voicer to get a bigger sound from the hammers without adding much lacquer. Coners explains that using less lacquer increases the body of the tone, and introduces fewer unwanted elements to the sound that must then be voiced out. This makes it easier to maintain the bank of Steinway concert grands while still catering to artists' individual tastes.

The hammers of older American pianos from the mid– to late 20th century tend to contain a lot of chemical hardeners, and today these pianos are likely to need new hammers in order to produce a good sound. Many technicians have been urging hammer makers to recapture the hammer and sound qualities of the early 20th century, and to use the most recent technical advances to get better tone from hammers. Hammer makers know a lot more than they did 40 years ago, and now produce a variety of hammers that don't rely on glassy brightness.

For a number of years, Dale Erwin, of Erwin Piano Restoration, in Modesto, California, has been working closely with Ronsen Piano Hammer Company president Ray Negron and the Wurzen Felt Company of Germany to take advantage of Wurzen's restoration of the original process for producing its famous Weickert felt. Erwin has been a proponent of developing a softer, more resilient hammer to recapture the classic, early 20th-century American piano sound, which, he says, will bring out the true tonal potential of rebuilt instruments from that era. Erwin says that high-quality felt is the basis for good hammers and the production of tone color. Negron is quick to point out, however, that even with the highest-quality materials, the machinery and processes used to make the hammers can radically affect the final product.

The same caution should be applied to the early Asian imports from the 1960s through the '90s, which can have excessively hard hammers that don't respond to traditional voicing techniques. The good news is that technicians such as Erwin are reporting great results with new, softer hammers on those instruments, too.—S.P.

*For a more in-depth look at the historical evolution of piano voicing, with links to recordings on YouTube, check out our **online article** on the subject at* **www.pianobuyer.com**.

---

fully prepared. However, the technician who installs new hammers in the field must possess the skills of the factory *and* field technicians to be able to set up the hammers correctly, then voice them to the customer's preferences.

Tonal Considerations When Purchasing a Piano

I encourage customers, prior to shopping, to attend concerts and listen to high-quality recordings of the

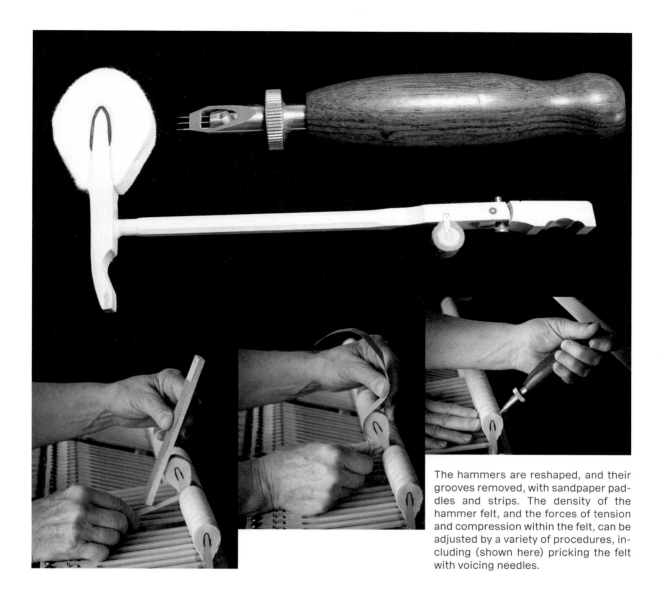

The hammers are reshaped, and their grooves removed, with sandpaper paddles and strips. The density of the hammer felt, and the forces of tension and compression within the felt, can be adjusted by a variety of procedures, including (shown here) pricking the felt with voicing needles.

type of piano music they typically play in order to establish a concept of tonal aesthetics. Older voicers called it "having a sound in your ear"—that is, establishing a mental standard of what you like with which you can evaluate the tone of the instruments you encounter.

I recommend that you purchase a piano that, on the dealer's floor, sounds reasonably close to what you desire. Don't buy a piano with unsatisfactory sound based on a promise that radical changes in its voicing will make it sound good in your home. It's true that the tone will be different in your home due to differences in environment; e.g., carpeting and drapery instead of the dealer's hardwood floor and bare walls, as well as the rooms' different sizes. But you're buying a piano whose tonal goal has been established by the manufacturer and has been built to that standard; you shouldn't expect anything more than minor voicing in the home to even out the tone or make small changes in its brightness, If a greater change in the instrument's tone *is* attempted, it may well not be effective.

There's one exception to this: A large piano can, within reason, be voiced to sound good in a smaller space (though the opposite is unlikely to be true). I have many clients with 9' grands in their living rooms, and many piano studios in universities have one or two 7' grands in rather small spaces. The concern that a piano that large will be too loud can be alleviated by regulation and judicious voicing.

The above notwithstanding, it's probably best to err a little on the mellow side when purchasing a new piano. The really bright-sounding piano in the showroom will get only brighter with time. It's easier to maintain the tonal quality of hammers that start out mellow because, eventually, they will naturally brighten with use to the desired level, and will tend to stay at that level longer. Overly bright hammers will require more voicing maintenance over time, and in extreme cases, can be responsible for broken strings.

The better the piano, the more voiceable its hammers and the more malleable its sound. Manufacturers have to make decisions about materials as they increase or decrease the quality of the product to meet various price points. The hammers in the least expensive models just won't produce the quality of sound heard from the more expensive instruments. This can make separating a piano's voicing issues from its tonal potential much more challenging for the consumer.

In addition, because tone depends not only on the quality and voicing of the hammers, but also on the other sound-producing parts of the instrument (such as the rim, soundboard, and bridges), one should have realistic expectations about smaller, less expensive pianos. No amount of voicing will make an entry-level grand sound like a 9' concert grand. And because hammers tend to revert to their originally designed tone, scaling deficiencies in older or smaller models that may have been hidden by careful voicing may return as harsh changes in tone when the voicing deteriorates, exposing awkward transitions in the scale.

Following purchase of a piano, it should be ready for touch-up voicing and regulating after having been played for 50 to 100 hours, depending on repertoire and on how much playing and touch-up it received in the store before purchase. After that, the tone and voicing will evolve throughout the life of the hammers.

Choose a technician experienced in voicing your particular brand, especially for performance-quality instruments. Many manufacturers have specific tonal goals for their instruments, and technicians who regularly work with those brands' hammers are more attuned to their expectations—and the expectations of the client who has chosen that brand based on its tone.

CLEANING AND POLISHING A PIANO'S FINISH

DAVE SWARTZ

THE PURPOSE of this article is to explain the proper care of the three most common piano finishes today: satin, high gloss, and open pore. Wood-finishing materials have changed dramatically in the last century. The earliest were made of oil-based varnish, rubbing oils, or shellac. Then, in the 1920s, lacquer became more prevalent, with synthetics such as polyurethane and polyester following later in the century as scientific advances were made. Water-based coatings also were and continue to be applied.

To best care for your piano's finish, you need to know what kind of finish it is, and what its special requirements are.

Satin Finishes

A satin finish reflects light but not images. Satin finishes may be of any color, including ebony (black), or wood tones such as cherry, mahogany, and walnut. Regardless of whether the finishing material is lacquer, polyester, or something else, the process of applying the finish is similar.

First, numerous layers of high-gloss material are applied; typically, each layer is lightly sanded before the next layer is applied. When an adequate thickness of material has been built up, the finish is left to cure for a while, then rubbed to a satin finish. The rubbing is done with #0000 steel wool or, in some instances, 600-grit wet/dry sandpaper or other abrasive. A rubbing lubricant, along with water on the abrasive applicator, serves as a buffer. The rubbing is done in one direction only, to create tiny grooves in the finish that diffract light (see photo). In this way, the original high-gloss sheen is knocked down to a hand-rubbed satin sheen that is dull but elegant.

Caring for this type of finish can be problematic, for two reasons. First, body oils from fingerprints can get trapped in the tiny finish grooves, and are not easily removed by a simple dusting. Second, if the finish is wiped in a circular motion, the fine grooves become uneven, disturbing the original even pattern of light reflection and thus ruining the satin effect. Over time, repeated polishing in the wrong direction can actually remove the tiny grooves and bring the finish down to the base of the high-gloss material. An example of this condition would be an older satin finish that now looks somewhat "semigloss" due to overwiping and overpolishing.

The adage "less is more" is applicable to caring for a satin finish. In most cases it is unnecessary to apply polishes or cleaners to remove ordinary dust or dirt—a simple dusting with a non-abrasive cloth is sufficient. If you want to remove fingerprints, a mild cleaner can be applied. A product specifically designed for this purpose is our Cory Pre-Polish Finish Cleaner, but you can also use a microfiber cloth dampened with warm water and Ivory liquid dish detergent, then a separate, dry microfiber cloth to remove any remaining moisture. Apply the cleaning liquid directly to the cloth, and be sure to wipe in a

Hand-rubbed satin finishes on ebony (above) and natural wood (right).

back-and-forth motion *only* in the direction of the satin "grain."

Another type of satin finish is created by adding a pigment to the high-gloss material, to suppress the high shine of the finish. This type of finish is often less expensive because it is usually not rubbed, but instead is left as is for a duller, matte appearance. Some dealers and rebuilding shops use this type of finish when refinishing a piano. The recommendation for care remains the same as for a rubbed finish, although the direction of wiping is not as critical.

Avoid using waxes, products with ammonia, oils, petroleum-based products, or grocery-store aerosols. These types of household cleaners will make the finish appear hazy, milky, or smeared.

High-Gloss Finishes

High-gloss finishes act as mirrors, reflecting both light and images, and the material most commonly used in today's high-gloss finishes is polyester. Pioneered in the 1960s, polyester finish is a two-part synthetic resin that completely hardens during curing, is resistant to cracks, and can't be broken down by solvents. Polyester finishes are the most durable of all piano finishes, but their hardness and resistance to solvents make them more difficult to repair when damaged.

Aside from damage repair, polyester finishes are easier to maintain than satin finishes, but still require proper care. Using ammonia, solvents, or waxes

generally will not damage the finish, but will create a smeary, uneven appearance as these contaminants build up over time. In addition, some polyesters themselves may not be of high quality, and will eventually haze over. If oil- or solvent-based polishes were previously used on the piano, or if its surfaces are dirty, a simple cleaning with a mild solution is recommended to remove the contaminants and dirt before polishing. Use my suggestions in the Satin Finishes section, above, to do a thorough cleaning before applying a polish. Once again, I recommend that you

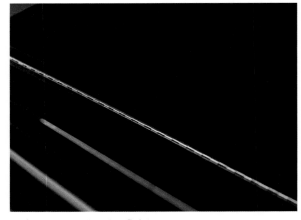

A high-gloss polyester finish.

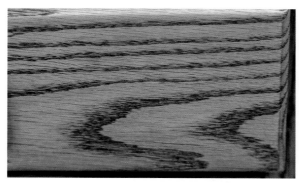 

Two examples of open-pore finishes.

use a clean, high-quality microfiber cloth (see below) when caring for a high-gloss finish, to avoid scratching or uneven results. More abrasive cloths can create surface scratches.

Some polishes are designed specifically for high-gloss finishes. Many piano manufacturers recommend our Cory Super High-Gloss Piano Polish, a water-based polish that contains no solvents, waxes, or harmful additives. This special, emulsified blend of polymers will not build up, smear, or leave other undesired results. It's worth stressing that oil and water don't mix—when using a water-based product such as ours after an oil-based product, it's paramount to first clean the surface for best results.

Other types of high-gloss finishes include polyurethane and lacquer. Polyurethane is a bit softer than polyester, and lacquer is softer yet. Care must be taken when using cleaners or polishes with these finishes—avoid those based on solvents, petroleum-based paraffin wax, or ammonia. Note that, although more easily damaged than polyester, lacquer is often considered the most beautiful of high-gloss finishes, and is used on some of the most expensive pianos.

Open-Pore Finishes

Open-pore finishes are used primarily on pianos with natural wood-veneered cabinets (i.e., not ebony). Though not as commonly used on pianos as satin and high-gloss finishes, open-pore finishes are often used as an alternative to satin on instruments made in Europe, as well as on furniture such as end tables, coffee tables, and bed headboards. An open-pore

finish is achieved using a sanding sealer and a coat or two of lacquer or polyurethane. However, it is not rubbed, nor is the grain completely filled, which gives an open-pore finish a sheen somewhere between satin and matte. The way to identify this type of finish is to examine it closely, to ascertain if the wood cells are exposed, and not filled (see photos).

There are many options for the care of open-pore finishes; I recommend conditioning and preserving with an oil- or petroleum-based product. Howard's and Old English are two brands that are popular in the furniture world. Our company, Cory Products, makes specific blends for piano finishes, such as Honey Oak, Natural Wood, and our very popular Harmony Detailing Oil. But regardless of which conditioning polish you use, be sure to remove any excess—otherwise it will collect dust and create a buildup of grime.

Should the finish be worn, or with visible bare wood due to gouging or scrapes, you can use products such as Old English Scratch Cover or Cory Scratch-Brite Fine Wood Restorer. Note that using products containing paraffin waxes may leave the finish tacky to the touch.

In all cases, avoid spraying any product on or near the piano's tuning pins or strings. The wisest choice is usually to first apply the product to the cloth, then the cloth to the wood.

Microfiber Cloths

Microfiber cloths are superior to other cloths for maintaining fine finishes, and are recommended for all finish care. However, not all microfiber cloths are created equal; the higher the quality, the better the cleaning results. Most microfiber cloths are made of 80% polyester and 20% polyamide, as polyester has an affinity for oil and polyamide has an affinity for water. You can judge the quality of a microfiber cloth in part by its weight, measured in grams per square meter (gsm). Good cloths start at around 200 gsm; the best are over 400 gsm. If the cloth is hemmed, make sure that the stitching contains no nylon, which will scratch the finish.

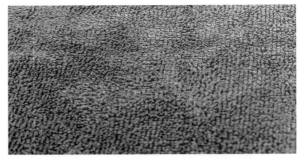

Microfiber cloths are recommended for all finish care.

BENCHES, LAMPS, ACCESSORIES, AND PROBLEM SOLVERS

Benches

In all likelihood, your purchase of a new piano will include a matching bench. Benches for consumer-grade pianos are usually made by the piano manufacturer and come with the piano. Benches for performance-grade pianos are often provided separately by the dealer.

Benches come in two basic types: *fixed-height* or *adjustable*. Consumer-grade pianos usually come with fixed-height benches that have either a solid top that matches the piano's finish, or a padded top with sides and legs finished to match the piano. The legs on most benches will be miniatures of the piano's legs, particularly for decorative models. Most piano benches have music storage compartments. School and institutional-type vertical pianos often come with so-called "stretcher" benches—the legs are connected with wooden reinforcing struts to better endure heavy use.

Both solid-top and padded benches work well. The padded benches tend to be a little more comfortable, especially for those who have little natural padding of their own. They tend to wear more quickly, however, and are subject to tearing. Solid-top benches wear longer but are more easily scratched.

Adjustable benches are preferred by serious players who spend hours at the piano, and by children

Padded Bench

Wood Top Bench

Adjustable Bench with Steel Legs

www.benchworld.com

Adjustable Artist Bench

Stretcher Bench

and adults who are shorter or taller than average. The standard height of a piano bench is 19" or 20". Adjustable benches typically can be set at anywhere from about 18" to 21". By adjusting the bench height and moving it slightly forward or backward, one can maintain the proper posture and wrist angle to the keyboard.

High-quality adjustable benches have a very heavy steel mechanism—so strong you could almost use it as a car jack! The duet-size bench (seats two) weighs well over 60 pounds. These benches are made of hard rock maple and come in most leg styles and finishes. The deeply tufted tops come in a heavy-duty vinyl and look like leather; tops of actual leather are available at additional cost. Both look great and wear well. The best ones, such as those made by Jansen, are expensive ($500 to $750) but are built to last a lifetime. Over the past few years, lesser-quality adjustable benches have come on the market. While these benches are adjustable within a similar range, the mechanisms aren't as hardy. They may be fine for light use, but most will not last nearly as long as the piano. A new style of adjustable bench, with steel legs, may be useful in high-use institutional settings.

A new type of adjustable bench on the market contains a hydraulic or pneumatic mechanism for raising or lowering the seat. There are different versions, but a typical one uses two nitrogen-gas cylinders, one on each side, and is good for 30,000 up-and-down cycles. The bench can be adjusted quickly and effortlessly by means of a handle on the side of the bench. This can be an advantage to players whose wrists are easily fatigued by turning the knob of the traditional or standard type of adjustable bench, or for musicians

who need to make height adjustments quickly and silently during a performance. These benches can also usually be set higher than the traditional kind. Most hydraulic or pneumatic benches are very stable, with metal legs (see photo), avoiding the wobbliness that can sometimes afflict four-legged wooden benches. Standard models range in price from $500 to $900; fancier versions, on which the metal is covered by wood, cost from $1,300 to $2,200.

Legs for both fixed-height and traditional adjustable benches are attached by a single bolt at the top of each leg. These bolts should be tightened anytime there is wobble in the bench. Don't over-tighten, however, as that might pull the bolt out of the leg.

Finally, if the piano you want doesn't come with the bench you desire, talk to your dealer. It's common for dealers to swap benches or bench tops to accommodate your preference, or to offer an upgrade to a better bench in lieu of a discount on the piano.

Lamps

Having adequate lighting for the piano music is critical. It's hard enough to learn how to read music without having to deal with a lack of illumination, or with shadows on the sheet music. The ideal solution is track lighting in the ceiling just above the player.

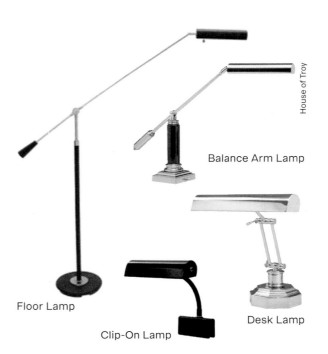

House of Troy

Balance Arm Lamp

Floor Lamp

Clip-On Lamp

Desk Lamp

House of Troy

Piano Lamps for all Piano Styles
www.houseoftroy.com 800-428-5367

Piano lamps are available through most piano dealerships as well as at lighting stores. A limited selection can also be found at The Home Depot and Lowe's.

Accessories and Problem Solvers

Only a few accessories are used with pianos, and most are available at your local piano dealership. You might consider:

- **Caster Cups**. Caster cups are small cups that go under the wheels of vertical and grand pianos to protect the floor or carpet. They come in plastic or a variety of woods, and in clear acrylic that allows the carpet or hardwood floor to show through. If the caster cups have felt on the bottom, however, be careful, as the dye from the felt can bleed into carpeting, especially if it gets damp.

Caster Cups

In many homes and institutions, however, this is not feasible. In those instances, a piano lamp may well be the answer.

Piano lamps fall into two major groups: floor lamps and desk lamps. Floor lamps arch over the piano and hover over the music rack, while desk lamps sit directly on the piano or are attached to the music rack itself. Desk lamps are subdivided into three groups: a standard desk lamp that sits atop a vertical piano directly over the music rack; a "balance-arm" lamp that sits off to the side on a grand piano's music desk and has a long arm that hovers over the music rack; and a clip-on lamp that attaches directly to the music rack itself (see illustrations).

Piano lamps come in a variety of qualities, sizes, styles, finishes, and bulb types. The better ones are usually made of high-quality brass, while the least expensive are often made of very thin brass or are simply brass-plated. The light from incandescent-bulb lamps tends to be a tad harsh, but the bulbs are less expensive than those for fluorescent lamps, which, though pricier, emit a softer light.

- **Piano Covers**. Used mostly in churches and schools (and homes with cats), piano covers are designed to protect the piano's finish from accidental damage, and are available to fit any size of piano. They come in vinyl or mackintosh (a very tight-weave fabric that is very water-resistant), brown or black on the outside, and a fleece-like material on the side that touches the piano. A thicker, quilted, cotton cover is available for use in locations where the piano is moved frequently or may get bumped.

Piano Covers

Bench Cushions

- **Bench Cushions**. Bench cushions are made in a variety of sizes, thicknesses (1" to 3"), fabrics, and colors. They are also available in tapestry designs, most with a musical motif, tufted or box-edged, and all have straps to secure them to the bench.

- **Pedal Extenders**. These extension devices are available for those whose feet do not comfortably reach the pedals. Some are nothing more than a brass pedal that bolts on to the existing pedal, while others are a box, finished to match the piano, that sits over the existing pedals and has pedals with rods to operate the piano's pedals.

Pedal Extenders

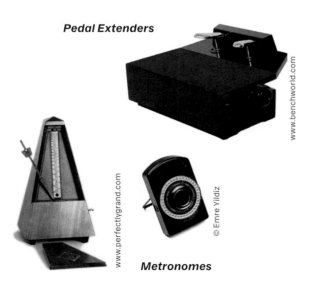

www.benchworld.com

www.perfectlygrand.com

© Emre Yildiz

Metronomes

- **Metronomes**. Many music teachers recommend using a metronome to improve students' timing. Any piano or musical-instrument dealership will generally have a wide selection, from the solid walnut, wind-up, oscillating metronome like the one your grandmother had on her piano, to a new, beeping digital model.

- **Grand Piano String Covers**. Wool string covers are available in a variety of colors that complement the piano's finish. When in place, they provide a reduction in sound volume, and protection against dust (and cats). Thicker sound-reduction covers and baffles are also available.

- **Lid and Fallboard Slow-Close Systems**. Raising and lowering the lid of a grand piano is frequently difficult, and can be downright dangerous. This is due to the combination of its weight, which can exceed 50 pounds, and its position, which makes it hard to reach. Enter a new product that solves at least the weight problem: Safety-Ease Lid Assist. Safety-Ease (now known as Magic Lid) consists of pneumatic cylinders that effectively counter-balance the weight of the lid and damp its movement so that it can be easily raised or lowered, even by a child. It mounts under the lid, between the lid hinges on the piano's rim, is finished in polished ebony to match most pianos, and requires no drilling or permanent installation. This unique system is sold and installed only by piano dealers or technicians. The installed price for small and mid-size grands is $500 to $600. More information is available at **www.magic-lid.com**.

  The fallboard (keyboard cover) can also be a danger, not so much for its weight or position, but for the swiftness of its fall and because, when it falls, little fingers are likely to be in its path. Many new pianos today come with a pneumatically or hydraulically damped, slow-close fallboard. For those that don't, aftermarket devices are available from piano dealers or technicians.

- **Touch-Weight Adjustment Systems.** *Touch* or *touch weight* refers to the pressure required to press a piano key. Too little touch weight, or touch weight that is uneven from note to note, makes a piano action difficult to control; too much touch weight makes a piano tiring to play, and can cause physical problems for the player over time. Touch-weight problems can be caused by poor action design, worn parts in older pianos, or incorrectly dimensioned replacement parts in restored pianos.

Historically, discussions, measurements, and adjustments in this area of piano technology have been about *static* touch weight—the force needed to make a piano key just begin to move slowly downward. Less well understood, and usually ignored, has been *dynamic* touch weight—the force required to press a key in actual normal, rapid playing. Here, the rapid movement of the key creates *inertia* (i.e., the tendency of a moving mass to keep moving in the same direction and at the same speed, and the tendency of a stationary mass to remain stationary.) Unlike static touch weight, which depends on the *relative* amount and positioning of mass on either side of the key's balance point, as well as on friction, dynamic touch weight depends on the *total* amount of mass in the system. Attempts to fix problems in static touch weight by adding mass to the front or rear of the key can cause problems with dynamic touch weight by creating excessive inertia.

Until fairly recently, technicians resorted to a patchwork quilt of homemade, trial-by-error remdies for problems with static touch weight; dynamic touch weight wasn't even on their radar. More recently, a greater understanding of touch weight has emerged, and more sophisticated techniques for solving touch-weight problems

are being developed. The gold standard among these techniques is that of David Stanwood, who developed the first system for mathematically describing, measuring, and solving problems related to dynamic touch weight. His system is applied by a network of specially trained technicians who, because of the comprehensive nature of the system and the remedies it suggests, tend to use it on higher-end instruments and those undergoing complete restoration. More information can be found at **www.stanwoodpiano.com**.

A simpler remedy, but only for heavy or uneven static touch weight on a grand piano, is a product called TouchRail, available through piano technicians. TouchRail is a rail with 88 individually adjustable springs that replaces a grand piano's key-stop rail. The springs press gently on the keys to the front of the balance point, enabling the technician to effectively "dial in" a desired touch weight and make it perfectly even from note to note. Because it's spring-based rather than mass-based, TouchRail won't add inertia to the action system, though of course it won't cure any pre-existing problems with excessive inertia, either. Installation requires no drilling, cutting, or other permanent modification of the piano, and the rail can be removed and replaced in seconds during routine piano service, just like a traditional key-stop rail. The installed price is $800 to $1,000. See **www.pitchlock. com** for more information.

TEN WAYS TO VOICE A ROOM

CHRISTOPHER STORCH

HAVE YOU NOTICED that your newly purchased piano doesn't sound quite the same as when you tried it in the showroom? The difference you notice between showroom and home may stem from the acoustics of the room in which the piano is placed. Not all problems with piano tone are best solved by voicing the instrument—it may be your room that needs voicing. Some of the factors that can significantly affect the sound of your piano room are: the size of the room, including ceiling height; the sound-absorbing and -reflecting materials in the room, which give it its reverberant character; and the number and orientation of objects in the room, which affect how sound is scattered or diffused.

Making the Distinction Between the Piano and the Room

It's important to distinguish between acoustical problems caused by the piano and those caused by the room. For instance, a problem of too much loudness is often caused by a piano that is too large for the room. This can be best addressed at or close to the piano, rather than by increasing the amount of sound-absorbing materials elsewhere in the room. On the other hand, such problems as harshness of tone, excess lingering sound, and hot and dead spots, can often be attributed to the room. Many of the following suggestions for loudness control or other acoustical adjustments are easily reversible; experiment with some of these before making more permanent changes to your piano or room.

Reverberation

Reverberation refers to the persistence of sound within a space after the source of the sound has stopped. Such prolongation of sound can help give music the qualities of blending, lushness, fullness, and breadth. Too much reverberation can make the music muddy and indistinct, and the buildup of reverberant sound can make the piano sound too loud. When there is too little reverberation, the room is said to sound "dry" or even "dead"; to compensate for this, the pianist might feel the need to overplay to achieve a lush, musical sound. In general, the larger the cubic volume of the space, the longer the reverberation time; the smaller the cubic volume, the shorter the reverberation time. The more sound-absorbing materials in the space, the shorter the reverberation time; the fewer such materials, the longer the reverberation time. The length of reverberation is a matter of personal preference. Some pianists like having the room reverberation be part of the sound of their piano playing; others prefer keeping the sound of the room to a minimum, enjoying primarily the clear sound of the piano as modulated by their technique.

Hot or Dead Spots

Hot spots and dead spots are places in the room where certain frequencies or notes, though played with the same force, stand out more than other frequencies or notes. Problems of this type are best solved by installing sound-scattering objects: bookcases, furniture, wall hangings, and so forth. Reorienting the piano or moving it slightly can also help.

Below are ten ways to mitigate problems in piano sound other than by voicing the instrument, beginning with some relatively simple things to do nearby the piano itself:

 Buy a piano that's the right size for the room.

The first and best way to avoid problems with room acoustics is to buy a piano that's the right size for the room. Too large a piano can overload a room with sound, while one that's too small may not be heard equally well in all parts of the space. A rule of thumb: Assuming a ceiling height of eight feet, the combined lengths of the four walls should be at least ten times the length of a grand piano or the height of a vertical. However, it's not always possible to follow this advice—in many cases, the purchase decision will be dictated more by musical needs or budget than by room size. A small piano, for example, may have performance problems inherent to the instrument's size, such as poor bass tone or an unresponsive action, even when it's the right size for the room. Or, if you're longing for a large grand's growling bass, be aware that, even though such a piano is perfectly capable of producing that sound, your room may not be able to support it.

When the piano's size is not a good match for the room, try voicing the piano, or experimenting with one of the following tips:

 Move or reorient the piano within the room.

Most rooms have three pairs of parallel surfaces: two sets of opposing walls, and the ceiling and floor. Parallel surfaces tend to produce standing waves—certain frequencies that sound much louder than others at some points in the room, but that are virtually inaudible at other points. Moving the piano away from room corners and partway along the length of a wall, and/or turning it at an angle this way or that, can sometimes mitigate this problem. You'll have to

experiment, listening at different places within the room. Remember that the piano's sound when you sit at the keyboard will be different from its sound elsewhere in the room.

 Use a piano cover to directly reduce loudness.

Typical cloth string covers designed for grand pianos—that is, covers that lie directly on the strings—will only marginally reduce sound volume, especially if they have only a single layer of cloth. Most reports say that thin string covers are effective only for the highest notes, to take the edge off the sound. Thicker, sound-attenuating string covers, custom-made for a particular model of grand piano, work better. An even more effective mute for a grand would be a full-size, quilted cover that reaches the floor. However, this will require closing the lid completely and placing the music rack atop the cover—though unattractive, in some situations this is the only practical way to reduce excess loudness. For a vertical piano, a blanket or section of carpet can be attached to the piano's back.

 Place sound-absorbing material inside the piano, between the soundboard and the wooden structural support beams.

You may be able to drastically reduce a piano's loudness by inserting blankets or foam rubber blocks between a grand's soundboard and its wooden case beams, or between a vertical's soundboard and wooden posts. One possibility is to purchase the foam in sheets and cut shapes to fit. Your piano technician may have experience in doing this, and may also be able to help you avoid damaging the soundboard or creating the buzzes that can accompany this technique—ask for pointers. This method of loudness control won't be possible if you have a grand outfitted with a humidity-control system or an electronic player-piano system.

 Place a rug under a grand piano to absorb sound.

The sound of a grand piano is sent out into the room via the lid, which is propped up at an angle on the stick—and by a considerable reflection by the floor of

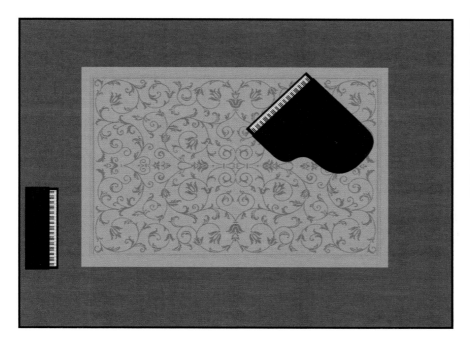

Moving the piano away from room corners and partway along the length of a wall, and/or turning it at an angle this way or that, can sometimes mitigate acoustic problems. Experiment and listen at different places within the room. If your floor is a sound-reflecting material, the loudness can be greatly reduced by placing a rug under the piano.

sound emanating from the underside of the sound-board. If your floor covering is a sound-reflecting material such as wood, stone, or tile, the loudness can be greatly reduced by placing a rug under the piano. To absorb even more sound, place a thick pad under the rug. Experiment with the size of the rug or carpet and its orientation under the piano. Other, more temporary solutions: place a dog bed or a collection of throw pillows under the piano.

6 Place objects under a grand piano to scatter sound.

Perhaps you don't want to absorb the sound coming out of the bottom of your grand piano, but just want to disperse it more evenly throughout the room. The space under a grand can be used for storage chests, plants, knickknacks, and the like.

Let's say you've tried some or all of these steps; you've noticed some improvement, but not enough. Here are some more advanced treatments for the room itself.

7 Cover or expose hard wall and/or window surfaces.

Glass tends to reflect high-frequency sound, while allowing lower frequencies to pass right through, never to return. A room with a lot of exposed glass will often sound harsh and bright, as if the treble notes are accentuated, but the problem may in fact be a lack of bass energy, or an imbalance between the bass and treble energy in the space. Covering these windows can help to absorb higher-frequency sound energy and thus restore the balance of bass and treble. Heavy fabric such as velour, sewn into gathers, works best to absorb sound. Sheer, semitransparent fabrics are much less effective, but can have subtle acoustical effects, if that's all that's required, and can be used to "fine-tune" the room.

Large areas of exposed bare walls and ceiling can produce a similar effect as glass, but are more effective at preserving bass energy. In a room that sounds too muddy—i.e., it makes music sound indistinct—sound-absorbing wall coverings such as tapestries, or hanging rugs, might be worth a try. Also available are fabric-wrapped, sound-absorbing panels that will work well in homes, though their "professional" look lacks the personal touch of one's own home furnishings.

In a space with high ceilings, hanging banners, flags, or other materials from the ceiling can cut down on reverberation.

Be aware that most household sound-absorbing materials do not work very well below about 200 Hz (about middle C). If your acoustical problem occurs below this frequency, look to other techniques or materials to solve it, including professional acoustical materials designed specifically to address low-frequency sound.

8 *Add or remove upholstered furniture and other sound-absorbing objects.*

Adding sofas, pillows, upholstered chairs, carpets, and other sound-absorbing décor can reduce excess reverberation and loudness, and removing such objects will increase them. Even placing cloths over coffee and side tables will cut down the reflection of sound just a little bit. Plush, overstuffed furniture produces the greatest sound-absorbing effect. Upholstered furniture of leather, wood, or metal has less effect.

9 *Add or remove sound-scattering wall hangings, objects, and furniture.*

Be careful not to add *too* many sound-absorbing objects to the room—it's possible to go too far, making the room sound too dead, dry, or soft. Sometimes you don't want to absorb sound—you merely want to scatter or diffuse it more evenly about the room. The sound will then be more natural and less "hollow" without necessarily losing reverberation and loudness. In scattering sound, your goal is to use objects both large and small with complex shapes to break up large expanses of flat surfaces. Again, some experimentation is in order. Examples of sound-scattering objects are bookshelves (not too full), tables, chandeliers, room-dividing screens, and sculpture. Designing a space with ceiling beams can also scatter sound.

You've tried everything! Below is one last word of advice.

10 *Hire a professional.*

Some of the acoustical phenomena described here can be confusing to the untrained. Even worse, some problematic combinations of piano and room may have more than one of these problems. If you've tried everything and still don't hear an improvement, consider seeking expert help from a piano technician or a room-acoustics consultant (acoustician). Such professionals may be able to help you design or furnish the space for the best sound, suggest appropriate acoustical materials, and direct you to local suppliers for those materials.

MOVING THE FAMILY PIANO

Russ Vitt

MOST OF US have seen or heard a humorous story of ordinary people attempting to move the heaviest thing ever made: a piano. Just thinking about it can give otherwise macho adults lower-back pain. A typical vertical piano weighs 300 to 500 pounds; some larger uprights can weigh over 800. Grand pianos typically weigh about 100 pounds per foot of length, but some concert grands weigh as much as 1,400 pounds. While pianos are abnormally heavy, with thousands of moving parts, they are also fragile. Additionally, many pianos have fine finishes that are sensitive to extremes of temperature and humidity. Then, to make things even more interesting, there are obstacles to maneuver, such as steps, turns, overhangs, hills, culs-de-sac, wet grass, and long gravel driveways. So, as someone who needs a piano moved, what are your options?

As the owner of a professional piano-moving company, I can't recommend moving a piano yourself. Risk of personal injury and damage to the instrument outweigh the advantage of saving a few dollars. Here are just a few of the many mistakes people make, and the dangers that await you if you try to do it yourself:

Letting the piano get away from you: Gravity can be a powerful tool when used properly, but it's dangerous if not respected. If someone slips or loses their grip, the piano will start moving by itself. In *The Piano Book*, Larry Fine tells the story of some friends who tried to move an upright piano. As they tipped the piano back, the bottom scooted away from them, causing the instrument to fall. The top edge gouged the wall and severed an electric cable, which started a fire that burned down the house. If something like this can happen in the home, imagine what gravity will do on steps or a steep outside grade. I'm sure you've seen those commercials in which a piano is being hoisted by crane and falls from a great height, breaking into smithereens. The truth, though, is that for many moves, particularly those above the second floor, hoisting by crane is much safer than moving a piano by hand. In some kinds of geography, additional equipment and creativity may be needed. One move we did in hilly San Francisco, on a street too steep for a truck to maneuver, required three professionals, two tow straps, an all-terrain vehicle, and an SUV! Don't think you can do this yourself.

Moving a piano without securing it to the vehicle: A piano sitting on a truck may seem just fine in the driveway, but a piano is not like a refrigerator, which is heavy mostly at its base. An upright piano's weight is evenly distributed from top to bottom, and some may even be top-heavy. Even a slight

A moving crew takes a baby grand piano out of a second story window because the steps were not an option. A forklift was used to secure the piano and lower it down.

turn or grade can encourage a piano to jump ship. One story has the proud piano owner playing his instrument in the back of a pickup as they ride down the road. When the truck turned at a traffic light, the piano, motivated by inertia to keep going straight, did a back flip out of the truck, whereupon it ceased being in one piece.

Moving a grand piano without removing the legs and lyre: We delivered a grand to a customer who thought he was being helpful when he removed the entire sliding-door assembly from the family room. He didn't realize that a grand piano is moved only after it's been laid on its side and its legs and pedal lyre have been removed. The caster wheels attached to the legs are designed for minor adjustments of location in-room, not for the driveway or the yard. Stories abound of grand pianos being dragged over cement, gravel, grass, deep carpeting, or in-floor heating ducts, only to have the legs snap off and the instrument collapse. In addition, a grand must be protected by the proper special equipment before it can be moved. The piano is placed on its side on a special moving board, and secured with straps and blankets. The lid is either removed or positioned to protect it from damage.

Almost as scary as moving a piano yourself—or scarier, depending on the outcome—but without the cost savings, is finding a nonprofessional mover. Typically, this category includes anyone who will move anything anywhere for one low price. They can be found online at what seems like a cheap price, and some of them demand payment before pickup. To make matters worse, sometimes these folks are merely brokers and have no truck or workers. They take your money, then find someone to do the job. There's a well-known saying: "The bitterness of poor service remains long after the sweetness of low price is forgotten." This is very true of piano moving.

Professional furniture movers are a step better, but you run the risk of being assigned to a driver who has little training or experience in moving a piano. Many drivers hate to see a piano in a shipment because they know pianos require special care. When the largest household mover in the U.S. bought another large mover in the 1990s, the wife of one of their top managers hired my company to move her piano. She knew the system, and wanted the comfort of knowing that the crew moving her cherished instrument moved several pianos every day, not several a year.

The best way to avoid unprofessional service is to look for a professional piano mover. You can find good companies online. (Yellow Pages ads are old-school; some professional movers, particularly those who provide interstate service, don't advertise in local books.) Just check a few important issues:

The name of a company that specializes in moving pianos will most often include the word "piano" or "keyboard." An interstate mover's website should offer its Department of Transportation (DOT) number, which indicates that it is regulated and has the required insurance and authorization. Some states also regulate intrastate movers, and require them to publish their state registration number in advertisements. Regulated or not, a company should be able, on request, to show you proof of insurance. The company's actual street address should accompany a local phone number. Check the company's Better Business Bureau rating at **www.BBB.org**. Check for its membership status in the National Association of Music Merchants (NAMM), the American Moving and Storage Association (AMSA), or that the owner is a member of the Piano Technicians Guild (PTG). How long a company has been in business will suggest whether it has been able to weather economic storms while continuing to satisfy its customers. A positive reference from one or more friends, family, or a professional such as a piano dealer or technician is always helpful. I suggest you exercise a reasonable

A steep hillside poses a problem for moving a piano.

A blizzard in Colorado made truck and parking access almost impossible. The truck ramps allowed the use of a shuttle truck (an ATV) to bring the piano up the steep and icy hill.

amount of due diligence, and try to use a company for which you have been given two or three referrals.

Long-distance moving presents its own set of options. Basic service involves a local piano mover picking up the piano and holding it in storage. Then the long-distance trucking company picks it up and takes it to the destination piano mover, who delivers it to the home. If you're moving your own household goods in a rental truck, you should have the local piano mover at the point of origin move the piano from the house into the truck and properly secure it, then have the local mover at the destination remove it from the truck and move it into the house. This method is usually the cheapest, the downside being that there are two or three different companies to deal with.

Better still is working with one company from start to finish. The office folks, the logo on the truck, and the uniforms on the moving personnel remain the same throughout your piano's travels. This way, you don't have to worry about complex scheduling problems or liability issues. For example, what happens if your rental truck or moving van is delayed? Will the local movers at the points of origin and destination still be available when you need them? If damage is discovered after your piano is moved

Hefting a heavy organ safely takes planning, coordination, and a few muscles.

into your new home, which of the three parties is responsible?

The best companies offer custom trucks and trailers specifically designed to transport pianos. Air-ride suspension, which keeps road vibrations and pot holes from shaking your piano apart, has proven to give the best ride. Proper load control, lift gates, and ramps further ensure that your piano is getting special care. Climate control is critical during especially warm or cold seasons; some finishes can be ruined if allowed to freeze. A professional piano mover handles all these variables for you.

When calling a long-distance moving company, be as specific as possible about any known difficulties associated with the move, such as difficult truck access in a rural or urban area, a very steep driveway, or no cell-phone service. Verify that the price is all-inclusive (includes moving the piano between house and truck), and not just for curbside delivery. Ask about any additional charges that might apply if, for example, you later decide to have the piano delivered to the second floor instead of the first.

Check your budget and schedule to determine the level of service you need. For long-distance moves, typically allow 30 days for pickup and another 30 days for delivery. If the move needs to be done more quickly, it will likely cost more; if you can give the mover more time, it will cost less. Most companies accept credit cards, which can allow you to spread the cost over several payments if necessary. Then sit back and enjoy a professional experience. Although a little more expensive than the nonprofessional kind, it will be less stressful for both you and your piano.

BUYING A DIGITAL PIANO
An Introduction

Alden Skinner and *Piano Buyer* Staff

IF, AFTER HAVING READ "**Acoustic or Digital: What's Best for Me?**," you've decided on a digital piano, the next step is to shop for and select the right model for your needs. There are currently some 200 models of digital piano on the market. Narrowing the field requires exploring some basic issues.

Style and Price

Digital pianos come in three basic physical styles: **slab**, **console** (also sometimes called vertical or upright), and **grand** (see illustrations). Which instrument style you choose will depend on use, space limitations, furniture requirements, and price.

Slab: A *slab* is simply a keyboard and, usually, pedal(s), without a stand. If you need to take the piano to a gig, or if home is a dorm room or a small studio apartment and you need to make the most efficient use of every square inch, you may opt for a slab that can be placed on a stand or table for practice, and stuck in a closet when not in use. Keep in mind, however, that slabs currently on the market weigh from 20 to 85 pounds, so be sure to choose one with a weight that you can handle.

Slabs generally come with a single pedal, but for many models, optional stands and three-pedal units are available. You may need to buy the slab, stand, and pedal unit separately and put them together, or a retailer you buy from may sell you all the parts as a package deal. Slab digital pianos start as low as $200, with most priced between $500 and $2,000, and a few as high as $7,000. An optional matching stand with integrated pedal assembly usually costs $200 to $300 more, but a simple, generic stand can be had for as little as $40. Note that some slabs don't come with a stand to hold your music; you might need to provide one.

Console: A *console* is a keyboard with a stand or cabinet that contains a built-in pedal assembly. A console may look like an upright acoustic piano or organ, or simply like a digital piano. Consoles generally have a stand and pedal assembly built in at the factory. However, as mentioned above, many slabs can effectively be turned into a console by separately buying a stand with an integrated pedal assembly.

The cabinetry of console models ranges from two flat side supports with a cross member for stability, to elegant designs that would look at home in the most posh surroundings. It's common for models in this category to be available in multiple finish options, including synthetic wood grain, real-wood veneers, and, on some of the better models, the lustrous polished ebony often found on acoustic pianos. Most of these models have the usual three pedals. Console digitals start at about $500, with most priced between $1,000 and $5,000, and a few as high as $10,000.

Grand: If the piano will be in elegant surroundings, you may choose a *grand*-style digital. Digital grands come in lengths of about three feet—just long enough to suggest the shape of a baby grand—to about five feet. Like some of the console models, these are often available in a variety of wood-grain finishes and the polished ebony finish common in

Digital consoles

Roland

Slab pianos

Yamaha

Digital grand

kawai

today's acoustic grands. You will usually pay a premium for the elegant furniture. Grands start at $1,500, with most priced between $3,000 and $10,000, and a few as high as $20,000.

Note that there is little or no relationship between an instrument's physical style and its musical features—slabs are often used on stage by professional musicians, and grand-shaped digitals may have features no better than the non-grand versions they're based on. However, the larger spaces enclosed by a grand-piano cabinet and some console cabinets can accommodate more, larger, and more advantageously positioned speakers, particularly bass speakers (woofers). This, and the sympathetic vibration of a wood cabinet, may result in better sound quality from the onboard speakers of some cabinet models than that found in digitals without cabinets, especially slabs.

Speakers, Headphones, and Stage Pianos

Most people who buy a digital piano do so, in part, so that they can play with headphones and not disturb

anyone. For that reason, *all* digital pianos come with headphone jacks. When used with headphones, most instruments' onboard (internal) speakers are silenced. Also, nearly all digital pianos can have the sound of their onboard speakers rerouted to an external amplifier and speakers if, for example, the onboard speakers are inadequate for the venue, or if you'd prefer to use the speakers of your home audio system.

Some slab digitals come *without* onboard speakers. These are called *stage pianos*, and are generally used by professional musicians in performance venues where an external amplifier and speakers are expected to be present. Not having onboard speakers saves a little bit in cost, weight, and space. However, if you're planning to use the instrument at home most of the time, the convenience of having at least some onboard speakers is generally worth the trade-off.

(Note: The *stage piano* category also includes a few models of electronic keyboard with fewer than 88 notes and/or with keys that are not weighted to feel like an acoustic piano. For our purposes, those models are not considered digital pianos and are not included in our database.)

C1 Air
DIGITAL PIANO

The range of digital pianos from KORG sets a new world standard in digital piano performance.

B1
DIGITAL PIANO

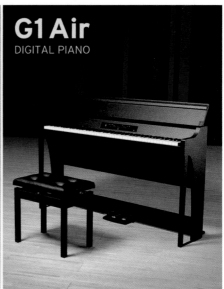

G1 Air
DIGITAL PIANO

LP-380
DIGITAL PIANO

KORG NEW. MUSIC. ALWAYS.

korg.com

Taking Stock of Your Musical Needs

Unless you expect to buy another piano in a year or so, you need to consider your long-term requirements. Who will be the piano's primary player today, and what are his or her musical interests and ambitions? If it's for the family, how long will it be until the youngest child has the opportunity to learn? Does Mom or Dad harbor any musical interests? If so, it's likely that one family member or another will use the instrument for many years to come. This argues for getting a higher-quality instrument, whose advantages of better tone, touch, and features will be appreciated over time.

If multiple players will use the instrument, it needs to meet the expectations of the most advanced player. At the same time, a beginner in the family will benefit from features that are of no interest to the advanced player, and still another family member may just want to fool around with the instrument once in a while. Easy-play features and educational software will keep these players happy—and you might be surprised how many people are enticed into learning to play as a result of these easy first steps. So, obviously, an individual player may search among a very narrow range of instruments, while a family may have to balance the different needs of several people. Fortunately, the wealth of available choices can easily accommodate any combination of individual and/or family needs.

Instrumental Voices (Sounds) and Ensemble Capabilities

Sounds in digital pianos are also known as *voices* or *tones*. Voices can include such sounds as:

- Individual musical instruments, such as piano, electric piano, guitar, flute, etc.
- Combinations of instruments, such as a string or brass ensemble
- Percussion sounds, such as snare drum or cymbals
- The human voice
- Unusual sound effects, such as gunshot or helicopter

Some digital pianos may contain more than one example of a particular type of voice, especially piano, such as bright- and mellow-sounding pianos, or pianos that mimic the tonal characteristics of several different well-known makes of concert grand.

Standard or *traditional* digital pianos are designed mainly to emulate the acoustic piano, with the optional accompaniment of one or more other voices. Most will allow you to split the keyboard so that the right hand plays a melody in one instrumental voice while the left hand plays an accompaniment in another (such as piano and string bass); or to layer the sounds so that two or more instrumental voices sound together (such as piano and strings) when each key is played. These days, even the least-expensive standard digitals usually have at least a few different piano voices, as well as a dozen or two other instrumental voices, such as harpsichord, church and jazz organ, vibes, and strings. Many models contain hundreds of voices, built-in rhythms, sound effects like *reverb* and *chorus*, and a metronome for keeping time, among other features.

Other, slightly more expensive models, called *ensemble* or *arranger* digital pianos, generally have all the features of standard digitals, but also come with two other major features: Easy-Play and Auto-Accompaniment. With *Easy-Play*, playing as little as a single key will trigger the sound of an entire chord. With *Auto-Accompaniment*, an entire musical combo or orchestra (strings, horns, percussion, etc.) will back you up as you play, and automatically change

its accompaniment to match your melody or changing chords. These backing tracks, known as *styles*, come in all kinds of musical forms, such as Swing, Latin, Rock, World, and so forth—with many different rhythms and special effects. The best of these styles are of a caliber that will please the most discerning ear.

You might not think you need the additional capabilities of an ensemble digital, but having them can enable the beginner, as well as family members who don't take lessons, to have a lot more fun and sound like pros with minimal practice. The instant gratification provided by auto-accompaniment might keep a player with low attention span more fully engaged. For an advancing player, the opportunities for musical creativity are significantly enhanced. On the other hand, if you're the only player and expect to play mostly classical piano music, you may not want to spend money on the ensemble feature.

When looking over the specs of digital pianos, it's easy to be impressed by the large number of voices that some models contain, and there was a time in the recent past when the number of voices was closely related to an instrument's quality and price. That's no longer necessarily true. First, the price of memory has plummeted to the extent that even the least expensive models can be outfitted with hundreds of voices. Second, the quality of the voices, which is related to the amount of memory they take up, varies considerably; more voices doesn't necessarily mean a better instrument. It's expensive for a manufacturer to create or purchase custom, high-quality sounds, and these sounds take up a lot of memory. When an instrument contains more than a few dozen voices, often most of the rest are from a standardized set of voices, sometimes usable only for playback of files created elsewhere, but not selectable from the instrument panel by the user; or from a company's library of legacy (older) voices; both usually using less memory, and therefore of lower quality than the company's latest offerings. That said, these additional voices can still come in handy for the power user who needs a certain unusual sound or combination of sounds, or for the playback of some music files that call for them. And ensemble digitals, with the diverse instrumentation contained in their many styles, can make good use of the extra voices. But most home users of standard digital pianos will find a dozen or two high-quality voices to be more than sufficient.

Keep in mind also that we've been speaking here only of an instrument's internal voices. These days, it's also possible to install additional high-quality piano and instrumental voices on your computer, and play them using your digital piano as a keyboard controller; or to download voices to the digital piano directly from the Internet via Bluetooth (both discussed later).

Piano Sound and Acoustic Piano Realism

Manufacturers create digital piano sounds either by recording actual pianos (known as *sampling*) or by using mathematical algorithms to mimic the acoustic properties of piano sounds (known as *physical modeling*). Some instruments employ a combination of the two methods. Whereas even the most expensive acoustic piano has only a single set of sound characteristics, many modestly priced digital pianos can reproduce the sounds of multiple sampled concert grands, pianos with different tonal characteristics, and imitations of vintage electronic keyboards, among others. Digital pianos that use physical modeling, and some that use sampling, may even allow the user to make extensive custom refinements to the built-in piano sounds.

Some kinds of music, especially classical, require a level of musical expression that traditional acoustic pianos have evolved to satisfy. For those who play, or plan to play, this music, the ability of a digital piano to imitate the sound, touch, and pedaling of an acoustic piano is important. For players of other kinds of music, however, the ability of a digital piano to sound or play like an acoustic one may be less important. Although virtually all digital pianos are designed to imitate acoustic pianos to *some* extent—that's why they're called *digital pianos*, not *electronic keyboards*—they vary considerably in how accurately and thoroughly they do so.

The better digital pianos more accurately imitate an acoustic piano by, among other things:

- Re-creating the piano's acoustical resonance, and the sympathetic vibrations of the strings of an acoustic piano's *unplayed* notes—that is, the keys the player *hasn't* struck—especially when the sustain pedal is depressed, as well as the sound of a vibrating string being silenced by a damper when a key is released: sounds that are subconsciously part of the acoustic-piano experience.

- Having a larger number of speakers, or speakers that are better positioned; or special features like a soundboard speaker system, in which an acoustic-piano–style soundboard is used as a "speaker."
- Containing higher-quality key sensors to more accurately translate the speed with which a key is depressed into sound volume; re-creating the acoustic-piano action's feel of "escapement" as a key is depressed, and having wooden keys with keytops that imitate the feel of ivory, which absorbs sweat and so is less slippery to the touch than plastic.
- Including three pedals that perform the same functions as on an acoustic grand (soft, sostenuto, sustain), and a sustain pedal capable of half pedaling, a pedaling technique used by advanced players.

Note that all of the models that we consider to be digital pianos have 88 notes, the keys are weighted, and, in virtually all of them, the touchweights are graded (i.e., the resistance to your touch gradually decreases from bass to treble) across the range of the keyboard—all just as in an acoustic piano. Instruments with fewer than 88 notes, or with semi-weighted keyboards that depend on springs for their weight, should be avoided by those looking for a realistic acoustic-piano experience.

Connecting to a Computer

Virtually all digital pianos can be connected to a personal computer, allowing you to:

- Use computer software and a printer to record, notate (write), edit, and print the music you play
- Use software that will, for example, help you learn to play piano, train your musical ear, or teach you music history
- Use your digital piano as a keyboard controller for playing virtual instruments (i.e., instrumental sounds that reside on your computer)
- Play duets or practice with someone in a different location

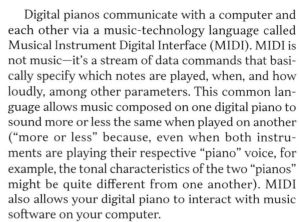

Digital pianos communicate with a computer and each other via a music-technology language called Musical Instrument Digital Interface (MIDI). MIDI is not music—it's a stream of data commands that basically specify which notes are played, when, and how loudly, among other parameters. This common language allows music composed on one digital piano to sound more or less the same when played on another ("more or less" because, even when both instruments are playing their respective "piano" voice, for example, the tonal characteristics of the two "pianos" might be quite different from one another). MIDI also allows your digital piano to interact with music software on your computer.

Most digital pianos connect to a computer via a cable that plugs into USB ports on both ends. (The USB port on the digital piano is technically known as *USB to Host*.) A few of the less-expensive models rely on an older method: a cable from the MIDI ports of the piano to a USB port on the computer. The newest method of connecting to a computer is wirelessly via Bluetooth.

Bluetooth and Internet Connectivity

An increasing number of digital pianos are now equipped with Bluetooth, to link to the Internet using your smartphone or tablet as a hotspot. This feature is still in its infancy, so many of its potential uses are not yet known; here are some of the ways it's currently being used:

- Stream virtually unlimited music, sounds, rhythms, and styles from the Internet, and play along with them and/or record them for later playback
- Access an app on your smartphone to change your digital piano's touch, tone, and tuning
- Access an app on your smart-phone for sophisticated recording in MIDI or digital audio
- Access sheet music from the Internet and use an app on your smartphone to turn pages
- Access apps and online video tutorials to learn to play piano, or to teach yourself a particular song
- Access the piano manufacturer's user guide, instructional videos, and apps to learn to use and customize your instrument

Recording and Playback

Most digital pianos allow you to record your playing for future playback. Here are some of the reasons you might want to do this:

- To critically review your own piano playing, possibly with a teacher
- To play a duet with a recording you previously made of yourself, or one made by someone else
- To create a "one-person band" by recording different instrumental parts from the same piece of music on separate tracks and combining them into a single performance
- To create a soundtrack for a home video

As mentioned earlier, digital pianos create and record music as a sequence of MIDI commands—thus the name *MIDI sequencer* for the most common form of internal recorder in a digital piano. This type of recording system is popular because it requires relatively little memory, and because of its simplicity and flexibility: If you later want to play the music back with different instrumental sounds, all you need do is specify the different voices, usually by pressing a button or two—you don't have to re-record the music.

Digital piano models vary in their internal recording (MIDI sequencing) capabilities from one track to about 16 tracks. However, the trend in the industry today is to output the music from the instrument to a computer, and to use computer software, not the piano's internal recorder, for sophisticated recording and music editing. This MIDI sequencing software is generally inexpensive, runs faster than the piano's internal recorder, and is constantly evolving in sophistication. Thus, most digital pianos today have no more than three to five internal recording tracks, and often as few as one or two. A minority of models still have as many as 16 tracks, and the larger number of tracks could be convenient if, say, you wanted to sketch out an idea requiring many instrumental voices and a computer wasn't nearby. But a few tracks will be more than enough for most nonprofessional users.

If you want to create a very high-quality recording, however, it's generally necessary to record in a digital audio format, such as MP3 or .WAV, instead of MIDI; that is, to record the actual sound, rather than just the MIDI commands. This used to be the exclusive province of specialized, expensive workstations, but the ability to record in digital audio has now trickled down to many digital piano models. This type of recording is much more memory-consuming than MIDI sequencing, so it's usually stored on a USB memory device, such as a flash drive, plugged into the piano. The recording can then be transferred to a computer, where you could use it, for example, as the soundtrack of a home video, or upload it to social media, or e-mail it to family and friends.

SELECTED OTHER FEATURES

External Flash-Drive Storage

Some digital pianos allow you to store your recorded music and other files on USB flash drives or memory cards plugged into a port provided for this purpose. (This port is technically known as *USB to Device*.) These may be files you've recorded, files you've downloaded from the Internet, or files of additional rhythm patterns and styles, additional voices, and user data such as the instrument's internal settings.

Vocal Support

Some digital pianos feature a microphone connection, on the theory that many who love to play also love to sing. At its most basic level, this feature simply uses the digital piano's audio system as a PA system for the singer. However, some models can also employ effects processing to enhance the performer's voice in some way, or can combine the vocal input with harmonizing to create four-part harmony. Some will also display karaoke lyrics, which, on some higher-end models, can also be output to a video display, such as a TV monitor. Without the vocal support feature, it would still be possible to run vocals through the instrument's speaker system via its line-in connection, but the microphone would require its own amplifier (or the use of an amplified mic), and the special effects mentioned above would not be available.

Educational Support

Some digital pianos include educational extras, such as digital piano lessons, a DVD, or a teaching app that can guide the beginner through a number of factory-installed or downloaded songs, even integrating with

Internet connectivity to provide interactive coaching. While not a substitute for a private teacher or class lessons, these materials can be very useful to those who have only a casual interest in learning to play, or whose budget for lessons is limited.

In this tutorial, we've only barely scratched the surface of the amazing features of today's digital pianos. You can read about these and other features in greater depth in our online-only **"Digital Piano Basics"** articles. Read on for information and tips about the process of shopping for a digital piano.

Shopping Options

Your shopping options depend on the type of digital piano you've decided to buy and the region you live in. In North America, different categories of instruments are available through different types of outlets. Furniture-style models, particularly the higher-end models manufactured by the largest suppliers, are available mostly through traditional bricks-and-mortar piano dealers, though increasingly they're finding their way into other types of outlet. The lower-priced console, slab, or stage models, and some of the less widely distributed brands, are available from a cross section of traditional bricks-and-mortar music retailers, club and warehouse chains such as Costco, consumer-electronics chains such as Best Buy, big-box instrument stores such as Guitar Center, and online retailers such as Amazon, Kraft Music, Musicians Friend, and Sweetwater Music. If you enter into a search engine the specific brand and model of instrument you're looking for, and the name of the city you live in or near, the search results will usually show both online and local sources for that model.

At a bricks-and-mortar retailer, prices are usually somewhat flexible, and negotiating the price of a digital piano is no different from negotiating the price of

an acoustic piano (as is discussed in "**Piano Buying Basics**," elsewhere in this volume). But wherever you shop, you'll find that many of the simpler console digitals and nearly all slab and stage-piano models that are sold through a variety of local and online stores are virtually always sold at the same price. This is due to a pricing model called *minimum advertised price* (or MAP), that's used for many categories of products.

A manufacturer's or distributor's MAP is the lowest price at which a dealer is allowed to advertise an item. Since prices are easily compared and all retailers want an even chance at winning your business, everyone advertises at the MAP. And since the MAP is typically lower than the price at which the dealer might have preferred to sell the item, the selling price is rarely lower than the MAP. Therefore, MAP has become the standard pricing for all non-piano-dealer models of digital piano. (Note: In practice, retailers will often get around the MAP advertising restriction by offering discounts on accessories when you buy the instrument. Also, the restriction is only on the *advertised* price, not the selling price. With online retailers, it may be possible to get a lower price if you can speak with a salesperson over the phone.)

In deciding where to buy, consider what level of service and support you require. Do you:

- Want to try out an instrument before buying?
- Need the help of a salesperson in choosing an instrument or in learning how to use it?
- Need someone to come out to your home to install or set up the instrument?
- Want local warranty support in case you encounter a problem?

If the answer to any of these is "yes," then you should buy from a piano dealer, or other bricks-and-mortar music dealer, as these services will not be available from online retailers, and will be minimal at best from mass merchandisers like Costco. To some extent this will limit the models available to you, as bricks-and-mortar dealers are more likely to stock models whose higher prices and profit margin can support the services they provide. On the other hand, if you're experienced at buying music technology online, pretty much know what you want, or are a beginner with few requirements and just buying something inexpensive, you may find it quicker, easier, and cheaper to buy online.

Tips for the Serious Shopper

If you're going to be shopping for an instrument among local bricks-and-mortar music retailers, the following shopping tips may be useful:

- *Calibrate your ears.* Before you shop, "calibrate" your ears by listening to recordings of solo piano. Listen to whatever type of music you enjoy—and use the headphones you bought for your digital piano. This will embed in your mind, as a benchmark, the sound of high-quality acoustic pianos.
- *Evaluate the tone.* Evaluating an instrument's tone is very subjective, and judging the tone of instruments that have a lot of voices can be overwhelming. Your best bet is to select the five or six instrument voices you think you'll use most, and make them the standard for comparison as you shop. If you choose the digital piano on which those voices sound best to you, it's likely you'll find the other voices satisfying as well. Take detailed notes and use them to establish your favorite(s).
- *Turn off effects.* Be aware that the default voice settings of most digital pianos include some degree of reverberation. This isn't a bad thing, but it's worthwhile to listen to the piano voice, and any you, with reverb and all other effects turned off. This will allow you to judge those voices without any coloration or masking from the effects.
- *Evaluate the touch.* Aside from sound, the most important element in the selection of an instrument is likely to be the feel of the action. You'll be selecting from a variety of actions that all try to emulate the feel of an acoustic piano—some lighter, some heavier. Just as there is no single correct piano sound, there is no single correct touch; rather, there is a range of acceptable touches. If you spend most of your playing time with a heavy action, then when you encounter an instrument with a lighter action, you'll play too heavily—and vice versa. The cure is to play as many instruments as possible, as often as possible. Listen to how each piano responds and adjust your touch accordingly. With experience, you'll learn to adapt.
- *Use the salesperson.* Digital pianos are really computers disguised as pianos, and like some

features of a PC, many of the capabilities of digitals are hidden from view, accessible by pressing a sequence of buttons or through multi-screen menus. While the owner's manual will explain how to access these features or sounds, it's impractical for you to study the manuals of every instrument under consideration. Enter the salesperson! This is one of those instances where a well-trained salesperson can be invaluable. But remember that the salesperson is not going home with you, so don't be swayed by his or her talent. Listen to what they have to say, but focus your attention on the instrument itself.

- **Used digitals.** Because digital-piano technology advances at a blistering pace relative to acoustic-piano technology, there is much less interest in used digitals than in used acoustics. Many of today's digital pianos eclipse the capabilities of the models of even five years ago. Combine this technological advancement with the fact that support of older instruments may be limited—electronics manufacturers are required to maintain replacement parts for only seven years after production ceases—and investing in older models becomes worthy of serious second thoughts.

MY OTHER PIANO IS A COMPUTER
An Introduction to Software Pianos

Alden Skinner

IF THE DIGITAL PIANO is thought of as a complete instrument that's ready to play right out of the box, piano software can be thought of as part of a "piano kit." The standard digital piano is completely self-contained in that it's made up of the memory and processing electronics required to produce the sound, the firmware (software residing on a chip) that is the source of the sound, a keyboard to control the sound, and, more often than not, the audio system needed to hear the sound. If viewed as separate components of a piano kit, however, a personal computer can take on the role of memory and processing, piano software becomes the sound source, a keyboard (very possibly your digital piano) provides control, and powered monitor speakers and/or headphones let you hear your new invention. If you have a digital piano (or an acoustic piano with hybrid features) and a personal computer (Mac or Windows), you already have most of the ingredients of a software-based piano.

The obvious question: If you already have a digital piano, why would you want to add a software piano? Most digital pianos are capable of producing more than one piano sound, but typically, all of these sounds are based on a single piano as a sample source. Think of it this way: If you could add a Bösendorfer, Blüthner, Fazioli, or Steinway to your palette of piano samples for only the cost of the software, would you do it? (I hear the sounds of pianos and computers being pushed together even now.) How about being able to virtually design your own instrument with piano software based on physical modeling? (*Physical modeling* is the use of mathematical algorithms to mimic the acoustic properties of piano sounds.)

Adding a software piano to your existing piano, or building your own piano from a "piano kit," is a bit more involved than putting your computer and your piano in the same room—but not by much. Let's take a look at the requirements on both the computer and piano sides. Since the requirements for the piano are pretty simple, we'll start there.

Digital and Hybrid Piano Considerations

If your existing piano is going to serve as the basis for your extended piano family, the minimum requirement is that it have MIDI-out capability—USB MIDI makes it slightly easier, but regular MIDI connections will do as well. The good news here is that all currently available digital pianos and most acoustic hybrid pianos already have, or can add, this capability. The next step is to be able to get your existing "host" piano to stop producing its own sound. For digital pianos, this consists of a brief trip to the owner's manual to learn how to set it up as a "controller" or "master" keyboard. Acoustic pianos must either be capable of "silent" mode or must be converted to enable it (see the article "**Hybrid Pianos**").

Computer Considerations

Requirements for the computer vary considerably, depending on the piano software used and the choices you make in software settings. Just as with digital pianos, sample-based software is highly dependent on the size of the computer's memory, while physical modeling software—which creates the sound in real time rather than retrieving an existing sound sample—primarily depends on the speed of the computer's processor. At a minimum, hardware requirements will involve processor type and speed, and the amount of random-access memory (RAM) and hard-disk space. These requirements range from packages that can run on most recent-vintage mid-range computers, to those requiring higher-speed multi-core processors, 8 Gigabytes (GB) of RAM, over 250 GB of free hard-disk space (preferably on a fast SSD drive), and a dedicated sound card. Either way, you need to check the hardware requirements of the individual software package you'd like to run to make sure it will work properly on your computer—or use it as an excuse to get a new computer.

Aside from making sure that you have enough memory to store and run these packages, processor and sound-card choices will also keep latency in check. Latency is how long it takes the computer to produce a sound from the time you press a key. When latency becomes noticeable, your brain doesn't know whether to slow your playing so that the sound can catch up, or to speed up to make the sound happen faster. Neither of these works. (Anyone who plays the pipe organ knows what latency is, and will adapt to it without a second thought.)

Software

This is where the real fun starts. There are currently dozens of software-piano packages available, at prices ranging from under $50 to over $500. These include both sample-based packages and packages based on physical modeling. There are products on the market for Mac, PC, and even mobile-device platforms. Several host acoustic pianos (i.e., the sources of the samples) are available via software, including instruments made by Bechstein, Bösendorfer, Blüthner, Fazioli, Kawai, Steingraeber, Steinway, and Yamaha. If you'd like to add some period instruments to your palette, there are also packages with samples from historical fortepianos.

If you're not particularly into computers, software pianos may not be for you. But if you enjoy even a mild bit of tinkering, and have dreamed of owning a collection of the world's finest pianos or even of "designing" your own piano, you may find software pianos an irresistible temptation. If you're interested in following the world of piano software, it's discussed in Piano World's "**Digital Pianos—Synths & Keyboards**" forum.

HYBRID PIANOS

Alden Skinner and Larry Fine

MENTION THE WORD *hybrid* today and most people think of cars that combine a traditional internal-combustion engine with an electric motor to improve gas mileage and reduce emissions. By definition, a hybrid—whether a rose, a breed of dog, or a car— is a composite: the result of the combination of two different backgrounds or technologies. Now the piano has joined the ranks of the hybrids.

A hybrid piano combines electronic, mechanical, and/or acoustical aspects of both acoustic and digital pianos, in order to improve or expand the capabilities of the resulting instrument. But while the term hybrid piano is relatively new, the practice of combining elements from acoustic and digital pianos is more than 25 years old.

A hybrid piano can be created from an acoustic or a digital piano, but we need to be clear about our definitions of *acoustic* and *digital*. The essential difference between acoustic and digital pianos is in how each produces sound. In an acoustic piano, a sound is produced by the mechanical act of a hammer hitting strings, which causes the strings to vibrate. In a digital piano, the sound is produced electronically, either by playing a recording of a note previously *digitally sampled* (recorded) from an acoustic piano, or by *physical modeling*, in which a mathematical algorithm closely approximates the sound of that note on an acoustic piano. (Here we're speaking only of that aspect of a digital piano that is designed to produce a piano-like sound. Digitals typically also can produce the sounds of many other instruments and non-instruments.)

Acoustic-based Hybrids: the MIDI Controller

The first hybrid pianos were not new instruments, but modifications of already existing acoustic pianos. In 1982, with the advent of the Musical Instrument Digital Interface (MIDI), a computer language for electronic musical instruments, instruments from different makers could "speak" to one another. Soon after, various kinds of mechanical contacts were invented for placement under the keys to sense keystroke information such as note, key velocity, and duration, and convert it into MIDI data. This MIDI information was then routed to synthesizers, which turned the information into whatever instrumental sounds the attached synthesizer was programmed to produce. When one instrument is used to control another in this manner through the transmission of MIDI information, the first instrument is called a *MIDI controller*. At the beginning, however, the sound of the acoustic piano could not be turned off, though it could be muffled in vertical hybrids.

Early mechanical key contacts were subject to breakdown, or infiltration by dust, and their presence could sometimes be felt by sensitive players, which interfered with their playing. The more advanced key contacts or sensors used today involve touch films or optical sensors that are more reliable and accurate, and add no significant weight to the touch. In time, too, mechanisms were invented for shutting off the acoustic piano sound entirely, either by blocking the hammers from hitting the strings, or by tripping (escaping) the action's train of force earlier than normal, so that the hammers lacked the velocity needed to reach the strings. Headphones would block out any remaining mechanical noise, leaving only the sounds of the electronic instrument.

Not surprisingly, most makers of these MIDI controller/acoustic hybrid systems have been manufacturers of electronic player-piano systems. The same MIDI sensor strip used under the keys of these systems for their Record feature (which allows players to record their own playing for later playback) can also transmit the MIDI information to a digital sound source: either an internal source that comes with the piano (a *soundcard*) or an external source, such as a synthesizer or a computer with appropriate software installed. All player-piano systems today allow, through MIDI control, for the accompaniment of the acoustic piano sound by digitally produced sound, be they other piano-like sounds, other instrumental sounds, or even entire orchestras.

In addition to the accompaniment function, it turns out that these hybrid systems in which the acoustic piano can be silenced potentially have another very practical function. If your playing is likely to meet with objections from neighbors or family, being able to silence the piano and then play as loudly as you want, while listening through headphones, can be very handy. Realizing this, the major player-piano manufacturers make the MIDI controller feature available—without the player piano—relatively inexpensively. These MIDI controllers include a MIDI sensor strip under the keys, or optical sensors for keys and hammers, but no hardware and electronics that would make the piano keys move on their own. Usually, these systems come with a *stop rail* or other mechanical device to prevent the hammers from hitting the strings, as well as an internal digital sound source and headphones. When you move a lever to stop the acoustic piano sound, you turn on the digital sound source, which is heard through the headphones. Yamaha calls their version of this instrument Silent Piano; a variant whose digital piano sound is broadcast by the acoustic piano's soundboard is called TransAcoustic. Kawai calls their hybrid piano series—including one model with a soundboard speaker system—AnyTime. PianoDisc calls their two add-on systems QuietTime and ProRecord; QRS's version is SilentPNO.

But the accompaniment and "silent" functions of a hybrid MIDI controller/acoustic piano are only the beginning of what it can do. Just as the MIDI signal can be sent to a synthesizer or soundcard, it can also be sent to a personal computer or transmitted over the Internet. Regardless of whether a MIDI controller originates in an acoustic or a digital piano, it enables the instrument to interact with music software to record, produce notation, control instrumental voices on a personal computer, or interact with other pianos in the same room or on different continents. The potential for hybrids in creating and teaching music is limited only by the imagination of the user. Notation softwares—e.g., MakeMusic's Finale, Avid's Sibelius, and GenieSoft's Overture—allow the hybrid piano's keystrokes to be converted to music notation. This notation can be edited, transposed, split into parts for different instruments, played back, and printed out. The possibilities for teaching are perhaps even more powerful. Taking a lesson from a teacher in a different state, or a master class from a performer in a different country, becomes feasible with hybrid technology, particularly when combined with the player-piano features. Exacting copies of performances can be sent to similarly equipped instruments for playback, and critiques—with musical examples—can be sent back to the student. Some systems enable this interaction in real time over broadband connections, complete with synchronized video.

As we've said, most of the activity in the field of acoustic hybrids has been among player-piano makers, whose offerings have been either specialized (Silent Piano) or add-ons (QuietTime, SilentPNO).

Kawai's silent/hybrid pianos are known as **AnyTime** (ATX).

However, MIDI capabilities are now standard in all acoustic pianos, vertical and grand, made by Story & Clark, a subsidiary of QRS, the only piano maker so far to have done this. If you add a stop rail to silence the piano (available from QRS) and a sound source, you could turn one of these instruments into a "silent" hybrid like those described above. But even without those additions, a Story & Clark piano can be used with a personal computer and music software for recording, notation, controlling computer-produced instrumental voices, or any of the myriad other uses possible with a MIDI controller.

All Story & Clark pianos come with a factory-installed PNOscan MIDI strip beneath the keys.

Digital-based Hybrids: Replicating the Acoustic Experience

Now, you may wonder: If you're going to use a piano to interact with a computer, play piano sounds silently, or make the sounds of other instruments, why bother with an acoustic piano at all? Why not just use a digital piano or keyboard of some kind? The reason: the *experience*. Digital pianos are long on functionality but short on, so to speak, atmosphere. For those used to the looks, touch, tone, or other, less tangible aspects of acoustic pianos, digital pianos, in their "pure" form, just don't cut it—so digital piano makers have spent a great deal of time, energy, and money trying to mimic one or more of these aspects of acoustic pianos. The closer they get to duplicating the experience of playing an acoustic piano, the more they earn the right to the designation *hybrid*—because, when you get down to it, the purpose of playing an acoustic piano *is* the experience.

The first aspect of acoustic pianos that digital piano makers mimicked was, of course, their looks—indeed, a large segment of the digital piano market consists of acoustic-piano look-alikes. But that alone isn't enough to earn the label *hybrid*. Next, the action mechanism of the acoustic piano found its way into the digital piano. Much engineering has gone into the numerous action designs in digitals, always in the attempt to make their feel and response as close as possible to those of a "real" piano. Many digital piano actions these days have weighted and/or wooden keys with ivory-like keytops, and other enhancements that

do a reasonable job of emulating an acoustic piano action; still, advanced pianists, especially players of classical music, are unlikely to be completely satisfied by most of these.

Some digital-piano models now use real or only slightly modified acoustic-piano actions to trigger the piano's sensors (the hammers are small and don't actually strike strings). With such an action, there's no need to simulate certain action processes, such as escapement, because, mechanically, those processes are what is actually occurring. The first instrument to be formally named a Hybrid Piano was Yamaha's AvantGrand series, unveiled in 2009. The AvantGrand elevated the digital piano to a new level with a number of hybrid technologies, first of which was a real piano action. All three AvantGrand models have grand-piano actions, but whereas the model N3X is also shaped like a grand, the cabinets of the lower-cost N1 and N2 are closer to that of a vertical piano (which brings up the interesting observation that whether to call a digital piano a "grand" or a "vertical" is not a simple decision). In 2012, Yamaha introduced the model NU1 Hybrid Piano, the first digital piano with a real vertical-piano action.

To emulate the feel of an acoustic-piano action, it's necessary to also address the feel of the dampers and pedals. When you depress the sustain pedal on most digital pianos, you're pressing a spring with constant tension. This is not how the sustain pedal feels on most acoustic pianos, in which the initial movement meets little resistance as the pedal takes up a bit of slack in the mechanism that lifts the dampers. Once the mechanism begins to actually lift the dampers, the resistance increases. Here again, the AvantGrand does a convincing job of conveying the feel and, perhaps more important, provides the degree of control available with an acoustic's sustain pedal, including half-pedaling and incremental control. Kawai's Novus NV10 Hybrid digital piano, which also uses an acoustic-piano action, goes a step further: Just as on an acoustic piano, the Novus's touch weight varies based on whether or not the sustain pedal is depressed.

One aspect of the traditional acoustic-vs.-digital argument that changes with the addition of a real piano action is the digital's advantage of rarely needing maintenance. While the AvantGrand, NU1, and Novus models will never need to be tuned, eventually their actions will require some degree of adjustment or regulation. (We'll bet the piano technician will be surprised when, on arriving to regulate an action, he or she finds that the "piano" is a digital.)

Of course, makers of digital pianos have put more effort into copying the tone of the acoustic piano than any other aspect. How they've done this is beyond the scope of this article, but an interesting technique used in some models (e.g., the Kawai CS11 and CA-98) is to add to the digital an acoustic-piano soundboard, set in motion by transducers, to augment the piano's conventional speakers and give the instrument a more natural tone. Others are the installation of elaborate speaker systems, and the use of sampled concert grands. An example is the N3X's four-channel sample set and 12-speaker audio system, which easily trick the ears into thinking that considerably more than four feet of piano are in front of you. The Avant Grand and NU1 models all use samples from Yamaha concert grands for their sounds; the Novus uses samples from a Shigeru Kawai concert grand.

But there's even more to copying the acoustic-piano experience than its looks, action, and tone, and this brings us to aspects that are more difficult to precisely quantify or describe. With the AvantGrand, one of these—the vibrations generated by the strings and transmitted throughout the instrument—has been duplicated. Yamaha has added this ingredient to the N2 and N3X by connecting transducers to the action to send the appropriate frequency and degree of vibration to the player's fingers through the keys. This is where the experience of playing becomes a bit spooky. Not unlike an amusement-park ride that convinces your brain that you're dodging asteroids while hurtling through space when you are, in fact, fairly stationary, the AvantGrand's Tactile Response System quickly convinces you that you're feeling the vibrations of nonexistent strings.

One area in which digital pianos are *not* intended to emulate acoustic instruments is that of price. Most hybrid pianos that can provide the sound of and, in some cases, the experience of playing a concert grand, are priced similarly to a company's least expensive acoustic grands and verticals. Actually, such comparisons are barely possible—the acoustics lack many of the digitals' features, such as onboard recording, USB memory, transposition, and alternate tunings.

Which Side Are You On?

As the market for hybrid pianos grows, buyers will increasingly have to choose between acoustic pianos with digital enhancements and digital pianos that try to re-create the acoustic experience. Decisions will be made by weighing the relative quality, and importance to the buyer, of action, tone, looks, and features, as well as price. More advanced classical pianists whose digital needs are modest, and buyers who, among other things, are looking to fill a living room with a large, impressive piece of furniture, will probably tend to stick with the acoustic-based hybrid, at least for now. Those whose musical needs are more general, or who have a strong interest in digital features, may find digital-based hybrids more cost-effective.

Another factor that may come into play is that of life expectancy. A good acoustic piano will typically function well for 40 or 50 years, if not longer. Few digital pianos made 15 to 20 years ago are still in use, due either to technological obsolescence or to wear. True, the relevant technologies have evolved, as has the design of digital pianos and the quality of their construction. However, if past experience is any guide, pianos that are largely acoustic but include digital enhancement may well last for many decades; digital pianos enhanced with acoustic-like features are unlikely to last as long.

The piano has evolved a great deal since Bartolomeo Cristofori invented it in 1700, and that evolution continues. Today it's possible to buy a piano with an ABS-Carbon action (Kawai), a carbon-fiber soundboard (Steingraeber Phoenix), or one that looks as if it was made for the Starship *Enterprise*. The hybrid piano's blending of acoustic and digital technologies is just another step—or branch—in that evolution.

Yamaha AvantGrand model **N3X**

BUYING AN ELECTRONIC PLAYER-PIANO SYSTEM

Larry Fine

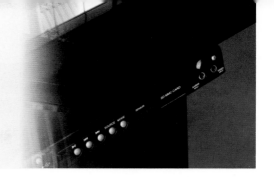

SOME OF YOU may have fond memories of gathering around Grandma's old upright player piano and pumping those huge pedals to make it play—until you could hardly walk! As with so many other devices, technology has revolutionized the player piano, replacing the pneumatic pressure and rolls of punched paper with electronics, smartphones, iPads, and MP3 files. Today, nearly one out of every four new grand pianos is sold with an electronic player-piano system installed.

The capabilities of these systems range from those that simply play the piano (often all that's desired for home use) all the way to those that allow composers to create, play, and print entire orchestral scores without ever leaving the piano bench. You can even watch a video of Billy Joel in concert on a screen built into your piano's music rack, or on your tablet or notebook, while, simultaneously, his performance, with orchestra, is faithfully reproduced on your own piano, "live" in your living room! The features and technological capabilities are already vast and are still evolving.

Before you begin to wade through the possibilities, you should carefully consider your long-term needs. Since many of the features of the more sophisticated systems are related to recording one's performance and composing, you should first decide whether or not you want the ability to record what you or others play on your piano, or to use the piano for music notation. In many typical family situations, the piano, just like Grandma's, is primarily used for children's lessons and for entertainment. If that's the case, one of the more basic systems, without recording capabilities, will likely be satisfactory. Most systems can be upgraded to add recording and other, more advanced features, should you later want to add those. However,

as technologies advance, it may become increasingly difficult to upgrade your older system.

Some player systems can be added (retrofitted) to any new or used piano; others are available only on a specific make of piano. When installed in a new piano, some systems must be installed by the piano's manufacturer, while others can be installed by the dealer or at an intermediate distribution point. A factory-certified local installer of a retrofit can usually match the quality of a factory installation. Installation is somewhat messy and must be done in a shop, not in your home; but when done correctly, it won't harm the piano or void its warranty.

The player systems currently on the market can be described as falling into two categories: those that are used mostly in situations requiring only low- to medium-quality playback reproduction, and those whose playback and/or recording functions are of audiophile quality and are intended for the most discriminating or high-level professional users. The first category includes systems by PianoDisc, Pianoforce, QRS, and most Yamaha Disklaviers. When used as playback-only systems, these are suitable for home entertainment, and for commercial use in restaurants, hotels, assisted-living facilities, etc. When outfitted with recording capabilities and/or

How a Typical Electronic Player-Piano System Works

Basic player systems consist of:

- a solenoid (electromechanical actuator) rail installed in a slot cut in the piano keybed (a shelf-like part of the piano that supports the keys and action)
- a processor unit and other electronics mounted out of sight under the piano
- Some models use a control box that plays MP3s, DVDs, and/or CDs (depending on the model), and is either mounted under the keybed at the front of the piano, or sits on or near the piano. In some models, the control box contains no disc drives and is hidden away under the piano, depending instead on your own CD player, MP3 player, or other device for the musical input. A remote-control device for operating the control box from a distance is also generally included with these units.
- In place of a control box, most newer models now use as the system's remote control an iPad or other tablet, or a smartphone, linked to a WiFi station such as Apple's Airport Express mounted out of sight under a grand piano or inside an upright. A number of apps are available for operating and calibrating the system.
- One or more amplified speakers are installed out of sight under the grand piano or inside the upright models—unless you choose a system configuration that uses your own speaker system.

The underside of a grand piano with solenoid rail (uncovered), power supply, and speaker installed.

QRS Music Technologies, Inc.

with a "silent" feature that mutes the acoustic piano's sound, they become more useful for students, and for lighter professional use for music notation or as a MIDI controller. The audiophile category includes the Steinway Spirio and the Disklavier Pro models. However, this classification scheme doesn't entirely do justice to home entertainment systems, which can be more sophisticated in other respects, such as versatility and functionality, than some audiophile systems.

The quality of a piano performance, either by a sophisticated electromechanical reproducing system or by a human being, greatly depends on the overall quality and condition of the instrument being played. Thus, an out-of-tune and/or ill-voiced piano with a poorly regulated action would result in an unpleasant listening experience, whether played by human or machine. This, of course, emphasizes the importance of regular and proper maintenance of the instrument. When buying a piano, the performance quality of the player-piano system will be limited, to a large extent, by the performance quality of the piano itself. Don't scrimp on the piano, just to be able to afford a player system for it.

On the solenoid rail, there is one solenoid for each key. There is also a solenoid for the damper pedal and, sometimes, one for the una corda (soft) pedal. Each solenoid contains a mechanical plunger that, when activated by an electronic signal, pushes against a key or against the pedal trapwork, causing the appropriate keys and pedals to move up and down. When playing, one track contains the datastream that controls the piano solenoids; the other track provides an instrumental and/or vocal accompaniment that plays through a stereo system or through amplified speakers that come with the player system. The accompaniment may be in the form of synthesized or sampled sounds, or actual recordings of live musicians. A wide selection of piano solos is also available.

Treasure it. Play it.
Stand in awe of it.
ENTERTAIN WITH IT.

SPIRIO

Presenting the first high-resolution *player piano* worthy of the revered STEINWAY & SONS name.
SPIRIO is a masterpiece of artistry, craftsmanship, and engineering that delivers all the nuance
and passion of live performances by today's most renowned musicians from classical to jazz to rock.
WWW.STEINWAY.COM/SPIRIO

STEINWAY & SONS

ONE STEINWAY PLACE, ASTORIA, NY 11105 TEL. 718.721.2600 STEINWAY.COM

QRS
SINCE 1900

QRS PNOMATION
Play - Practice -Perform - Produce
The Perfect Player Piano Experience Is Here

THE BEST PLAYER SYSTEM IN THE WORLD
THE BEST MUSIC, THE BEST TECHNOLOGY, THE BEST ENTERTAINMENT VALUE

- Easier to navigate, log in, play, setup and enjoy.
- **Existing player system upgrade kits available even for competitors systems.**
- Designed to deliver whisper quiet playback without sacrificing full dynamic playback when you want it.
- **Multiple User Interface Options - Tablets, Phones, PC's, Android, IOS, Apple Watch, Amazon Echo, IR.**
- Custom record, audio playback & playlist setups.
- **Bluetooth Audio, Bluetooth MIDI and Wi-Fi make setup and access a breeze.**

AN UNRIVALED MUSIC LIBRARY

- Solo & Concert series content delivers impeccable reproduction, dynamics & control.
- Patented QRS SyncAlong where piano plays along with original artists.
- Over 100 years of piano content & production experience.
- Seamless integration and content differentiation within the App.
- Improved music tracking with cloud content sharing and archiving.
- All Access Music Plans or buy by the song, playlist or album.
- Patented PNOscan optical record technology (Optional).
- Add Key-Stop Headphones to practice in silence.

Patented QRS SyncAlong Technology allows your QRS PNOmation to play along with an original artists DVD.

QRS continues to offer paths to its newest technology and music, ensuring your investment is protected and relevant for years to come.

ELECTRONIC PLAYER SYSTEMS

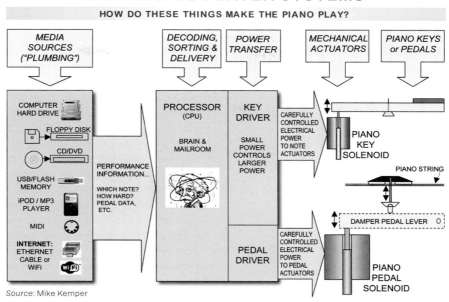

HOW DO THESE THINGS MAKE THE PIANO PLAY?

Source: Mike Kemper

For recording, keystroke and pedaling information are recorded in MIDI format by a sensor strip installed beneath the keys and sensors attached to the pedals. Some systems also record hammer motions. This information can be stored for later playback on the same piano, stored on other media, sent to other MIDI-compatible devices, or imported into a computer.

The same sensors used for recording can turn the piano into a MIDI controller. Add headphones, a device for mechanically silencing the acoustic piano, and a sound card or other tone generator, and you essentially have a hybrid acoustic/digital piano you can play late at night without disturbing anyone. Because this feature can be used independently of the player piano, most manufacturers of these systems make it available separately under such names as Silent Piano (Yamaha), QuietTime or ProRecord (PianoDisc), SilentPNO (QRS), and AnyTime (Kawai). Of course, the MIDI controller can also be used with or without a tone generator to send a MIDI datastream to a computer for use with composing and editing software, among other applications. (For more information, see the article **"Hybrid Pianos"** elsewhere in this volume.)

Common Features

Basic player-piano systems share a number of features:

- live playback of piano music with a good reproduction of the artist's performance. The keys, and in some systems the pedals, actually move up and down.
- playback of piano music with a full band, orchestral, and/or vocal accompaniment (yes, it will sing!)
- a repertoire of thousands of songs and the ability to download music from the Internet
- connectivity to home audio or home-theater systems
- remote control

Other capabilities, in a variety of applications, are considered valuable tools for composers, educators, and students, as well as performers. They include:

- a system of sensing key and pedal motions that can capture and record the nuances of a live performance for later playback or editing
- playing every instrument of the orchestra (and then some!), using the piano keyboard coupled with an onboard and/or outboard sound module

- the ability to import and export performances through a variety of wired and wireless connections, including MP3s, iPads, the Internet, etc.
- synchronizing a solo-piano performance on your piano with a commercially available CD or DVD of a famous performing artist
- Internet radio that streams data specifically formatted for the player system, for a virtually unlimited supply of musical input
- connectivity to most computers, facilitating music editing, enhancing, and printing
- connecting to teachers and other players anywhere in the world via the Internet

In addition to bundling some amount of music software with the purchase of their systems, most manufacturers record and separately sell software for their systems as MP3 downloads from a website, or as CDs or DVDs. A significant caveat is that one manufacturer's software may, by design, not work unconditionally with another manufacturer's hardware.

Questions to Consider

To list and compare the wide variety of features and capabilities offered by each of the many player systems would be beyond the scope of this article. However, the most significant concerns, aside from price, are the following. Ask your dealer or installer about the ones that interest or concern you.

- **Installation:** Can the system be installed in (retrofitted to) any piano, or is it exclusive to a particular brand of piano? If exclusive, this will limit your options as to what brand of piano to buy.
- **Music Source:** Do you have a preference of source of music for the system: smartphones, Internet downloads, iPads and other tablets, MP3s, CDs, etc.? This will influence your choice of system brand and configuration.
- **Recording:** Do you need recording capability, or the ability to use the system as a MIDI controller? The addition of an acoustic-piano silencing mechanism will allow you to play silently with headphones, or to connect to a computer to edit and transcribe music, among other benefits.
- **Playing Softly:** How well does the system play softly without skipping notes and without excessive mechanical noise? This is especially important if you plan to use the player piano for soft background music. If so, be sure to try out the system at a low volume level to be sure it meets your expectations.
- **Music Software:** How well does the available music software satisfy your needs?
- **Equipment:** Do you need a system with a CD player and/or iPad included, or will you be supplying your own? Do you need speakers or a video monitor, or will you be connecting the system to your own stereo system or home theater?
- **Software Compatibility:** Can it play the music libraries of other manufacturers' systems? It's important to note, however, that because competitors sometimes change their formats and encryption, the ability to play the data format of a particular competitor's software may not be guaranteed.
- **Dynamic Resolution:** How many gradations of volume can the system record and play back? Most systems record and play back in 127 increments, which is more than sufficient for most uses. Some pre-recorded CDs play back with as few as 16 levels of expression—still probably enough for casual use, but you should test out the type of music you expect to listen to, to hear if it meets your musical expectations for dynamic resolution. A few systems can handle 1,000 or more increments. This may be desirable for high-level professional or recording applications, or for the most authentic playback of complex classical compositions. Likewise, some systems have higher processor speeds that scan the system a greater number of times per second for higher resolution. Some record by sensing only key movements, while others, for greater accuracy, also sense hammershank movements. It's important to note that some systems that are theoretically capable of playing back with high resolution nonetheless come with music that has been prerecorded at lower resolution. Music can never be played back at a level of sound quality higher than that at which it was recorded.
- **Pedals:** Which pedals are played by hardware (solenoids) and which, if any, are mimicked by software? Hardware provides a more authentic piano performance, but duplication of pedal functions by software is simpler. Most important is hardware support for the sustain (damper)

pedal, and all systems currently provide that. Only a few also provide hardware for the soft pedal (less important), and fewer still for the sostenuto (middle) pedal (unimportant).

- **Damper Pedal Performance:** Does the system record multiple damper-pedal positions, allowing for pedaling techniques such as "half-pedaling," or does it simply record an "on" or "off" position? As with dynamic resolution, the recording and playback of multiple pedal positions is desirable for an authentic performance experience. The on/off mode is sufficient for casual or simple uses.
- **Pedal Functionality:** Some add-on (retrofit) systems, when installed, may alter the functionality or feel of the pedals, especially the middle pedal. If possible, try playing a piano on which a similar player system is installed to see if the pedal operation is okay for you. If only the middle pedal is affected, it might not matter to you, because this pedal is rarely used
- **Options:** What special features, advantages, and benefits are included or are optionally available? Examples include the ability to synchronize the piano with commercially available MP3s, CDs, and DVDs, features used for teaching purposes, a built-in video monitor, subscriptions to Internet music libraries or streaming radio that make available virtually unlimited input to your piano, bundled music software, and so forth.
- **Upgradability:** To what extent is the system upgradable? Most systems are highly upgradable, but the upgradability of some entry-level systems may be limited.

How Much Player-Piano Systems Cost

The costs of electronic player-piano systems vary enormously, not only from one system to the next, but even for the same system, depending on where it is installed and other factors.

A dealer has several ways of acquiring an add-on (retrofit) player system, which can affect the price at which the system is sold. Factory-installed systems—installed while the piano itself is being manufactured—are the least expensive for the dealer to acquire. Several large piano manufacturers are authorized to do this. In addition, the companies that make the player systems may factory-install them in brands that they own; for example, QRS PNOmation

in Story & Clark pianos, and PianoDisc in Mason & Hamlin instruments. When installed this way, the difference in price between the piano alone and the piano plus player system may be moderate. The next more expensive options are when the player system is installed at an intermediate distribution point before reaching the dealer, or when a larger dealer, in his or her own shop, installs a system in a piano already on the showroom floor—with most brands of piano, either of these can be done. These installations require more labor that those done while the piano is being manufactured. More expensive yet is when the smaller dealer must hire a local independent installer to install a system in a piano that is on the dealer's showroom floor. The most expensive option is to have a system installed in a piano you already own. In that situation, you also incur the expense of having the piano moved to and from the installer's shop.

The cost can also vary because player systems are often used by dealers as an incentive to buy the piano. The dealer will charge well for an expensive piano, then "throw in" the player system at his or her cost. Or vice versa—the dealer lets the piano go cheaply, then makes it up by charging list price for the system. The more modular systems can also vary in price, according to which options and accessories the dealer includes.

For all these reasons, quoting prices for player systems without knowing the context in which they're installed and sold is difficult. Nevertheless, as a rule of thumb, one of the more popular, typically configured, factory-installed QRS or PianoDisc systems with playback and accompaniment might add $5,500 to $7,000 to the piano's street price, with recording capability adding another $1,500 or so. However, for the reasons given above, prices 20% lower or higher aren't unusual.

As for systems available only as factory installations, Yamaha Disklavier grands generally cost $10,000 to $15,000 (street price) more than the same Yamaha model without the player system. At the time of this writing, the Steinway Spirio is about $25,000 more expensive than the Steinway piano alone. The retail prices of these systems are included under their companies' listings in the online **"Model & Pricing Guide"** at **www.pianobuyer.com.**

Mike Kemper, a Los Angeles-based piano technician and expert on electronic player-piano systems, contributed to the original version of this article.

BRAND & COMPANY PROFILES

THIS SECTION contains brief descriptions of most brands of new acoustic and digital piano, and electronic player-piano system, distributed nationwide in the United States. Brands that are associated with only a single dealer, or otherwise have marginal distribution, are omitted unless I believe them to be significant in some respect. To save space, and to avoid publishing details that go out of date too quickly, many of the profiles have been shortened somewhat from their online versions. For the more complete and current versions, including more complete contact information (distributor, address, phone, e-mail), and for current model and price information, see our website, **www.pianobuyer.com**.

ACOUSTIC PIANOS

BALDWIN

www.baldwinpiano.com

Baldwin Piano & Organ Co. was established in Cincinnati in 1862 as a retail enterprise and began manufacturing its own line of pianos in 1890. Throughout most of the 20th century, the company was considered one of the most successful and financially stable piano makers in the United States. Beginning in the 1980s, however, the quality declined, especially as a result of the relocation of action manufacturing to Mexico. In 2001, a combination of foreign competition and management problems resulted in bankruptcy, and purchase by Gibson Guitar Corporation.

Baldwin currently manufactures vertical pianos for the U.S. market in a factory it owns in Zhongshan, China, where it also maintains a major presence in the Chinese domestic, and other international, piano markets. It also contracts with Parsons Music, a large, well-respected manufacturer associated with a chain of music schools and stores in Hong Kong and China, to have grand pianos made under the Baldwin name.

The company ceased regular piano production at its only remaining U.S. factory, in Trumann, Arkansas, at the end of 2008, though the facility remains open as a U.S. distribution and service center. Pianos sold in the U.S. now bear only the Baldwin name; all other piano names Baldwin owns and has recently used, such as Hamilton, Wurlitzer, Chickering, Howard, and D.H. Baldwin, have been retired.

Baldwin has re-created versions of most of its former U.S. vertical models at its facility in Zhongshan. In most instances, both the cabinet styling and the musical scale designs of the former models have been copied. The Baldwin grands made by Parsons Music have some similarities to the former U.S.-made Artist grands in terms of cabinet styling and material specifications, but the scale designs have been changed. Premium features include a maple rim, sand-cast plate, solid Alaskan Sitka spruce soundboard, duplex scaling, real ebony-wood sharps, German Röslau music wire, German Abel hammers, and a slow-close fallboard. All grand models are now available in a hand-rubbed, satin ebony finish.

Baldwin has licensed the Magic Lid slow-close grand lid system, which is now standard on several of its grand models.

BECHSTEIN, C.

including W. Hoffmann
www.bechstein.de

Bechstein was founded in 1853 by Carl Bechstein, a young German piano maker who, in the exploding world of piano technology of his day, had visions of building an instrument that the tradition-bound piano-making shops of Berlin were not interested in. Through fine workmanship and the endorsement of famous pianists, Bechstein soon became one of the leading piano makers in Europe, producing over 5,000 pianos annually by 1900. The two World Wars and the Depression virtually destroyed the company, but it was successfully rebuilt. In 1963 Bechstein was acquired by Baldwin, and in 1986 Baldwin sold it to Karl Schulze, a leading West German piano retailer and master piano technician, who undertook a complete technical and financial reorganization of the company. In the early 1990s, Bechstein acquired the names and factories of Euterpe, W. Hoffmann, and Zimmermann. Pianos with these names are currently being sold in Europe, but only W. Hoffmann is sold in North America. In 2006 Bechstein purchased a controlling interest in the Czech piano maker Bohemia, and integrated it into a new entity called C. Bechstein Europe Ltd.

Bechstein says that all C. Bechstein-branded pianos are manufactured in Seifhennersdorf, Germany, and that W. Hoffmann pianos are made in the Czech Republic. With few exceptions, Bechstein prefers not to divulge where the components for its instruments are made, a policy that frustrates some industry observers who seek transparency. However, the company says that, whatever the origin, all parts are inspected and made to conform to its rigid standards; in my experience, all models, including the less expensive ones, continue to receive praise for their high quality.

C. Bechstein pianos are available in two levels of quality. The regular verticals and partially redesigned versions of the old grand models now comprise a lower-priced Academy (A) series. They were previously branded Bechstein (B), instead of C. Bechstein, a distinction that has been eliminated. The 51½" Concert 8 (one of my all-time favorite verticals), several smaller verticals, and the fully redesigned grands (models D, C, B, M/P, and L), comprise the higher-priced line. The company says that both lines are made in Germany, though for cost-effectiveness some parts and components may originate in the Czech Republic.

The differences between the A series and the regular C. Bechsteins appear to be primarily in tonal philosophy and cabinetry. Regular C. Bechstein grands were designed with a higher tension scale for better projection, and with various components that the company believed would result in the greatest usable palette of tonal color. The grand soundboard is installed after the inner and outer rims are joined. The ribs are tapered after being glued to the soundboard, and the heavy-duty rim posts are dovetailed and embedded in the rim. With the less-expensive, traditional, A-series grands, the rim parts are joined, and the soundboard and ribs installed, in a more efficient, less time-consuming manner than with the regular, higher-priced models. The same quality wood and strings are used in both.

The company uses its own Silver Line action in the A series and, in the regular series, its Gold Line action, which is made to slightly stricter tolerances. As part of its global strategy, the company uses multiple suppliers for nearly all parts; parts for the Gold Line action come from Renner in Germany, while Silver Line parts are sourced from several countries, including China. Both actions appear to be well made, and both are of the Renner design, with the smooth, responsive touch characteristic of that design.

The cabinetry of the regular C. Bechstein models is much sleeker and more sophisticated than the plain A series, though both cabinets are finished to the same standard. The regular plates receive the royal hand-rubbed finish; the other plates are just spray-finished in the conventional manner.

When the two lines are compared side by side, there are differences in their finished quality and performance level. Although the A-series pianos are, generally speaking, very good instruments, it's apparent that they are not prepped at the factory to the same standard as the higher-priced pianos.

C. Bechstein grands are impeccably made, and are "orchestrally" voiced, a concept that the company says is related to the change of timbre at different velocities of touch. According to Bechstein, customers who do not explore this feature of tonal design often prematurely assume that the piano is voiced too bright for the American taste. The company maintains that since voicing is a matter of overall piano design, their pianos are voiced at the factory to their tonal standard and should not be significantly altered. Some customers may still prefer the slightly warmer sound of the A-series grands, which are also about half the price of the regular C. Bechstein models.

Bechstein engineers oversee production of the Bechstein-designed W. Hoffmann line of pianos in the company's Czech facility. This is a mid-priced line intended to compete with other mid-priced pianos from Eastern Europe and Japan. Currently it consists of grands and verticals in three series. The Tradition- and Professional-series instruments are entirely made in the Czech Republic. The Professional series has a higher level of design and components, and more customized musical preparation by the company's most experienced craftspeople. The Vision-series pianos are assembled in the Czech Republic, but their strung backs (the instruments' structural and acoustical parts) are imported from China.

BLÜTHNER

including Haessler. See also Irmler and Rönisch.
www.bluthnerpiano.com
www.bluethner.ca

Blüthner has been making pianos of the highest quality in Leipzig, in the eastern part of Germany, since 1853, and though nationalized in 1972, always remained under the management of the Blüthner family. Until 1900, Blüthner was Europe's largest piano factory. During World War II, the factory was bombed, but after the war the East German government allowed the Blüthner family and workers to rebuild it because the Blüthner piano was considered a national treasure (and because the Soviet Union needed quality pianos). With the liberation of Eastern Europe, Blüthner is again privately owned by the Blüthner family. Blüthner builds about 100 verticals a year in four sizes, and 500 grands a year in six sizes.

Blüthner pianos incorporate several unique technical features. With aliquot stringing, the notes in the highest treble section (about the top two octaves) have four strings each instead of three. The extra string is raised slightly above the others and vibrates only sympathetically. The effect, heard mainly in medium to forte playing, is similar to that of a duplex scale, adding tonal color to the treble and aiding the singing tone. Another feature concerns the angled hammers, which may at first look odd, though the

reason may not be readily apparent. It turns out that the angled hammers are actually cut at an angle to match the string line and mounted straight on the shanks instead of being cut straight and mounted at an angle like other brands. The company says that the effect is to more evenly distribute the force of the blow across both the strings and the hammers, and to make a firmer connection with the backchecks, which are also positioned in a straight line. Visually, the effect is an even, rather than a staggered, hammer line.

With voicing, Blüthner pianos have a very full sound that is warm, romantic, and lyrical, generally deeper and darker than some of their German counterparts. Sustain is good, but at a low level of volume, giving the tone a refined, delicate character. The action is a little light, but responsive. The pianos are built of superb materials, and are favorably priced compared to some of their competitors.

In the 1990s a Haessler line of pianos was added to the Blüthner line. (Haessler is a Blüthner family name.) Created to better compete in the American market, Haessler pianos have more conventional technical and cosmetic features than Blüthner pianos and cost about 25 percent less. For example, the grands are loop-strung instead of single-strung, there is no aliquot stringing, and the hammers are cut and mounted in the conventional way. Case and plate cosmetics are simpler. The pianos are made in the Blüthner factory in Germany to similarly high quality standards.

In 2016, Blüthner added to its line a hybrid-piano option, known as "e-volution," (see **Hybrid Pianos**, elsewhere in this volume). This option, which comes with an optical MIDI strip, a digital sound source, and a piano-silencing system, can be added to any Blüthner upright or grand piano model. A piano outfitted with the e-volution system can be played as an acoustic piano, as a digital piano (with the sound of a Blüthner concert grand), or as both at the same time. It can also stream music via Bluetooth from another source through its built-in Bose sound system.

Blüthner also owns the Irmler brand (see under **Irmler**), and the Rönisch and Hupfeld brands (see under **Rönisch**).

BÖSENDORFER

www.boesendorfer.com

Bösendorfer was founded in 1828 in Vienna, Austria, by Ignaz Bösendorfer. The young piano maker rose to fame when Franz Liszt endorsed his concert grand after being unable to destroy it in playing, as he had every other piano set before him. Ignaz died in 1858 and the company was taken over by his son, Ludwig. Under Ludwig's direction, the firm greatly prospered and the pianos became even more famous throughout Europe and the world. Ludwig, having no direct descendants, sold the firm to a friend, Carl Hutterstrasser, in 1909. Carl's sons, Wolfgang and Alexander, became partners in 1931. Bösendorfer was sold to Kimball International, a U.S. manufacturer of low- and medium-priced pianos, in 1966. In 2002 Kimball, having left the piano business, sold Bösendorfer to BAWAG Bank, Austria's third largest financial institution. The bank encountered financial troubles unrelated to Bösendorfer and sold the piano company to Yamaha in 2008. Yamaha says it will not be making any changes to Bösendorfer's location or methods of production, and that its sales network will continue to be separate from Yamaha's. Bösendorfer manufactures fewer than 500 pianos a year, with close to half of them sold in the U.S.

Bösendorfer makes a 52" upright and eight models of grand piano, from 5' 1" to the 9' 6" Imperial Concert Grand, one of the world's largest pianos. The company also makes slightly less expensive versions of four grand models known as the Conservatory Series (CS). Conservatory Series grands are like the regular grands except that the case receives a satin finish instead of a high polish, and some cabinet details are simpler.

One of the most distinctive features of the grands is that a couple of models have more than 88 keys. The 7' 4" model has 92 keys and the 9' 6" model has 97 keys. The lowest strings vibrate so slowly that it's actually possible to hear the individual beats of the vibration. Piano technicians say that it is next to impossible to tune these strings by ear, although electronic tuning aids can help accomplish this. Of course, these notes are rarely used, but their presence, and the presence of the extra-long bridge and larger soundboard to accommodate them, add extra power, resonance, and clarity to the lower regular notes of the piano. In order not to confuse pianists, who rely on the normal keyboard configuration for spatial orientation while playing, the keys for these extra notes are usually covered with a black ivorine material.

The rim of the Bösendorfer grand is built quite differently from those of all other grands. Instead of veneers bent around a form, the inner rim is made in solid sections of spruce and beech that are joined together. The outer rim has a solid core of quartersawn spruce that is grooved by Bösendorfer craftsmen so that it can be bent around the inner rim; after bending, the grooved sections are filled with spruce inserts. Because spruce is better at transmitting than reflecting sound, the extensive use of spruce in the rim has the effect of making the rim an acoustical extension of the soundboard, causing the entire body of the piano to resonate. This, along with the scale design, may be why Bösendorfers tend to have a more delicate treble, and a bass that features the fundamental tone more than the higher harmonics. Although the stereotype that "Bösendorfers are better for Mozart than Rachmaninoff" may be an exaggeration (as evidenced by the number of performing artists who successfully use the piano in concert for a wide variety of music), the piano's not-so-"in-your-face" sound is certainly ideally suited for the classical repertoire, in addition to whatever else it can do.

In recent years, Bösendorfer has made some refinements to its designs. The relatively newer 6' 1", 7', and 9' 2" models have been designed specifically to appeal to pianists looking for a more familiar sound. These models, now called the Vienna Concert (VC) series, have redesigned scaling and soundboard for greater sound projection, improved sustain, and a wider range of tonal color and dynamics. In all models, however, the distinctive Bösendorfer sound is still readily apparent.

In the past few years, Bösendorfer has introduced a number of interesting instruments in new cabinet styles. These include a Porsche-designed modern piano in aluminum and polished ebony (it can be special-ordered in any standard Porsche finish color); the Liszt, Vienna, and Chopin models of Victorian-styled pianos; and limited-edition models, such as the Liszt Anniversary, Beethoven, Mozart, Hummingbird, and Schönbrunn. Perhaps not to be outdone by Porsche, in 2009 Bösendorfer produced a model commissioned and designed by Audi on the occasion of that automaker's 100th anniversary.

The Bösendorfer model 200 is optionally available with a Yamaha Disklavier Enspire installed.

BOSTON

www.steinway.com/boston

In 1992 Steinway launched its Boston line of pianos, designed by Steinway & Sons and built by Kawai.

Steinway's stated purpose in creating this line was to supply Steinway dealers with a quality, mid-priced piano containing some Steinway-like design features for those customers "who were not yet ready for a Steinway." In choosing to have a piano of its own design made in Japan, Steinway sought to take advantage of the efficient high-technology manufacturing methods of the Japanese while utilizing its own design skills to make a more musical piano than is usually available from that part of the world.

Sold only through select Steinway dealers, Boston pianos are currently available in three sizes of vertical and five sizes of grand. All are made in Japan, except the school studio model UP-118S PE, which is made in Kawai's Indonesian factory.

In 2009, Steinway launched the Performance Edition of the Boston piano with enhancements to the instruments' design and specifications, including a grand inner rim of maple for increased structural integrity and improved tone, the patented Octagrip® pinblock for smoother tuning and more consistent torque, and improvements to hardware and keytop material, among other things. Performance Edition models have model numbers ending in PE. In 2016, the company introduced Performance Edition II grands (PE-II), containing further improvements, including bubinga veneer on the inside rim of all ebony grands, improved finishes, a new plate color, and other cosmetic changes; and a lower-tension scale, resulting in a very clear bass, better treble sustain, and more transparency in the tenor range.

A number of features in the Boston piano are similar to those in the Steinway, including the above-mentioned maple inner rim, vertically laminated bridges for better tonal transmission, duplex scaling for additional tonal color, rosette-shaped hammer flanges to preserve hammer spacing, and radial rim bracing for greater structural stability. The Boston grand action is said to incorporate some of the latest refinements of the Steinway action. Cabinet detailing on the Boston grands is similar to that on the Steinway. Boston hammers are made differently from both Kawai and Steinway hammers, and voicers in the Kawai factory receive special instruction in voicing them. All Boston grand models come with a sostenuto pedal; all verticals have a practice (mute) pedal, except for the model UP-118S PE, which has a bass sustain.

Boston pianos are used by a number of prestigious music schools and festivals, including Aspen, Bowdoin, Brevard, Ravinia, and Tanglewood.

Steinway guarantees full trade-in value for a Boston piano at any time a purchaser wishes to upgrade to a Steinway grand.

BRODMANN
www.BrodmannPianoUSA.com

Joseph Brodmann was a well-known piano maker in Vienna in the late 18th and early 19th centuries. Ignaz Bösendorfer apprenticed in Brodmann's workshop and eventually took it over, producing the first Bösendorfer pianos there. The modern-day Brodmann company was founded in 2004 by two former Bösendorfer executives. Brodmann, they say, was originally planned as a possible second line for Bösendorfer, but when that company abandoned the idea, the two executives pursued it on their own.

Brodmann says its mission is to produce a piano with high-end performance characteristics at an affordable price by using European components in key areas, strict quality control, and manufacturing in countries with favorable labor rates.

There are three lines of Brodmann piano, all manufactured, in whole or in part, in China by Parsons Music. The Professional Edition (PE) pianos, made entirely in China, are designed in Vienna and use European components. Several vertical models use carbon-fiber action parts, for greater uniformity and dimensional stability, and all grand models are now available with optional carbon-fiber actions. For quality control, Brodmann has its own employees from Europe working in the factory.

The Conservatory Edition (CE), for the more price-conscious buyer, is also made entirely in China, from parts sourced globally, and receives Brodmann quality control.

The Artist Series (AS) models, introduced in 2011 and available only in the larger grand sizes (including a concert grand) and the largest upright size, are based on German scale designs. They are partially made in China, then shipped to the Wilh. Steinberg factory (also owned by Parsons Music), in Eisenberg, Germany, where the Röslau strings and Renner actions are installed, and all musical finishing work is performed by German artisans. The rim is made of maple; the soundboard, ribs, and pinblock are from Bolduc, in Canada; and the piano uses a Renner action, Kluge keyboard, and Renner hammers.

BUSH & GERTS

en.bushgerts.com
This company is seeking U.S. distribution.

The original Bush & Gerts Piano Company was founded in 1884 by Chicago businessman William H. Bush; his son William L. Bush, who had trained in organ and piano making; and John Gerts, a master piano builder from Germany. In addition to its high-quality pianos, Bush & Gerts was best known for the establishment of the Bush Temple of Music, a Chicago landmark that, for a time, served as the company's headquarters and housed its music conservatory. William L. Bush was also known for his tireless campaigning against the "stencil piano"—a piano bearing a name other than that of its maker—a fraudulent and confusing practice common in the piano industry of early 20th century America.

In 1924, Bush & Gerts was acquired by the Haddorff Piano Company, of Rockford, Illinois, which from then on manufactured Bush & Gerts instruments. Haddorff was acquired by Conn in 1940, and production of Bush & Gerts pianos effectively ceased about 1942, when most piano production nationwide was commandeered by the U.S. government for the war effort.

Since 2015, Bush & Gerts pianos have been made in Shanghai, China, for the Asian market. Components are sourced from the German companies Abel (hammers), Röslau (strings), and Strunz (soundboard), among others.

CHERNOBIEFF

www.chernobieffpiano.com

Reminiscent of some piano designs attempted 200 years ago, Chernobieff's Mammoth is one of the most unusual pianos being built today. Dubbed a Vertical Concert Grand, Mammoth's model VCG stands 7' 2" tall, weighs 1,200 pounds, and has the scale design and sound of a 9' concert grand.

The piano's immense structure includes six laminated wooden back posts and a welded steel frame, yet despite its bulk, the instrument appears quite attractive in its custom-made cabinet of Brazilian cherry. The soundboard and ribs are of Sitka spruce. The action, invented specifically for this piano, appears superficially to be like that of a vertical, but actually contains the double-escapement feature of a grand piano action.

Inventor-builder Chris Chernobieff got his start assembling dulcimer and harpsichord kits, and branched out into piano service and rebuilding about 20 years ago. Inspired by other technicians who built their own pianos, Chernobieff asked, "Why not me?" Having spent the last several years designing and building the Mammoth, he now has plans for a 6' vertical and some innovative grand models.

CLINE—see Hailun

CRISTOFORI

including Paul A. Schmitt
www.cristoforipianos.com

Originally issued under the name Opus II, the Cristofori and Paul A. Schmitt (formerly Lyrica) brands are a joint undertaking by Jordan Kitt's Music, which owns and operates four piano dealerships in the D.C. and Atlanta markets; and Schmitt Music, which has more than a dozen locations throughout the Midwest and in Denver. About 15 years ago, wanting to improve their entry-level product offerings, the two companies combined forces to negotiate upgrades of product features and quality control directly with the factory. Today, although the brands are identical, Cristofori is sold only in Jordan Kitt's stores, Paul A. Schmitt in Schmitt Music stores. Bartolomeo Cristofori (1655–1731) was, of course, the inventor of the piano.

The Cristofori and Paul A. Schmitt lines, which come in numerous sizes, styles, and finishes, are manufactured by Pearl River, China's largest piano manufacturer. They are differentiated from Pearl River's own line of pianos by upgraded specifications such as the use of highest-quality German Röslau strings; all-spruce veneered soundboards of premium Siberian spruce; a different selection of cabinet styles; and a full, transferable warranty. U.S. technicians inspect every Cristofori and Paul A. Schmitt piano at the Pearl River factory prior to crating and shipping.

CUNNINGHAM

www.cunninghampiano.com

Cunningham Piano Company began manufacturing pianos in 1891 and, in its time, was the largest piano maker in Philadelphia. The original Cunningham factory ceased production in December 1943. The company was reopened in December 1945 as a piano rebuilder and retailer. Today, Cunningham specializes in the restoration of high-quality American and European pianos, and produces the new Matchless Cunningham.

Designed by Frank Emerson, the Matchless Cunningham is based on the original Cunningham scale designs. "Matchless" is used in reference to an offer made by Patrick Cunningham over a century ago: that he would pay $10,000 to anyone who could build a better piano. Because no one ever took him up on his offer, Cunningham labeled his piano the Matchless. Today, Matchless also refers to a unique combination of high-quality parts and an American scale design, assembled in China at the Hailun factory. Cunningham regularly sends technical staff to the factory to oversee production, and each piano undergoes a thorough final preparation by Cunningham in Philadelphia.

The special Heritage Series incorporates art cases that reflect late Victorian styling. Customers have the option of customizing certain aspects of the cabinetry based on their personal preferences.

ESSEX

www.steinway.com/essex

Essex pianos are designed by Steinway & Sons engineers and are made in China by Pearl River. Steinway introduced its Essex line of pianos in early 2001 with a limited offering of models made by Young Chang, and the brand kept an unusually low profile in the piano market for a number of years. In 2006, a major relaunch of Essex included a new and very complete line comprising 35 grand and 31 vertical models and finishes. Steinway has a permanent office in Shanghai, China, and full-time employees who inspect the pianos made in the Asian factory.

Today, two grand sizes and three vertical scales are made. The studio model is available in seven different and striking cabinets designed by Steinway & Sons and renowned furniture designer William Faber. These models incorporate various leg designs (including cabriole leg, spoon leg, and canopy-styled tapered leg and arm designs) and hand-carved trim (such as Acanthus leaf and tulip designs, and vertical bead molding), highly molded top lids, picture-frame front panels, and stylized, decorative music

desks. The 48" upright comes in a traditional style in three finishes, two with chrome hardware, along with Empire and French styles. The Essex grands are available in 5' 1" Classic and French Provincial styles and 5' 8" Classic style. They come in a variety of regular and exotic veneers in high polish polyester and satin luster (semigloss) finishes.

Like Steinway's Boston pianos, the Essex line was designed with a lower tension scale and incorporates many Steinway-designed refinements. Included in these are a wide tail design that allows the bridges to be positioned closer to the more lively, central part of the soundboard, smoothing out the break between bass and treble. This and a thinner, tapered solid-spruce soundboard, and other scaling differences, produce a tone with a longer sustain. Other Steinway-designed features include an all-wood action with Steinway geometry, and with rosette-shaped hammer flanges, like those used in Steinway grands, to preserve hammer spacing; pear-shaped hammers with reinforced shoulders and metal fasteners; vertically laminated bridges with a solid maple cap; duplex scale; radial bracing (in grands); and staggered backposts (in verticals).

Steinway guarantees full trade-in value for an Essex piano toward the purchase of a Steinway grand within 10 years.

ESTONIA

www.estoniapiano.com

Piano-making in Estonia goes back over 200 years under German influence, and from 1850 to 1940 there were nearly 20 piano manufacturers operating in the country. The most famous of these was Ernst Hiis-Ihse, who studied piano making in the Steinway Hamburg and Blüthner factories and established his own company in 1893. His piano designs gained international recognition. In 1950 the Communist-dominated Estonian government consolidated many smaller Estonian piano makers into a factory managed by Hiis, making pianos under the Estonia name for the first time. The instruments became prominent on concert stages throughout Eastern Europe and, amazingly, more than 7,400 concert grands were made. However, after Hiis's death, in 1964, the quality of the pianos gradually declined, partly due to the fact that high-quality parts and materials were hard to come by during the Communist occupation of the country. After Estonia regained its independence in 1991, the factory struggled to maintain production. In 1994 Estonia pianos were introduced to the U.S. market.

In 1994 the company was privatized under the Estonia name, with the managers and employees as owners. During the following years, Indrek Laul, an Estonian recording artist with a doctorate in piano performance from the Juilliard School of Music, gradually bought shares of the company from the stockholders until, in 2001, he became sole owner. Dr. Laul lives in the U.S. and represents the company here. Estonia makes 200 to 300 pianos a year, all grands, mostly for sale in the U.S.

Since becoming owner, Dr. Laul has introduced so many improvements to the piano that it has become practically a different, much higher-level instrument. In the short time Estonia pianos have been sold here, they have gathered an unusually loyal and devoted following. The pianos have a rich, warm, singing tone and a wide dynamic range; are very well constructed and well prepared at the factory; and there is hardly a detail that the company has not examined and impressively perfected. The price has risen over the years, but they are still an unusually good value among higher-end instruments.

FANDRICH & SONS

www.fandrich.com

In the late 1980s, Darrell Fandrich, RPT, an engineer, pianist, and piano technician, developed a vertical piano action designed to play like a grand, for which 10 patents were issued. In July 2013, a new patent application was filed in the U.S. (along with an application for future international patents) on an improved version of the action. You can see an illustration of the original Fandrich Vertical Action™, an explanation of how it works, and some history of its development in the third and fourth editions of *The Piano Book* and on the Fandrich & Sons website.

Since 1994, Fandrich and his wife, Heather, have been installing Renner-made Fandrich actions in selected new pianos, selling them under the Fandrich & Sons label. Over the years, the Fandrichs have installed their actions in over 300 instruments from various makers. At present, the action is being installed in 52" Pearl River uprights featuring Lothar Thomma scale designs (under the Fandrich & Sons

label), and, by special order, in 51" Steingraeber uprights (under the Steingraeber & Söhne label). The converted pianos are available directly from the Fandrichs, as well as from their Canadian representative, in Montreal (contact the Fandrichs for information). They also sell some grands (with regular grand actions) under the Fandrich & Sons name.

Fandrich & Sons grands are also manufactured in China by Pearl River. These pianos feature Lothar Thomma scale designs, and are remanufactured at the Fandrich & Sons facility in Stanwood, Washington. The company offers three sizes of grand piano in two configurations: Standard (S) and Enhanced (E), the latter with Heller bass strings from Germany and/or Abel hammers, depending on customer preference. The tone of the S model is said to be powerful, dark, and sonorous; the E model, in contrast, is more brilliant and transparent. All models feature precision touchweighting using the Fandrich-Rhodes Weightbench™ system, which enables precise control of action inertia as well as traditional up- and downweight; redesigned pedal-lyre and trapwork systems; and a very extensive high-end preparation.

The Fandrichs are passionate about their craft and choose the brands they work with carefully for musical potential. In addition to making standard modifications and refinements to remedy perceived shortcomings in the original Chinese-made instruments, the Fandrichs are inveterate tinkerers always searching for ways to make additional improvements, however subtle. As a result, many who play the pianos find them to be considerably more musical than their price and origin would suggest.

FAZIOLI

www.fazioli.com

As a youth, Paolo Fazioli, of Rome, Italy, studied music and engineering, receiving advanced degrees in both subjects. He briefly attempted to make a living as a concert pianist, but instead joined his family's furniture company, rising to the position of factory manager in the Rome, Sacile, and Turin factories. But his creative ambitions, combined with his personal search for the perfect piano, finally led him to conclude that he needed to build his own piano. With advice and financial backing from his family, in 1977 Fazioli assembled a group of experts in woodworking, acoustics, and piano technology to study and scientifically analyze every aspect of piano design and construction. The following year, prototypes of his new instruments in hand, he began building pianos commercially in a factory housed at one end of the family's Sacile furniture factory, a top supplier in Italy of high-end office furniture.

In 2001, Fazioli built a new, expanded, modern piano-production facility, and in 2005 opened an adjoining 198-seat concert hall with a stage large enough for a chamber orchestra, where he maintains a regular concert schedule of well-known musicians who perform there. The concert hall is designed so that it can be adjusted acoustically with movable panels and sound reflectors to optimize the acoustics for performing, recording, or testing, and for different kinds of music, musical ensembles, and size of audience. The hall is used for the research and testing of pianos—every instrument Fazioli makes is tested here. In addition to these activities in the concert hall, the new factory also contains a department for ongoing research in piano design in cooperation with a number of educational institutions.

Fazioli builds only grands, about 150 per year, in six sizes from 5' 2" to 10' 2", the last one of the largest pianos in the world, with the further distinction of having four pedals. Three are the usual sustain, sostenuto, and una corda. The fourth is a "soft" pedal that brings the hammers closer to the strings—similar to the function in verticals and some older grands—to soften the sound without altering the tonal quality, as the una corda often does. A unique compensating device corrects for the action irregularity that would otherwise occur when the hammers are moved in this manner. The fourth pedal is available as an option on the other models. Fazioli also offers two actions and two pedal lyres as options on all models. Having two actions allows for more voicing possibilities without having to constantly revoice the hammers. A second pedal lyre containing only three pedals can be a welcome alternative for some pianists who might be confused by the presence of a fourth pedal.

All Fazioli pianos have inner and outer rims of maple, and seven-ply maple pinblocks from Bolduc, in Canada. The pianos have Renner actions and hammers and Kluge keyboards. The bronze capo d'astro bar is adjustable in the factory for setting the strike point and treble string length for best high-treble tone quality, and is removable for servicing if necessary; and the front and rear duplex scales can be tuned to maximize tonal color. A newly patented action rail structure is more resistant to moisture, and provides a more uniform touch across the keyboard. Also newly patented are double- and triple-layer, moisture-resistant soundboards, available by special order for pianos that will be used in extreme climates. The pianos are impeccably prepared at the factory, including very fine voicing—even perfect tuning of the duplex scales.

The company says that a critical factor in the sound of its pianos is the scientific selection of its woods, such as the "resonant spruce" obtained from the Val di Fiemme, where Stradivari reportedly sought woods for his violins. Each piece of wood is said to be carefully tested for certain resonant properties before being used in the pianos. Similarly, three different types of wood are used for the bridge caps, each chosen for the most efficient transmission of tonal energy for a particular register.

A series of stunning art-case pianos is a testament to the ability of the Fazioli artisans to execute virtually any custom-ordered artistic variation on the six Fazioli models.

FEURICH

www.feurich.com

This German piano manufacturer was founded by Julius Feurich in 1851, in Leipzig. At its height in the early 20th century, the company employed 360 people, annually producing 1,200 upright and 600 grand pianos. Feurich was the first German manufacturer to produce an upright with an under-damper system, and was also a member of the so-called Group of Five—the leading German manufacturers who joined forces to provide selected renowned pianists with concert instruments worldwide. Like many German manufacturers, however, Feurich lost its factory during World War II. Following the war, the fourth generation of the Feurich family rebuilt in Langlau, in what became West Germany.

In 1991, Bechstein purchased Feurich and closed the Langlau factory, but in 1993 the name was sold back to the Feurich family. For a time, production was contracted out to other German manufacturers, including Schimmel, while the Feurich family marketed and distributed the pianos. In 1995, Feurich opened a new factory in Gunzenhausen, Germany. Under the direction of the fifth-generation Julius

Feurich, the family-owned company once again began producing its own pianos.

In 2011, Feurich was acquired by Wendl & Lung, headquartered in Vienna, Austria, which distributed a line of pianos under that name made to their specifications by Hailun, in China. The Wendl & Lung pianos went through further development, and additional models were added to the line, before being rebranded as Feurich. Julius Feurich is no longer involved with the company.

There are currently two lines of Feurich instruments on the market. Utilizing a separate production line within the Hailun factory in Ningbo, China, Feurich produces a line of high-quality, affordable uprights and grands distinguished by their strict quality control, the use of European tonewoods, and modern innovations, such as Paulello rust-free music wire. Feurich experts are present in the factory at all times, in order to perform a full quality-control inspection before shipping. In 2015, a new Feurich-designed action and keyboard was introduced for all Feurich uprights, and other new improvements and design modifications have been made on all the instruments.

The second line is made in Vienna, Austria. The first model in this line is the 48" model 123 Vienna upright. The strung back for this model is made in China by Hailun, but with a new design, more advanced CNC milling, and with Paulello rust-free strings. All other parts are European. The level of detail in the design can be seen in features such as the compensation in the action for the different proportions and leverages required for black and white keys, owing to their different lengths. The Feurich High-Speed KAMM Action, designed by master piano builder Udo Kamm, also features a new, patented system of springs and rollers that enable extremely fast repetition for an upright piano. The pianos are meticulously regulated and voiced in Vienna.

Feurich offers an optional fourth pedal on their grand pianos. The Harmonic Pedal is essentially the inverse of a sostenuto: instead of holding up the dampers of notes struck prior to depressing the pedal, it holds up all *but* those notes. This allows the player to create sympathetic resonance between strings, even while playing staccato.

FÖRSTER, AUGUST

www.august-foerster.de

The August Förster factory was founded by Friedrich August Förster in 1859 in Löbau, Germany, after Förster studied the art of piano building. During the years of control by the government of East Germany, the factory was managed by the fourth-generation piano builder, Wolfgang Förster. After the reunification of Germany and privatization, Wolfgang and his family once again owned their company. August Förster GmbH is now managed in the fifth generation by Wolfgang's daughter, Annekatrin Förster.

With a workforce of 40 using a great deal of hand labor, Förster makes about 120 grands a year in four sizes, and 150 verticals a year in three sizes. The pianos are very well built structurally, and the cabinets are elegant. Rims and pinblocks are of beech, soundboards of solid mountain-grown spruce, and bridges are of hardrock maple (without graphite). Each string is individually terminated (single-strung). The actions are made by Renner with Renner hammers. A sostenuto pedal is standard on all grand models.

The tone of August Förster grands is unique, with a remarkable bass: dark, deep, yet clear. As delivered from the factory, the treble is often quite bright, and for some American tastes might be considered a bit thin—it is a less complex sound that emphasizes clarity. This, however, can be modified somewhat with voicing and a good dealer preparation. The instruments are quite versatile, at home with Mozart or Prokofiev, classical or jazz. The 6' 4" model is often said to have an especially good scale. The concert-quality 7' 2" and 9' 1" models are well balanced tonally, and over the years have been endorsed by many famous artists. The Renner actions are very responsive and arrive in exacting regulation. The new 53" model 134K anniversary upright, intended for pianists who don't have space for a grand, has such grand-piano–like features as a full sostenuto; a large, adjustable music desk; and black keys of real ebony.

Most of the comments regarding the quality of materials and workmanship of the Förster grands also apply to the verticals. The cabinet of the vertical is of exceptional width, with extra-thick side panels of solid-core stock. Counter bridges are used on the outside of the soundboard to increase its mass. The verticals have a full set of agraffes, and all the hardware and handmade wood parts are of elegant quality. The actions are built by Renner. The verticals possess the same warm, rich, deep bass tone as the grands.

GEYER, A.

www.geyer-pianos.com

The A. Geyer brand and factory were established by the Geyer family in 1877, in Eisenberg, Thuringia, Germany, and the brand was well known in the late 19th and early 20th centuries, when Eisenberg was a significant center for piano building. In time, the Geyer factory became the Wilh. Steinberg factory, which continues to produce pianos today.

Today, A. Geyer is a new company, with headquarters in Wiesbaden, Germany. The company's founders are Christoph Schulz, a fifth-generation German piano maker; Frederik Steffes, the former owner of the Wilh. Steinberg factory; and Colin Taylor, formerly with Bösendorfer and Brodmann. Although the company is new, the three founders bring to it decades of combined experience in piano manufacturing, and a vision, they say, to create a piano wonderful in sound, touch, and style, with outstanding value for the money.

Although the pianos are designed in Germany, A. Geyer production is located near Hangzhou, in Zhejiang Province, China, a region just outside of Shanghai that has become a center of piano manufacturing. The company founders believe that their knowledge and experience of traditional German methods of piano making, combined with local Chinese resources, can result in a better piano at lower cost.

Currently, A. Geyer makes three upright pianos and five grands. All pianos use carefully selected Chinese parts that are subject to strict quality controls. German Wurzen felt is used for the upright hammers, and Abel hammers for the grands. All pianos have a solid-spruce-core veneered soundboard and Japanese Suzuki strings. The actions and keyboards have been designed by the company's German master piano builder. All pianos are inspected by the company's technicians before leaving the factory.

GROTRIAN

including Wilhelm Grotrian

www.grotrian.de

Friedrich Grotrian was born in 1803 in Schöningen, Germany, and as a young man lived in Moscow, where he ran a music business and was associated with piano manufacturing. Later in his life he teamed up with C.F. Theodor Steinweg, son of Heinrich Steinweg, to build pianos. Heinrich had emigrated to the U.S. about 1850, soon to establish the firm of Steinway & Sons. Theodor followed in 1865, selling his share in the partnership to Wilhelm Grotrian, son of Friedrich, who had died in 1860. Thereafter, the firm became known as Grotrian-Steinweg. (In a legal settlement with Steinway & Sons, Grotrian-Steinweg agreed to use only the name Grotrian on pianos sold in North America.) Even as early as the 1860s, Grotrian pianos were well known and highly respected throughout Europe. Each successive generation of the Grotrian family maintained the company's high standards and furthered the technical development of the instrument.

In 2015, a majority interest in the Grotrian Piano Co. was purchased by Parsons Music Group, a Hong Kong–based piano manufacturer. Grotrian says that all pianos bearing its name will continue to be made in Braunschweig, Germany, and that the Parsons investment will be used to expand manufacturing capacity to better serve the burgeoning Asian piano market. A member of the sixth generation of the Grotrian family is a shareholder, and will continue to participate in managing the company.

Grotrian grands have beech rims, solid spruce soundboards, laminated beech pinblocks, Renner actions, and are single-strung. Grotrian prides itself on what it calls its "homogeneous soundboard," in which each piece of wood is specially chosen for its contribution to the tone. The cast-iron plate is attached with screws along the outer edges of the rim, instead of on the top of the rim, which the company says allows the soundboard to vibrate more freely. The vertical pianos have a unique star-shaped wooden back structure and a full-perimeter plate to ensure the instrument's structural and tonal stability over time.

The treble of Grotrian pianos has extraordinary sustaining characteristics. It also has a pronounced sound of attack, subtle and delicate. The tenor is darker than many other brands. The bass can be powerful, but without stridency. Overall, Grotrian pianos have a unique, expressive sound and are a pleasure to play. Over the years, many European royal families have appointed Grotrian to supply pianos to the court, and many well-known pianists have endorsed or expressed appreciation for Grotrian pianos.

Grotrian makes five sizes of grand and six sizes of vertical piano. New "studio" versions of grand models 192 (6' 3") and 208 (6' 10"), made for institutions, have scratch-resistant cabinet finishes, wider music desks, and more impervious soundboard finishes. At the Braunschweig factory, Grotrian also makes a lower-cost line with a beech back frame but no back posts, and a simpler cabinet. It's available in a 43½" model in polished ebony with legs, and in 43½" and 45" models for institutional use, with satin finishes but without legs.

In 2018, Grotrian introduced two lines that are even more affordable: Wilhelm Grotrian and Wilhelm Grotrian Studio. These instruments combine German Grotrian designs with "global sourcing and global manufacturing," including soundboards of lightweight Alaskan spruce. The two new lines have the same tone color, touch, and performance; the only difference between them is that the Wilhelm Grotrian Studio models come in simpler cabinet designs for the more price-conscious buyer.

The Wilhelm Grotrian line comprises four sizes of vertical piano—46", 48", 49", 52"—and three sizes of grand: 5' 7", 6' 2", and 6' 11". The Wilhelm Grotrian Studio line consists of three sizes of vertical—45½", 47", 48"—and two sizes of grand: 5' and 5' 5".

HAESSLER—see Blüthner

HAILUN

including Cline and Emerson
www.hailun-pianos.com

Hailun is a little different from most of the other Chinese companies selling pianos in the U.S.: Its founder and owner, Chen Hailun, is an entrepreneur in the Western style, and deeply involved in every aspect of the business. Originally a maker of molds for industrial use, in 1986 Chen got into the piano business when piano manufacturers started to use his services to make piano parts. In 1998 he bought out the government's position in his company to better control quality and hiring decisions. He began

assembling entire pianos in 1995, and the assembly facility converted to a full-scale piano manufacturing facility in 2000. Today, the Hailun factory has over 400,000 square feet of production capacity and 800 employees. A 200,000-square-foot expansion project is underway to accommodate distribution in the U.S. market. Additionally, a new cabinet factory is now complete and began production in 2008. In addition to making pianos under the Hailun name, the company also makes the Feurich brand, and also makes pianos or components under contract for several other manufacturers and distributors. Hailun recently conducted an Initial Public Offering of stock on the Shenzen Stock Exchange. Currently, the Hailun line consists of four vertical sizes (mostly larger uprights) and five grand sizes.

Over the years, much of Chen's technical efforts have gone into maximizing the precision and stability of the pianos and parts his company makes. This is evidenced by the substantial investment in computer-controlled machinery used for precision cutting; the design of keys, keybeds, and other parts to resist warping; and the fact that grand piano actions are actually interchangeable between instruments of the same model (this requires an unusually high level of precision). The pianos themselves exhibit good quality control and intelligence in design. In terms of materials, the company uses maple in grand piano rims, a feature indicative of higher quality and arguably necessary for the best sound.

Hailun America is in the process of introducing several new grand and vertical models under the Emerson brand name (formerly the Hailun Vienna Series). The W.P. Emerson Co. was founded in 1849 by William P. Emerson, later changing its name to the Emerson Piano Co. Located in Boston, the company became a meeting place of old-world artisans and new-world technology, and grew into one of the largest and most reputable piano manufacturers of its time, selling its pianos throughout the world.

Emerson pianos are designed by an international team of piano designers close to the Hailun factory, and are manufactured by Hailun. The wood for its soundboards is sourced from the North Austrian Alps. The grands are designed with a wide tail, vertically laminated maple bridges, a slightly firmer touch, and faster action speed. Each purchaser of an Emerson may, within 18 months of purchase, request that a special highly qualified technician, known as a Vienna Concert Technician, spend a full day of concert-level regulation and voicing on the piano at the customer's home.

In 2011, Hailun introduced a slow-close piano lid in all its grand piano models. Graphically named the Hailun Limb Protection System (HLPS), this is a version of the Magic Lid retrofit system, described elsewhere in this publication, built into the piano at the factory. HLPS allows even a child to easily lift the otherwise heavy lid of a grand piano without danger, and prevents a falling lid from crashing down onto arms and hands. A version of HLPS, called HLPS Plus, and available only in the Emerson models, allows the user to adjust a grand piano lid to any position without the need for a lid propstick. Apart from the safety benefit, HLPS Plus allows the user to modulate sound projection by adjusting the lid position.

Hailun has introduced the Hailun Dream Assurance Program, in which the company guarantees, subject to certain limitations, that the sound of any purchased Hailun piano will be to the customer's liking or, within 90 days of purchase, the company will exchange the piano for another of the same model. Under the company's Gold Service Program, Hailun dealers are obligated to provide each customer with one free service call between 60 and 180 days after purchase of a piano.

Hailun America is reintroducing the Cline brand to the U.S. market in the form of entry-level models made by Hailun. Chester L. Cline began selling pianos in Tacoma, Washington, in the 1880s, and produced pianos under his own name beginning in 1889. He eventually expanded his retail chain throughout the Northwest and, in the 1920s, into California, becoming one of the largest piano dealers in the West. In the 1980s and '90s, pianos bearing the Cline name were made by several manufacturers of entry-level pianos.

Today, Cline makes 46½" and 48" verticals and a 4' 11" grand. The grand comes with the HLPS lid-support system. Owners of Cline pianos in North America are entitled to receive a trade-in credit of the full amount paid for the instrument toward the purchase of a new grand made by Hailun, Emerson, or Petrof (all of whom share a common distributor).

HALLET, DAVIS & CO.

www.halletdavispianos.com

This famous old American piano brand dates back to at least 1843 in Boston, and has changed hands many times over the years. It eventually became part of the Aeolian group of piano brands, and instruments bearing the name were manufactured at Aeolian's Memphis plant until that company went out of business in 1985. Subsequently, North American Music began producing Hallet, Davis, & Co. pianos, first in Korea, and now in China.

The Heritage Collection is made by the Beijing Hsinghai Piano Group, Ltd. (see Beijing Hsinghai), the Signature Collection by Pearl River. The upper-level pianos, known as the Imperial Collection II, are manufactured by Parsons Music, a factory associated with a large chain of music stores in China and Hong Kong, and one of the largest producers of pianos in China.

HARDMAN, PECK & CO.

www.hardmanpiano.com

Hugh Hardman established the Hardman Piano Company in New York City in 1842. Leopold Peck joined the company in 1880, and became a partner in 1890, at which time the company was renamed Hardman, Peck & Company. In the early 20th century, Hardman, Peck was sold to the Aeolian Corporation, which eventually moved to Memphis, where it remained until it went out of business in 1985. Today's Hardman, Peck pianos are manufactured in China by the Beijing Hsinghai Piano Group. The piano line offers a selection of vertical and grand pianos in a variety of styles and finishes to meet the needs of entry-level and mid-level pianists.

HARRODSER

www.harrodser.de
This company is seeking U.S. distribution.

The original Harrodser piano was a collaboration between the 19th-century pianomaker W. Danemann and the young British pianist Harold Bauer. The two met in 1893, and finding they had much in common, Danemann designed a piano for Bauer, and Bauer hired the C. Bechstein company to custom-produce it under the name Harrods. Thereafter, Bauer toured with the piano, which led to sales of custom-built Harrods pianos for the wealthy. (Bauer's father, Robert Bauer, had actually built his own "Harrodser" piano as early as 1840. When, years later, it was damaged, Bechstein restored it, thus leading to the commission in the 1890s to produce the Harrods piano for Harold Bauer.)

At the outbreak of World War I, Harold Bauer emigrated to the U.S., and the production of Harrods pianos ceased. Then, in 1931, Bauer moved to Düsseldorf, Germany, where he established a piano factory and began manufacturing pianos under the name Harrodser (meaning "Harrods forever"). Production was interrupted by World War II, but resumed in 1945.

In 1941, Harold Bauer died, and control of the company passed to his son, Bain, who continued to improve the piano and increase production. By the 1970s, some 500 Harrodser uprights and 200 grands were being made annually. Later in the century, in response to the pressures of globalization, the company established manufacturing facilities in Indonesia. More recently, in 2012, the company signed an agreement with a production partner in Shanghai, China. The piano brand is now distributed throughout China and in many other countries.

HEINTZMAN & CO.

including Gerhard Heintzman
www.hzmpiano.com

Heintzman & Co. Ltd. was founded by Theodore August Heintzman in Toronto in 1866. By 1900, Heintzman was one of Toronto's larger manufacturing concerns, building 3,000 pianos per year and selling them throughout Canada and abroad through a network of company stores and other distributors. The pianos received high praise and won prizes at exhibitions. Even today, technicians frequently encounter old Heintzman pianos built in the early part of the 20th century and consider them to be of high quality. In the latter decades of the century, Heintzman, like other North American brands, struggled to compete with cheaper foreign imports. The factory finally closed its doors in 1986 and relocated to China. At first the company was a joint venture with the Beijing Hsinghai Piano Group, but when the Chinese government began allowing foreign ownership of manufacturing concerns, the Canadian partner bought back majority ownership and took control.

The new company, known as Heintzman Piano Company, Ltd., is Canadian owned and managed and has a private, independent factory dedicated to producing Heintzman-brand pianos. Heintzman makes pianos to the original Canadian Heintzman designs and scales

using some of the equipment from Canada. The company even uses some components from Canada, such as Bolduc soundboards, in grands and larger verticals. The factory makes about 5,000 pianos per year.

Verticals for export to North America typically start at 48", and both verticals and grands contain a mixture of parts from China, Canada, the U.S., and Germany. New in 2013, and aimed at a slightly more upscale audience, is the Royal series of verticals and grands, with two-tone cabinet trim and inlays on the inside of the lid.

Heintzman Piano Company also makes the slightly less expensive Gerhard Heintzman brand. This line uses less expensive materials and components, such as Japanese hammers and a veneer-laminated spruce soundboard in the verticals (a Bolduc soundboard in some of the grands). The polished ebony grands have a silver plate and trim.

HESSEN, J.F.

www.jfhessenpiano.com

In 2002, the Chinese piano manufacturer Artfield purchased a majority interest in Feurich from its owner, Julius Feurich, whose company had been making pianos in Germany since 1851. Artfield made exact copies of all the Feurich equipment and scale designs, and has since been manufacturing and distributing pianos in China under the Julius Feurich name. In 2008, Artfield transferred the Feurich company back to Julius Feurich in exchange for additional production equipment, but retained the right to use the Julius Feurich name in China. Now Artfield has hired Stephan Kühnlein, a production manager in Julius Feurich's former company (no longer in business), and other former Feurich employees, to complete the manufacture of pianos in Altenstadt, Germany, to the original Feurich designs. These pianos are to be called "J.F. Hessen," the "J.F." referring to Julius Feurich, and "Hessen" referring to the German state, Hesse, in which Altenstadt is located. Julius Feurich is not involved with the company.

Most of the assembly of J.F. Hessen pianos is performed in China by Artfield, and the pianos are similar to those Artfield makes under the Julius Feurich name. For the J.F. Hessen pianos, however, the nearly completed instruments are shipped to Germany, where the hammers are installed and all musical finishing work, such as tuning, voicing, and action regulating, is performed to German standards. The pianos contain the usual high-quality components often found in German pianos: Renner actions (standard in grands, optional in verticals), Renner or Abel hammers, Strunz Bavarian spruce soundboards, Röslau strings, and sharps of real ebony wood. Due to the amount of German materials and labor in the final product, the pianos qualify for "made in Germany" status under German law.

HOFFMANN, W.—see Bechstein, C.

HUPFIELD—see Rönisch

IRMLER

including Schiller
www.irmler-piano.com
www.bluethner.ca

Irmler is a sister company of Blüthner, and Irmler pianos are distributed through the Blüthner dealer network. The brand is available in two series: Studio and Professional.

The Studio series is largely made in a factory in China owned by Irmler. The pianos are then shipped to the Blüthner factory in Germany, where Abel hammers are installed and the pianos are inspected and adjusted as needed, prior to shipping to dealers. The pianos have Delignit pinblocks and veneer-laminated spruce soundboards. The grand rims are of Chinese oak and the grand actions are made with Renner parts. The Studio-series verticals include a number of models with interesting, modern cabinet designs.

The Professional series, also known as Irmler Europe, is assembled in Germany using strung backs (structural and acoustical elements) from Samick in Indonesia and cabinets from Poland. The pianos have Delignit pinblocks and solid spruce soundboards. Grands have rims of maple and beech, action parts by Renner (U.S. distribution only), and duplex scaling. Vertical actions are by Detoa.

The Irmler Studio series is also available from some dealers under the Schiller brand name, with a slightly modified cabinet; prices are comparable to those for Irmler.

KAWAI

including Shigeru Kawai
www.kawaius.com
www.shigerukawai.com

Kawai was founded in 1927 by Koichi Kawai, an inventor and former Yamaha employee who was the first person in Japan to design and build a piano action. While Kawai is second in size to Yamaha among Japanese piano manufacturers, it has a well-deserved reputation all its own for quality and innovation. Nearly all Kawai grands and taller uprights are made in Japan; most consoles and studios are made in Indonesia.

One of Kawai's most important innovations is the use of ABS Styran plastic in the manufacture of action parts. More than 40 years of use and scientific testing have shown this material to be superior to wood for this purpose. ABS does not swell and shrink with changes in humidity, so actions made with it are likely to maintain proper regulation better than wood actions. The parts are stronger and without glue joints, so breakage is rare. These parts are present in every Kawai piano. In the current Millennium III action found in some models, the ABS is reinforced with carbon fiber so it can be stronger with less mass. Having less mass to move (that is, less inertia), the action can be more responsive to the player's intentions, including faster repetition. Certain contact surfaces on the action parts are also micro-engineered for ideal shape and texture, resulting in a more consistent touch. Although it took a number of years to overcome the idea that plastic parts must be inferior, there is essentially no dispute anymore among piano technicians on this subject.

At present there are three basic series of Kawai verticals. The console models, all approximately 44" in height, are available in a variety of cabinet styles, all with the same internal workings. The action in this series is slightly smaller than a full-size action, so it will be slightly less responsive. However, it is more than sufficient for beginner or casual use. The studio series consists of the 46" school model UST-9, made in Indonesia, with the Millennium III action; an angled, leather-lined music desk to better hold music; and a stylish, reinforced bench; and the model 907, essentially the UST-9 in a fancy, furniture-style cabinet. The K series of uprights, 45" to 53" in height, include Millennium III actions, tapered soundboards, steel-reinforced keybeds to prevent warping, slow-close fallboards, and adjustable benches. Some of the larger models also have ivory-like keytops and a sostenuto pedal, and several models are available in the AnyTime (ATX) series as silent/hybrid pianos. See the article on **Hybrid Pianos** for details.

Kawai makes two series of grand pianos: GX (formerly RX) and GL (recently created by consolidating the GM and GE lines). The GX line, which is sold in North America in a version known as the BLAK series, is the most expensive and has the best features. It is designed for the best performance, whereas the GL series is designed more for efficiency in manufacturing, with fewer refinements. All the GX pianos feature a radial beam structure, converging together and connected to the plate using a cast-iron bracket at the tenor break. This system makes for a more rigid structure, which translates into better tone projection. The GX rims use alternating layers of two different hardwoods, one chosen for tonal power, the other for warmth. The soundboards in the GX models are tapered for better tonal response; and the rims are thicker and stronger than in the GL models. The Kawai Millennium III actions used in both series now have hammer-shank stabilizers, designed to retain power by keeping the shank from wavering under a heavy blow. All GX pianos have agraffes, duplex scaling, lighter hammers (less inertia), and Neotex synthetic ivory keytops; and come with a slow-close fallboard. The GX grands get more precise key weighting, plus more tuning, regulating, and voicing at the factory. The cabinetry is nicer looking and of better quality than that of the GL series pianos, with the polished ebony models in the new BLAK series receiving a UV-cured, scratch-resistant coating on the music rack.

Kawai's quality control is excellent, especially in its Japanese-made pianos. Major problems are rare, and other than normal maintenance, after-sale service is usually limited to fixing the occasional minor buzz or squeak. Kawai's warranty service is also excellent, and the warranty is transferable to future owners within the warranty period (a benefit that is not common these days). When expertly voiced, Kawai grands are quite versatile musically. In part because the touch is so good, they are often sought by classical pianists as a less-expensive alternative to a high-end piano. There is also a thriving market for used Kawais. (If you're considering buying a used Kawai, please read the section on gray-market pianos in the article **"Buying a Used or Restored Piano,"** elsewhere in this publication.)

The Shigeru Kawai line of grands represents Kawai's ultimate effort to produce a world-class piano. Named after Kawai's former chairman (and son of company founder Koichi Kawai), the limited-edition (fewer than 300 per year) Shigeru Kawai grands are made at the separate facility where Kawai's EX concert grands are built.

Although based on the Kawai RX designs, the Shigeru Kawai models are "hand made" in the extreme. Very high-grade soundboard spruce is air-dried for multiple years, then planed by hand by a worker who knocks on the wood and listens for the optimum tonal response. Ribs are also hand-planed for correct stiffness. String bearing is set in the traditional manner by planing the bridges by hand instead of having pre-cut bridges pinned by machine. Bass strings are wound by hand instead of by machine. Hammers are hand-pressed without heat for a wider voicing range, and the hammer weights are carefully controlled for even touch. Hammer shanks are thinned along the bottom so that their stiffness is matched to the hammer mass. These procedures represent a level of detail relatively few manufacturers indulge in.

Each buyer of a Shigeru Kawai piano receives a visit within the first year by a Kawai master technician from the factory in Japan. These are the same factory technicians who do the final installation of actions in pianos, as well as the final voicing and regulation. According to those who have watched them work, these Japanese master technicians are amazingly skilled. Because the Shigeru Kawai pianos have been on the market only since 2000 and in very limited quantities, many piano technicians have yet to service one. Those who have, however, tend to rank them among the world's finest instruments, and Shigeru Kawai pianos are often chosen by pianists participating in international piano competitions.

KAYSERBURG—see Pearl River

KINGSBURG

www.kingsburgpianosusa.com
www.kingsburgpiano.com.cn

Yantai Kingsburg Piano Co., Ltd., formerly known as Yantai Longfeng, was established in 1988. It is located in a temperate area of northern China that is said to be ideal for piano making because of its moderate humidity level. The same factory, under previous ownership, made pianos for the West under various brand names for many years.

All Kingsburg pianos have been designed by well-known piano-design master Klaus Fenner, and scales have been further developed by a piano-design expert from a highly regarded overseas piano manufacturer. Components are sourced from around the world: from Germany, Röslau piano wire, Abel hammers, and Dehonit pinblocks; from the Czech Republic, Detoa actions; and from Japan, tuning pins and ivory-like mineral keytops. All pianos now feature sharps of real ebony wood and come with a slow-close fallboard. Interesting design features include longer keys on upright models for more a grand-like playing experience, brass-bar duplex scale, and the company's exclusive Tri Board solid spruce soundboard, which, in the taller verticals, is unattached to the piano back at the bottom, for better bass tone and improved tuning stability. Kingsburg has also invested in computerized manufacturing equipment and advanced scale-design software.

At present, the Kingsburg line comprises four sizes of upright and three sizes of grand. Custom styles and finishes are also available.

KNABE, WM.

www.knabepianos.com

Founded in Baltimore in 1837 by Wilhelm (William) Knabe, a German immigrant, Wm. Knabe & Co. established itself in the 19th and early 20th centuries as one of the finest piano makers in America. Over the years, Knabe pianos have left an important mark on the music field, including over 40 years as the official piano of the Metropolitan Opera, sponsoring Tchaikovsky's appearance at the opening of Carnegie Hall, and their places inside the White House and Graceland. Today, Knabe is the official piano of the American Ballet Theatre at the Met.

As part of the consolidation of the American piano industry in the early 20th century, Knabe eventually became part of the Aeolian family of brands. Following Aeolian's demise in 1985, the Knabe name became part of Mason & Hamlin, which was purchased out of bankruptcy in 1996 by the owners of PianoDisc. Around 2000, Samick acquired the Wm. Knabe & Co.

name from PianoDisc. (Note: "Knabe" is pronounced using the hard K sound followed by "nobby.")

Knabe piano are available in three series: Concert Artist, Academy, and Baltimore. Highlighting the Concert Artist series are the 5' 8" and 6' 4" grand models, which have been redesigned based on the original 19th- and early 20th-century Knabe scale designs and cabinet styles in use when the company was based in Baltimore. Features include sand-cast plates, lacquer semigloss wood finishes, Renner actions on larger grands, German hammers, and rims of maple and oak. The verticals feature unique cabinet designs with bird's-eye maple and mahogany inlays, rosewood key inserts, and tone escapement. Originally made in Korea, most Concert Artist pianos are now made in their entirety in Indonesia, but are still uncrated in the U.S., where they are inspected, tuned, regulated, and voiced before being shipped to dealers.

The Academy series features a maple or beech inner rim (grands); a premium soundboard of solid white spruce; German hammers; a Samick Premium Action; satin lacquer semigloss wood finishes; and a Samick-made hornbeam action rail (larger verticals). The Academy series also includes two institutional studio uprights.

The Baltimore series offers a more modestly priced alternative to the institutional Academy series or upper-end Concert Artist series. This line features an all-spruce "surface tension" (veneered) soundboard. The grands provide a full sostenuto pedal, slow-close fallboard, fully adjustable music desk and rack, multiple finishes in both satin ebony and wood tones, and, recently, a new designer grand with accents of Bubinga or African Pommele. The verticals showcase a wide range of sizes and cabinet styles, including wood tones in French cherry, traditional mahogany, and Renaissance walnut.

MASON & HAMLIN

www.masonhamlin.com

Mason & Hamlin was founded in 1854 by Henry Mason and Emmons Hamlin. Mason was a musician and businessman and Hamlin was an inventor working with reed organs. Within a few years, Mason & Hamlin was one of the largest makers of reed organs in the U.S. The company began making pianos in 1881 in Boston, and soon became among the most prestigious of the Boston piano makers. By 1910, Mason & Hamlin was considered Steinway's chief competitor. Over the next 85 years, Mason & Hamlin changed hands many times. (You can read the somewhat lengthy and interesting history in *The Piano Book*.) In 1996 the Burgett brothers, owners of PianoDisc, purchased Mason & Hamlin out of bankruptcy and set about reestablishing manufacturing at the six-story factory in Haverhill, Massachusetts. The company emphasizes limited-quantity, hand-built production, and currently manufactures from 200 to 350 pianos per year. Daily tours are offered to visitors.

Since acquiring the company, the Burgetts have brought back most of the piano models from the company's golden Boston era (1881–1932) that originally made the company famous. Refinements have been made to the original scale designs and other core design features. The redesign of several older models was an especially interesting and costly project: in the process, the engineering staff resurrected the original design of each model, constructed new rim presses, standardized certain features, refined manufacturing processes, and modernized jigs, fixtures, templates, and machinery, improvements that afterward were applied to the company's other models. The 50" model 50 vertical piano has also been reintroduced and redesigned, with longer keys for a more grand-like touch, and improved pedal leverage. Internal parts for the verticals are made in Haverhill, then assembled in the company's Sacramento factory, where it also installs PianoDisc systems.

All Mason & Hamlin grands have certain features in common, including a wide-tail design; a full-perimeter plate; an extremely thick and heavy maple rim; a solid spruce soundboard; a seven-ply, quartersawn maple pinblock; and the patented tension-resonator Crown Retention System. The tension resonator (illustrated in *The Piano Book*), invented by Richard Gertz in 1900, consists of a series of turnbuckles that connect to specific points on the inner rim. This system of turnbuckles is said to lock the rim in place so that it cannot expand with stress and age, thereby preserving the soundboard crown (curvature). (The soundboard is glued to the inner rim and would collapse if the rim expanded.) While there is no modern-day experimental evidence to confirm or deny this theory, anecdotal evidence and observations by piano technicians tend to validate it because, unlike most older pianos, the soundboards of old Mason & Hamlins almost always have plenty of crown.

In the early part of the 20th century, Wessell, Nickel & Gross was a major supplier of actions to American piano manufacturers, including Mason & Hamlin. Over the years, the name fell into disuse. In 2004 Mason & Hamlin revived the name by registering the trademark, which now refers to the design and specifications of Mason & Hamlin actions. The company manufactures a new line of carbon-fiber action parts of strikingly innovative design, which the company makes available to its dealers and to rebuilders as a high-performance upgrade to the traditional wood action. The company explained that it has moved to using composite parts because of the inherent shortcomings of wood: it's prone to breakage under constant pounding, the parts vary in strength and mass from one piece of wood to the next, and wood shrinks and swells with changing temperature and humidity. Composite parts, on the other hand, are more than ten times as strong as wood; are built to microscopic tolerances, so they are virtually identical; and are impervious to weather. According to the company, material scientists predict that in the benign environment of a piano, the minimum life expectancy of composite parts is 100 years. The Wessell, Nickel & Gross composite action is now standard on all new Mason & Hamlin pianos.

Mason & Hamlin grands are available in satin and high-polish ebony finishes, and in several standard and exotic wood finishes in high polish. Satin finishes are lacquer, the high-polish finishes are polyester. Most sizes are also available in a stylized case design called Monticello, which has fluted, conical legs, similar to Hepplewhite style, with matching lyre and bench. In 2009 Mason & Hamlin introduced the Chrome art-case design, in polished ebony with chrome and stainless-steel case hardware replacing the traditional brass hardware. This design also has art-deco case styling, a silver plate, and a new fallboard logo in a modern font. This modern-font logo, along with a new slow-close fallboard, is standard on all new Mason & Hamlin grands.

In 2014, to commemorate the company's 160th anniversary, Mason & Hamlin introduced the Cambridge Collection. Model designs in this series feature two-toned cabinets in hand-rubbed finishes of polished ebony and either bubinga or Macassar ebony. On the grands, the hand-selected exotic veneers appear on the fallboard, the music desk, the lid underside, and the inner rim; on the verticals, they appear on the upper and lower front panels.

The tone of Mason & Hamlin pianos is typically American—lush, singing, and powerful, not unlike the Steinway in basic character, but with an even more powerful bass and a clearer treble. The designers have done a good job of making a recognizable Mason & Hamlin sound that is consistent throughout the model line. The 5' 8" model A and 5' 4" model B have particularly powerful bass registers for pianos of their size. The "growling" power of the Mason & Hamlin bass is most apparent in the 7' model BB. The 6' 4" model AA is a little better balanced between bass and treble, one reason why it is a favorite of mine.

In recent years many companies have turned to China and other international sources for parts and materials, for several reasons: a domestic source is no longer available, to save money, to increase the security of supply, and, in some cases, to increase quality. Among makers of high-end pianos, Mason & Hamlin has been pioneering in this regard, though it is not the only company to do so. The company's worldwide sourcing of parts and materials, along with its investment in modernized equipment, has made the Mason & Hamlin a better instrument while keeping the piano's price at a reasonable level. It's a very good value among high-end instruments.

PALATINO

www.palatinousa.com

Although Palatino may be a relatively new name to the piano world, it is not a newcomer to the music business. For almost 20 years, parent company AXL has manufactured a full range of musical instruments under its own name and under a variety of other, recognizable brand names, including cooperative ventures with Schimmel and Renner. The company has a highly automated factory that employs CNC routers from Japan and Germany, and imports high-quality materials and components for its pianos from around the world.

Palatino makes over 10,000 pianos annually in two categories: Classic and Professional. Features common to all Palatino pianos include a German or Canadian solid spruce soundboard, German Röslau steel strings, and hard rock-maple pinblock. In addition, Professional-series pianos have a Renner-style action and hammers; the Classic series uses

British-designed customized BPA-style actions and hammers.

Based on personal observation and dealer reports, Palatino pianos appear to have good quality control and are prepared well at the factory before being shipped to dealers. The AXL factory is known as being one of China's higher-grade facilities for the manufacture of musical instruments.

PARSONS MUSIC

www.parsonsmusic.com
www.parsonsmusic.com.cn

Parsons Music Corporation, headquartered in Hong Kong, was founded in 1986 by Terence and Arling Ng as a small music-lesson studio. Since then it has become China's largest music retailer, with more than 100 retail locations and 80 music schools throughout China and Hong Kong. In 1997, the company expanded into manufacturing pianos and other musical instruments, and is now the third largest piano maker in China.

At present, all of the pianos Parsons makes for sale in this part of the world are made for and distributed by other companies under those companies' own brand names. However, Parsons manufactures and sells, in China and Hong Kong, its own house brands, Yangtze River, Toyama, and Schönbrunn; manufactures the brand Barrate & Robinson, which it licenses the right to sell in China; has a strategic alliance with Kawai, in which Parsons distributes Kawai pianos in China, and manufactures select Kawai models for sale only in Parsons Music's stores in China; is the majority shareholder of the German piano makers Grotrian and Wilh. Steinberg and manufactures some of the Wilh. Steinberg models in China; and cooperates in the manufacture of the Pianoforce electronic player-piano system, and distributes it in China and Hong Kong. Parsons Music's commitment to piano manufacturing is also demonstrated by its ownership of an iron-plate foundry, a wood-processing facility, and even the forests in which the wood for its instruments is grown. In recent years, Parsons has become known within the piano-manufacturing community as the source of some of the best-made pianos from China.

PEARL RIVER

including Ritmüller and Kayserburg
www.pearlriverusa.com
www.ritmullerusa.com
www.kayserburgusa.com

Established in 1956, Pearl River Piano Group has become the largest piano manufacturer in the world, with a production of over 120,000 pianos annually by more than 2,000 workers. The company builds pianos under the Pearl River, Ritmüller, and Kayserburg names, as well as under a few other names for OEM contracts with distributors such as Cristofori (with Jordan Kitt's Music) and Essex (with Steinway). (See separate listings under those names.)

Pearl River is the best-selling piano brand in China, and is exported to more than 120 countries. After a successful IPO in 2012, the formerly government-owned company began construction of a new, state-of-the-art, 3.5 million sq. ft. factory, to which it will complete a transition in 2018. The factory combines traditional craftsmanship with advanced CNC digital machinery, and complies with European high-level technology and process standards. Pearl River has been operating a European company headquarters in Germany since 1995.

In recent years, Pearl River has revised and streamlined its model line with the assistance of European and American piano-design consultants. Many new models have been introduced, while older models have been reviewed and modified. Currently, Pearl River verticals range from 43" console models in a variety of furniture styles; to a series of studio models, including a school-friendly institutional style with special casters and a full-length music desk; to upright models up to 51½" in height. Pearl River grands come in six sizes, from 4' 11" to 9', and have been redesigned over the last several years to include features such as vertically laminated beech bridges with solid beech caps, lighter touchweights, German hammer felt, beech rims, and new scale designs.

Pearl River also makes pianos under the Ritmüller name, a brand that originated in Germany in 1795. A European master piano designer was engaged in 2007 to design, from the ground up, a line of higher-end pianos that would be distinct from the Pearl River line. These instruments were introduced in North America in 2009 under the Ritmüller name.

Ritmüller pianos come in three distinct price categories: Premium, Performance, and Classic. The Premium models feature solid spruce soundboards, Renner hammers, hornbeam actions, beech rims, and real ebony sharps, among other higher-quality features. *Piano Buyer*'s reviewers have auditioned several of the new grand models and have been consistently impressed. The Performance models, introduced in 2014, feature unique scales, offset backposts, ebony sharps, high-quality hammers made with German felt, and a veneered and tapered all-spruce soundboard. The Classic series, introduced in 2011, is a line of lower-cost instruments currently comprising three vertical models. They feature a veneered all-spruce soundboard and German Röslau strings.

In 2013, Pearl River brought to North America the upper-level Kayserburg Artists series. These instruments are handmade by two dozen of Pearl River's most experienced craftsmen, personally managed by European piano experts, in what can be described only as a small "German" piano workshop inside a large Chinese piano factory. The Kayserburg Artists craftsmen have all completed a rigorous training that includes studying the world's finest pianos and working side by side with visiting European craftsmen. The Kayserburg Artists pianos contain such high-end features as soundboards of tight-grained, solid European spruce, Renner hammers, Laoureux (French) damper felt, German Röslau strings, vertically laminated beech bridges with wood cores and solid beech caps, German natural keytops, and genuine ebony sharps.

PERZINA

including G. Steinberg
www.perzina-america.com
www.freeburgpianos.com

The Gebr. Perzina (Perzina Bros.) piano company was established in the German town of Schwerin in 1871, and was a prominent piano maker until World War I, after which its fortunes declined. In more recent times, the factory was moved to the nearby city of Lenzen and the company became known as Pianofabrik Lenzen GmbH. In the early 1990s the company was purchased by Music Brokers International B.V. of the Netherlands. Eventually it was decided that making pianos in Germany was not economically viable, so manufacturing was moved to Yantai, China, where, under license, Perzina verticals and grands were made for a number of years by another company. In 2003, Music Brokers International established Yantai-Perzina, a joint-venture factory in Yantai, where it now builds Perzina pianos.

Perzina verticals have several interesting features rarely found in other pianos, including a "floating" soundboard that is unattached to the back at certain points for freer vibration, and a reverse or concave soundboard crown. (There may be something to this; Perzina verticals sound very good, particularly in the bass.) The veneered soundboards are made entirely of Austrian white spruce, and the hammers are from C. Bechstein, in Germany.

A new line of Perzina grand pianos was introduced in 2011, designed and manufactured by Perzina in cooperation with a major European manufacturer. All contain veneered soundboards of Austrian white spruce, duplex scaling, and Abel hammers, among other high-quality components. All models come with a slow-close fallboard, and an adjustable artist bench. The distributor says that each grand is unpacked in the U.S., inspected, and adjusted as necessary before being shipped to the dealer.

The company's European headquarters says it ships many European materials to Yantai, including Degen copper-wound and Röslau strings, Delignit pinblocks, Renner and Abel hammers, English felts, European veneers, and Austrian white spruce soundboards. New manufacturing equipment is from Germany, Japan, and Italy. According to the company, all the piano designs are the original German scales.

The Perzina factory also manufactures G. Steinberg (formerly Gerh. Steinberg) pianos for distribution in the U.S. Gerhard Steinberg began making pianos in Berlin in 1908. The firm he established changed hands several times during the 20th century, most recently in 1993, when it was acquired by Music Brokers International. G. Steinberg grands are lower-cost versions of Perzina grands. They use standard factory hammers instead of Abel hammers, and the cabinets are cosmetically simpler. The verticals, also a lower-cost alternative, are of an entirely different scale design from that of Perzina verticals, and do not use Perzina's floating soundboard design.

PETROF

www.petrof.com

The Petrof piano factory was founded in 1864 by Antonin Petrof in Hradec Králové, an old, historic town 100 kilometers east of Prague, in the present Czech Republic. Five generations of the Petrof family owned and managed the business, during which time the company kept pace with technical developments and earned prizes for its pianos at international exhibitions. The Czechs have long been known for their vibrant musical-instrument industry, which also includes makers of brass, woodwind, and stringed instruments.

In 1947, when all businesses in the Czech Republic were nationalized by the state, the Petrof family was forced out of the business. In 1965 Petrof, along with other piano manufacturers, was forced to join Musicexport, the state-controlled import-export company for musical instruments. Since the fall of the Soviet Union and the liberation of Eastern Europe, the various factories that were part of Musicexport have been spun off as private businesses, including Petrof, which is once again owned and controlled by the Petrof family. Currently Petrof manufactures 5,000 vertical pianos and 900 grands annually.

Petrof manufactures six grand piano models, named (in size order) Bora, Breeze, Storm, Pasat, Monsoon, and Mistral, from 5' 2" to 9' 2" in length. Most component parts are produced by Petrof or other Czech factories, and hammers are from Renner or Abel. These pianos also boast several interesting features: The soundboard is custom-tapered and asymmetrically crowned for optimal resonance; the treble bridge is capped with genuine ebony for better transmission of treble tone; front and rear duplexes are tuned for tonal color; pianos are single-strung for tuning stability; an adjustable bolt has been added from the plate to the wooden cross block for additional tuning stability; and a decorative veneer has been added to the inner rim.

Petrofs are known for their warm, rich, singing tone, full of color. The pianos are solidly built and workmanship is good. After careful preparation, the pianos can sound and feel quite beautiful and hold their own against other European brands. Wages in the Czech Republic have risen in recent years, and with it the price of Petrof pianos, but the company has placed a greater emphasis on quality control and enhanced features in the new models in order to meet the higher expectations that come with higher prices.

PLEYEL

www.pleyel.com

This company is seeking U.S. distribution.

Ignace Pleyel, an accomplished musician and composer, patron of music, and publisher, began manufacturing pianos in 1807 with the aim of adapting instruments to the new requirements of the composers and musicians of his day. By the time of his death in 1831, Pleyel pianos were known and exported throughout the world. His son, Camille, an accomplished pianist, continued the family business and brought it to new heights of success. As part of his work, Camille established the legendary music salons that served as a focus for the Parisian music scene of his time and where many famous musicians and composers were heard for the first time. It was at one of these concerts, in 1832, that Frederic Chopin made his Paris debut, and he played his final concert there in 1848. Chopin was always very loyal to Pleyel, and was the company's best ambassador. In addition to Chopin, who is closely associated with Pleyel pianos, other notable users included Claude Debussy, Cesar Frank, Edward Grieg, Charles Gounod, Felix Mendelssohn, and Maurice Ravel. In 1927 the company established the Salle Pleyel, an important Paris concert venue.

The ingenuity of Pleyel's innovations was expressed through many patents and inventions. For example, the company first introduced iron bracing into a piano in 1826, was the first to bring the upright piano to France, and is credited with inventing the sostenuto in 1860.

Over the years, Pleyel acquired the piano names of former French makers Rameau, Gaveau, and Erard. From 1971, these names were made under contract by Schimmel in Germany, returning to France in 1994. In 2000, a private investor associated with the Salle Pleyel acquired the Pleyel trademarks under the name Manufacture Française de Pianos and moved the factory to the south of France, where for several years it produced high-quality instruments using a combination of high-tech machinery and hand craftsmanship. In 2008, the company downsized and moved to a location in the outskirts of Paris, not far from its original factory and the Salle Pleyel, where it concentrated on building a small number of designer instruments. In 2013, Pleyel ceased manufacturing, and moved to a workshop in Paris dedicated to the restoration of antique pianos.

In 2016, Pleyel began a partnership with Algam, a leading musical-instrument distribution company in Europe. In 2017, Algam acquired the Pleyel brand, and launched two series of pianos for the international market: the Heritage collection of upright and grand pianos, made in Indonesia; and the Haute Facture collection of high-end grands, made in France.

PRAMBERGER

www.smcmusic.com

The Pramberger name was first used by Young Chang for its premium-level pianos under license from the late piano engineer Joseph Pramberger, who at one time was head of manufacturing at Steinway & Sons. When Pramberger died, in 2003, his estate terminated its relationship with Young Chang and signed up with Samick. However, since Young Chang still holds the rights to its piano designs, Samick has designed new pianos to go with the name.

The J.P. Pramberger Platinum piano is a higher-end instrument, formerly made in Korea, and now made in Indonesia under Korean supervision using the CNC equipment acquired by Samick during its partnership with Bechstein. It is then shipped to the U.S. for inspection, tuning, regulating, and voicing before being shipped to dealers. Several American technicians who had known and worked with Joe Pramberger went to Korea at Samick's request to design this piano. Benefiting by work previously done by Bechstein engineers at the Samick factory, they began with a modified Bechstein scale, then added several features found on current or older Steinways, such as an all-maple (or beech) rim, an asymmetrically tapered white spruce soundboard, vertically laminated and tunneled maple and mahogany bridges with maple cap, duplex scaling, a Renner/Pramberger action, and Renner or Abel hammers. One of the technicians told me that the group feels its design is an advancement of Pramberger's work that he would have approved of.

The Pramberger Signature (formerly known as J. Pramberger) is a more modestly priced instrument from Indonesia whose design is based on the former Korean-built Young Chang version. The Pramberger

Legacy, the newest addition to the Pramberger line, has a veneer-laminated "surface tension" soundboard, and provides a reasonably priced option for the budget-minded consumer. These models were formerly sold under the Remington label.

RAVENSCROFT

www.RavenscroftPianos.com

Handcrafted in Scottsdale, Arizona by piano builder Michael Spreeman, the Ravenscroft piano entered the market for high-end performance pianos in 2006. Two models are available, the 7' 3" model 220 and the 9' model 275. A custom-built model 275 is currently the official piano at the Tempe Center for the Arts.

While the general trend in the industry seems to be toward outsourcing to less expensive suppliers, Spreeman says his concept is the exact opposite. Appealing to the niche market of high-end consumers, Spreeman's approach is more along the lines of the early European small-shop builders, with an emphasis on quality and exclusivity.

The case and iron frame of the Ravenscroft piano are constructed in Germany by Sauter to Ravenscroft specifications and shipped to the Arizona facility. The Renner action and Kluge keys of each piano are computer-designed to optimize performance. The rib scale, soundboard, bridges, and string scale are designed by Spreeman, who meticulously hand-builds each instrument with his three-person team.

Currently, only four to six pianos are produced yearly, with pricing beginning at $230,000 for a model 220, and up to $550,000 for a model 275 with "all the extras," including titanium string terminations, exotic veneers, intarsia, artwork, and inlays of precious stones. Most instruments are custom ordered and can take up to a year to complete.

RITMÜLLER—see Pearl River

RÖNISCH

including Hupfeld
www.roenisch-pianos.de
www.hupfeld-piano.com
www.bluethner.ca

In 2009, the German piano manufacturer Blüthner purchased the Rönisch and Hupfeld brands and, to manufacture them, set up a new legal entity and a factory next door to the Blüthner factory in Leipzig, Germany.

Rönisch was established in Dresden in 1845 by Carl Rönisch. In his day, Rönisch was a pioneer in piano building, and his instruments were sold throughout the world. Rönisch's son sold the company after World War I, and production was moved to Leipzig after the Dresden factory was bombed in 1945. During the Communist era, the company was taken over by the state and combined with other piano factories; it became privately owned again in the 1990s.

Since purchasing the brand, Blüthner has redesigned the pianos, which are now made in three sizes of vertical and three sizes of grand, in dozens of styles, woods, and finishes. Musically, and in terms of their quality, Rönisch pianos are very similar to Haessler, another Blüthner brand, but the cabinet styles and finishes offered are different. The pianos are entirely made in Germany, with such parts as rims, beams, and cabinets supplied by Blüthner, and other high-quality parts from European suppliers. Although new to North America, Rönisch pianos have been very popular in other parts of the world for decades. Approximately 600 verticals and 300 grands are made each year.

Ludwig Hupfeld became involved in the musical instrument business in 1892, and purchased the Rönisch company in 1918. (Today, Hupfeld is a subdivision of Rönisch.) Hupfeld was one of the earliest and best-known makers of reproducing pianos—advanced pneumatic player pianos of the early 1900s that faithfully recorded the nuances of the playing of recording artists—and other automatic musical instruments.

Hupfeld pianos are made in two editions: Hupfeld Europe and Studio. The Hupfeld Europe line is entirely made in Europe, with strung backs and cabinets from Romania, and key and action assembly, final regulation, voicing, and inspection done at the Rönisch factory in Germany. The Studio line is made in Indonesia, using cast-iron plates, actions, and keys from Indonesian suppliers, and hammers, strings, pinblocks, and felt from Germany. The instruments are then sent to the Rönisch factory in Germany for final regulation, voicing, and inspection.

SAMICK

See also Wm. Knabe, Pramberger, and Seiler
www.smcmusic.com

In 1958, in South Korea, Hyo Ick Lee founded Samick as a Baldwin distributor. Facing an immense challenge in an impoverished and war-torn country, in the early 1960s, using largely imported parts, Lee began to build and sell a very limited quantity of vertical pianos. As South Korea's economy improved, Lee expanded his operation, and in 1964 began exporting to other parts of the world, eventually becoming one of the world's largest piano manufacturers, now making most parts in-house. Over the next several decades, Samick expanded into manufacturing guitars and other instruments and opened factories in China and Indonesia, where it shifted much of its production as Korean wages rose.

The company says that "Samick" means "three benefits" in Korean, symbolizing the management's wish that the activities of the company benefit not only the company itself, but also its customers and the Korean economy.

Samick Music Corporation (SMC), the North American sales and marketing arm of the Korean company, distributes Samick, Pramberger, Wm. Knabe, and Seiler pianos in North America (see separate listings for the other brands). Most Samick-made pianos destined for the U.S. market are made in Indonesia. SMC has a warehouse and office facility in Tennessee, at which it uncrates, inspects, tunes, regulates, and voices its upper-level pianos before shipping them to dealers.

Most dealers of Samick-made pianos carry the Wm. Knabe, Pramberger, and/or Seiler lines. The company's offerings under the Samick brand name are limited to three sizes of grand piano that the company calls its International Series. These models are made in Indonesia using the same German computerized manufacturing (CNC) equipment employed for the upper-level models of its other brands. These models have solid white-spruce soundboards.

In the 1980s Klaus Fenner, a German piano designer, was hired to revise the Samick scale designs to make the pianos sound more "European." Most Samick pianos now being made are based on these designs. Most Samicks also have veneer-laminated soundboards, which the company calls a "surface tension" soundboard—essentially, a solid spruce soundboard sandwiched by two very thin veneers. With Klaus Fenner's technical advice, Samick pioneered the use of this soundboard in early 1980, and it is now used by others as well. Tonally, it behaves much like a solid spruce soundboard, but won't crack or lose its crown.

Quality control in Samick's South Korean and Indonesian factories has steadily improved over the years, and the Indonesian product is said to be almost as good as the Korean. The company says that new CNC machinery installed in 2007 has revolutionized the consistency and accuracy of its manufacturing. Many of Samick's Indonesian pianos are priced similarly to low-cost pianos from China.

SAUTER

www.sauter-pianos.de

The Sauter piano firm was founded in 1819 by Johann Grimm, stepfather to Carl Sauter I, and has been owned and managed by members of the Sauter family for six generations. The factory produces about 500 vertical and grand pianos a year in its factory in the extreme south of Germany, at the foot of the Alps. Structural and acoustical parts are made of high-quality woods, including solid Bavarian spruce soundboards and beech pinblocks. Actions are made by Renner. The keybed is reinforced with steel to prevent warping, and all pianos are fully tropicalized for humid climates. The larger verticals use an action, designed and patented by Sauter, that contains an auxiliary jack spring to aid in faster repetition. Sauter calls this the R2 Double Escapement action. (Although the term double escapement does not apply here as it has historically been used, the mechanism has some of the same effects.)

Sauter pianos are especially known for their lush, full, singing tone, and for the variety of finishes and styles in which they are available, many with intricate detail and inlay work. It is common to find such rare woods as yew, burl walnut, pyramid mahogany, and genuine ebony in the cabinets of Sauter pianos, as well as special engravings, which can be customized to any customer's desires. Sauter's M Line of vertical pianos features exclusive cabinet detailing and built-in features such as a hygrometer to measure relative humidity.

The company also has introduced versions of its 48" upright and 6' 11" and 7' 6" grands with cabinets designed by the famous European designer Peter Maly. Some recent designs include the 48" upright Vitrea, after the Latin word for glass, with a veneer of greenish glass covering the front of the cabinet; Vivace, a 6' 11" grand in a contemporary style with steel leg frame and inlays of stainless-steel squares on the rim; and Ambiente, a 7' 6" grand that is asymmetrically curved on both the bass and treble sides. In the recent past, Sauter has won several prestigious design awards for its Peter Maly–designed pianos.

SCHILLER—see Irmler

SCHIMMEL

including Wilhelm Schimmel and Fridolin Schimmel
www.schimmel-piano.de

Wilhelm Schimmel began making pianos in Leipzig in 1885, and his company enjoyed steady growth through the late 19th and early 20th centuries. The two World Wars and the Depression disrupted production several times, but the company has gradually rebuilt itself over the past 70 years while earning a strong reputation for quality. In 2016, the Chinese piano maker Pearl River purchased a majority interest in Schimmel, in which the Schimmel family remains shareholders. Today, Schimmel is managed by Hannes Schimmel-Vogel, the husband of Viola Schimmel. One of Europe's most prolific piano makers, Schimmel makes about 2,500 verticals and 500 grands per year.

Among European piano manufacturers, Schimmel has been a pioneer in the use of computer-aided design and manufacturing. The company has used its Computer Assisted Piano Engineering (CAPE) software to research, design, and implement virtually every aspect of making a piano, from keyboard layout and action geometry to soundboard acoustics and scale design. According to Schimmel, the combination of CNC machinery and handcraftsmanship leads to better results than handwork alone. Schimmel also believes that precision is aided by controlling as much of the production process as possible.

For that reason, Schimmel produces its own piano-cabinet components and its own keyboards, which it also supplies to other German piano makers.

Schimmel's model line is organized into five categories: Konzert (K) and Classic (C), both made entirely in Germany; the Schimmel International series, made in Germany from parts sourced globally (this series is no longer exported to North America); Wilhelm Schimmel (formerly known as Vogel), made in Poland; and Fridolin Schimmel, made in China by Pearl River.

The company says that the purpose of the Konzert series is to expand the Schimmel line upward to a higher level of quality than it had previously attained, whereas the Classic series represents models that have been tested over time and are solid, traditional, high-quality instruments, but without all the latest refinements. The Konzert-series uprights are based on a more sophisticated philosophy of construction than the Classics, and incorporate triplex scaling and other advanced design features. Schimmel's philosophy for these uprights was to design them to be as much like the grands as possible. The treble scales, in fact, are exactly the same as in the Konzert grands. All uprights have adjustable gliders (to adjust to unevenness in the floor) and come with a matching adjustable bench.

All Konzert grand models are scaled to use the model 280's concert-grand action. The case sides are angled slightly to accommodate a larger soundboard, and all have tunable front and rear duplex or triplex scales for greater tonal color. Other advanced features include: improved soundboard and bridge materials, more time spent voicing the instruments in the factory, sharps of real ebony, and mineral white keytops to mimic the feel of ivory. The largest grands have reinforced keys for optimal energy transmission.

The Konzert grands were designed, in part, to add color to the tone; sustain is also very good. The pianos are being delivered to U.S. dealers voiced less bright than in the past, as this is what the American ear tends to prefer. As for the verticals, the smaller models tend to have very big bass for their size, with a tone that emphasizes the fundamental, giving the low end a warmer character.

In 2002, Schimmel acquired the PianoEurope factory in Kalisz, Poland, a piano-restoration and manufacturing facility. This factory makes the Wilhelm Schimmel brand, named for the company's founder.

Schimmel says that although the skill level of its Polish employees is high, the lower wages and other lower costs available in Poland result in a piano approximately 30% less costly than comparable Schimmel models. Wilhelm Schimmel grand pianos feature full Renner actions, with other parts mainly made by Schimmel, in Braunschweig or in Kalisz. The Wilhelm Schimmel pianos, though designed by Schimmel, don't have all the refinements and advanced features of the latest Schimmel models. Nevertheless, they have received praise from many quarters for their high-quality workmanship and sound.

The Fridolin Schimmel line is named for Wilhelm Schimmel's younger brother, who emigrated to America in 1890, and in 1893 established his own piano-manufacturing business, in Faribault, Minnesota. Fridolin Schimmel instruments feature scales, actions, and cabinets designed by Schimmel in Germany, and are made to high quality standards by Pearl River in China.

SCHULZ, GEBR.

www.schulz-pianos.com

The Schulz family has been involved in the German piano industry for more than five generations, in both manufacturing and trade. In 1888, the brothers Albert and Franz Schulz established the brand Gebr. Schulz (Schulz Bros.). The brand and company quickly became the strongest brand in the Rheingau, a county in the German state of Hesse, near Frankfurt and Wiesbaden.

In 2014, Frederik Steffes and Christoph Schulz established Steffes & Schulz to make the Gebr. Schulz brand internationally available. Steffes is the former owner of the Wilh. Steinberg factory, and Schulz is a member of the fifth generation of the Schulz family and a highly respected piano designer and technician. Their stated aim is to use their decades of combined experience in piano manufacturing "to create a piano wonderful in sound, touch, and style, which provides outstanding value for the money." To that end, the company has set up a production chain that combines modern design skills and high-tech manufacturing techniques with traditional German craftsmanship and quality control.

Currently, the company offers its G (German) line of pianos. The cabinets of G models are made in China, and, depending on the model, some sound-producing elements are made in Germany, some in China. The actions are installed, and final musical preparation is done, in Germany by specially trained and certified technicians.

SCHULZE POLLMANN

www.schulzepollmann.com
www.namusic.com

Schulze Pollmann was formed in 1928 by the merger of two German piano builders who had moved to Italy. Paul Pollmann had worked first with Ibach, then with Steinway & Sons (Hamburg), before opening his own piano factory in Germany. He later moved to Italy, where he met Albert Schulze, another relocated German piano builder. Pollmann managed the combined firms until 1942, and was followed by his son Hans, who had managed the piano maker Schimmel before returning to his father's firm. Recently, the company relocated a short distance to San Marino, a tiny city-state entirely surrounded by Italy.

In North America, Schulze Pollmann offers two series of pianos: Masterpiece (grands) and Studio (verticals). The Masterpiece Series pianos, available only by special order, are made entirely in Italy and San Marino, and contain Delignit pinblocks, Renner actions and hammers from Germany, and Ciresa solid red-spruce soundboards from the Val di Fiemme, in Italy. The company uses both sophisticated technology and handwork in its manufacturing. All soundboards have finger-jointed construction to optimize stability and prevent cracking. Many of the cabinets have beautiful designs and inlays. The Studio series is partially made in Asia and finished off, including deluxe cabinetwork, in San Marino.

The uprights are well built and have a warm, colorful sound with a good amount of sustain. The treble is not nearly as brittle sounding as in some other European uprights. Schulze Pollmann grands are likewise very nicely crafted and arrive at the dealer in good condition, needing only solid preparation to sound their best.

SCHUMANN

www.schumannus.com

One of China's oldest piano manufacturers, Nanjing Schumann was founded in 1956 as Nanjing Moutrie, originally to manufacture the Moutrie piano brand. The Schumann brand was added in 1984. The factory covers 650,000 square feet and produces nearly 10,000 pianos annually.

The company says that its pianos are modeled after the "German piano tradition," with German components used in the production process. Examples include Röslau strings, German hammer felt, and imported German beechwood for pinblocks. The uprights have agraffes, and the grands sport bird's-eye maple veneer on the inner rim. All models include a veneered all-spruce soundboard, a slow-close fallboard (keyboard cover), silver/chrome hardware, and an adjustable padded bench.

SEILER

including Johannes Seiler
www.seilerpianousa.com

Eduard Seiler, the company's founder, began making pianos in 1849, in Liegnitz, Silesia, then part of Prussia. By 1923 the company had grown to over 435 employees, was producing up to 3,000 pianos per year, and was the largest piano manufacturer in Eastern Europe. In 1945 and after World War II, when Liegnitz (now Legnica) became part of Poland, the plant was nationalized by the Polish Communist government, and the Seiler family left their native homeland with millions of other refugees. In 1954, Steffan Seiler reestablished the company in Copenhagen under the fourth generation of family ownership, and began making pianos again. In 1962 he moved the company to Kitzingen, in Bavaria, Germany, where it resides today. Steffan Seiler died in 1999; the company was managed by his widow, Ursula, until its sale to Samick in 2008. Seiler now produces about 1,000 pianos annually.

Beginning in 2010, Samick expanded the Seiler line to cover several additional price points to suit a wider range of buyers. The top-level, SE-series instruments continue to be handcrafted at the Seiler factory in Kitzingen, Germany, just as they have been for many years. These come in two styles, Classic and Trend. The construction and specifications of the two styles are the same, but the Trends look a bit more modern, and sport a silver-colored plate and chrome hardware, whereas the Classics have the traditional gold- or bronze-colored plate and brass hardware.

Both are available in dozens of special furniture styles with beautiful, exotic woods and inlays.

The mid-level Seiler pianos, the ED models, are also known as the Eduard Seiler line. The pianos are manufactured entirely at Samick's Indonesian factory, using German CNC machinery, to the exact scales and specifications of the hand-built German models, though with different keys and action parts. The custom model ED-186A, a specially prepared, limited-production version of the 6' 2" model ED-186, is for the higher-level player who seeks a musical response greater than that generally found in regular factory-produced instruments. This model uses hand-selected Renner action parts, and higher-quality keys, keyframe, and hammers, all assembled, regulated, and voiced by Samick's Senior Technical Advisor at the company's facility in Tennessee. This model, as well as model ED-168HS (Heritage), will be part of Seiler's new Elite series. These pianos receive special care and attention from technical personnel in the Tennessee facility.

In 2013, the Johannes Seiler line was introduced. Though it features cabinetry as beautiful as that of its more expensive brethren, this lower-cost line has its own scale design not shared by other Samick-owned brands, and is produced entirely in the company's Indonesian facility, using Samick's premium action and hammers from Abel.

Seiler uses a combination of traditional methods and modern technology. The scale designs are of relatively high tension, producing a balanced tone that is quite consistent from one Seiler piano to the next. Although brilliant, the tone also sings well, due to, the company says, a unique, patented soundboard feature called the Membrator system, used in Seiler's SE and ED lines: The perimeter of the soundboard is sculpted to be thicker and heavier in mass than the central portion of the board, forming an internal frame within the soundboard itself. The lighter, inner area becomes the vibrating membrane—a diaphragm on its own—unimpeded by the larger soundboard's attachment to the inner rim. Seiler says that its use of the Membrator system, as well as effective rib positioning, improves the soundboard's efficiency in radiating sound. It's easy to identify the Membrator by the tapered groove around the perimeter of the board. The grands have wide tails, for greater soundboard area and string length. The German Seiler pianos feature Bavarian spruce soundboards, multi-laminated Delignit pinblocks, quartersawn beech bridges, full Renner actions, and slow-close fallboards.

At both the German and Indonesian factories, strung backs are inspected and cabinet parts carefully fitted to ensure that all specifications have been met to precise tolerances. Soundboard mass distribution and rib positioning are under strict quality control, to achieve consistency in the soundboard's acoustical properties. Pre-stretching of the strings is done several times, followed by multiple tunings, to ensure maximum stability. Hammer alignment, voicing, and key weighting and balancing are all carefully performed by experienced Seiler technicians, both at the factory and at the company's Tennessee distribution facility, before shipment to dealers.

Seiler's 52" model SE-132, 49" model ED-126, and 52" model ED-132 are all available by special order with the optional Super Magnet Repetition (SMR) action, a patented feature that uses magnets to increase repetition speed. During play, tiny magnets attached to certain action parts of each note repel each other, forcing the parts to return to their rest position faster, ready for the next keystroke.

STEINBERG, G.—see Perzina, Gebr.

STEINBERG, WILH.

www.Wilh-Steinberg.com

This company, operating under the name Thüringer Pianoforte, was formed after the reunification of Germany by the merger of several East German piano companies, the oldest of which traces its origins back to 1877. Since July 2013, the company has been owned by Parsons Music., a Hong Kong–based piano manufacturer. In addition to its own pianos, Thüringer makes several other European piano brands under OEM agreements. The company also specializes in custom cabinets and finishes. Piano production is about 500 verticals and 50 grands per year.

Wilh. Steinberg pianos are made in two levels of quality. The higher-quality level is the Signature series. These pianos are made in Germany with actions by Renner and keyboards by Kluge. Cabinets for the verticals are made by Thüringer in its own facilities; grand cabinets are supplied by Parsons Music.

The lower-cost models, known as the P line (model numbers beginning with P), were formerly made under the Eisenberg brand name, a name no longer in use. P-line models are entirely made by Parsons Music in China using Thüringer designs.

STEINGRAEBER & SÖHNE

www.steingraeber.de

Bayreuth is famous the world over for its annual summer Wagner festival. But tucked away in the old part of town is a second center of Bayreuth musical excellence and one of the world's best-kept secrets: Steingraeber & Söhne. The company was founded in 1852 by Eduard Steingraeber, though its roots date back to the 1820s, when Eduard's father and uncle opened a workshop for square pianos and organs in the city of Neustadt. Eduard was an innovative piano designer, exhibiting his first full-size cast-iron frame at the world exhibition in Paris in 1867. From 1872 on, Steingraeber was associated with, and built pianos for, Franz Liszt and Richard Wagner, and in 1873 opened its first concert hall in Bayreuth.

Steingraeber is one of the smaller piano manufacturers in the world, producing fewer than 80 grands and 60 verticals per year for the top end of the market. It is owned and operated by sixth-generation family member Udo Schmidt-Steingraeber, who still makes pianos using the traditional methods of his forebears at the company's present factory, which it has occupied since 1872.

Steingraeber makes three sizes of vertical piano, from 48" to 54", and five sizes of grand, from 5' 7" to the 8' 11" concert grand. An interesting option on the vertical models is their "twist and change" panels: two-sided top and bottom panels, one side finished in polished ebony, the other in a two-toned combination of a wood veneer and ebony. The panels can be reversed as desired by the piano owner to match room décor, or just for a change of scenery. Steingraeber pianos have a unique sound, with an extensive tonal palette derived from a mixture of clarity and warmth.

Steingraeber is known for its many innovative technical improvements to the piano, one of which is a new action for uprights, available in all three vertical-piano models. This SFM action, as it is called, contains no jack spring, instead using magnets to return the jack more quickly under the hammer butt for faster repetition. Another innovation, introduced in 2013, is the optional sordino pedal, which inserts a thin strip of felt between hammers and strings. Popular in early 19th-century grand pianos, the purpose of this feature is not, as in most modern pianos, to damp the sound almost completely, but rather to create a distant, ethereal sound, and thus to expand the instrument's expressive possibilities. On a Steingraeber piano, the sordino can either replace the sostenuto as the middle pedal or, be operated by a fourth pedal or a knee lever. A knee lever can also be employed to activate the so-called Mozart Rail, which reduces both the hammer-blow distance and the key-touch depth to simulate the sound and touch of the pianos of Mozart's day. Steingraeber pianos can also be special-ordered with a carbon-fiber soundboard, and with the Phoenix system of bridge agraffes (see **www.hurstwoodfarmpianos.co.uk** for more information on the Phoenix system).

In addition to its regular line of pianos, Steingraeber makes a piano that can be used by physically handicapped players who lack the use of their legs for pedaling. A wireless (Bluetooth) pedal actuator is operated by biting on a special denture.

STEINWAY & SONS

www.steinway.com

Heinrich Engelhardt Steinweg, a cabinetmaker and piano maker from Seesen, Germany, emigrated with his family to the United States in 1850, and established Steinway & Sons in 1853. Within a relatively short time, the Steinways were granted patents that revolutionized the piano, and which were eventually adopted or imitated by other makers. Many of these patents concerned the quest for a stronger frame, a richer, more powerful sound, and a more sensitive action. By the 1880s, the Steinway piano was in most ways the modern piano we have today, and in the next generation the standards set by the founder were strictly adhered to. (The early history of Steinway & Sons is fascinating, and is intimately connected to the history of New York City and the piano industry in general. You can read a summary of it in *The Piano Book*; there are also several excellent books devoted to the subject.)

In the 1960s the fourth generation of Steinways found themselves without any heirs willing or able to take over the business, and without enough capital to finance much-needed equipment modernization; eventually, in 1972, they sold their company to CBS. CBS left the musical instrument business in 1985, selling Steinway to an investment group. In 1995 the company was sold again, this time to Conn-Selmer, Inc., a major manufacturer of brass and woodwind instruments, and the combined company (called Steinway Musical Instruments, Inc.) was taken public on the New York Stock Exchange. In 2013, Paulson & Company, a private-equity firm led by Queens native John Paulson, purchased the public company and took it private once again. Paulson has said that he is committed to continuing the quality-first approach on which Steinway has built its reputation. Steinway also owns a branch factory in Hamburg, Germany, which serves the world market outside of the Americas, and two major suppliers: the Herman Kluge company, Europe's largest maker of piano keys; and the O.S. Kelly company, the only remaining piano plate foundry in the U.S.

Steinway makes two types of vertical piano in three sizes: a 45" model 4510 studio, a 46½" model 1098 studio, and a 52" model K–52 upright. Models 4510 and 1098 are technically identical, with differences only in the cabinets: the former is in a period style for home use, the latter in an institutional cabinet for school use or less furniture-conscious home use. In all three models, the middle pedal operates a sostenuto mechanism. All Steinway verticals use a solid spruce soundboard, have no particleboard, and in many other ways are similar in design, materials, and quality of workmanship to Steinway grands. Actions are made by Renner. Model K–52 in ebony, and model 1098 in ebony, mahogany, and walnut, come with an adjustable artist bench, the others with a regular bench.

Steinway makes six sizes of grand piano. All ebony, mahogany, and walnut grand models come with an adjustable artist bench, the others with a regular bench.

The 5' 1" model S is very good for a small grand, but has the usual limitations of any small piano and so is recommended only where space considerations are paramount. The 5' 7" model M is a full six inches longer, but costs little more than the S. Historically one of Steinway's more popular models, it is found in living rooms across the country. Its medium size makes the tone in certain areas slightly less than perfect, but it's an excellent home instrument.

The 5' 10½" model L has been replaced with the model O of the same size. Model O was first produced in 1902, but discontinued in 1924 in favor of the model L. Changes over time in both engineering and musical taste, as well as a desire to better synchronize the offerings of the New York factory with Hamburg (where the model O was never abandoned), seemed to dictate a return to the O. The main difference between the two models is in the shape of the tail—the L has a squared-off tail, the O a round tail—but this can also affect the soundboard and bridges and therefore the tone.

Reintroduction of the model O followed by one year the reintroduction of the legendary 6' 2" model A. First offered in 1878 and discontinued in New York in 1945, the model A revolutionized piano making by featuring, for the first time, the radial rim bracing and one-piece bent rim construction now used in all Steinway grands. Over the years the model A has gone through several makeovers, each of slightly different size and scaling. The version being reintroduced was made in New York from 1896 to 1914 and is the same size as the model A that has been made at the Hamburg factory for more than a century. Models O and A are suitable for larger living rooms, and for many school and teaching situations.

The 6' 10½" model B is the favorite of many piano technicians. It is the best choice for the serious pianist, recording or teaching studio, or small recital hall. Small design changes and other refinements to this model in recent years have brought a steady stream of accolades. The 8' 11¾" model D, the concert grand, is the flagship of the Steinway line and the piano of choice for the overwhelming majority of concert pianists. It's too large for most places other than the concert stage.

Steinway uses excellent materials and construction techniques in the manufacture of its grands. The rims, both inner and outer, are made in one continuous bend from layers of maple, and the beams are of solid spruce. The keybed is of quartersawn spruce planks freely mortised together, and the keys are of Bavarian spruce. The pinblock consists of seven laminations of maple with successive grain orientations of 45 and 90 degrees. The soundboard is of solid Sitka spruce, the bridges are vertically laminated of maple with a solid maple cap, and all models have duplex scaling.

It is well known that Steinway's principal competition comes from used and rebuilt Steinways, many of which come in exotic veneers or have elaborately carved or customized "art cases." The company has responded by expanding its product line to include modern-day versions of these collector's items. The

Crown Jewel Collection consists of the regular models in natural (non-ebonized) wood veneers, many of them exotic. They are finished in a semigloss that Steinway calls Satin Lustre. In addition to satin and semigloss finishes, all regular Steinway grands are also now available in polyester high-polish ebony, lacquer high-polish ebony, and polyester high-polish white.

Limited Edition models, issued at irregular intervals, are reproductions of turn-of-the-century designs, or pianos with artistic elements that make them unique. A currently-available Limited Edition model, honoring the 70th anniversary of the birth of John Lennon, is the Imagine Series, a white piano that incorporates artwork by Lennon, along with other design elements.

During the early 1900s, ownership of art-case Steinways became a symbol of wealth and culture. Steinway has resumed this tradition by regularly commissioning noted furniture designers to create new art-case designs, usually around a theme. For example, in 1999 Frank Pollaro designed an art case called Rhapsody to commemorate the 100th anniversary of the birth of George Gershwin. The piano featured a blue-dyed maple veneer adorned with more than 400 hand-cut mother-of-pearl stars and a gilded silver plate. In 2016, another Pollaro-designed art-case model, the Fibonacci, was sold, for a record-setting $2.4 million, as Steinway's 600,000th piano. Each year sees new art-case pianos from Steinway, and they are truly stunning.

As another way of capitalizing on the popularity of older Steinways, the company also operates at its factory the world's largest piano rebuilding facility for the restoration of older Steinways. *The Piano Book* contains a great deal of additional information on the purchase of older or restored Steinways. See also **"Buying a Used or Restored Piano"** in this publication.

The underlying excellence of the Steinway musical designs and the integrity of the construction process are the hallmarks of the Steinway piano. Steinway pianos at their best have the quintessential American piano sound: a powerful bass, a resonant midrange, and a singing treble with plenty of tonal color. Although other brands have some of these characteristics, it is perhaps the particular combination of harmonics that comprise the Steinway's tonal coloration that, more than anything else, distinguishes it from other brands and gives it its richness, depth, and power. The construction process creates a very durable and rigid framework that also contributes to the power of its sound.

As mentioned earlier, Steinway owns a branch factory in Hamburg, Germany, established in 1880. The "fit and finish" (detailing) of the pianos at this factory is reputed to be better than at the one in New York, although pianists sometimes prefer the sound of the New York Steinway. Traditionally, the Hamburg factory has operated somewhat autonomously, but more recently the company has been synchronizing the two plants through technical exchanges, model changes, jointly built models, and materials that are shipped from New York to Hamburg. It's possible to special-order a Hamburg Steinway through an American Steinway dealer; or an enterprising American customer could travel to Europe, buy one there, and have it shipped back home.

In 2016, in a major development for the company, Steinway unveiled its own electronic player-piano system, Spirio. For details, see **Steinway Spirio** in the section on electronic player-piano systems.

STORY & CLARK

www.qrsmusic.com

Hampton Story began making pianos in 1857 and was joined by Melville Clark in 1884. The business settled in Grand Rapids, Michigan, in 1901, where it remained, under various owners, until about 1990, when a new owner moved the company to its present location in Seneca, Pennsylvania. Over the years, pianos were manufactured under a number of different names, including, in recent years, Story & Clark, Gulbransen, Hobart M. Cable, Hampton, and Classic. In 1993 Story & Clark was purchased by QRS Piano Rolls, Inc., now QRS Music Technologies, Inc. (Ironically, QRS itself was founded in 1900 by Melville Clark, of the Story & Clark Piano Co. of old.) QRS, historically the nation's major source of music rolls for traditional player pianos, now manufactures an electronic player-piano system, called PNOmation, that can be retrofitted into any piano (see "**Buying an Electronic Player-Piano System**").

Story & Clark offers two series of pianos, each series including verticals and grands made to its specifications by various Asian manufacturers. The Heritage Series is a popularly priced line of verticals and grands with a Storytone II soundboard—Story & Clark's name for a veneer-laminated, all-spruce soundboard. The Signature Series, also with both vertical and grand models, feature premium features, such as Renner hammers, Röslau strings, maple and mahogany rims, solid brass hardware, Bolduc tapered soundboards of solid spruce, sand-cast plates, and advanced low-tension scales. The Signature models have cabinet designs that offer lots of detail for the money and coordinate with major furniture trends. In spite of their beauty, the company says, these pianos are also appropriate for school and commercial applications.

In keeping with the tradition, established by Hampton Story and Melville Clark, of integrating the latest technology into pianos, all Story & Clark pianos now come equipped with QRS's latest connected systems. Grand pianos, and the 48" model H7 Academy upright, all have a PNOmation Studio reproducing-piano system, which includes the PNOmation[3] playback system, the PNOscan™ record system, a keystop rail to prevent the hammers from striking the strings in Practice (Silent) mode, and a specially designed piano speaker. Most vertical pianos are standardly equipped with a connected PNOscan Studio system, which includes PNOscan, the PNOmation[3] controller, a keystop rail, a specially designed piano speaker, headphones, and one year of PianoMarvel interactive piano lessons. The addition of these systems to every Story & Clark acoustic piano gives customers the potential to have all the features of a digital piano and more.

VAUGHAN

www.en.vaughanpiano.com
This company is seeking U.S. distribution.

In 1876, Tim Vaughan, a member of the third generation of a piano-making family, founded the German Vaughan Piano Co., in Bonn. At first, the pianos were made only in small quantities, but production increased in the early 20th century, and the company moved to Munich in 1910, where it built a larger factory, and began mass production in 1920. In 1925, it also began mass production of piano parts and accessories, such as keyboards and hammers. After World War II, Vaughan expanded internationally, and eventually, in 2006, to Asia. In 2015, Vaughan established a production facility in Hangzhou, Zhejiang Province, China, to serve the global market.

Vaughan says that it is a diversified piano manufacturing company that integrates scientific research and development with production, sales, and service. It uses advanced German production equipment and components, has hired German piano-manufacturing experts as consultants, and meets international technical standards for production and quality control.

WALTER, CHARLES R.

www.walterpiano.com

Charles Walter, an engineer, was head of Piano Design and Developmental Engineering at C.G. Conn in the 1960s, when Conn was doing important research in musical acoustics. In 1969 Walter bought the Janssen piano name from Conn, and continued to make Janssen pianos until 1981. In 1975 he brought out the Charles R. Walter line of consoles and studios, based on his continuing research in piano design. Walter began making grands in 1997.

The Walter Piano Company is fairly unique among U.S. piano manufacturers in that it is a family business, staffed by Charles and his wife, several of their grownup children, and various in-laws, in addition to unrelated production employees. The Walters say that each piano is inspected and signed by a member of their family before being shipped. Dealers and technicians report that doing business with the Walters is a pleasure in itself.

The Charles R. Walter line consists of 43" and 45" studio pianos in various decorator and institutional styles, and 5' 9" and 6' 4" grands. Note that both vertical models have full-size actions and are, in fact, identical studio pianos inside different cabinets. Walter calls the 43" model a "console" because of its furniture styling, but due to its larger action, it will outplay most real consoles on the market.

Although Mr. Walter is not oblivious to marketing concerns, his vertical piano bears the mark of being designed by an engineer who understands pianos and strives for quality. The pianos are built in a traditional manner, with heavy-duty, full-length spruce backposts; a solid spruce soundboard; and Delignit pinblock. Exceptionally long, thick keys that are individually lead-weighted provide a very even feel across the keyboard. The scale design is well thought out and the bass sounds good most of the way to the bottom. The cabinetry is substantial, contains no particleboard, and is beautifully finished. Some of the fancy consoles in particular, such as the Queen Anne models, are strikingly beautiful. The pianos are well prepared at the factory and so need minimal preparation by the dealer.

The vertical pianos now use Renner actions, but a Chinese-made action is available as a lower-cost option, reducing the price of the piano by about $2,000. The Chinese parts are virtually indistinguishable from the Renner parts, but they make the action feel just slightly lighter due to differing spring tensions.

The Walter 5' 9" and 6' 4" grands were designed by Del Fandrich, one of the nation's most respected piano-design engineers. Both models have high-quality features such as a maple rim, Renner action, Kluge keys, Delignit pinblock, tapered solid spruce soundboard, and Abel hammers (Ronsen hammers in the 5' 9" model). The 5' 9" grand also has a number of innovative features: A portion of the inner rim and soundboard at the bass end of the piano are separated from the rest of the rim and allowed to "float." Less restricted in its movement, the soundboard can reproduce the fundamental frequencies of the lower bass notes more as a larger piano does. A special extension of the tenor bridge creates a smoother transition from bass to treble. Eight plate nosebolts increase plate stability, helping to reduce energy loss to the plate and thus increase sustain. Inverted half-agraffes embedded in the capo bar maintain string alignment and reduce unwanted string noise. The Walter grands are competently built and play very well.

WEBER—see Young Chang

WERTHEIM

www.wertheimpianousa.com

Wertheim pianos were first produced in Germany from 1875 to 1908, and then in Richmond, Australia, a suburb of Melbourne, from 1908 to 1935. Approximately 18,000 uprights and grands were made during the Richmond period. They were popular, all-purpose pianos with a good reputation for easy maintenance, and were used in a wide variety of settings, including homes, schools, and public halls. The most famous exponent of the Wertheim brand was Dame Nellie Melba, who frequently requested Wertheim pianos for her performances.

The Wertheim brand is currently owned and distributed to the international market by John Martin, who revived it in 2002. In his more than 46 years in the music industry, Martin has owned full-line retail music stores, managed a buying group for music-store retailers, and manufactured and distributed Wertheim pianos. Martin says that Wertheim's aim is to make the best-value, top-class pianos, using the best designs, materials, and workmanship, and working with leading piano designers and technicians from Germany, the U.S., Australia, and New Zealand.

Most Wertheim pianos for the North American market are made by AXL Musical Instrument Co., in Shanghai, China, which also manufactures the better-known Palatino brand. These Wertheims come in three series: Gold (model numbers beginning with W), Euro (WE), and Platinum (WP). The Gold-series models are for the budget-conscious buyer, Euro and Platinum for those desiring higher performance and quality. All contain German Röslau strings, solid spruce soundboard, and an 18–ply pinblock. The Gold and Euro series models use a Chinese action, the Platinum series models use a Renner action, with the option of a Wessell, Nickel & Gross composite action. The Euro and Platinum series have German Strunz soundboards and Renner hammers, and real ebony wood sharps. Currently available in North America are three vertical and three grand sizes, each available in several popular finishes, and with some variation in cabinet design.

New in 2017 is the Wertheim/Fandrich (WF) series. These models, designed by internationally recognized piano designer Del Fandrich, are assembled in Wertheim's own new factory in Shanghai from the best internationally sourced components by workers who, the company says, are rewarded for high quality rather than high volume. The new models will be positioned to fill the mid- to upper range of the piano market.

YAMAHA

www.yamaha.com

Torakusu Yamaha, a watchmaker, developed Japan's first reed organ, and founded Yamaha Reed Organ Manufacturing in 1887. In 1899, Yamaha visited the U.S. to learn how to build pianos. Within a couple of years he began making grand and vertical pianos under the name Nippon Gakki, Ltd. Beginning in the 1930s, Yamaha expanded its operations, first into other musical instruments, then into other products and services, such as sporting goods and furniture, and finally internationally.

Export of pianos to the U.S. began in earnest about 1960. In 1973, Yamaha acquired the Everett Piano Co., in South Haven, Michigan, and made both Yamaha and Everett pianos there until 1986. In that year, the company moved its piano manufacturing to a plant in Thomaston, Georgia, where it made Yamaha consoles, studios, and some grands until 2007, when a depressed piano market and foreign competition forced it to close its doors. Yamaha pianos sold in the U.S. are now made in Japan, China, and Indonesia. Yamaha also owns the renowned Austrian piano maker, Bösendorfer.

Yamaha's console line consists of the 43" model b1, in continental style, with a laminated soundboard; and the 44" models M460 and M560 in furniture style (freestanding legs), representing two levels of cabinet sophistication and price. All are internally similar (except for the soundboard) and have a compressed action typical of a console, which means that the action will not be quite as responsive as in larger models.

The studio line consists of the popular 45" model P22 in institutional style (legs with toe blocks) with school-friendly cabinet; the furniture-style version P660; and the 45" model b2, with a less-expensive institutional-style cabinet. All studio models are internally similar, with a full-size action. All Yamaha verticals under 48" tall are now made in the company's Indonesian factory.

The uprights are the very popular 48" model U1; the 48" model b3, which is made in Indonesia and has the same scale design as the U1; and the 52" model U3. A new Super U series of uprights (YUS1, YUS3, and YUS5) have different hammers and get additional tuning and voicing at the factory, including voicing by machine to create a more consistent, more mellow tone. The YUS5 has German Röslau music wire instead of Yamaha wire, also for a mellower tone. This top-of-the-line 52" upright also has agraffes, duplex scaling, and a sostenuto pedal (all other Yamaha verticals have a practice/mute pedal). The U- and YU-series uprights are all made in Japan and come with soft-close fallboards.

Yamaha grands come in several levels of sophistication and size. The Classic Collection consists of the 5' model GB1K, the 5' 3" model GC1M, and the 5' 8" model GC2. The GB1K has simplified case construction and cabinetry, no duplex scale, and the middle pedal operates a bass-sustain mechanism. It does have a soft-close fallboard. It is currently the only Yamaha grand sold in the U.S. that is made in Indonesia. The GC1M and GC2 have regular case construction, duplex scale, soft-close fallboard, and sostenuto pedal.

The Conservatory Classic and Conservatory Concert Collections of C-series grands were replaced in 2012 with the CX series, consisting of the 5' 3" model C1X, the 5' 8" model C2X, the 6' 1" model C3X, the 6' 7" model C5X, the 7' model C6X, and the 7' 6" model C7X. The new CX series incorporates some of the design elements of the limited-production CF series (see below) into the higher-production C-series pianos to create a sound more like that of a high-end American or European instrument. Features include a European spruce soundboard crowned using CF-series technology, a thicker rim and bracing, German music wire, additional time spent voicing, regulating, and tuning by very skilled craftsmen, and some changes in cabinet design. Both the C and CX models have advanced construction, scaling, and cabinetry, including a true sostenuto pedal, soft-close fallboard, vertically laminated bridges with maple or boxwood cap, and keytops of Ivorite™, Yamaha's ivory alternative.

The CF Series, one of two Yamaha Premium Collection lines, comprises the 9' model CFX (replacing model CFIIIS), and the 6' 3" model CF4 and 7' model CF6 (respectively replacing, in the U.S., models S4B and S6B, which will remain available by special order only). The pianos in this collection are made in a separate factory to much higher standards and with some different materials: e.g., maple and mahogany in the rim, which is made more rigid, for greater tonal power, than in the other collections; higher-grade soundboard material; a treble "bell" (as in the larger Steinways) to enhance treble tone; German strings, and hammer and scaling changes, for a more mellow tone; as well as the more advanced features of the other collections. The result is an instrument capable of greater dynamic range, tonal color, and sustain than the regular Yamahas. Yamaha says that the CF series represents 19 years of research and development by its craftsmen, designers, and engineers. The Yamaha concert grand is endorsed and used by a number of notable musicians, including Olga Kern, Michael Tilson Thomas, Chick Corea, Elton John, and Frederic Chiu.

The second Premium Collection line, added in 2017, is the SX Series, positioned between the CX and CF lines and comprising the 6' 1" model S3X, the 6' 7" model S5X, and the 7' 6" model S7X. The SX series uses the same soundboard and scale-design approach as the flagship CFX model; has a completely new hammer design derived from testing more than 100 prototypes; and, most significant, has a new, thicker rim construction in which the wood is treated with a patented accelerated-aging process called Acoustic Resonance Enhancement, to give the piano a warmer, more romantic sound with a wider range of expression.

The price differences between the SX and CF models are related to their production processes: the CF instruments are fully handcrafted, whereas the SX pianos are built with a combination of handcraftsmanship and innovative technologies. Yamaha says that SX pianos are intended especially for institutions and smaller concert venues, the CF models for larger concert halls.

Yamaha grands have historically been a little on the percussive side and have been said not to "sing" as well as some more expensive pianos. On the other hand, Yamaha has long been the piano of choice for jazz and popular music, which may value clarity and brightness more than the other qualities mentioned. In recent years, however, Yamaha has been trying to move away from this image of a "bright" piano whose sound is limited to jazz. First with its larger grands, and later with the smaller ones, Yamaha has changed such things as bridge construction and hammer density, and provided more custom voicing at the factory, to bring out a broader spectrum of tonal color. Now, with its Premium Collection models, and the innovative soundboard, hammer, and rim technologies used in their design and construction, Yamaha has come fully into the world of instruments suited for classical music (as well as jazz).

Both Yamaha's quality control and its warranty and technical service are legendary in the piano business. They are the standard against which every other company is measured. For general home and school use, piano technicians probably recommend Yamaha pianos more often than any other brand. Their precision, reliability, and performance make them a very good value for a consumer product.

There is a thriving market for used Yamahas. If you're considering buying a used Yamaha, please read "**Buying a Used or Restored Piano**" in this publication.

Yamaha also makes electronic player pianos called Disklaviers, as well as a variety of hybrid acoustic/digital instruments—including Silent Piano (formerly called MIDIPiano), the AvantGrand series, and the model NU1, that account for a substantial percentage of the company's sales. These products are separately described in the articles "**Buying an Electronic Player-Piano System**," "**Hybrid Pianos**," and in the **Yamaha Disklavier profile** for electronic player pianos.

YOUNG CHANG

including Weber and Albert Weber
www.youngchang.com
www.weberpiano.com

In 1956, three brothers—Jai-Young, Jai-Chang, and Jai-Sup Kim—founded Young Chang and began selling Yamaha pianos in Korea under an agreement with that Japanese firm. Korea was recovering from a devastating war, and only the wealthy could afford pianos. But the prospects were bright for economic development, and as a symbol of cultural refinement the piano was much coveted. In 1962 the brothers incorporated as Young Chang Akki Co., Ltd.

In 1964 Yamaha and Young Chang entered into an agreement in which Yamaha helped Young Chang set up a full-fledged manufacturing operation. Yamaha shipped partially completed pianos from Japan to the Young Chang factory in Incheon, South Korea, where Young Chang would perform final assembly work such as cabinet assembly, stringing, and action installation. This arrangement reduced high import duties. As time went by, Young Chang built more of the components, to the point where they were making virtually the entire piano. In 1975 the arrangement ended when Young Chang decided to expand domestically and internationally under its own brand name, thus becoming a competitor. Young Chang began exporting to the U.S. in the late 1970s, and established a North American distribution office in California in 1984.

Weber & Co. was established in 1852 by Albert Weber, a German immigrant, and was one of the most prominent and highly respected American piano brands of the late 19th and early 20th centuries. During the consolidation of the American piano industry in the early 20th century, Weber became part of the Aeolian family of brands. Following Aeolian's demise in 1985, Young Chang acquired the Weber name.

In 1995, in response to rising Korean wages and to supply a growing Chinese domestic market, Young Chang built a 750,000-square-foot factory in Tianjin, China, and gradually began to move manufacturing operations there for some of its models. Today, the Tianjin facility produces Young Chang and Weber pianos, and components for the Albert Weber line, which is assembled in South Korea.

Hyundai Development Company, a Korean civil-engineering and construction firm, acquired Young Chang in 2006. The company says that Hyundai Development has brought the necessary capital for factory renovations and has instituted new advanced industrial quality-control systems.

In 2008 Young Chang hired noted American piano designer Delwin D. Fandrich to undertake a redesign of the entire Young Chang and Weber piano line. Highlights include extensively redesigned cast-iron plates, new string scales, new soundboard and rib designs, and a new hammer-making process. Fandrich says that all of these features and processes contribute to his goal of building instruments with improved tonal balance and musicality, and provide opportunities to standardize manufacturing processes for better quality control.

Along with the redesign, former multiple piano lines were consolidated into just three lines: the Young Chang (Y) and Weber (W) series are entry- and mid-level instruments made in China, and the Albert Weber (AW) line comprises upper-level models made in Korea. The AW grands have lower-tension scales, maple rims, and Renner actions, and higher-quality hammer felt, soundboard material, and veneers (on wood-veneered models). The Y and W grands have lauan rims and Young Chang actions.

The AW verticals use slightly better materials than the other verticals for the cabinets, hardware, music wire, and keys, though in general the differences are smaller than with the grands.

The Young Chang and Weber pianos distinctly differ from one another: the Weber models have a low-tension scale and softer, cold-pressed hammers, and the greater warmth and romantic tonal characteristics that often accompany that type of scale; the Young Chang models have a higher-tension scale and firmer cold-pressed hammers, and the greater brightness and stronger projection of a more modern sound. The Weber line, also known as the Premium Edition, also has agraffes in the bass section of the verticals, and beveled lids on the grands.

Young Chang also owns Kurzweil Music Systems, a manufacturer of professional keyboards and home digital pianos, which it acquired in 1990.

DIGITAL PIANOS

BLÜTHNER E-KLAVIER

www.bluthnerpiano.com

Blüthner, one of the world's preeminent piano makers, has released its first line of digital pianos, called the e-Klavier. (For company background, see the Blüthner listing under Acoustic Pianos.) Engineered and manufactured in Leipzig, Germany, the e-Klavier line currently consists of a slab, three standard verticals, a decorator vertical called the Pianette, a vertical called Homeline with a solid wood cabinet, and two grand-shaped models.

Blüthner says it has developed a unique approach to sampling and sound modeling, called Authentic Acoustic Behavior, that allows the e-Klavier to reproduce the effect of the aliquot (fourth) string of Blüthner's acoustic pianos. This system also permits the reproduction of advanced harmonics, such as the coincidental partials produced when two notes are played simultaneously, and the sound the dampers make when lifting off the strings. The e-Klavier actions, sourced from Fatar, feature escapement, and wooden keys with "ivory feel" in some models. In the near future, users will be able to download new sounds to the e-Klaviers via the Internet at no charge, and store the sounds of turn-of-the-century Blüthner pianos and other Blüthner models of interest.

The e-Klavier 2 and 3 also contain an actual piano soundboard, which enables these instruments to produce certain aspects of acoustic-piano tone that are difficult or impossible to simulate by purely electronic means.

CASIO

www.casiomusicgear.com

Kashio Tadao established Casio in 1946. Originally a small subcontractor factory that made parts and gears for microscopes, Casio built Japan's first electric calculator in 1954, which began the company's transformation into the consumer-electronics powerhouse it is today. Perhaps best known for its calculators, digital cameras, and watches, Casio entered the musical instrument business with the launch of the Casiotone in 1980.

Casio's current line of digital pianos consists of vertical and slab models under the Privia and Celviano labels. Four of the five Privia slabs offer an optional stand-and-pedal module that turns them into three-pedal pianos with support for half-pedaling. At a mere 24 or 25 pounds, they are also some of the lightest digital pianos available. The AP and GP models are marketed under the Celviano label. All Casio digital pianos use a three-sensor, weighted, and scaled (graded) Tri-Sensor hammer action with ebony- and ivory-feel keys. Casio digital pianos are available at music retailers, consumer electronics stores, warehouse clubs, and online.

DEXIBELL

www.dexibell.com

Dexibell, made in Italy, was established in 2013 by the R&D and engineering team of the former Roland Europe, with financial backing from parent company Proel S.p.A., an Italian manufacturer of leading brands of professional audio and lighting equipment, musical instruments, and accessories. In 2017, after several years of international success, Proel began distributing the Dexibell brand in North America.

Dexibell uses a suite of patented technologies, called T2L (True to Life), to increase acoustic-piano realism in its instruments. First, whereas the industry standard for sound resolution is 16-bit/44.1kHz (CD quality), Dexibell uses 24-bit/48kHz resolution, resulting in 256 times greater sound resolution and clarity. Second, in comparison to the industry-standard sampling time per note of five seconds or less, Dexibell's samples run for 15 seconds, capturing virtually the entire natural decay of a note, and eliminating the need for the artificial looping found in most of today's digital pianos. Last, Dexibell's Quad Core sound engine contains 320 digital oscillators, allowing for virtually unlimited polyphony and sympathetic resonance.

Dexibell partnered with Ferrari's design firm to create a look for its instruments that is uniquely Italian, with sleek curved lines, and striking color options that include black, white, red, pink, and blue, in matte and polished finishes.

Dexibell produces digital pianos, keyboards, and organs. Its digital piano line is called VIVO (Italian for *alive*), and is available in home, portable, and stage versions. Most are Bluetooth-equipped, record and play digital audio, and come with two original apps: the VIVO Editor, for modifying any of the instruments' sound elements, and XMURE, for recording songs and play-along backing tracks with smart accompaniment.

DYNATONE

www.dynatoneusa.com

Dynatone, headquartered in Seoul, South Korea, was founded in 1987 as the Electric Instruments Division of the global semiconductor manufacturer Korean Electronics Company (KEC), and was the first maker of electric musical instruments in Korea. It became an independent company in 2000. In addition to digital pianos and MIDI keyboards, Dynatone makes percussion, string, woodwind, and brass instruments, which it exports to more than 30 countries.

Dynatone is offering in the U.S. market vertical and grand models, some as standard digitals and some as ensemble models. The cabinets come in a variety of finishes and distinctive, contemporary designs, including some with smaller, sleeker designs suitable when space is limited. The new ROS V.5 Plus sound engine contains the clean, realistic sound of a 12-megabyte grand piano sound sample. The wooden-key, triple-sensor, Real Hammer Action (RHA-3W) uses the hammer weight, not springs, to reproduce the touch and feel of an acoustic piano. The flagship model VGP-4000 digital grand is one of the only digital pianos on the market to contain a player-piano feature, and its USB memory stick can store a library of 1,300 songs. All Dynatone models come with a three-year parts and labor warranty.

FLYCHORD

www.flychord.com

Flychord is a subsidiary of a company headquartered in Shenzhen, Guangdong Province, China. Flychord currently offers two models in the U.S., the DP330 and DP420K, both ensemble verticals. The DP330 has 500 voices and 210 auto-accompaniment styles. The DP420K, with 40 voices and 50 styles, is more limited as an ensemble instrument, but with its triple-sensor and ivory-textured keys, support for half

pedaling, and more elegant furniture styling, it has greater acoustic-piano realism in performance and appearance.

Flychord pianos are distributed in the U.S. by a network of sales agents—piano dealers, studios, and schools—who have demonstrator models to show potential buyers, but who do not stock the instruments themselves. When the customer places an order with the sales agent, the instrument is delivered directly from Flychord, which also handles any future warranty issues. The instruments are also available for purchase from Amazon.com, and directly from the Flychord website.

GALILEO

www.galileopianos.com

Galileo is a division of Viscount International, an Italian company that traces its roots back to accordion builder Antonio Galanti, who built his first keyboard instrument in 1890. Today, Viscount is run by the fourth generation of the Galanti family, and distribution in the U.S. is handled by members of the fifth generation. Viscount also makes Physis digital pianos and Viscount organs.

The Galileo collection of digital pianos includes verticals, grands, and ensembles in a variety of colors, finishes, and elegant Italian styling.

Galileo recently introduced VEGA high-definition sound-generation technology, currently available on its new YP and GYP series of digitals.

KAWAI

www.kawaius.com

For company background, see the Kawai listing under Acoustic Pianos.

A renowned builder of acoustic pianos for over 90 years, Kawai entered the digital piano market in 1985. Today, Kawai's digital pianos comprise four main model lines: Concert Performer (CP), Concert Artist (CA), Classic Series (CS), and CN Series. Other digital models include the CE220, CL26, and KDP110. Portable digitals include the ES8 and ES110, and professional models include the MP Series stage pianos and the VPC1 virtual piano controller.

Kawai created the first hybrid digital instrument to use a transducer-driven soundboard for a more natural piano sound, a feature available in the CS11 and the flagship CA98. Many Kawai models offer USB digital audio recording and playback. Recently, Kawai introduced the first of its Novus line of hybrid instruments, the NV10. This new model features an actual grand-piano action, with modified hammers and optical sensors.

Several different types of action appear in Kawai digital pianos. Kawai is well known for its wooden-key actions for digital pianos, the current versions of these being the Grand Feel (GF), GFII, RM3II, and AWA PROII, these actions available in upper-end models. The Responsive Hammer II (RHII), RHIII, and RH-Compact actions use an industry-standard graded hammer design with plastic keys, and are found in the lower-cost and portable models.

Kawai's main lines of digital piano are sold through a network of authorized local dealers; several models are also available from Kawai's online store. Professional products and other digitals are sold through a combination of authorized online and bricks-and-mortar retailers.

KORG

www.korg.com

Korg was founded in 1962 to produce its first product, an automatic rhythm machine, and in 1972 entered the electronic-organ market. The LP-10 stage piano appeared in 1980, and its first digitally sampled piano, the SG1, was introduced in 1986. Korg now offers nine models of 88-key digital piano. The company also sells its home digital pianos online.

KURZWEIL

www.kurzweilmusicsystems.com

Legendary American inventor Ray Kurzweil, perhaps best known for having developed a reading machine for the blind, and hailed by Forbes magazine as "a modern-day Edison," launched Kurzweil Music Systems in 1983, following conversations with Stevie Wonder about the potential for combining the control and flexibility of the computer with the sounds of acoustic instruments. The result, in 1984, was the Kurzweil K250, recognized as the world's first digital piano. In 1990, Boston-based Kurzweil Music Systems was purchased by Young Chang, which continues to operate the division today. (See the Young Chang listing under Acoustic Pianos.)

All Kurzweil home pianos feature the award-winning PC3X sound engine. Kurzweil piano models also feature USB and audio inputs to allow easy expansion via iPads and other external peripherals. Kurzweil pianos and keyboards are available through a combination of musical instrument dealers, piano-specialty stores, and online sources.

LOWREY

www.lowrey.com

Early research by Chicago industrialist Frederick C. Lowrey produced a working model of an electronic sound source in 1918. The company bearing his name made organs for many years and, for a brief time in the 1980s, pianos. In 1988, Lowrey joined the Kawai family of companies, and is a developer and distributor of Lowrey Virtual Orchestra and digital piano products designed for the consumer market.

NORD

www.americanmusicandsound.com
www.nordkeyboards.com

The Nord Piano is a professional stage piano that comes with a library of more than 1,000 sounds on a DVD, or downloadable from the Nord Piano website to the instrument via USB. Nord Keyboards are made in Sweden by Clavia DMI AB.

OMEGA

www.kainopianos.com

Omega is the brand name used in the U.S. for Kaino digital pianos. Established in 1986, Kaino, located in Guangzhou, China, began as a manufacturer of portable keyboards. In 1996, the company expanded to manufacture a full line of 88-note digital pianos, quickly becoming a major provider of keyboards throughout China. In 2010, the Omega brand was established for distribution in North America and Europe.

PHYSIS

www.viscountinstruments.us

Physis is a division of Viscount International, an Italian company that also makes Galileo digital pianos, among other brands. It has factories and research facilities in San Marino and Italy.

Physis uses physical modeling as the sound source for its instruments. Instead of recorded samples, physical modeling uses advanced mathematical algorithms to reproduce the physical properties of sound, and requires immense computational power that, until recently, was not technologically available. Two international patents have been granted for the Physis technology.

The Physis physical model combines more than 100 elements of the traditional acoustic grand piano sound; e.g., hammer density, string resonance, soundboard size, damper noise, duplex vibration, etc. One of the key advantages of physical modeling is that these elements can be modified by users to create their own unique sounds, and the resulting models can be shared with others, allowing for their continuing evolution. Other advantages include unlimited polyphony, unlimited pedal resolution, and the greater expressiveness that results from the real-time interaction of the physical elements.

Some Physis models have wooden keys with ivory-like keytops and triple sensors, for better expression and a more natural, realistic feel. The H- and V-series pianos have a customizable, multitouch, glass-panel interface that gives the user control of all items on the panel, including display colors. These models also have USB thumb-drive connections for audio and data storage and playback. The Pro and Stage versions are ergonomically designed for portability, and allow maximum flexibility of inputs and outputs.

Physis pianos are sold through a network of professional music retailers.

ROLAND

www.rolandus.com

Ikutaro Kakehashi started down the path to Roland Corporation at the age of 16, when he began repairing watches and clocks in postwar Japan. However, his enthusiasm for music meant that his business soon evolved into the repair of radios. In 1954, Kakehashi opened Kakehashi Musen (Kakehashi Radio). Once again, his interest in music intervened, this time leading to his development of a prototype electric organ. In 1960, Kakehashi Radio evolved into Ace Electronic Industries. The FR1 Rhythm Ace became a standard offering of the Hammond Organ Company, and Ace flourished. Guitar amplifiers, effects units, and more rhythm machines were developed. In 1972, Kakehashi left Ace and established Roland Corporation. The first Roland product was a rhythm box.

In 1973, Roland introduced its first all-electronic combo piano, followed in 1974 by the world's first electronic piano with a touch-sensitive keyboard. Japan's first genuinely digital pianos for home use were released by Roland in 1975 as part of the early HP series. In 1983, Roland released the very first digital pianos with MIDI.

When introduced in 1986, the RD–1000 stage piano was Roland's first entry in what would become the digital piano category. Today, Roland offers more than two dozen models of digital piano covering every facet of the category: slab, vertical, grand, ensemble, and stage instruments.

Of particular interest to those looking for educational features is Roland's HPi model, which includes a substantial suite of educational capabilities supported by an LCD screen mounted on a music desk. The LX models add traditional-looking vertical pianos to the line.

The Roland V-Piano was the first digital piano to rely entirely on physical modeling as its tonal source. Physical modeling breaks down the sound of a piano note into discrete elements that can be represented by mathematical equations, and creates the tone in real time based on a complex series of calculations.

The HP models are the core of Roland's offerings in home digital pianos; the latest models, including the new GP607 and GP609 digital grands, share the company's hallmark SuperNATURAL® piano sound engine, premium Progressive Hammer Action with Escapement, and built-in Bluetooth wireless capability, and differ from each other primarily in the specifications of their audio systems and cabinet-types.

SAMICK

www.samickdigital.com

Established in 1958, Samick Musical Instrument Mfg. Co. Ltd. is one of the world's leading producers of pianos and guitars (see Samick under Acoustic Pianos). The company has factories in China, Germany, Indonesia, Korea, and the U.S.

Samick is in the process of revamping its digital piano line, and currently sells one vertical and two grand models. The grands are ensemble digitals with six or eight speakers; the vertical has four speakers and an acoustic-piano–style soundboard. All three have Fatar keyboards with triple-sensor keys and are equipped with Bluetooth.

SUZUKI

www.suzukimusic.com

Suzuki sells its line of digital pianos on its website, through other online outlets, and through Costco. Models change frequently.

WILLIAMS

www.williamspianos.com

Williams digital pianos are available from Guitar Center stores and the Musician's Friend e-commerce website. The company offers five models, including two verticals, two slabs with optional stand, and one ensemble grand. The sounds on Williams instruments are from the Williams Custom Sound Library, a large collection of high-definition sounds carefully sampled from sought-after acoustic, electric, and vintage keyboards, and unique to Williams digital pianos. Also unique to Williams pianos is the Mod/FX control interface, which enables authentic rotary effects on organs and vibrato on electric pianos. All models come with a free introduction to McCarthy Music educational software.

YAMAHA

usa.yamaha.com

For company background, see the Yamaha listing under Acoustic Pianos.

Yamaha Corporation is the world's largest producer of musical instruments. Yamaha entered the world of electronic instruments in 1959, when it introduced the first all-transistor organ. Jumping ahead to 1983, the introduction of the first Yamaha Clavinova, the YP-40, marked the beginning of what we now call the digital piano. Today, Yamaha's three dozen or so models of digital piano (not counting different finishes) constitute the broadest range of any manufacturer.

Clavinova digital pianos include the standard CLP line, the ensemble CVP line, and the app-driven, learn-to-play, CSP line, and are available only through piano dealers. The Modus models (model numbers beginning with F, H, and R), Yamaha's series of designer digitals, are functionally similar to the CLP line but with modern-looking cabinets. (The Modus H01 and H11 are perhaps the most striking visual designs among digital pianos.) Arius (model numbers beginning with YDP) represents Yamaha's entry-level line of digital verticals.

The CP and CP stage models are intended for situations that require a portable instrument. Available at several price points, they are suitable for a wide range of applications, from live performance to studio recording. Some of the models in this line feature Yamaha's Spectral Component Modeling (SCM) technology, or a combination of SCM and Advanced Wave Memory (AWM) sampling.

Yamaha's apps for iPad, iPhone, and iPod Touch are unique in the digital-piano world. The NoteStar app brings sheet music into the 21st century, and puts you in the band with real audio backing tracks that you can slow down or transpose. MusicSoft Manager lets you manage the content of your CVP Clavinova, while Repertoire Finder provides complete keyboard setups for songs you want to play.

Seven different actions are used in Yamaha digitals. In order of increasing quality, they are: Graded Hammer Standard (GHS), Graded Hammer (GH), Graded Hammer 3 (GH3), Natural Wood (NW), Natural Wood Stage (NW-Stage), Natural Wood Linear Graded Hammer (NW-LGH), and the real grand piano action used in the AvantGrand models.

A few years ago, Yamaha introduced its Avant-Grand hybrid piano. For more information about this instrument, see the article "**Hybrid Pianos**" elsewhere in this publication.

ELECTRONIC PLAYER-PIANO SYSTEMS

PIANODISC

www.pianodisc.com

PianoDisc, based in Sacramento, California, is a leading manufacturer of player-piano and optical MIDI sensor and record systems. The company, in business since 1988, offers retrofittable systems that can be installed in virtually any acoustic piano, grand or vertical, new or used. A number of piano manufacturers offer factory-installed PianoDisc systems, and a large network of PianoDisc dealers and certified technicians throughout the U.S. and many other countries offer installation services.

PianoDisc manufactures three core player-piano systems featuring its iQ technology: Prodigy iQ Entertainment, Prodigy iQ Interactive, and Prodigy iQ QuietTime. The Prodigy iQ Entertainment system is the most popular and least expensive, and provides playback-only capabilities. The Prodigy iQ Interactive system also provides playback functionality and, with the addition of an optical MIDI strip, allows the user to record performances and interact with MIDI music apps such as PianoDisc iQ Player (described below), Garage Band, Symphonix Evolution, and Piano Marvel, to name a few. The Prodigy iQ Quiet-Time system is essentially an iQ Interactive system, but the addition of a manually activated mechanical mute rail to prevent the piano's hammers from striking the strings eliminates the normal acoustic-piano sound. The user can then listen through headphones (provided) without being disturbed by surrounding sounds, and/or play without disturbing others. Although most buyers use their own smartphones, tablets, or computers to control their iQ systems, PianoDisc offers several media-player packages that include Apple's popular iPad devices.

At the heart of the PianoDisc Prodigy iQ player system is SilentDrive HDII, a high-resolution solenoid system that features integrated Bluetooth audio and MIDI for fast wireless connections, easy operation, and additional connection flexibility. With 1,024 levels of expression, SD HDII can replay piano performances with highly accurate articulation, even at very low volume.

All PianoDisc Prodigy iQ systems come with a complimentary music and video library consisting of nearly 500 songs and 15 video performances, valued at $1,400. When a customer registers a PianoDisc warranty, he or she receives a $175 coupon that can be used toward the purchase of music or videos from PianoDisc's large library. Recently, PianoDisc began offering single-song downloads from its Music Store, in addition to downloads of entire albums.

The introduction of the PianoDisc iQ Player app (free for iOS devices) makes it easier and more enjoyable to operate all of the music and video features offered by the Prodigy iQ Player Piano system. This powerful app permits the user to download music or video performances from the PianoDisc Music Store directly into the app, and automatically downloads the free music library. The Player app also lets you download and play MIDI files on the Prodigy iQ system, stream free PianoDisc Radio stations, create playlists, record MIDI performances, and much more.

PianoDisc also manufactures two optical MIDI and Record systems, ProRecord and ProScan. These systems feature optical sensors, installed under the keys of the piano, that transmit information about the notes played: i.e. velocity, duration, pedal effects, etc. This information, called MIDI data, can then be recorded using a MIDI app (e.g., Symphonix Evolution) or MIDI computer software program (e.g., Finale), or sent to another MIDI device or keyboard.

Whereas ProScan is simply a MIDI sensor strip, ProRecord also has a built-in sound module that contains 88 high-quality digital instruments and numerous other features and functions, including recording capabilities, metronome functions, transpose and tempo adjustments, digital effects, and much more. With Bluetooth-ready integration, ProRecord can pair quickly and easily with an iPad or iPhone using the free ProRecord app and the very user-friendly interface. All of the features and functions of the ProRecord system can be accessed from the ProRecord app, eliminating the need to look down at the small display screen and buttons of the ProRecord control box.

Both ProRecord and ProScan can be integrated into an iQ player system, or used without the player-piano function to create a standalone digital piano or MIDI controller. Additionally, both systems can be fitted with an optional mute rail, which transforms the system into a QuietTime, or "silent," system for private practice.

PIANOFORCE

www.pianoforce.com

Pianoforce EU, of Bratislava, Slovakia, has been developing and manufacturing front-end controllers for the player-piano systems of other companies since 1995. In 2005, Pianoforce was first offered as a complete system in the pianos of selected piano makers. In 2006, it was introduced as a kit retrofittable to any piano, new or old. Designed and built by Pianoforce in Europe, the kit is ordered through a piano dealer, and is typically installed in a new piano at a distribution point or at the dealer location.

Pianoforce says that its system differs from those of its competitors in that the main rail component also contains all the controlling electronics, eliminating the need for a lot of complicated wiring and making for a neater, simpler installation. Also, a technician using the remote handset can customize the system to the piano and to the customer's preferences through the adjustment of many playing parameters, such as solenoid force, note release, and pedal release. These custom settings can then be saved in the controller. With the help of a small sensor mounted on the soundboard, the system automatically calibrates itself to the piano's sound. The combination of automatic calibration and manual setup ensures the best playback performance for each individual piano.

In 2007 Pianoforce introduced its Performance controller. The controller contains some of the most advanced features available in a player piano, such as the ability to read the softwares of other systems—including Yamaha Disklavier, QRS (except Sync-Along), and Web Only Piano—plus standard MIDI files; and onboard connections to the Internet via an Ethernet or wireless hookup. There are three USB ports for greater versatility, such as plugging in flash drives or an external hard drive. There is an optical digital stereo output and a dedicated subwoofer output line. The system can now be controlled remotely, via WiFi, with the user's Android or Apple device, and Internet streaming radio is available 24/7 with piano accompanied by original audio tracks.

More recently, Pianoforce has introduced the Stealth Performer controller, which allows the controller to be hidden away, out of sight. With WiFi remote control, all of the functionality of the original Performance controller is available, but no hardware is visible on the front of the piano.

The system comes with 2GB of internal memory (expandable to 8GB), preloaded with approximately 20 hours of piano music.

KEESCAN, an optional recording feature, uses optical sensors to record key and sustain-pedal movements. Also available is the AMI box, which facilitates connection of a microphone, iPod, and other USB devices. In addition to the system's ability to play other makers' softwares, Pianoforce is building its own library of CDs.

SilentPlay, Pianoforce's newest feature, combines KEESCAN, the new SP1 sound module, and a special muting rail to permit silent play of the customer's vertical piano, while giving the performer unparalleled digital sound through headphones or speakers. Connection to a computer gives a composer complete control over his or her compositions, from editing individual notes to saving new music for later replay.

QRS PNOmation

www.qrsmusic.com

PNOmation, and the new PNOmation Studio, are electronic player-piano reproducing systems that can be installed in virtually any piano, grand or vertical, new or used. Most manufacturers endorse the PNOmation system, and will install it, at a dealer's request, at one of their manufacturing or distribution points. Standard installation is also available at a dealer location by a QRS-trained and -certified technician. QRS also installs the system in many major brands of piano at its own U.S. factory. The factory installation conceals unnecessary wires, electronics, and the solenoid rail cover, for a more pleasing appearance, and the operation and feel of the piano's original pedal trapwork are retained.

Traditionally, electronic player pianos have been defined by the type of control box at the front of the piano, or by the controller's capabilities. PNOmation differs in integrating the core features of every controller, including the music, into the PNOmation engine, thereby eliminating confusing options as well as the need to have a box hanging under the piano or on the lyre. Instead of offering a modular approach to the equipment required for various features, PNOmation offers all features standard, and a modular approach to their use. For example, the user can log in to the PNOmation system through any web-enabled device, pull up the system's embedded web-app user interface, and begin to play the piano. For those more comfortable with inserting their music selections into the device, music can be delivered via a USB thumb drive; then you need only push Play on the system's remote control, or the Play button on the unit itself.

When PNOmation is integrated with the PNOscan optical sensor strip—a leading technology for recording performances on an acoustic piano—and a keystop rail to prevent the piano's hammers from striking the strings, the piano becomes a PNOmation Studio. The PNOscan strip doesn't touch the keys—it uses only reflected light to continuously measure key and pedal movements. By integrating PNOscan with PNOmation in a one-time setup operation, one need only play the piano and the piece is recorded—no login, no need to push Record or Stop. Just pull up a bench and play, and your performance is saved both locally (named according to your preset preferences) and uploaded to your personal QRS PNOcloud account. The file can also be sent to your favorite editing program or e-mailed to a friend—all without boxes or wires. Purchase of PNOscan also entitles the buyer to one year's worth of free piano lessons from the online piano-teaching software Piano Marvel.

Key to PNOmation's flexibility is the fact that it is simultaneously delivered in both a standalone-network mode, with its own network serving its own user interface, and in a network mode in which PNOmation is a client on your home network. One advantage of this arrangement is that if your home network is down, the PNOmation features can still be accessed. Other advantages include ease of setup, network updates, cloud account links, learning, archiving, and video streams.

As a client on a home network, a PNOmation-equipped piano can be controlled by accessing the web-app user interface via iPhone, iPad, iTouch, Android, Mac, Google Chrome browser, Kindle Fire, or any other similar piece of technology, as well as via the more unique Apple Watch and Amazon Echo. The web app gives the user full control of all parameters of the system and how music is played, so there is rarely a reason to call in a technician to make adjustments. Some customers are concerned only with whether a song is a solo performance or a performance with background music, which they can determine from the web-app screen. Other customers may want to manipulate a MIDI file to change the tempo or tuning, and some may want to upload a recorded performance to view or change. None of this is possible with an off-the-shelf MP3 playback engine, but all of it is easily done with QRS's PNOmation app. The QRS system also includes integrated Bluetooth MIDI and Bluetooth Audio. This gives you the ability to wirelessly use third-party apps in conjunction with your PNOscan, or third-party speaker systems for playback.

The web app also offers the customer several new ways to control the PNOmation engine, including better-controlled release of the sustain pedal, to give it a soft landing and eliminate the potential thump heard with the release of the damper tray. The same controlled-release technology has also been applied to the keys, improving the PNOmation's already quiet playback while adding much more lifelike fingering. Other features include trill timing compensation, delay compensation, pitch correction, and MIDI-output curve maps. While most customers will use the default settings, those who want to dial in the perfect performance will be able to do so.

QRS has been in the business of player-piano content since 1900, and offers one of the best player-piano libraries on the market, including SyncAlong, which allows the piano to play along with original artist content. All of the data that control the movements of the piano keys and pedals are in a non-compressed MIDI format (a high-definition MIDI format will soon be released). All music available for PNOmation—soon to number more than 10,000 tracks—can be purchased one song at a time or by the album, or users can purchase an All-Access Plan that provides access to the entire QRS music library and extends the warranty. QRS also offers an upgrade option for legacy QRS products and for competitors' systems that have a MIDI input, giving them many of the advantages of the latest PNOmation system.

STEINWAY SPIRIO

www.steinway.com

In 2016, Steinway officially launched the Spirio electronic player-piano system. Spirio is directly installed in a Steinway piano at the time of manufacture, ensuring no alteration in the exterior appearance of the instrument. Except for the power cord, Spirio requires no visible hardware on the piano. At the present time, Spirio is available on only three Steinway models, all in high-polish polyester finish: model B (available worldwide), model M (available in the

U.S. and Canada), and model O (available in select European and Asian markets). The system adds about $25,000 to the list price of the instrument. At present, a recording option is not available.

This high-resolution system uses proprietary software to measure hammer velocity up to 800 times per second at up to 1,020 dynamic levels, as well as proportional pedaling for the damper and soft pedals at up to 100 times per second for as many as 256 pedal positions. As a result of this high-resolution sampling, delicate damper and keyshift pedaling, subtle phrasing, and soft trills are reproduced with great accuracy. Steinway says that the system's superior playback is a result of a combination of numerous patented developments, including closed-loop proportional pedaling, immunity to varying line voltages, sophisticated thermal compensation, and proprietary high-resolution drive techniques.

While many older player-piano systems use compressed, low-resolution MIDI data files, Steinway says that the Spirio catalogue is recorded at the highest resolution possible from any system available today. The library contains thousands of tracks—including classical, jazz, and contemporary—all recorded live by accomplished Steinway Artists in Steinway's master recording studio, and new music is continually being added. Playlists, themes, and genres are curated by Steinway & Sons, drawing on the company's extensive musical expertise. In a first for the player-piano industry, Steinway's entire catalog of performances is provided to Spirio owners at no additional charge. Spirio users access the library through the Steinway & Sons App on their iOS device—an iPad is included in the Spirio purchase price.

YAMAHA DISKLAVIER

www.yamaha.com

Disklaviers are Yamaha (and now Bösendorfer) pianos that have been outfitted with an electronic player-piano system. These mechanisms are installed only in new Yamahas and the Bösendorfer model 200, and only at the Yamaha and Bösendorfer factories. They cannot be retrofitted into older Yamahas or any other brand.

Disklavier differs from most other player-piano systems in that its features, and the sophistication of the key, hammer, and pedal sensing, vary, depending on which Disklavier version is associated with the particular piano model purchased. For a number of years, the E3 has been the standard Disklavier version in the U.S. In 2016, it was replaced by the Enspire. However, many instruments with the E3 system are still on dealers' showroom floors.

The Enspire is available in the larger Yamaha upright models and in nearly all of the grand models, and is offered in three system variations: CL, ST, and PRO. The CL (Classic) is a playback-only system that omits the recording and Silent System functions found in the ST and PRO, and is offered only in the entry-level grand model GB1K, and only in select markets.

ST (Standard) systems are included in upright Disklaviers and in most grands under 6'. These systems have a noncontact optical sensing system featuring continuous grayscale shutters for each key, and window-style shutters on each hammer (grands only). Optical sensors are also used for the damper, soft, and sostenuto pedals. This sensor system allows users to capture their own performances in standard MIDI format. In addition, a built-in Silent System allows users to silence the acoustic-piano sound and, through headphones, access the instrument's digital sounds, which include binaurally captured samples of a CFX concert grand. A patented DSP servo-drive system monitors and controls key and pedal movements in real time to automatically compensate for environmental changes, or any other movement that doesn't correlate with performance data.

PRO systems, found in all grands over 6', are high-resolution systems that, in addition to the optical sensors mentioned in regard to the ST system, incorporate continuous grayscale shutters on each hammer to measure their speed and position. The additional sensors allow for even greater recording and performance accuracy: 1,024 levels of key and hammer velocity and 256 increments of pedal position. Enspire PRO systems also use an advanced DSP servo-drive system, called AccuPlay, to monitor and adjust performance reproduction.

Unlike the E3 system, the Enspire doesn't have a control-box style user interface, relying instead on a discreet control panel nearly invisible to the user. However, all functions and features can also be accessed and controlled by any compatible HTML5 browser; Yamaha recommends using an Apple iOS or Android device.

Enspire comes with 500 built-in songs, many of them in Yamaha's PianoSoft Audio format, which features stereo audio recordings that play in sync with piano performances. Users also have access to over 6,000 additional titles for purchase through the Yamaha MusicSoft online store, directly accessible through the instrument's user interface.

Yamaha also offers Internet streaming services for the Disklavier Enspire, including Disklavier Radio, which provides over 30 channels of streaming piano music 24 hours a day; and DisklavierTV, a video streaming service that allows users to view live and on-demand musical performances that play in sync with their piano.

Additional Enspire features include:

- An included USB WiFi adapter that permits peer-to-peer connectivity with a mobile device or connectivity to a network via WPS
- Automatic system calibration and troubleshooting
- Digital tone generator with 16 playable voices and 480 ensemble voices (256-note polyphony)
- Direct-to-USB audio recording function
- V-sync technology, which allows users to create video recordings that sync to recorded piano performances
- USB storage connectivity
- MIDI connectivity via standard MIDI ports or USB
- Coaxial digital output

For simple playback, most player-piano systems now on the market are probably equally recommended. The Disklavier, however, has a slight edge in reliability, and its recording system is more sophisticated than most of the others', especially in the larger grands. For this reason, it is often the system of choice for professional applications such as performance and teaching, and much of Yamaha's marketing efforts are directed at that audience.

Two examples are especially noteworthy. Yamaha supports the Minnesota International e-Competition, in which contestants gather in several cities and play Disklavier concert grands. Their performances are recorded using Video Sync, then sent to judges in another location, who, rather than listen to recordings, watch and listen to the music reproduced perfectly on other Disklavier pianos.

A similar concept is a technology called Remote Lesson, which debuted in spring 2010 after years of development and testing. A student takes a lesson on one Disklavier while a teacher located far away teaches and critiques on a second Disklavier connected via the Internet, student and teacher communicating with each other in real time via videoconferencing.

Yamaha maintains a large and growing library of music for the Disklavier, including piano solo, piano with recorded "live" accompaniment, piano with digital instrumental accompaniment, and PianoSmart arrangements. The system will also play standard MIDI files types 0 and 1.

About the Staff and Contributors

Larry Fine, *Piano Buyer*'s Publisher and Editor, is the author of *The Piano Book: Buying & Owning a New or Used Piano.* Fine has been involved in the piano industry for over 40 years. He lives in San Diego, California.

Ori Bukai owns and operates Allegro Pianos in Stamford, Connecticut, which specializes in the sale of new and restored high-end pianos. Visit his website at **www.allegropianos.com**.

Brian Chung is Senior Vice President of Kawai America Corporation and a leading proponent of the benefits of making music. He is also a pianist, and co-author of *Improvisation at the Piano: A Systematic Approach for the Classically Trained Pianist.* Visit his website at **www.brianchung.net**.

Steve Cohen owns Jasons Music Center (**www.jasonsmusiccenter.com**), in Glen Burnie, Maryland, a third-generation, family-owned piano dealer, and has been a consultant to the piano industry for over 40 years. He is also *Piano Buyer*'s Contributing Editor and Piano Industry Consultant, and lead appraiser for its Seller Advisory Service.

For over five decades, **Delwin D. Fandrich** has worked as a piano tuner, rebuilder, researcher, designer, and builder. He has served as principal design and technical consultant for leading pianomakers worldwide. Fandrich has presented technical classes and seminars around the world, and has authored numerous technical articles in the *Piano Technicians Journal.* He can be reached at **ddfandrich@gmail.com**.

David G. Hughes, RPT, has been a piano technician and rebuilder for more than 40 years. He regularly instructs at both regional seminars and national conventions of the Piano Technicians Guild. In 2001 he founded Vintage Case Parts, a firm specializing in the manufacture of classic Steinway furniture components for the rebuilding trade. He can be reached **www.davidhughespiano.com**.

Stuart Isacoff is an award-winning writer, pianist, composer and lecturer who performs and lectures across North America and Europe. He is the author of *When the World Stopped to Listen* (Knopf, 2017), as well as the highly acclaimed *A Natural History of the Piano* (Knopf, 2011) and *Temperament* (Knopf/Vintage, 2003). His website is **www.stuartisacoff.net**.

Mike Kemper is a Los Angeles-based piano technician and expert on electronic player-piano systems. He can be reached at **mkbizmail@icloud.com**.

Since 1982, **Karen E. Lile** has been co-owner, with Kendall Ross Bean, of Piano Finders, a San Francisco Bay–area piano appraisal, brokerage, and rebuilding firm. See their website at **www.PianoFinders.com**.

George Litterst is a nationally known music educator, clinician, author, performer, and music-software developer. He is the coauthor of several musical applications for iPad, Mac and PC, including SuperScore Music, Home Concert Xtreme, Classroom Maestro, and Internet MIDI. These applications work with technology-equipped pianos and are available from TimeWarp Technologies at **timewarptech.com**.

Dr. Owen Lovell, *Piano Buyer*'s Piano Review Editor, is Assistant Professor of Music at Georgia College. He can be reached at **owen@pianobuyer.com**.

Over the past 35 years, piano technician **Sally Phillips** has worked in virtually every aspect of the piano industry: service, retail, wholesale, and manufacturing. In her role as a concert-piano technician, she has tuned and prepared pianos for concert and recording work in such venues as Town Hall, Alice Tully Hall, and the Kennedy Center, and for the Cincinnati Symphony Orchestra, the BBC Concert Orchestra, and the Vienna Philharmonic. At present, Phillips lives in Georgia and works throughout the southeastern U.S. She can be contacted at **sphillipspiano@hotmail.com**.

Bill Shull, RPT, M. Mus., restrung his first piano at age 15, and for 38 years has maintained a piano service business, including a small rebuilding shop, in southern California. Shull founded the Period Piano Center, **www.periodpianos.org**, to promote the conservation of transitional-modern pianos, support research projects such as the early-Steinway documentation project, exhibit representative pianos, and develop an online database of historic pianos at **www.historicalpianosociety.org**.

Alden Skinner was involved in both the manufacturing and retail sides of the piano business for over 20 years. He currently works in the high-end audio/video industry.

Chris Solliday, RPT, services the pianos at several institutions, including Lafayette College and Lehigh University. He lives in Easton, Pennsylvania, and can be reached through his website at at **www.csollidaypiano.com**.

Chris Storch, RPT, is an acoustician with 25 years' experience in the areas of architectural acoustics, noise and vibration control, and environmental noise abatement. Some of the more prominent projects on which he has consulted include Verizon Hall, in Philadelphia; Sibelius Hall, in Lahti, Finland; LG Arts Center, in Seoul, South Korea; and Fox Cities Performing Arts Center, in Appleton, Wisconsin. Storch is a 2009 graduate of the Piano Technology program at the North Bennet Street School, in Boston. He tunes and services pianos in the Boston area, and conducts research in piano acoustics in his spare time. He can be reached at **chrisstor@aol.com**.

Dave Swartz, RPT, is owner of Cory Products. He can be reached through his company website, **www.corycare.com**.

Russ Vitt is owner of Modern Piano Moving, the country's first door-to-door nationwide piano mover. The company has warehouse locations throughout the U.S., with headquarters in Sullivan, Missouri. For additional information, see its website at **www.modernpiano.com**.

GENERAL PIANO INFORMATION

Nontraditional Materials and the Piano

Steve Brady, RPT

In existence for over 300 years, the piano is considered as "traditional" a musical instrument as the violin or guitar. From its beginnings as a mere subspecies of harpsichord, the *gravicembalo col piano e forte* has evolved into the modern grand piano, and in the process has changed dramatically in size, weight, sound, and the materials of its construction. Indeed, many of the materials used in pianos today were, at one time or another, considered "nontraditional," even experimental.

The Technology-Equipped Piano Goes to School: Not Your Grandmother's Piano
The Yamaha Disklavier, Long-Distance Learning, and More

George Litterst

Not long ago, I addressed—from my home in Massachusetts—an audience of Colorado piano teachers who had gathered at the Metropolitan State University of Denver. After greeting them, I sat down at the piano and performed Chopin's Étude in E Major, Op.10, No.3. During my performance, I actually played two pianos simultaneously: my own Disklavier grand piano, which is located in my home studio, and a similar piano in Denver. This long-distance performance was made possible by the video-conferencing technology of Skype and the record, playback, and MIDI features of the Yamaha Disklavier.

The Benefits of Laminated Soundboards

Delwin D. Fandrich

The soundboard remains one of the least-understood components of the modern piano. All sorts of claims—some of them bordering on the magical—are made for how the soundboard is made and for the wood traditionally used for its construction. While many of these claims make excellent advertising copy, they have little to do with how a piano actually works. This lack of understanding has impeded the acceptance of a beneficial advance in piano design: the laminated soundboard.

Dealer Preparation of New Pianos:
Should I Buy a Piano "Out of the Crate"?

Steve Cohen and Piano Buyer staff

Some shoppers request a new piano fresh out of the crate instead of a "floor sample," based on the misconception that a crated piano must be in perfect condition, whereas a piano that has been handled by the dealer and other shoppers is somehow compromised. In reality, the opposite is true: The extra tunings, the small amount of breaking-in of the action by prospective buyers, the optimizing of regulation and voicing by the dealer's technician, a little attention to cosmetics—all provide value to the wise shopper, who thus will always prefer a floor model to an unseen instrument still in its crate or box.

Plus, numerous reviews of acoustic pianos and digital pianos

USED & RESTORED PIANOS

How to Inspect a Used Piano Before Buying

Excerpted from The Piano Book, *Fourth Edition, by Larry Fine*

Unless you're very rich and can afford to keep a piano technician on retainer full time, chances are that at some point in your searching for a used piano, you're going to have to go it alone. Knowing that you'd rather not stare dumbly at the piano, I've prepared a little inspection routine for you. A thorough inspection of a piano must really be a joint effort with a technician. This inspection, however, will teach you a lot about the piano, enable you to talk intelligently with your technician, and make you feel a useful and involved participant instead of a passive bystander.

Rebuilding the New York Way

Sally Phillips

From 1789 to the present, over 100 different companies, most of them now long gone, have manufactured pianos in New York City. This extensive piano-manufacturing presence made New York the ultimate piano town. While many of those older pianos are still in use, many others have or soon will have reached the end of their useful life, and will need rebuilding if their owners—families, churches, schools, museums, universities—want to continue to use them as musical instruments. To serve that need, the piano-building tradition of a century ago lingers on in the many fine rebuilding shops of present-day New York.

Buying a Used Steinway

Excerpted from The Piano Book, *Fourth Edition, by Larry Fine*

As an aid to those buying a used Steinway, I have listed all models of Steinway pianos made in New York City since the firm's inception in 1853. This reprint also includes the list "Ages of Steinway Pianos," from which one can look up the year of manufacture of any Steinway piano by its serial number; and discussions of Teflon bushings and verdigris, two issues that frequently arise in connection with used Steinways.

Upright Cabinet Styles in American Piano Manufacturing, 1880–1930

Martha Taylor

From about 1880 to 1930, when piano manufacturing was one of the nation's most important industries, pianos were produced in a staggering array of cabinet styles, many of them highly intricate, embellished, and decorated, others dull and pedestrian. The cabinet styles were closely related to the social and economic climates of the period—to changes in values in an emerging consumer culture, and to economic cycles that affected the quantity, styles, and quality of the pianos made during that time. This article is an overview of the styles of the upright pianos of the period, and their historical context.

Dealers Speak About Their High-End Brands

Various Piano Dealers

In order to give prospective buyers of high-end pianos a better sense of the individual personalities of these brands, we will occasionally provide selected dealers, technicians, and pianists the opportunity to describe the musical and other qualities of the high-end brands they represent, service, or play. The brands presented will vary from issue to issue. As you'll see, although different writers often describe the same brands in very different ways, over time certain common themes emerge.

Technicians Speak About the High-End Pianos They Service

Various Piano Technicians

Piano technicians who eventually drift toward the high-end market are usually people who appreciate quality, strive for excellence, and can even be called connoisseurs. Their mission is to provide the pianist with a sublime, inspiring, creative, and enjoyable experience every time he or she plays the instrument. Each technician in this article has extensive hands-on experience with the specific brand(s) he writes about. All of them strive for quality and perfection, and have intimate relationships with the pianos, inside and out. Although you'll recognize common ground in these technicians' opinions, there are also differences, and each speaks only for himself.

"Fit and Finish" Improvements at Steinway & Sons:
A Photo Essay

Larry Fine

Due to its position for more than a century and a half as maker of America's preeminent concert piano, Steinway & Sons has often been a lightning rod for controversy and criticism, some of which have been played out in an unusually public way. It seems only right, therefore, that Steinway's improvements should also be given prompt coverage. In that spirit, the following photo essay, with photos supplied by Steinway & Sons, describe some of the recent changes and improvements I saw at the Steinway factory.

One by One:
Boutique Piano Builders in the 21st Century

Steve Brady

For several decades in the 20th century, most of the larger piano makers cast their own plates, bent their own rims, glued up their own soundboards and pinblocks, and manufactured their own action parts. Some makers took such vertical integration to the point of owning their own forests and sawmills. Now, however, in the 21st century, specialization has once again become commonplace. Along with this specialization, a remarkable breed of craftsperson has begun to build high-quality grand pianos in a workshop setting, defying the conventional wisdom that pianos must be made in large quantities by large corporations.

The All-Steinway Program vs. The Diverse-Inventory Approach to Buying Pianos for an Institution

Sally Phillips and Anne Garee

When an institution is ready to purchase a large number of new pianos, one of the major decisions to be made is whether to buy all from a single manufacturer, or to maintain a diverse inventory of instruments of many brands. The decision has artistic, technical, financial, institutional, and, often, political dimensions. On the single-brand side, probably best known is the All-Steinway School program, in which more than 150 institutions participate. The College of Music at Florida State University is one of the largest music schools in the country to maintain a diverse inventory of many brands. In this article, proponents of the two schools of thought put their best feet forward to explain the reasons behind their respective choices.

Are "Hand-Built" Pianos Becoming Obsolete?

George F. Emerson

Piano Buyer asked veteran piano designer George F. Emerson—whose 48-year piano-industry career has included employment with Baldwin, Mason & Hamlin, and, most recently, Hailun—to comment on how globalization and the computerization of manufacturing have affected the piano industry, and whether there is still a place for expensive, "hand-built" instruments. Following Emerson's remarks are responses from representatives of several companies that manufacture "hand-built" pianos. Finally, Emerson has the last word.

German Piano Makers Face the Music of Globalization

Derek Scally

Each Spring, Frankfurt, Germany, hosts Musikmesse, one of the world's largest gatherings for the international music industry. European piano makers convene there every other year. Our correspondent attended the 2016 gathering, at a time of great change for the German piano industry.

Plus, numerous reviews of acoustic pianos and digital pianos

PIANO CARE, MOVING & ACCESSORIES

Piano Moving & Storage
Excerpted from The Piano Book, *Fourth Edition, by Larry Fine*

Why Not to Move a Piano Yourself. Movers like to tell stories like this one: A young woman asked her father to help her move a piano from one place to another in her house. Her father got a couple of his friends to come along and they brought a dolly. While they were lifting the piano — a full-size vertical — it tipped back too far and got away from them. While it was falling, its upper corner dug down through the wall. The trench it made was deep enough to sever an electric conduit, which shorted and began to burn. The "movers" were unable to stop the fire, which also spread to the floor below, another person's apartment. After the fire department was done, there was little left of the two apartments and the piano.

How To Make a Piano Room Sound Grand
Lewis Lipnick

This article goes into some detail about the various factors that affect room acoustics for pianos, including room size, ceiling height, placement of the piano in the room, floor coverings, and reflection, diffusion, and absorption of sound.

Advertiser Index

Company	Page No.	Company	Page No.
Allegro Pianos	116	Palatino	6
Bechstein, C	96	Pearl River	8
Benchworld	166	Period Piano Center	77
Blüthner	112	Petrof	137
Bösendorfer (Yamaha)	111	PianoDisc	203
Brodmann	68	Piano Finders	78
Bush & Gerts	44	PianoMart.com	71
Clavier Companion	189	Piano Technicians Guild	126
Cooper Music	18	Piano World	19
Cory Products	148	Pierce Piano Atlas	62
Cunningham Piano Co.	95	Pleyel	43
Dampp Chaser Piano Life Saver	149	Pramberger (Samick)	31
Dexibell	183	QRS	200
Dynatone	187	Randy Potter School of Piano Technology	148
e-Klavier (Blüthner)	4	Reeder Pianos	63
Fazioli	107	Rick Jones Pianos	52
Förster, August	121	Ritmüller (Pearl River)	32
Grotrian	104	Roland	IBC
Hailun	28	Samick	36
Harrodser	146	Sauter	iii, 117
Hollywood Piano Co.	47	Schimmel	118
Hoffmann, W.	72	Schumann	14
House of Troy	167	Seiler (Samick)	108
Jordan Kitt's/Cristofori	3	Spirio (Steinway)	199
Kawai, Shigeru	140	Steinberg, Wilh.	35
Kayserburg (Pearl River)	13	Steingraeber & Söhne	115
Kingsburg	26	Steinway & Sons	IFC
Knabe, Wm.	2	Vaughan	48
Korg	181	Wertheim	38
Mason & Hamlin	123	Wessell, Nickel, & Gross	90
Modern Piano Moving	20	Yamaha	xii
North Bennet Street School	150		

Photo Credits